Beginn
Expressior

Beginning
Expression® Web

Zak Ruvalcaba

Wiley Publishing, Inc.

Beginning Expression® Web

Published by
Wiley Publishing, Inc.
10475 Crosspoint Boulevard
Indianapolis, IN 46256
www.wiley.com

Copyright © 2007 by Wiley Publishing, Inc., Indianapolis, Indiana

Published simultaneously in Canada

ISBN: 978-0-470-07315-5

Manufactured in the United States of America

10 9 8 7 6 5 4 3 2 1

Library of Congress Cataloging-in-Publication Data is available from the publisher.

For general information on our other products and services please contact our Customer Care Department within the United States at (800) 762-2974, outside the United States at (317) 572-3993, or fax (317) 572-4002.

Wiley also publishes its books in a variety of electronic formats. Some content that appears in print may not be available in electronic books.

I would like to dedicate this book to my wife, Jessica; my daughter, Makenzie; my son, Zaven; and the newest addition to our family, my son, Zayden, for putting up with my many faults. I love my family more than anyone can possibly know.

About the Author

Zak Ruvalcaba has been researching, designing, and developing for the Web since 1995. He holds a Bachelor's Degree from San Diego State University and a Master of Science in Instructional Technology from National University in San Diego. He served as Creative Director with EPIC Solutions until 1998. His expertise in developing Web applications led him to a position as Manager of Web Development at SkyDesk, Inc., where he developed Web applications for such companies as Gateway, HP, Toshiba, IBM, Intuit, Peachtree, Dell, and Microsoft. He's worked for such companies as ADCS Inc. and Wireless Knowledge as a wireless software engineer developing .NET solutions for companies including Mellon Financial, Goldman Sachs, TV Guide, Healthbanks, Gartner, Inc., Microsoft, Qualcomm, and Commerce One. Currently, he holds a position with MiraCosta College in Oceanside, California, supporting internal and external .NET applications. His skill set includes technologies and languages including (X)HTML, XML, JavaScript, CSS, ASP, ASP.NET, VB.NET, C#, ADO.NET, Web Services, SQL, T-SQL, and ActionScript. He is a Macromedia Certified Professional (MMCP), a Microsoft Certified Application Developer for .NET (MCAD), and a Microsoft Certified Solutions Developer for .NET (MCSD). He teaches and holds design lectures on various technologies and tools including Dreamweaver, Flash, ASP.NET, ADO.NET, and Web Services for the San Diego Community College District and Palomar College.

Credits

Senior Acquisitions Editor
Jim Minatel

Development Editor
Kevin Shafer

Technical Editors
Gregory Beamer and Spike Xavier

Copy Editor
Nancy Rapoport

Editorial Manager
Mary Beth Wakefield

Production Manager
Tim Tate

Vice President and Executive Group Publisher
Richard Swadley

Vice President and Executive Publisher
Joseph B. Wikert

Compositor
Laurie Stewart, Happenstance Type-O-Rama

Proofreader
Ian Golder

Indexer
Robert Swanson

Anniversary Logo Design
Richard Pacifico

Acknowledgments

Writing a book is a tremendous effort and takes dedication and patience from all who are involved. A sincere "Thank you" to my Acquisitions Editor, Jim Minatel, for being on top of this book and for ensuring that *Beginning Expression Web* is one of the first Expression Web books to market. I'd also like to thank Kevin Shafer, Tim Tate, Spike Xavier, and Greg Beamer for their diligence toward making this book a success.

Contents

Contents

Contents

Contents

Contents

Contents

Introduction

Ten years ago, when I used FrontPage for the first time, I was amazed at how far ahead of its time the program was. The ability to work with tables, visual formatting, styles, and pinpoint accurate designs truly amazed me. I was a skeptic when it came to visual editors, and preferred Notepad whenever possible. FrontPage changed that in me, and made me look at Web development in a whole new light.

Still, many considered FrontPage a simple visual editor that accomplishes little but aid in the development of static Web pages. The mindset is that visual editors lack the true complexity that it takes to create rich and powerful Web applications that encompass client-side technologies such as HTML, CSS, and JavaScript, while leveraging server-side technologies such as ASP.NET.

Enter Expression Web. As FrontPage's successor, Expression Web obliterates that stigma by captivating the developer in a vast, intuitive, and feature-rich environment. Whether you're designing a Web site for personal use, a government institution, or a private organization, Expression Web's tools are geared to aiding in the development of feature-rich, accessible, and captivating Web pages.

Who This Book Is For

If you've picked up this book, chances are you're interested in the world of Web design and development and, more specifically, how Expression Web can help you succeed in these endeavors. Whether you're a seasoned developer, a print designer looking to expand your base of knowledge to the Web, an existing FrontPage user looking to see what the fuss is about, or a home user who simply aims at creating a family Web site, Expression Web offers the features and flexibility to get you on your way quickly and effortlessly. This book introduces you to the many features available through Expression Web.

What You Need to Use This Book

To work through and run the samples in this book, you must have the following:

- ❑ A computer running the Windows operating system.
- ❑ The .NET Framework 2.0. (The .NET Framework 2.0 will be installed along with Expression Web. You can download it separately from http://www.asp.net.)
- ❑ Expression Web. (A trial version can be downloaded from Microsoft's Web site at http://www.microsoft.com/products/expression.)
- ❑ A database such as Microsoft Access or the free Microsoft SQL Server 2005 Express Edition.
- ❑ Internet Information Services (IIS) is needed for the validation and authentication examples in Chapter 14, "Securing Your Web Applications." You will also need IIS to install WebDAV as described in Chapter 3, "Working with Web Sites."

All of the files required for working with the examples in this book can be downloaded from our Web site at http://www.wrox.com/dynamic/books/download.aspx.

Conventions

To help you get the most from the text and keep track of what's happening, a number of conventions have been used throughout the book.

Try It Out

The "Try It Out" section is an exercise you should work through, following the text in the book.

1. They usually consist of a set of steps.

2. Each step has a number.

3. Follow the steps through with your copy of the database.

> **Boxes like this one hold important, not-to-be forgotten information that is directly relevant to the surrounding text.**

Tips, hints, tricks, and asides to the current discussion are offset and placed in italics like this.

As for styles in the text:

❏ Important new terms and important words are *highlighted* when we introduce them.

❏ Keyboard strokes are shown like this: Ctrl+A.

❏ File names, URLs, and code within the text are shown like this: `persistence.properties`.

❏ Code is presented in the following two ways:

```
In code examples, we highlight new and important code with a gray background.
```

```
The gray highlighting is not used for code that's less important in the
present context, or has been shown before.
```

Project Files

As you work through the examples in this book, you will need the project files that accompany the book. The entire set of project files used in this book is available for download at `http://www.wrox.com`. Once at the site, simply locate the book's title (either by using the Search box or by using one of the title lists), and click the Download Code link on the book's detail page to obtain all the project files for the book.

Because many books have similar titles, you may find it easiest to search by ISBN; for this book the ISBN is 9780470073155.

Once you download the files, just decompress them with your favorite compression tool. Alternately, you can go to the main Wrox code download page at `http://www.wrox.com/dynamic/books/download.aspx` to see the files available for this book and all other Wrox books.

Errata

We make every effort to ensure that there are no errors in the text or in the code. However, no one is perfect, and mistakes do occur. If you find an error in one of our books (such as a spelling mistake or faulty piece of code), we would be very grateful for your feedback. By sending in errata you may save another reader hours of frustration and at the same time you will be helping us provide even higher quality information.

To find the errata page for this book, go to `http://www.wrox.com` and locate the title using the Search box or one of the title lists. Then, on the book details page, click the Book Errata link. On this page, you can view all errata that has been submitted for this book and posted by Wrox editors. A complete book list including links to each book's errata is also available at `www.wrox.com/misc-pages/booklist.shtml`.

If you don't spot "your" error on the Book Errata page, go to `www.wrox.com/contact/techsupport.shtml` and complete the form there to send us the error you have found. We'll check the information and, if appropriate, post a message to the book's errata page and fix the problem in subsequent editions of the book.

p2p.wrox.com

For author and peer discussion, join the P2P forums at `p2p.wrox.com`. The forums are a Web-based system for you to post messages relating to Wrox books and related technologies and to interact with other readers and technology users. The forums offer a subscription feature to e-mail you topics of interest of your choosing when new posts are made to the forums. Wrox authors, editors, other industry experts, and your fellow readers are present on these forums.

At `http://p2p.wrox.com` you will find a number of different forums that will help you not only as you read this book, but also as you develop your own applications. To join the forums, just follow these steps:

1. Go to `p2p.wrox.com` and click the Register link.
2. Read the terms of use and click Agree.
3. Complete the required information to join, as well as any optional information you wish to provide, and click Submit.
4. You will receive an e-mail with information describing how to verify your account and complete the joining process.

You can read messages in the forums without joining P2P, but to post your own messages, you must join.

Once you join, you can post new messages and respond to messages other users post. You can read messages at any time on the Web. If you would like to have new messages from a particular forum e-mailed to you, click the Subscribe to this Forum icon by the forum name in the forum listing.

For more information about how to use the Wrox P2P forums, be sure to read the P2P FAQs for answers to questions about how the forum software works, as well as many common questions specific to P2P and Wrox books. To read the FAQs, click the FAQ link on any P2P page.

Introducing Microsoft Expression Web

There was a time in the not-so-distant past when a designer aiming to create Web pages needed only a basic knowledge of Hypertext Markup Language (HTML) and a robust, reliable, and feature-rich text editor such as Notepad. Okay, so the latter is an exaggeration, but let's face it. Web pages were simple then, containing limited tags used purely for formatting fonts, setting paragraph and line breaks, adding lists, placing images, and occasionally including tabular data.

The relative simplicity of creating Web pages, then, led to the increased visibility and use of the Web. Gone are the days of adding a few tags to a blank document in Notepad, saving the file with an .html extension, and then opening that page within a browser to see the finished product. With increased usage came new ways of formatting and structuring content in a Cascading Style Sheet (CSS). Scripting languages such as JavaScript were introduced in an effort to improve the usability of Web pages, validate forms, detect browsers, create cookies, and more. As the Web became the perfect medium for sharing and disseminating information, users became much more finicky, demanding support for audio, video, and even animation.

Beyond these simplicities however, Web pages grew to unbelievable proportions. The Web is no longer a simple medium used merely for informational purposes. Rather, users can now expect to do their banking, buy cars, shop for food, collaborate, and much more, online. We now work with Web pages that are responsible for extracting content from databases, Extensible Markup Language (XML) files, and more.

Developing for the Web no longer involves a simple understanding of HTML, a handy text editor, and a browser. Instead, developers are increasingly required to learn other complex technologies such as CSS, JavaScript, ASP.NET, VB.NET, C#, SQL, XML, and much more. But, with the introduction of so many Web technologies just over the last decade alone, how has the Web, and, more specifically, how has developing for the Web increased beyond a level that so few could have ever predicted during the Web's infancy? The answer lies in visual editors such as Microsoft Expression Web.

Microsoft Expression Web facilitates the development of Web pages visually. Even better, it fosters visual development of Web applications. While knowledge of the aforementioned Web technologies is encouraged, it's not required with Expression Web. Expression Web allows the developer to structure and format content, and even connect to and interact with database/XML data visually using a series of task panes, wizards, toolbars, and toolboxes. With Expression Web, years of learning and mastering complex authoring and programming languages are now cut down to a matter of days and 16 convenient chapters.

Your journey through Expression Web begins here with an introduction to the product. Specifically, you will do the following:

❑　Become familiar with the Expression Web interface

❑　Learn about the many options available within the menu bar

❑　Understand the role of Task Panes

❑　Use and customize toolbars

❑　Learn to recognize and use the Development window, the tag selector, the development area, the tabbed file chooser, and the Design, Split, and Code views

Throughout the book, certain Expression Web Task Panes, toolbars, windows, and more will be referenced by name. By the end of the chapter, you will have a solid understanding of where these components are located. You'll know which component accomplishes which task and when to use each. This will serve as a foundation for other, more complex processes throughout the book. Let's get started!

Familiarizing Yourself with the Interface

Opening Expression Web for the first time reveals a program that looks and, in many cases, functions much like other Microsoft products. Falling in line with the "familiarization through consistency" approach, Expression Web at first glance closely resembles other Office products such as Word, Publisher, and even its predecessor, FrontPage.

Initially, you'll notice Expression Web's Multiple Document Interface (MDI), where numerous windows (otherwise known as *Task Panes*), the Document window, toolbars, menus, and so on, converge within a single parent window shown in Figure 1-1.

The beauty in the MDI approach, as you may have seen by now in other Office products, is that the Task Panes and toolbars aren't fixed to the environment (otherwise known as *docked*). Instead, the toolbars and Task Panes that facilitate the majority of property modifications for your Web pages can be undocked, moved to a different area of the development environment, and then re-docked to that particular area. You can also choose to not dock a Task Pane or toolbar and instead leave it floating on top of other toolbars and Task Panes within the development environment. Figure 1-2 provides an example of how you might choose to customize the development environment.

To get an idea of just how easy it is to dock and undock toolbars and Task Panes, try rolling your cursor over the title bar of a particular Task Pane or toolbar. Your cursor will change to the Move cursor. Now, click, hold, and drag the Task Pane or toolbar out of its area and move it to another area within the environment. As long as the area supports the docking of that particular Task Pane or toolbar, it should snap automatically into place.

As you can see by the callouts in Figure 1-1, Expression Web's user interface offers the following five major components:

❑ The menu bar

❑ The Document window

❑ Task Panes

❑ Toolbars

❑ Context menus (not shown)

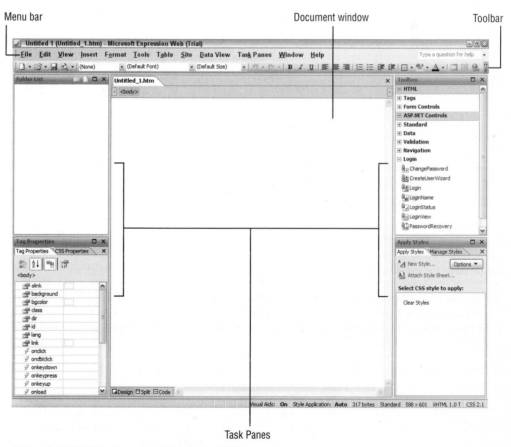

Figure 1-1: Multiple Document Interface (MDI)

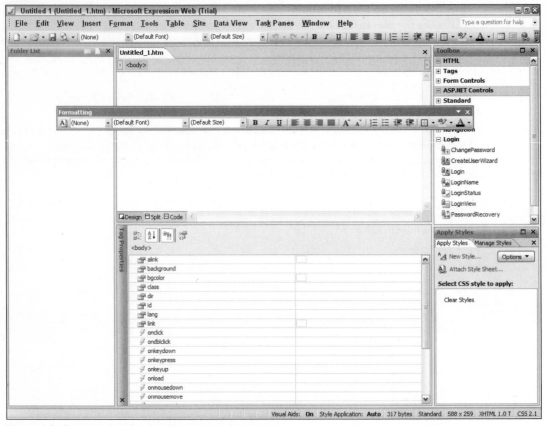

Figure 1-2: Customizing the development environment

While you may be surprised to learn that development of Web pages within Expression Web flows through just these five components, it's true! The menu bar, the Development window, the myriad of Task Panes and toolbars, and the context-sensitive menus represent 100 percent of the Expression Web development environment. The catch (yes, there's a catch) is that these five components trickle down other forms of functionality — for example, the component toolbars. However, there are 17 different toolbars that you may decide to use to work with anything from page formatting using CSS to page structuring using tables. Task Panes are another example. While I mentioned that Task Panes represent core functionality within Expression Web, I have yet to mention that there are 18 Task Panes that you can utilize based on the task at hand.

While I'll certainly cover the myriad of Task Panes, toolbars, and so on, as the book unfolds, this chapter is meant as a gentle introduction to the many components that make up the Expression Web development environment. This chapter should help you identify the Folder List or Tag Properties Task Pane, identify the Tools menu item, recognize the Document window, and even recognize what the Common toolbar is so that, in later chapters, when you read about opening a particular toolbar, accessing a particular menu item, or even opening a Task Pane, it will come as naturally as blinking.

The Menu Bar

Arguably, the most crucial component included within Expression Web is the menu bar. Like most Microsoft products, the menu bar allows for simple file-based operations such as opening a document, saving a document, printing, closing, cutting, copying, pasting, and much more. Unlike other Office products, however, the menu bar also includes numerous other options that are specific to Expression Web.

For example, the Task Pane menu item, which I touched on in the previous section, enables you to open any one of the 18 Task Pane windows within Expression Web. Like the Task Pane menu item, the Site menu item is also specific to Expression Web, enabling you to choose options for managing a Web site, opening and creating reports, copying a Web site, and more.

In all, there are 12 menu items within the menu bar. The following table provides a basic outline of each menu item and its common usage.

Menu Item	Usage
File	Use options within the File menu for performing common file-based operations such as creating a new document, opening an existing document, saving a document, opening a site, closing a site, launching the Site Publishing Wizard, importing and exporting files and sites, previewing your page in the browser, printing, opening recent files and sites, and exiting the program.
Edit	You can use options within the Edit menu to perform common word-processing operations such as cutting, copying, pasting, deleting, selecting all, launching the Find and Replace dialog, and more. Other non–word-processing features offered within this menu include checking files in and out (when versioning is enabled), accessing various code-only options (while in Code view), and undoing and redoing changes to a particular page.
View	As an Expression Web user, you can access options within the View menu for customizing the look and feel of the development environment. For example, you may decide to show the Design, Split, or Code views within the Document window. Perhaps you'd like to turn on and off options for viewing Visual Aids, Formatting Marks, Rulers, the Grid, and more. Options for showing and hiding the Folder list, Navigation pane, and the various toolbars also reside within the View menu.
Insert	Anything that you might want to insert into your Web pages can be found within the Insert menu. Need to insert a particular HTML tag or ASP.NET control? Maybe insert a Hyperlink, bookmark, picture, file, interactive button, or a symbol? All of this and more can be inserted via this menu.

Continued

Menu Item	Usage
Format	Once you've inserted an element into your Web page, you'll undoubtedly want some way of modifying its properties. While Expression Web supports a wide variety of methods for physically editing the properties of elements that you'll eventually add to your Web pages (Task Panes, toolbars, and so on), the Format menu provides a central list of options for modifying all properties for CSS, tables, behaviors, layers, fonts, and more.
Tools	The Tools menu can be considered a central repository for functionality that will ultimately improve the usability, accessibility, performance, and professionalism of your Web pages. For example, options within the Tools menu include a spelling dictionary, a thesaurus, accessibility checker, browser compatibility validation, CSS reports, an HTML optimizer, and various options for working with add-ins and macros.
Table	As you'll learn, tables are a traditional approach to structuring Web pages easily, with very little effort. When working with tables, you can access features within the Table menu to insert or draw a table; insert columns, rows, or cells within an existing table; delete rows, columns, or cells; split and merge cells; and more.
Site	While this topic won't begin to reveal itself until later, the concept of Web sites is an important one. If you're new to Web development, habit may drive you to simply open a file and begin editing it directly within Expression Web. While this is certainly acceptable, it's important to understand that you'll be missing out on many features that make Expression Web unique. By working with Web sites, Expression Web offers numerous management features, including file check in and check out, versioning, automatic visual navigation, the ability to copy an entire Web site to a Web hosting provider, site reports, and more. All of these features, including the ability to define site settings, can be found within this menu item.
Data View	As you progress through the book, one of the topics that you'll arrive at is that of extracting data from a database and presenting that data within a Web page. The set of options within the Data View menu facilitates the addition of user interface components for working with that extracted data.
Task Panes	As mentioned earlier, Expression Web includes more than 20 different Task Panes that facilitate a rich development workflow for the end user. Whether you want to work with CSS, JavaScript Behaviors, or HTML Tag Properties, or browse the folder list for your Web site, the Task Panes menu contains a Task Pane that is right for the job. Because a large portion of Expression Web's features stem from the functionality offered by the various Task Panes, I cannot begin to provide detailed coverage of all of them in this chapter. Instead, each Task Pane is covered as its related chapter unfolds.

Menu Item	Usage
Window	Like other Office products, Expression Web allows you to open more than one instance of the program at the same time. Doing so allows you to work with numerous projects at once. You can open a new Expression Web window by simply choosing the New Window option from the Window menu. Furthermore, the Window menu also manages Document window instances (covered with more detail in the next section). Rather than using the tabbed file chooser, you can simply select the Document window of choice from this menu. Additionally, you can close all Document window instances at once by choosing the Close All Pages option.
Help	As the name implies, various help-related links are contained within this menu. Other options within this menu include links for accessing the Expression Web home page, the Microsoft contact page for submitting questions or comments, the Web site for downloading Expression Web extensions and updates, and even a link to a Microsoft Expression Web page that contains links to developer blogs and community forums.

> Remember that the goal here isn't to place each and every menu item under a micro-scope. With hundreds of menu options available, it would be nearly impossible to remember them all by simply reading one chapter. Instead, I discuss what most of these menu items do when it's relevant to the topic of a given chapter. Also, assume that a lot of these menu items represent common operations that you'll most likely use shortcut keys for instead. In addition, some of these menu items are duplicate representations of an operation that you may find easier to perform via a toolbar or Task Pane window; thus, you can see why I'm holding off covering these menu items in depth.

The Development Window

Quite possibly, the most important window included within Expression Web's framework is the Document window. Simply put, the Document window is where all of the magic happens, or more specifically, where all of your creative energy will be focused. It's where you'll structure, format, and add interactivity and dynamic components to your Web pages visually, in code, or both. As you can see from Figure 1-3, the Document window is made up of the following components:

- ❑ The development area
- ❑ The tabbed file chooser
- ❑ Show Design, Split, and Code views
- ❑ The Quick Tag Selector

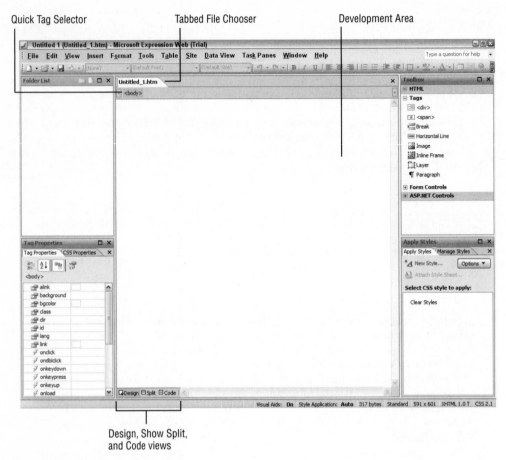

Figure 1-3: The Document window

The Development Area

Of the four major components included with the Document window, the development area is where you'll focus the majority of your attention. When you create a new Web page for the first time (as you'll see in Chapter 2), the development area appears as a blank white page waiting for you to add structuring components, formatting components, images, animations, and more.

Of course, you can also customize whether various development aids are shown within the development area. For example, assuming you wanted to display rulers and a grid within the development area, you'd need only to place your cursor within the development area and select View ⇨ Ruler and Grid ⇨ Show Ruler and View ⇨ Ruler and Grid ⇨ Show Grid, respectively. Selecting both of the options enables both a ruler and a grid within the development area.

Additionally, you may want to set the default page size of the development area. Doing so would allow you to develop your Web pages around a particular screen resolution. To set the page size, again place your cursor within the development area and choose View ➪ Page Size ➪ 760 × 420 (800 × 600, Maximized). You'll quickly notice that the development area adjusts its width and height (represented by a dashed line) to accommodate the particular page size. The addition of the rulers, grid, and custom page size are highlighted in Figure 1-4.

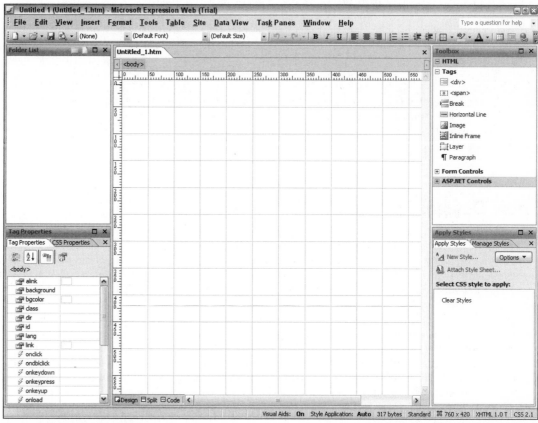

Figure 1-4: Development area

> Setting a page size is common in Web development. Current statistics show that roughly 54 percent of Internet users browse under a 1024 × 768 screen resolution, followed by 28 percent at 800 x 600, 10 percent at 1280 × 1024, and 4 percent at 1152 × 864. What this means is that as long as you target your Web pages for the least common denominator, or more specifically the option we selected of 760 × 420 (800 × 600, Maximized), roughly 96 percent of your users will be able to see your Web pages without having to scroll horizontally.

The Tabbed File Chooser

As your Web sites grow, so will the volume of Web pages that you need to manage. In some instances, you'll need to work on more than one Web page at the same time. This is where the tabbed file chooser comes into play. The tabbed file chooser allows you to open and work with numerous Web pages at once. As you open or create files, new tabs appear within the tab strip, each representing its own Document window instance. When you have more than one file open at the same time, browsing between the files is simply a matter of choosing the particular file, represented by its individual tab.

Closing a tab/page is easy. To close the tab/page, simply choose the small Close icon (represented by the small x) in the far right of the tab strip, or in the top-right corner of the Document window, also shown in Figure 1-3.

> **Remember that there's always more than one way to accomplish any task in Expression Web. Another way to close a page is to choose File ⇨ Close. Or, if you'd like to close all open tabs/pages at the same time, simply choose Window ⇨ Close All Pages.**

Show Design, Split, and Code View

One of the nice aspects of Expression Web is that it doesn't assume anything of its user. It doesn't care if you're a designer who prefers to structure and format Web pages visually. It also doesn't care if you're a developer who prefers to tinker with the code. In fact, it allows you to set what view you want to see for a particular situation via the Show Design, Split, and Code View set of options.

As you'll notice, the Show Design View option is shown to the user by default. For this reason, a blank white page is shown initially when a new page is created. If you prefer to work in a code environment, however, simply choose the Show Code View option. In this scenario, the development area changes, enabling you to manipulate the code that is produced. Furthermore, assuming you have the ability to build Web pages visually as well as the ability to tinker with the code, you may decide to choose the Show Split View option. Doing so splits the development area into two halves. As you can see from Figure 1-5, the top half displays the code, whereas the bottom half displays the visual environment.

So, why does Expression Web support two modes of development? The answer is simple. Some developers have the ability to work with HTML directly in code, while others prefer to work with the page visually. In the end, it doesn't matter. Even if you prefer to work with the page visually, in the end, the result is a series of tags that is produced automatically for you by Expression Web within the Code view. The browser, knowing nothing of the visual design, instead parses the carefully crafted tags associated with the page and presents to the user what the developer intended.

As an example of how Expression Web writes the code for you, try choosing File ⇨ New ⇨ HTML to create a new blank Web page. Immediately choose the Show Split View option. Now select Table ⇨ Insert Table. The Insert Table dialog box will appear. Accept the defaults and click OK to close the dialog box. Observe that a table is added to the page. More importantly, however, notice the code that is generated within the Code view.

> It's important to note that when you click the New Page icon in the Folder List Task Pane, the new page is created as default.htm. If you select File ⇨ New ⇨ HTML to create a new file, the new page is created as Untitled_1.htm.

The code that's produced here is what's parsed by the browser. The browser has no understanding of what you're developing visually. Instead, it parses the <table>, <tr>, and <td> tags, and associated properties of the table, and attempts to display within the browser something close (if not exact) to what you developed visually within Expression Web.

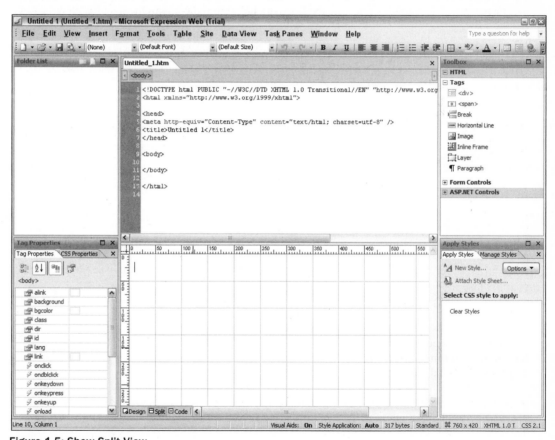

Figure 1-5: Show Split View

The Quick Tag Selector

As you build your Web pages visually within the Design view, you'll quickly find that you either need to place your cursor within a specific tag or manipulate properties of a particular tag while in Design view. The Quick Tag Selector (located just above the development area and just below the Tabbed File Chooser) displays a hierarchal list of tags from where your cursor is positioned in both the Design and Code views. This allows you to select a particular tag, manipulate its properties, or even wrap the tag with a new tag without having to switch to the Code view.

In the previous section you added a table within the development area in an effort to see code that was produced by Expression Web. But visually, how would you be able to select the `<td>` tag? The answer lies with the Quick Tag Editor. To select the `<td>` tag from the Quick Tag Editor, first place your cursor within the table. Immediately, the Quick Tag Selector changes to display the hierarchal tag list `<body><table><tr><td>`. Finally, select the `<td>` tag within the Quick Tag Selector. You'll quickly notice that the inner portion of the table becomes highlighted.

Although the benefits of this approach don't become immediately visible, they will become evident as your Web pages grow in complexity. Assume for a moment that you were working with a complex table-based structure where tables within your Web pages happen to be nested within each other. The Quick Tag Selector would be particularly handy in a situation such as this because you could easily select a nested table simply by selecting the `<table>` tag within the hierarchy of tags within the Quick Tag Selector.

The functionality offered by the Quick Tag Selector isn't limited to simple selections. You'll quickly notice that if you roll over a particular tag, an expander arrow appears. Selecting the expander arrow offers a submenu with other options, highlighted in Figure 1-6.

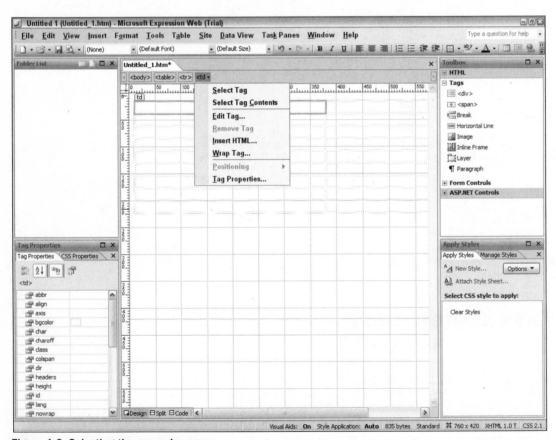

Figure 1-6: Selecting the expander arrow

The following table shows the options offered within the tag's submenu.

Option	Description
Select Tag	Selects the particular tag, enabling you to apply properties to the tag. Does not select the contents within the tag.
Select Tag Contents	Selects all of the content within the selected tag and not the actual tag.
Edit Tag . . .	Launches the Quick Tag Editor in Edit mode. The Quick Tag Editor enables you to quickly manipulate the properties of the particular tag as if you were in Code view without actually having to switch to Code view.
Remove Tag	Some HTML tags are represented by a single tag and, therefore, can be removed by simply choosing this option. Other tags (such as the `<table>`, `<tr>`, and `<td>` tags) rely on one another to function properly. Since this is the case, removing them is not an option because it would render the tags invalid by the browser.
Insert HTML . . .	Launches the Quick Tag Editor in Insert mode. While in this mode, the Quick Tag Editor allows you to freely insert code within the currently selected tag.
Wrap Tag . . .	Launches the Quick Tag Editor in Wrap mode. While in this mode, the Quick Tag Editor allows you to freely insert code that will end up wrapping the currently selected tag, as long as the resulting HTML is valid. If the HTML is not valid, Expression Web alerts you of the invalid entry.
Positioning	Choose one of the options within this submenu to apply an inline positioning style to the currently selected tag. Possible options include absolute, fixed, relative, and static. Positioning properties will be covered with more detail in Chapter 7, "Advanced Page Structuring by Using Layers and CSS."
Tag Properties . . .	Selecting this option launches a Tag Properties dialog box for the particular selected tag. The properties that appear within this dialog are similar to the properties that appear within the vertical list in the Tag Properties Task Pane, covered in the next section.

Task Panes

For the most part, all of your creative energy will be focused toward the development area within the Document window. However, without the collection of Task Panes that Expression Web offers, normal tasks such as quick browsing of files within a Web site, simple tag property modifications, centralized CSS style management, and drag-and-drop of common HTML and ASP.NET controls would consume much of the development time. To alleviate the burden Expression Web has conveniently separated all of the common functionality that developers will need the most access to into smaller user interfaces known as *Task Panes*.

Out-of-the-box Expression Web displays the Folder List Task Pane in the upper left, the Tag and CSS Properties Task Panes in the lower left, the Toolbox Task Pane in the upper right, and the CSS Styles Task Panes in the lower right. Of course, you're not limited to this set of Task Panes. As touched on earlier in the chapter, Expression Web includes a collection of Task Panes all conveniently located under the Task Panes menu item. In all, there are 18 Task Panes making up functionality that ranges from CSS property modification to an integrated compatibility check Task Pane. The following table briefly outlines the purpose of each Task Pane included with Expression Web.

Task Pane	Purpose
Folder List	Launches the Folder List Task Pane. Use this Task Pane to conveniently display a list of files and folders within your Web site. The files and folders within this list can be cut, copied, renamed, and deleted just as if you were working within Windows Explorer.
Tag Properties	As you'll see throughout the book, every selectable element within the development area has a set of modifiable properties. These properties are centrally listed within the Tag Properties Task Pane.
CSS Properties	When working with CSS, the CSS Properties Task Pane can be used to quickly manipulate properties for a class, ID, or tag redefinition quickly without having to launch the Modify Style dialog box each and every time.
Layout Tables	In addition to inserting and drawing tables within the development area, Expression Web supports a Layout Tables mode, which provides developers with a handy set of visual aids that make designing and working with tables easier and more efficient.
Apply Styles	Launches the Apply Styles Task Pane. When working with Cascading Style Sheets (CSS), the Apply Styles Task Pane is where you'll create new styles and apply existing ones to elements within your Web pages.
Manage Styles	Once you've added and applied styles to elements within your Web pages, you need some way to manage them. The Manage Styles Task Pane does just that. It provides a central interface for viewing a list of and modifying the styles within your Web sites.
Behaviors	Launches the Behaviors Task Pane. As you'll see in Chapter 8, "Adding Interactivity with Behaviors," behaviors are Expression Webs' alternative to writing JavaScript by hand. By simply inserting a behavior, functionality such as browser and plug-in checks, jump menus, pop-up messages, pop-up windows, and more become available to you.
Layers	Launches the Layers Task Pane. Use this Task Pane as a visual way to manage Layers within Expression Web. As you'll see in later chapters, Layers are a forward thinking alternative to structuring Web pages using CSS.

Task Pane	Purpose
Toolbox	All elements, whether they're HTML tags, form controls, ASP.NET controls, or SharePoint controls, are listed within the Toolbox Task Pane. Launching this Task Pane reveals a broad collection of controls that you can effortlessly select and drag out onto the development area.
Data Source Library	Launches the Data Source Library Task Pane. Use this Task Pane as a way to manage connections to data sources such as local or remote XML files or even Access, SQL Server, Oracle, and so on, databases.
Data Source Details	Once a data source has been defined, the fields/columns within the particular data source appear as a list within this Task Pane. The Data Source Details Task Pane makes it simple for a developer to quickly select and drag out bindings for a Web page to a data source.
Conditional Formatting	Launches the Conditional Formatting Task Pane. Use this Task Pane as a visual way to add server-side functionality to your Web pages. For example, you may decide to create a login page, a search page, or even an administrative dashboard for your organization. The features offered within this Task Pane facilitate this functionality.
Find 1	Launches the Find 1 Task Pane. Use this Task Pane as a way of searching for and even replacing text, code, and even HTML within a page, a group of pages, or the entire site.
Find 2	Launches the Find 2 Task Pane. Use this Task Pane as a second search when you don't want to clear the results of the Find 1 Task Pane.
Accessibility	Launches the Accessibility Task Pane. Use this Task Pane to perform accessibility checks against your Web pages/site. The Accessibility Checker dialog currently supports Web Content Accessibility Guidelines (WCAG) Priority 1 and 2 and Section 508 compliance validation. You may also choose to display errors, warnings, recommendations, or all three.
Compatibility	Launches the Compatibility Task Pane. Use this Task Pane as a way to validate your Web page/site against a particular browser version. You can also use this Task Pane to validate your Web page/site against a particular CSS version.
Hyperlinks	Launches the Hyperlinks Task Pane. Use this Task Pane as a way to check for broken links within your Web pages, collection of Web pages, or your entire Web site. This interface conveniently lists all broken links and provides a central method for editing/fixing broken links.
CSS Reports	Launches the CSS Reports Task Pane. Use this Task Pane to perform broad CSS validation checks on your Web pages.

Toolbars

So far, you've learned that the menu bar can be used when you need to insert or modify elements within your Web pages. In the previous section, you saw that Task Panes offer specific property modification options to particular elements that you happen to be working with within the development area. While these options are perfectly acceptable for use, it's important to understand that there's an easier, more visual way of inserting, modifying, and working with elements within your Web pages in what are known as *toolbars*.

If you're no stranger to Office applications, then there's no doubt that you've used toolbars. Toolbars, which are usually fixed under the menu bar and above the Document window, provide a visual approach (through the use of icons) for inserting, modifying, and managing specific types of elements within the development area. For example, if you're working with tables, you may decide to show the Tables toolbar. Alternatively, if you're working with CSS, you may decide to show the Style and Style Application toolbars. Or, if you're working within the Code view in Expression Web, you may decide to keep the Code View toolbar floating near or around where you're typing in code. Doing so would allow you quick, visual access to commonly accessed features without your having to fumble around through a massive collection of menus and submenus, which can be the case when working with the menu bar.

> Out-of-the-box, Expression Web docks the Common toolbar under the menu bar and just above the Document window. Obviously, you're not limited to having just this toolbar open. Furthermore, the toolbar doesn't have to be docked in this location. As mentioned earlier in the chapter, toolbars, like the Task Panes and the menu bar, can be undocked and repositioned anywhere within the Expression Web interface. Alternatively, you may decide not to re-dock a toolbar, but rather to keep it floating for easier access.

There are numerous ways of showing a particular toolbar, but probably none easier or more straightforward than choosing the toolbar you want to use from the View ⇨ Toolbars menu. As Figure 1-7 indicates, I've opened and docked the Common, Style, Style Application, and Tables toolbars. I also have the Code View toolbar open. However, this toolbar is floating, whereas the others are docked.

Once the toolbar is open and visible, a simple click of the icon performs the operation that the icon represents. For example, if I open the Tables toolbar and click the Draw Table icon (the first icon to the left in the Tables toolbar), I should expect to immediately be able to draw a table onto my Web page.

> It's important to understand that icons won't always be enabled within a particular toolbar. An icon's availability depends on the context for which you plan to use that feature that is ultimately offered by that icon. For example, if I haven't inserted a Layer into my Web page, I shouldn't expect options offered within the Positioning toolbar to become enabled. Additionally, unless I've already inserted a table, I shouldn't expect table formatting features offered within the Tables toolbar to become available either.

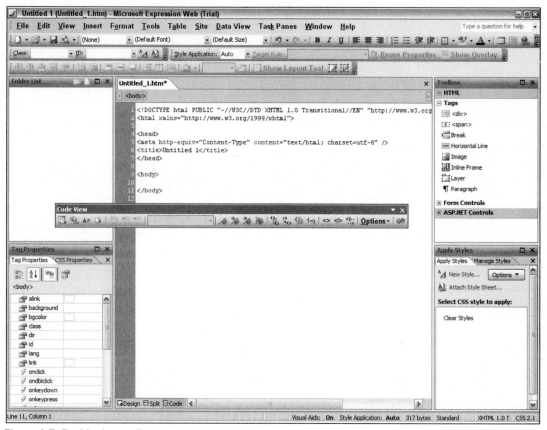

Figure 1-7: Positioning toolbars

Once a toolbar is open, you're not forced to use or even see the icons within the toolbar. There may be instances where you find that you'll never use a specific icon, and just its presence becomes a distraction. In this situation, you can hide specific icons within the toolbar.

You can hide specific icons within a toolbar by first rolling your mouse over the expander arrow located to the far right of the toolbar. The tool tip that appears should read "Toolbar Options." Click it. The Add or Remove Buttons menu option appears. Now, click the expander arrow that appears from the Add or Remove Buttons submenu. The name of the toolbar appears just to the right of the expander arrow. Click it. A list of available icons (representing functionality within the toolbar) appears in a list. Finally, check or uncheck the icons, representing the functionality that you may or may not want to use. When finished, your customized list may resemble Figure 1-8.

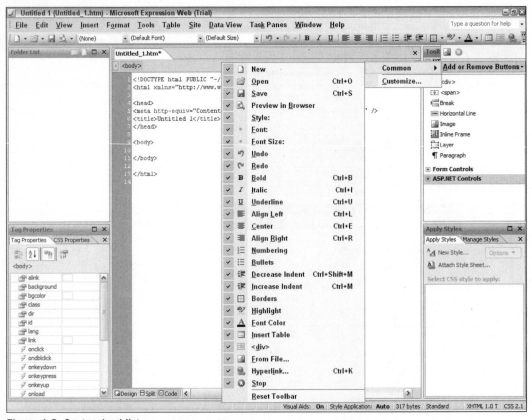

Figure 1-8: Customized list

You also probably noticed the Customize option that appeared when you selected the expander arrow from the Add or Remove Buttons submenu. Clicking this option (which is also available by choosing View ➪ Toolbars ➪ Customize) launches the Customize dialog. It's within this list of toolbars that you're presented with a complete list of 11 toolbars (minus the Menu Bar option, which enables or disables the menu bar at the top of the page). Also, it's important to understand that, like the Task Panes, the toolbars are specific to the type of element you happen to be working on within the development area. The following table provides a complete list of toolbars, including a brief description of their uses.

Toolbar	Usage
Standard	Lists standard document features such as the ability to create a new document, open an existing document, save, find, cut, copy, paste, undo, redo, and insert a table, hyperlink, layer, and more.
Formatting	Lists standard formatting features such as the ability to quickly show the CSS Task Pane, adding headings, fonts, font sizes, bold, italic, underline, alignments, lists, indentations, font colors, and more.

Toolbar	Usage
Code View	Provides functionality for working with code in Code view. Features such as adding bookmarks, selecting tags and parent tags, showing line numbers, and more, are displayed within this toolbar.
Common	Lists the most commonly used features within Expression Web. This is essentially a streamlined list of features taken from both the Standard and Formatting toolbars. This is one toolbar you'll probably always want open.
Dynamic Web Template	When working with dynamic templates, use the Dynamic Web Template toolbar to visually add and manage editable regions, region labels, and more.
Master Page	Similar to the Dynamic Web Template toolbar, the Master Page toolbar offers features for working with ASP.NET Master pages.
Pictures	Use the Pictures toolbar to quickly add and manipulate images within your Web pages. Options within this toolbar include the ability to rotate, crop, and set the contrast, brightness, opacity, and color of an image. When working with Image Maps (images that may contain multiple hyperlinks defined as hotspots), the hotspot set of tools is also available within this toolbar.
Positioning	When working with Layers, use the Positioning toolbar to set the Layer's position from the left, top, right, and bottom of the browser. You may also decide to set the width and height of the Layer within this toolbar, as well as the Z-Index, or stacking order of the Layer in relation to other Layers in your Web page.
Style	Use the Style toolbar to quickly apply classes or IDs to elements of your Web pages. You can also initiate the process of creating a new style or attaching an existing style sheet from this toolbar. Remember, this functionality is also offered within the Apply Styles Task Pane.
Style Application	Use features within this toolbar to set how CSS should be applied to the page. Options include Auto (Expression Web creates a new style whenever you manipulate formatting properties) or Manual (you are responsible for manually building styles when formatting elements within your Web pages).
Tables	Offers features for working with HTML tables. Options include the ability to draw tables, add columns and rows, split and merge cells, align content within cells, set background colors, auto-format a table using predefined styles, and the ability to visually switch to Layout mode.

Context Menus

Some of the most under-used features within Office applications are the context menus. Context menus are extended features, built into the environment, that you can access by right-clicking within a specific area in the application. The features that are offered within these menus depend on the context in which they are accessed, hence the name context menus.

In Expression Web, the toolbar, the Task Panes, the title heading within a Task Pane, the tag selector, the tabbed file chooser, and rulers all have selectable options within a context menu. However, the most dynamic context menu that you'll find yourself using more often than not is the context menu that appears within the development area.

As you progress through the book, the discussions will certainly cover options that are available within the many context menus. For now, let's do a simple cut-and-paste example using the development area's context menu.

You can follow along simply by first typing some text within the development area. I'll type **Hello World**. Highlight the text by selecting one end of it and dragging over to the other end. Now, right-click onto the selected text and choose Cut from the context menu. The text disappears. Finally, right-click onto the development area and choose Paste. The text reappears.

Summary

As you've learned in this chapter, Expression Web includes a myriad of toolbars and Task Panes, and a feature-rich and flexible Document window within its framework. While the discussion in this chapter has briefly highlighted the features offered by these toolbars, Task Panes, and the Document window, the overall goal of this chapter wasn't to provide a high-level understanding, but rather a gentle introduction and a chance of simple familiarization with some of the components that you will ultimately end up using while building your Web pages.

As the chapters progress, you'll undoubtedly be using the development area, the Task Panes, the toolbars, the menu bar, and even the myriad of context menus quite often. For now, at the very least, you understand the terminology, and more important, you'll be able to identify each component within the Expression Web framework by name.

Now that you've had a formal introduction to Expression Web, let's move forward with actually building a Web page. This is exactly what you'll get to do in Chapter 2. The Development window, the Task Panes, the menus, and more will begin to become clear as you begin to use them next.

Building a Web Page

Chapter 1 provided a real taste for some of the functionality that you'll be exposed to within Expression Web. You saw the potential provided by the Document window, in conjunction with the development area, the tag selector, the tabbed file chooser, and the Design, Split, and Code views. Combine that with a robust set of toolbars, flanked by a feature-rich set of Task Panes, and it would be hard to argue that Expression Web is not ahead of the game when it comes to visual Web development.

In this chapter, you will build on the gentle introduction provided in Chapter 1. You will have an opportunity to get your hands dirty with Expression Web by building your own Web page. Specifically, you will do the following:

❑ Expand on what you learned in Chapter 1 by building your first Web page

❑ Learn how to set page properties for a Web page

❑ Understand how to format text-based elements within a Web page

❑ Preview your Web pages within a browser directly from Expression Web with one click of a button

By the end of this chapter, you'll have your first Web page built. Granted, the page will be a simple representation of what you'll ultimately be building in later chapters. It will, at the very least, provide you with a solid foundation to other, more advanced concepts available through Expression Web later. Let's get started!

Creating a New Web Page

When working with Expression Web, it's important to understand what options are available to you when creating and working with Web pages. In this chapter, you will work with a single Web page. You'll create a new page, save it, add elements to that page, apply some formatting techniques, and then preview your work in the browser. While this method will be fine for this simple, introductory chapter, it's important to understand that this is not necessarily the ideal way to work.

Generally, Web developers like to create Web pages that include a multitude of text, images, media, and perhaps even links to other Web pages. Because this is the case, you'll want to keep all of these "assets" within the context of a single folder, otherwise known as a *Web site*. This way, when you need to add an image, reference a media element, or even link to another document, all of these assets are conveniently located in the same place as the file you're working on. Again, for the sake of simplicity, you'll work with individual Web pages within this chapter. Beginning with Chapter 3, "Working with Web Sites," however, the focus switches to that of working with Web sites.

With that said, it's time to create your first Web page. You can create a new Web page within Expression Web by choosing File ⇨ New. The New dialog will appear, as shown in Figure 2-1.

> **As is the case with nearly every option in Expression Web, you can also create a new page or access the New dialog by choosing the New Document icon within the Common toolbar (first icon from the left in the toolbar, represented by a blank white page icon).**

As you'll learn throughout the rest of this section, you can quickly create new HTML, ASP.NET, and CSS pages by expanding the submenu that appears when you mouse over the expander arrow icon available from the File ⇨ New menu. As you'll see in Chapter 3, you can also add folders, create a new Web site, and even launch this same New dialog by selecting the Page option that also appears from the submenu. Again, this point is made as a matter of thoroughness and also as a way of highlighting the fact that there are numerous ways of accomplishing the same task within Expression Web.

The New dialog offers the following functionality:

❑ *Page / Web Site Tabs* — Selecting one of these tabs customizes the New dialog's interface to support the creation of either a new page or a new Web site. The new Web site interface will be covered in depth in Chapter 3.

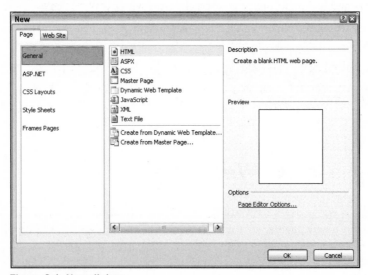

Figure 2-1: New dialog

❑ *Page / Web Site Categories* — Allows you to choose between General, ASP.NET, pre-built CSS structured layouts, pre-built CSS pages useful for formatting, and frame pages. As the chapters progress, you'll certainly explore all of these options. For now, choose the General category.

❑ *Page Type List* — Displays a custom list based on the selection made within the Page category selection list. When the General category is selected, options for creating a new HTML, ASP.NET (.aspx), CSS, Master Page, Dynamic Web Template, JavaScript, XML, or Text File become available. For our purposes, choose the HTML option.

❑ *Description* — Provides a simple text-based explanation for the selection made within the Page Type List.

❑ *Preview* — Use the Preview window to see an iconic representation of what the various CSS Layouts and frame pages will look like before you actually select them and click OK.

❑ *Options* — Offers the Page Editor Options hyperlink. Clicking this link launches the Page Editor Options dialog box, which enables you to customize various aspects of the development environment. When working with ASP.NET and Master Pages, a second option is offered just under the Page Editor Options hyperlink, allowing you to choose the type of language that you'd like to use when building and working with the page.

With the General category selected and the HTML option highlighted, click OK to close the New dialog. Instantly, a new Document window instance appears. The page is now ready for text, images, media, and so on. Before you begin adding content to the page, however, it's important to save the document. To save the document, choose File ⇨ Save As. The Save As dialog appears, similar to Figure 2-2.

The Save As dialog allows you to browse to a location on your computer to save the document to. If you have recently defined Web sites, selecting the Web Sites option within the category menu offers a list of recently defined Web sites where the new file may be saved to. Again, Web sites will be discussed with more detail in Chapter 3.

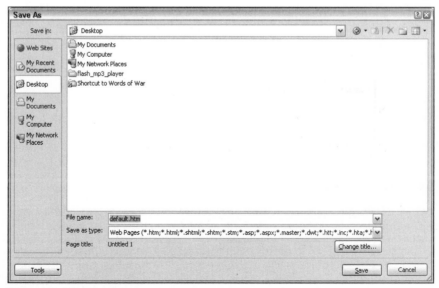

Figure 2-2: Save As dialog

For the sake of simplicity, choose the Desktop option and accept the default name of the page as `default.htm`. Before you click the Save button, however, change the page title from the default Untitled 1 to something that reflects the page you are working with. To do this, click the "Change title . . ." button. Immediately, the Set Page Title dialog appears. Enter the text **Welcome to Vecta Corporation** and then click OK to set the page title. Now, the page can be saved by clicking the Save button. Immediately, the page is saved, and the Document window's tab name changes from Untitled 1 to `default.htm`.

> **It's important to understand the role of the page title. Aside from appearing in the title bar within the browser, the page title also plays a key role in search engine ranking. A descriptive page title (one that includes keywords about what the company does, for example) will always benefit you more in the search rankings than one that includes a less descriptive one.**

Now that the new page has been created and, more important, saved to the desktop, you are now ready to begin adding elements such as text, images, and media to the page. Before you do, however, there may be certain properties associated with the page (otherwise known as *page properties*) that you will want to configure. Page properties are covered next.

Setting Page Properties

Now that the page has been created, you might think about configuring some basic page-level properties. For example, Expression Web offers a Page Properties dialog box (available by selecting the Format ➪ Properties option) that allows you to set generic, page-level properties such as the title of the page, keywords that should be associated with your page, background images and colors, page margins, system variables, the default language of the page, and more. In general, the Page Properties dialog offers the following tabs:

- ❑ General
- ❑ Formatting
- ❑ Advanced
- ❑ Custom
- ❑ Language

The following five sections discuss each option in greater detail.

General Properties

As you can see from Figure 2-3, you can use the properties offered within the General tab to set the title of the page, keywords that should be associated with your page, and even a background sound that should play when the page is loaded within the browser.

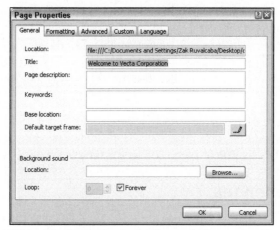

Figure 2-3: Properties in the General tab

The General category lists the following set of properties:

- ❏ *Location* — A read-only value indicating the full path to your saved file.

- ❏ *Title* — Sets the title of the page. This title ultimately appears within the title bar of the browser. Because you already set the page title when you saved the document, the text "Welcome to Vecta Corporation" is shown within the text box.

- ❏ *Page description* — Sets the description metatag. You can use this property to provide a short, plain-language description of the document. Ultimately, it's used by search engines to describe your document and is particularly important if your document has very little text, is a frameset, or has extensive scripts at the top of the page.

- ❏ *Keywords* — Sets the keywords metatag. Keywords are used by search engines to index your document and they ultimately play a part in how your page is ranked. Typically, you'd include keywords as a way of supplementing words included within the page title or document body, or as a way of including synonyms and alternates of title words.

- ❏ *Base location* — Sets the base location for all links within the page. For example, assume that the absolute address for an image on our site is `http://www.vectacorp.com/header.gif`. Rather than typing the full path every time you want to include an image within your page, you can instead set the Base location property here as `http://www.vectacorp.com`. Now, when inserting images on the page, you just have to specify the relative address as `header.gif`, and the browser automatically looks for that file using the full URL, or `http://www.vectacorp.com/header.gif`.

- ❏ *Default target frame* — Use the "Default target frame" selector as a way of setting the target browser that links should open within. For example, you may want all links within your site to open in the same browser, a new browser, a parent frame (when working with framesets), or a new whole page by default. When this is the case, you'd simply click the small icon (with a pencil on it) to launch the Target Frame dialog box. Within the Target Frame dialog box you can then specify whether to open within the same frame, whole page, new window, or parent frame.

❑ *Background sound location* — Sets the location to a sound file on your computer that should play in the background of the Web page. Expression Web supports the major file types including .wav, MIDI (.midi), Real Network's RealAudio (.ra), Apple's .aif, and more.

❑ *Background sound loop* — Sets how many times (if any) the audio file should loop in the background of the Web page. If you'd like the sound file to loop indefinitely, ensure that the Forever checkbox is selected.

While you do not have to set any of the properties within the General tab, it is wise to always set the Title, Page description, and Keywords properties. As mentioned previously, these three elements are important because they relate to page ranking in Internet search engines.

Formatting Properties

As you can see from Figure 2-4, you can use the properties offered within the Formatting tab to set a background image or color for your Web page; watermark the background image (if one is applied); and set the default text, hyperlink, visited, active, and hovered color of hyperlinks for your Web page.

Figure 2-4: Properties in the Formatting tab

The Formatting category lists the following set of properties:

❑ *Background picture* — Enable this checkbox and then browse to an image on your computer to set that image as the background of your Web page. By default, the image will tile (repeat) across the page. If this is not the desired result, you should use a larger image. Or, you can set the background-repeat property to no-repeat.

❑ *Make it a watermark* — Enable this checkbox to set the CSS background-attachment property as fixed. The code will be similar to style="background-image: url('Images/header .gif'); background-attachment: fixed".

❑ *Background color* — Sets the background color of your Web page. If a background image is applied along with a background color, the background image takes precedence. The default is white.

- ❏ *Text color* — Sets the default color for text within your Web page. The default is black.

- ❏ *Hyperlink color* — Sets the default color for hyperlinks within your Web page. The default is blue.

- ❏ *Visited hyperlink color* — Sets the default color for visited hyperlinks within your Web page. The default is purple.

- ❏ *Active hyperlink color* — Sets the default color for active hyperlinks within your Web page. The default is red.

- ❏ *Hovered hyperlink color* — Sets the color for hyperlinks when a user moves the mouse over the link. The default is red.

Again, setting properties within the Formatting tab is optional. However, you should always set the text and various hyperlink color properties because your users will be interacting with these elements the most. More information on these properties is available in Chapter 3, "Working with Web Sites," where linking is examined in much more detail.

Advanced Properties

As you can see from Figure 2-5, you can use the properties within the Advanced tab to set the default top, left, bottom, and right margins of your Web page. If these properties are left blank, the browser renders approximately 10 to 15 pixels of space between the edge of the document border and the content within your Web page.

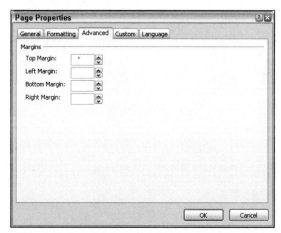

Figure 2-5: Properties in the Advanced tab

The Advanced category lists the following set of properties:

- ❏ *Top Margin* — Sets the amount of space in pixels that should appear between the top-most edge of your content and the top edge of the browser window.

- ❏ *Left Margin* — Sets the amount of space in pixels that should appear between the left-most edge of your content and the left edge of the browser window.

❑ *Bottom Margin* — Sets the amount of space in pixels that should appear between the bottom-most edge of your content and the bottom edge of the browser window.

❑ *Right Margin* — Sets the amount of space in pixels that should appear between the right-most edge of your content and the right edge of the browser window.

Again, setting properties within the Advanced tab is optional, but be aware that, unless you manually set these properties to 0, a default value of 10 to 15 pixels is automatically rendered by the browser.

Custom Properties

As you can see from Figure 2-6, you can use the properties within the Custom tab to set both system and user variables for the Web page. These variables are represented in code as metatags and are a useful way, for a developer, to include content that either describes the page (for example, the page type and default encoding), or as a way of forcing the Web server to handle a particular page with specific metatags differently than pages that do not include these metatags.

The Custom category lists the following properties:

❑ *System variables* — You can use the Add button located to the right of this list to add the HTTP-EQUIV metatag to your Web page. By default, Expression Web adds the `<meta http-equiv="Content-Type" content="text/html; charset=utf-8" />` tag, which sets the content type and default encoding of the Web page. Once you've added a system variable, you can modify it or remove it by clicking the respective button located just to the right of the System variables list.

❑ *User variables* — Similar to the System variables list, you can use the User variables list as a way to add customized metatags to your Web page. Because these metatags can contain information that describes the page, as a developer, you might add these custom user variables as a way to initiate a particular action by the Web server, depending on the variable set for the page.

Again, properties within the Custom tab are completely optional and are seldom used.

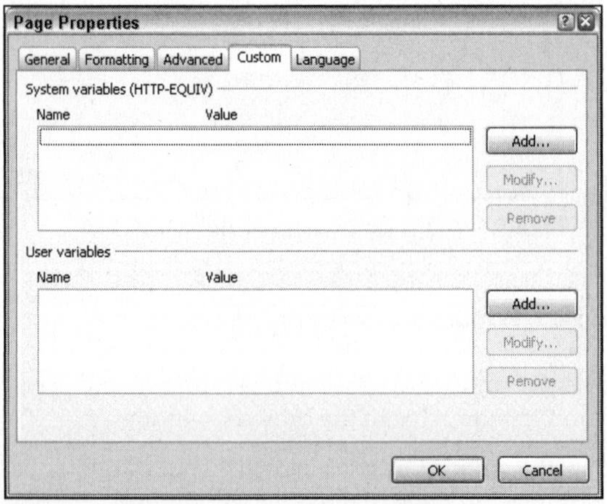

Figure 2-6: Properties in the Custom tab

Language Properties

As you can see from Figure 2-7, you can use the properties within the Language tab to set the default language and encoding type of the Web page.

The Language category lists the following properties:

❑ *Page language* — Sets the default language of the page. This creates the `<meta http-equiv="Content-Language" content="en-us" />` tag where the value `en-us` represents English (U.S.).

❑ *HTML encoding* — Sets the HTML encoding type of the Web page. By default, Expression Web automatically includes this metatag for you as `<meta http-equiv="Content-Type" content="text/html; charset=utf-8" />`. Essentially, this sets the content type as a Text/HTML document and sets the encoding type as UTF-8.

Unless you want to change the default language or encoding type of the page (you probably wouldn't), the properties within this category will rarely be accessed.

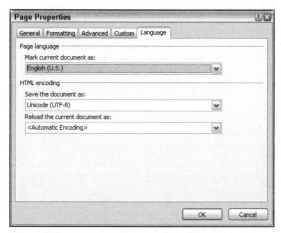

Figure 2-7: Properties in the Language tab

Working with Text

Now that a new page has been created and saved, and you've seen some of the many properties that can be set for the page, let's turn our attention to a topic that you may find just a bit more compelling: adding content to the page. The next few sections examine just that: adding and formatting text within Expression Web. Specifically, you will do the following:

❑ Copy, paste, and insert text from an external source into your Web page

❑ Learn about line breaks and paragraph breaks

- ❑   Apply headings
- ❑   Choose a font
- ❑   Set font sizes
- ❑   Apply text styles
- ❑   Align and indent text
- ❑   Work with ordered and unordered lists
- ❑   Highlight and set the text color
- ❑   Apply borders
- ❑   Insert a horizontal line
- ❑   Check the spelling of your document

Copying, Pasting, and Inserting Text from an External Source

In most cases, habit may drive you to simply place your cursor into your Web page and start typing. While this method is perfectly acceptable, let's assume for this section that you've either pre-typed the content that will appear within your Web page in a separate program, or that a content manager has created the content, saved it within a text file, and given it to you for placement on the Vecta Corp. home page. If this is the case, you must apply methods available within Expression Web for including that content within the page.

There are numerous methods for adding content from external sources within a Web page in Expression Web. Possibly the simplest would be to open the text file (open the `content.doc` file located within the `Assets` folder for this chapter's project files), select all of the text within the file, copy it, and then switch over to Expression Web and choose Edit ⇨ Paste. Doing so would take all of the content that you've copied from the external text file and include it within an HTML `<p>` tag in the development area of your Web page. While using this method certainly has its advantages, it's not encouraged because Expression Web preserves all of the formatting that was applied (if any) within the external text file.

So, what's the problem with this approach? The answer lies in how Microsoft Word structures and formats content within the program. Word uses technologies such as XML and CSS to structure and format even the simplest bits of text within the program. When you copy and paste from Word, all of that markup (sometimes markup that isn't even needed for the page to look decent) is also copied over, resulting in a bloated rendition of the page. If you're in a hurry and need to create a Web page quickly, then maybe this approach is OK. If, however, you like to be in command of the styles and formatting that are generated by Expression Web, the Edit ⇨ Paste option isn't the way to go. Figure 2-8 shows the design and the code that are produced when choosing the Edit ⇨ Paste option.

As you can see from Figure 2-8, Expression Web produces some hefty code (document-wide style sheets, `<span>` tags with inline styles applied, redefined `<h1>` tags, and more) to make the page look exactly the way it looked like in Word. Again, if you're in a hurry and need to quickly create a document, then perhaps this option is for you. If, on the other hand, you like to control the formatting of the text within Expression Web, you can choose the Edit ⇨ Paste Text option instead. Choosing the Paste Text option as opposed to the Paste option launches the Paste Text dialog box, similar to Figure 2-9.

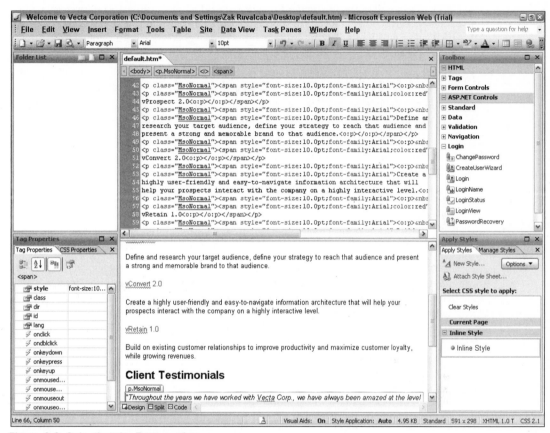

Figure 2-8: Selecting the Paste option

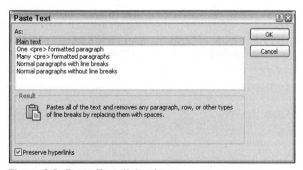

Figure 2-9: Paste Text dialog box

The Paste Text dialog box is for those developers who prefer not to preserve any of the formatting that was applied to content copied from an external source. As you can see from Figure 2-9, options within this dialog box include the following:

❑ *Plain text* — Pastes all of the text and strips out any and all formatting and paragraph and line breaks. Essentially, you get one big block of plain text. This option is ideal for those developers who are used to working with content managers that over-format documents within word processing applications.

❑ *One <pre> formatted paragraph* — Pastes all of the text into a preformatted text (<pre>) tag. This option preserves basic paragraph and line breaks, but still removes formatting (text colors, sizes, and so on) from the pasted text. This is not the best option in most cases because you cannot later add style tags to format the text differently without a major reworking of the text.

❑ *Many <pre> formatted paragraphs* — Similar to the previous option. The difference here is that Expression Web will enclose empty lines within their own <pre> tags. This is also not a good option in most cases because this just separates out the problem rather than solving it.

❑ *Normal paragraphs with line breaks* — Pastes all of the text, but preserves paragraph breaks by replacing them with line breaks.

❑ *Normal paragraphs without line breaks* — Pastes all of the text, but replaces any line breaks with paragraph breaks.

> **Another option that appears within this dialog box is the checkbox to preserve hyperlinks. Because hyperlinks aren't considered a formatting element, Expression Web gives you the opportunity to preserve them when copying and pasting from an external document. Simply check this box to enable them, or uncheck the box to disable them. If the box is unchecked, the text that is pasted in place of the actual hyperlink is the full text-based path.**

For this example, and as a lead-in to the next section, let's choose the "Plain text" option and click OK. As you can see from Figure 2-10, the text is pasted into the document, but this time any text formatting, paragraph, and line breaks that may have carried over from the previous document are completely stripped out.

In this scenario, the developer is given complete control over the formatting properties of the page.

Of course, there are a few other options for including text within your Web page. The first is to simply take the file from Windows Explorer and physically drag it into the Web page. Depending on the type of file you are dragging in and the content that the file contains, the Paste Text dialog box may or may not appear. At any rate, this is a quick-and-easy way of adding content within a file to your Web page.

The second method is to choose the Insert ⇨ File option. Selecting this option launches the Select File dialog box, where you're given the opportunity to browse for and select the external document whose content you want to include within your Web page.

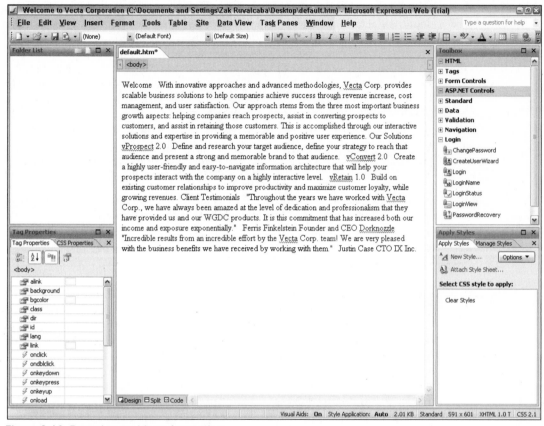

Figure 2-10: Pasted text without formatting

Line Breaks and Paragraph Breaks

In the previous section, the Edit ➪ Paste Text option was chosen as a way of including text with no formatting within a Web page. While this option seemed unnecessary, and for the amount of content you copied over, it probably was, I took this approach as a way to demonstrate the topic of adding line breaks and paragraph breaks here.

Paragraph breaks (represented by the <p> tag) are a block-level structuring technique for content within your Web pages. When you set aside an element or a collection of elements within a paragraph break, you're then able to apply block-level formatting properties such as alignments, lists, indents, and more to the element or collection of elements on the Web page.

Adding a paragraph break is easy. Simply highlight the element or group of elements that you want to wrap within a paragraph, and choose the Paragraph <p> option from the Formatting menu located within either the Common or Formatting toolbars, similar to Figure 2-11.

As soon as the paragraph option is applied, the highlighted element within the development area is wrapped within a <p> tag, represented visually by the black border and red/grey shaded areas that represent the spacing that's automatically rendered above and below the element that's marked as a paragraph. When you're ready to create other individual paragraph breaks, simply place your cursor after the element and click Enter. You'll notice that the two elements are separated into two separate paragraph breaks.

Line breaks (represented by the <br /> tag) differ from paragraph breaks in that they don't wrap around elements and don't facilitate the addition of block-level formatting. Instead, line breaks (considered *empty elements* because they don't wrap content) are used simply as a way to add a break within lines of text. To add a line break, you'd simply place your cursor after the element where you want to create the line break and press Shift+Enter. You'll immediately notice that text shifts down to the next line.

Figure 2-12 shows how the finished page might look once paragraph and line breaks are added to all of the text within the page.

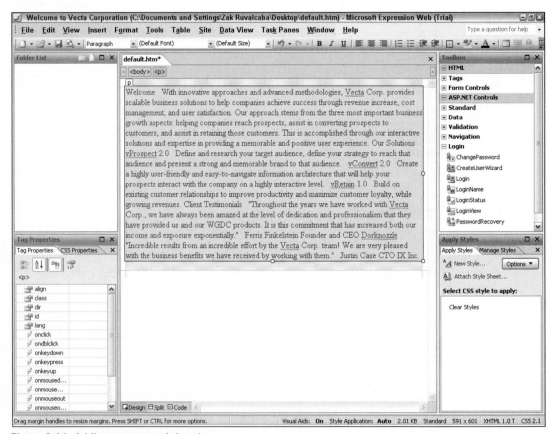

Figure 2-11: Adding a paragraph break

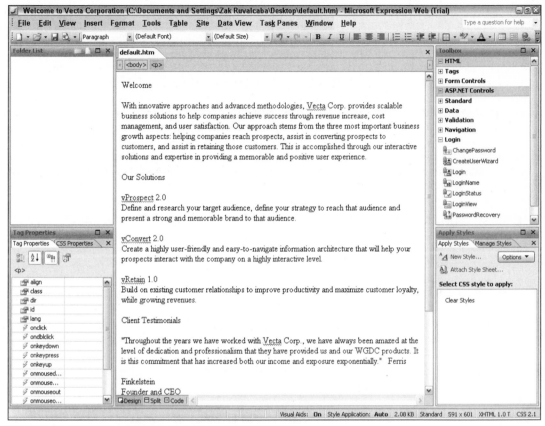

Figure 2-12: Finished page with paragraph and line breaks

Applying Headings

With paragraph and line breaks now firmly in place, you can turn your attention to the various formatting options that exist within Expression Web. The sections that follow discuss formatting options such as setting the typeface, font color, size, and more. For now, however, let's consider the formatting options that exist within the Common toolbar, and apply headings to some of the elements within your Web page.

In the previous section, you saw how easy it was to apply a paragraph break to an element within a Web page by simply choosing the Paragraph <p> option from within the Formatting menu in the Common toolbar. While following along in the previous section, you may have also noticed that just below the Paragraph <p> option in the formatting menu exist six options for setting headings within your Web pages. These headings, defined as Heading 1 (<h1>), Heading 2 (<h2>), Heading 3 (<h3>), Heading 4 (<h4>), Heading 5 (<h5>), and Heading 6 (<h6>), allow a developer to insert paragraph-like functionality into an element within a Web page.

While the paragraph option simply wraps a specific element with the <p> tag, allowing a developer to work with other block-level formatting options later, headings define pre-built formatting properties (such as a type face, color, and size), but are treated much like the paragraph tag in terms of the spacing that's offered above and below the element. By default, all headings are defined with the Times New Roman typeface and are black in color. What varies is the size. Depending on the heading that you select, the size can vary from a small font (Heading 6) to a much larger font (Heading 1).

To demonstrate the use of headings, highlight an element on the Web page (the Welcome text) and choose the Heading 3 <h3> option from the Formatting menu. Immediately, the <p> tag that once wrapped the element is converted to an <h3> tag, and the text within the tag appears bigger, bolder, and darker than the text that was there previously. Additionally, you can highlight the text elements for "Our Solutions" and "Client Testimonials" separately, and apply the same option (Heading <h3>) from the Formatting menu. The result will appear, similar to Figure 2-13.

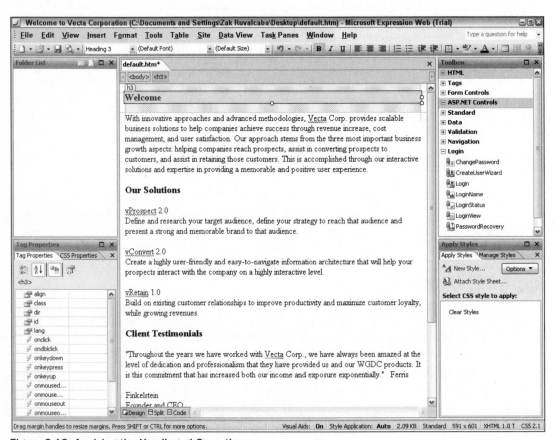

Figure 2-13: Applying the Heading <h3> option

By default, headings are rendered by the browser as black in color and Times New Roman. Again, the size is fixed based on the particular option that you select. However, you're not stuck with these properties. In Chapter 5, "Page Formatting Using Cascading Style Sheets," you see just how easy it is to redefine these headings with custom properties that you specify.

Choosing a Font

One of the biggest adjustments that people have to make when making the transition from word processing applications such as Microsoft Word to a program like Expression Web is that they have only a limited number of fonts to choose from.

When you're working in Word, choosing a font can be a daunting task because there are hundreds to choose from. The user is limited only by the number of fonts available on his or her computer. Because the font is also embedded in the file when it's saved, the user doesn't have to worry about the recipient of the file having the same font to accurately view the stylized file.

Again, Web pages are a completely different animal. When you build a Web page, everything is referenced. Images, media elements, and even font faces are referenced from the user's computer. When you browse to a Web page, the developer of that Web page is assuming that you have the particular font on your computer. If you don't have it, the browser displays the content of that Web page using whatever default font you've set up within the browser, typically Times New Roman.

For the most part, Expression Web supports three different font faces: Arial, Times New Roman, and Courier. It's safe to assume that if you apply one of these three font faces to the text within your Web pages, you'll never have any problems. This isn't to say that you can never use any font that you want. For example, if you're building an intranet site where you know for a fact that everyone's computer within the organization has the same fonts installed, you might decide to pick a font other than the three mentioned.

To apply a font to text within a Web page you'd simply highlight the text by clicking, holding, and dragging until all of the text is selected, or press Ctrl+A to access the Select All command within the Edit menu. Next, select the appropriate font within the Font menu located just to the right of the Formatting menu in the Common toolbar. Immediately, the text changes to the font option you selected, similar to Figure 2-14.

You probably noticed that the three common fonts are conveniently listed as the first three fonts within the list. This is done to prevent you from having to repeatedly scroll through an enormous list of fonts when you'd be accessing only the same three anyway.

You probably also noticed that fonts are listed in groups of threes. For example, when you selected Arial, it wasn't just Arial; it was Arial, Helvetica, sans-serif. This is known as a *font family*. Applying a font family as opposed to an individual font is a safe way of guaranteeing that your users will always see a similar font, regardless of whether they have the font installed on their computers or not. For example, if the user, for some odd reason, doesn't have Arial installed on his or her computer, the browser will automatically try to use Helvetica instead. If Helvetica isn't available, it will pick the next best sans-serif font. This would always protect the developer from content being shown in a serif font such as Times New Roman.

You're probably wondering if you can create your own font family that initially includes the font of your choice, followed by other standard fonts such as Arial, Helvetica, and so on. The answer is "yes." In this way, you can try the font of your choice, and, if the user doesn't have that font installed on his or her computer, the browser would immediately try the fonts that are more common such as Arial or Helvetica.

You can accomplish this by creating your own font family, available by choosing the Customize Font Family option located as the fourth option below the three font families in the Font menu within the Common toolbar. When you select this option, the Page Editor Options dialog box appears with the Font Families tab selected. To create your own font family, simply select the fonts from the "Add font" list, clicking the Add button along the way. When you're finished, you'll have a new font family available within the "Select font family" list box, similar to the one shown in Figure 2-15.

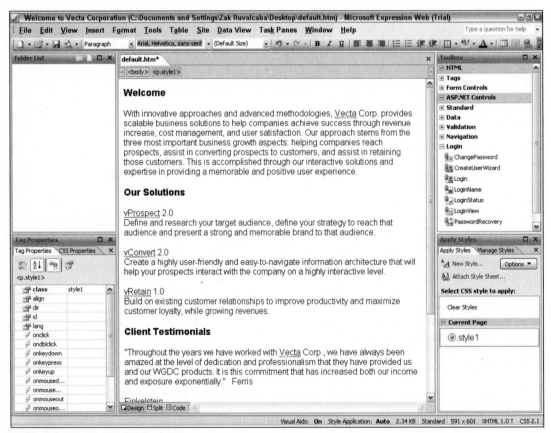

Figure 2-14: Font option text change

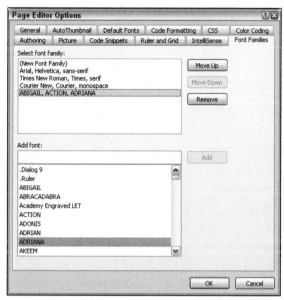

Figure 2-15: New font family

As you might have guessed, the option you selected would assume that the user has the specific font installed on his or her computer. While the chances are good that the user won't have it, you don't have to worry too much because the browser would simply default to either Arial or to the next best sans-serif font. Clicking OK closes the Page Editor Options dialog box and, more important, includes your new font family within the Font menu in the Common toolbar.

Setting a Font Size

Now that you've successfully set the font face for your Web page, you'll probably also want to set the size. Setting the size of text within your Web pages is just as easy as setting a heading or choosing a font. Because the font size list is conveniently located directly to the right of the font face list, setting the font size is simply a matter of highlighting the text that you want to change the size for, and then choosing a size option from the Font Size menu.

The easiest way to set the font size for text within your Web page would be to select all (Ctrl+A) of the text within that page and then choose the appropriate size from the Font Size menu. However, in this case, this isn't an option; after all, you wouldn't want to change the size of your headings. Instead, let's choose all of the paragraph breaks that contain text. To do this, hold down the Ctrl key and then select all of the <p> tags (the small tab that appears in the upper-left corner of the paragraph) within the Web page. When you're finished, all of the paragraphs (excluding the headings) will be selected, similar to Figure 2-16.

Now, to apply the font size for these paragraphs, choose the "small" option from the Font Size menu. Instantly, all of the paragraphs change to 12pt.

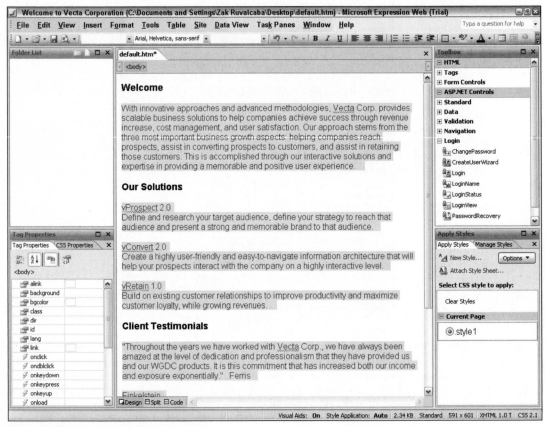

Figure 2-16: Selecting all the paragraphs

The Font Size menu within Expression Web includes seven commonly used font sizes ranging from the xx-small option of 8pt to the xx-large option of 36pt. Fortunately, you're not limited to these seven font sizes. As you'll learn in Chapter 5, "Page Formatting Using Cascading Style Sheets," CSS opens a whole new world of font sizes. The seven that are listed within this menu are simply the ones that you'll find yourself using most often.

Text Styles

Three options that you may have noticed right away within the Common toolbar are the Bold, Italic, and Underline icons. Similar to other Office applications, selecting text within your Web page and then choosing these icons will cause that text to be styled in bold, italics, and even underline.

For example, choose the text element "vProspect 2.0" and then select the Bold icon within the Common toolbar. Instantly, the text becomes darker and appears to stand out from the other elements. You can repeat this process two more times for the elements "vConvert 2.0" and "vRetain 1.0." Now, you might want to italicize text (for example, the client testimonials that appear near the bottom of the page). To do this, click, hold, and drag your cursor from the opening quote in the first client testimonial over and down to the last quote in the same testimonial. Next, choose the italic icon within the Common toolbar. Instantly, the text is italicized. Repeat this process for the second client testimonial so that, when you're finished, your page resembles Figure 2-17.

> While you're certainly free to underline text just as you bolded and italicized it, you should refrain from doing so. Because underlines are synonymous with hyperlinks, underlining text that isn't a hyperlink can pose a usability problem. You most certainly wouldn't want to frustrate your users by offering a text element that resembles a link, only to have the users click that text element and wonder why they aren't being redirected to what they think might be another Web page.

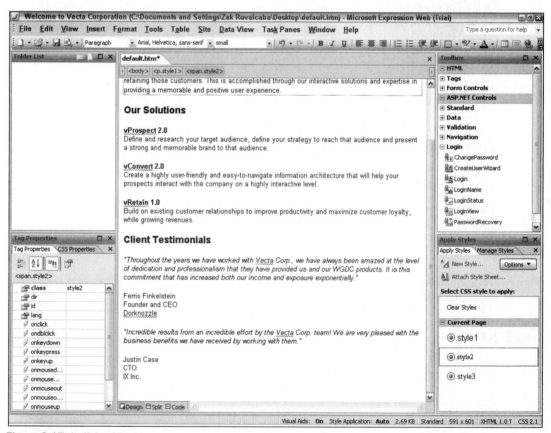

Figure 2-17: Italicized text

Text Alignment and Indentations

Just to the right of the text styles (bold, italic, and underline) within the Common toolbar are three options for aligning text within your Web page. As you can see, the three icons moving from left to right allow you to align a block of text either to the left, center, or right of the page, providing that the text block resides within a paragraph break. To demonstrate how alignments work, select each heading and click the center align icon within the toolbar. The result forces the heading to center itself within the Web page, as shown in Figure 2-18.

Moving forward in the toolbar are text indent icons. Located just to the right of the numbering and bullet list icons, the text increase and decrease indent icons allow you to indent and remove indentations for text within your Web pages. As an example, select the two paragraphs of text that contain the client, title, and company just underneath each client testimonial. With both paragraphs selected, click the Increase Indent Position icon within the toolbar. The result of the text indent and the center alignment is also shown in Figure 2-18.

Of course, if you need to remove the indentation, you'd only need to choose the Decrease Indent Position icon. Doing so removes the indentation from the text.

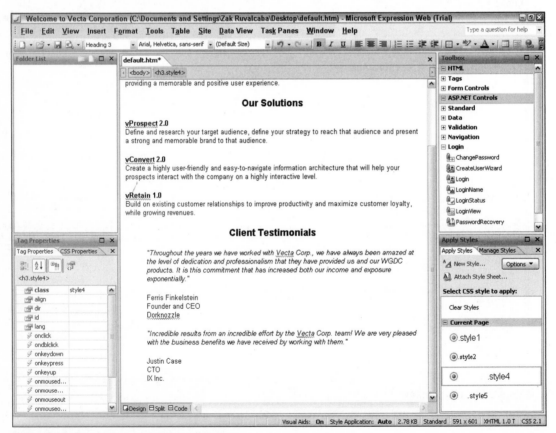

Figure 2-18: Text indent and center alignment

Working with Lists

One text-formatting feature you may be interested in is the ability to work with lists. Located to the right of the alignment icons and to the left of the indent icons, the icons within the toolbar for numbered and bulleted lists allow you to structure text within a numbered or bulleted list. To see how lists work, select the three solution paragraphs within the Web page and choose the icon for a bulleted list. As you can see from Figure 2-19, the three solutions within the Web page are displayed in a bulleted list.

As you may have also noticed, the three <p> tags that used to wrap each solution are now combined together into one <ul> tag. The <ul> tag stands for "unordered list" and is the tag used for bulleted lists. If you place your cursor within each solution, you'll see that it's wrapped within the <li> tag. The <li> tag, which is short for "list item," is the tag used within the <ul> tag to set aside a particular item as being part of that list.

Of course, you're not limited to working with bulleted lists. If you'd prefer to have a numeric list, you could simply highlight the <ul> tag that wraps the three solutions and then choose the numbered list icon within the toolbar. Doing so would create a numeric list starting at 1 and ending at 3.

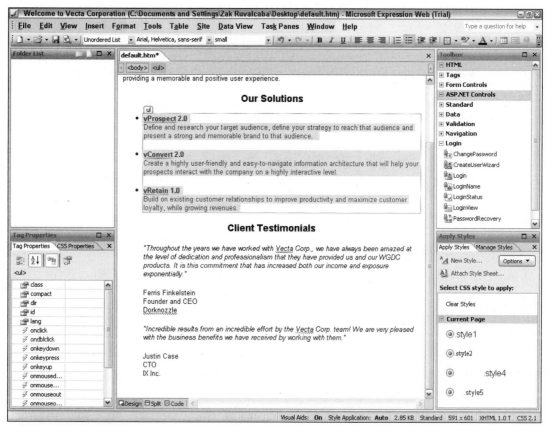

Figure 2-19: Bulleted list

You probably noticed that when working with bulleted lists, by default, Expression Web displays solid black circles. While these are the traditional representations of bulleted lists, you're certainly free to customize your own style. To do this, choose Format ⇨ Bullets and Numbering (or right-click onto the <ul> tag to access the context menu and choose the List Properties option). Choosing this option launches the List Properties dialog box, similar to Figure 2-20.

As you can see from Figure 2-20, the dialog box is separated into the following four tabs:

❑ *Picture Bullets* — Selecting this tab configures the List Properties dialog box in a manner that allows you to browse for and use a custom image as the bullet. When you specify a custom image to use as a bullet, Expression Web adds an inline style (discussed in more depth in Chapter 5) within the <ul> tag that redefines the look of the default bullet. The code resembles <ul style="list-style-image: url("Images/custombullet.gif")">.

❑ *Plain Bullets* — Shown by default, the Plain Bullets tab offers options that allow you to remove bulleting altogether, applying the default, solid, black bullets, the disc style bullet, or the squared style bullets.

❑ *Numbers* — Select the Numbers tab when you want to configure your list to use numbers, letters, or Roman numerals. You can also set the starting number by using the scroll list widget to increase or decrease the starting point of the numeric list.

❑ *Other* — Access the Other tab when you want to set the final type of list supported by Expression Web: the *definition list*. The definition list, which comprises the <dl>, <dd>, and <dt> tags, allows you to create a list that looks similar to a dictionary listing. This option is seldom used.

When you've finished making changes within the List Properties dialog box, simply choose the OK button to close the dialog box and apply the new list properties to the selected elements within your Web page.

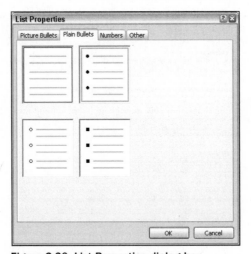

Figure 2-20: List Properties dialog box

Highlighting and Setting the Text Color

One of the topics yet to be discussed is that of working with text colors. In Expression Web, colors are applied to text via the two icons located just to the right of the indentation icons within the toolbar.

The first icon, Highlight, allows you to apply a highlight (also known as a *background color*) to text within your Web page. To see how highlighting is applied, select the first heading on the Web page ("Welcome") and choose the Silver (grey) color from the menu of colors that appears once you click the expander arrow icon located just to the right of the Highlight icon in the toolbar. You'll notice that as soon as the color is chosen, the silver color is applied to the heading's background. Repeat this process twice more until the other two headings ("Our Solution" and "Client Testimonials") have the silver color applied as their backgrounds similar to Figure 2-21.

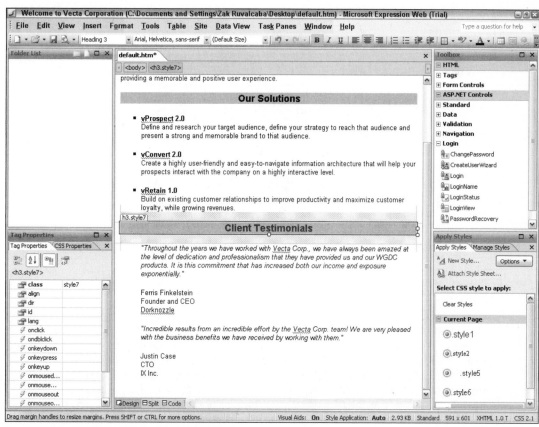

Figure 2-21: Applying color to the background

Similar to the process of applying a text highlight is the process of applying a text color. The text color differs from the highlight option in that it applies the color to the text element itself, rather than to the background of the element. For example, if you want to change the color of the headings to a bluish color, you only need to select the text element, and choose a blue color from the menu that appears when you click the expander arrow located to the right of the Font Color icon within the toolbar. Applying the color to the other headings is easier. Because the color is already preselected for you, you'd only need to select the other headings and then click the icon to apply the blue color.

By default, the color menu displays a list of 16 standard colors. Of course, you're not limited to just these 16. You may decide to choose from a list of 216 Web-safe colors, or you may even decide to pick from the millions of system colors. To access these colors, you simply click the expander arrow icon located just to the right of either the Highlight or Font Color icon within the toolbar. When the color menu appears, select the More Colors option. Doing so causes the More Colors dialog box to appear, as in Figure 2-22.

As you can see from Figure 2-22, the More Colors dialog box displays a complete list of the 216 Web-safe colors.

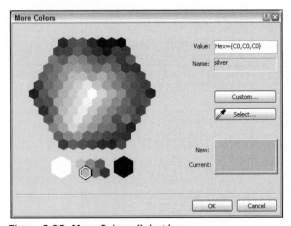

Figure 2-22: More Colors dialog box

"Web-safe" is a reference used when referring to the spectrum of 216 colors that are guaranteed to work on a 256 color (8-bit) computer. When colors were introduced to the Web in the early to mid 1990s, the majority of developers were designing their Web pages on antiquated systems that at best had an 8-bit video card installed. Because the hardware couldn't support a range beyond 256 colors, a Web-safe spectrum of 216 colors was introduced to make Web page colors as compatible across the board as possible. Today, these systems are rare, and the need to rely on the Web-safe color spectrum has diminished greatly. Realistically, the only time you'd need to rely on the 216 Web-safe colors is when development is targeted to small form-factor devices such as a PDA or cell phone.

If you'd prefer to sample a color from the development environment, you can choose the Select button. Doing so changes your cursor into the eye dropper. Now, try rolling your cursor around the development environment. You'll quickly notice that the New color pane within the More Colors dialog box changes to reflect the color that you're rolling into. When you want to change the cursor back, simply click the eye dropper within the Current color pane. This keeps the color at its current state and returns your cursor back to normal.

If you'd prefer to choose from the millions of colors that your computer supports, you can choose the Custom button. Doing so launches the Color dialog, similar to Figure 2-23. It is within this dialog that you are able to browse the spectrum of millions of colors that your computer supports.

When you've identified a color to use, select it, and then click the OK button to close the Color dialog box. Once the Color dialog is closed, you'll immediately notice that the New color pane within the More Colors dialog displays the selected color. Click OK to close the More Colors dialog box and apply the color to the selected element within your Web page.

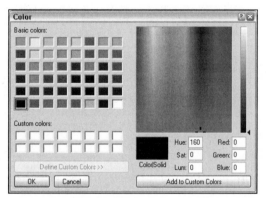

Figure 2-23: Color dialog

Applying Borders

You might also consider adding borders to your Web pages. Borders, when used appropriately, can add a simple, aesthetically pleasing line that surrounds an element in your Web page.

As an example of how borders can be used within Expression Web effectively, let's surround the background color that you applied in the previous section with a border. To do this, place the cursor within the first heading and choose the Outside Borders icon located just to the right of the Indent icon and just to the left of the Highlight icon. As you can see from Figure 2-24, a solid blue line now surrounds the heading.

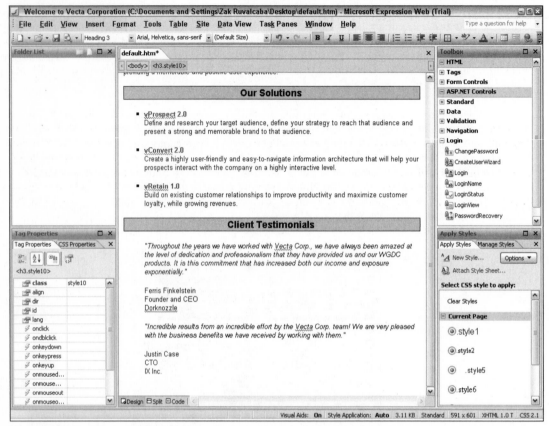

Figure 2-24: Applying a border

Unfortunately, Expression Web doesn't visually support changing the color of the border. The border's color is set based on the text color that's applied to the element within the paragraph/heading. Because the element within the heading was set to blue in the previous section, it's the color that's applied to the border automatically for you.

You can repeat the process two more times to add surrounding borders to the other headings within the Web page.

You probably also noticed that the Borders icon offers an expander arrow that, when selected, offers a menu of other border options. By default, Expression Web displays the Outside Borders icon, but as you can see from the menu that's offered when the expander arrow is selected, options exist for setting outside borders, a border at the top only, left only, right only, and bottom only, as well as options for setting inner borders when working with tables and an option for removing borders altogether.

Inserting a Horizontal Line

The final element that you might think about adding to your Web page is a horizontal line. Represented by the <hr> tag, the horizontal line (*horizontal rule* is the actual term) adds a simple line that spans horizontally for a given width across the page. To see how a horizontal line is applied, position the cursor at the end of the document and choose Insert ⇨ HTML ⇨ Horizontal Line. As you can see from Figure 2-25, a line is added (represented by the <hr /> tag) to the Web page.

By default, the horizontal line is displayed at a width of 100 percent. (That is, it spans the entire width of the browser window.) Furthermore, the horizontal line doesn't display as a solid line, but rather displays with what's known as *shading* (a slight beveled look that gives the appearance of a drop shadow). If you want to adjust the width of the horizontal rule, and perhaps disable the shading property, you'd only need to manipulate some of the properties that appear within the Tag Properties dialog box. However, if you're new to HTML and aren't familiar with the values that the properties listed within the Tag Properties Task Pane accept, you may choose to manipulate the properties using a visual dialog box instead.

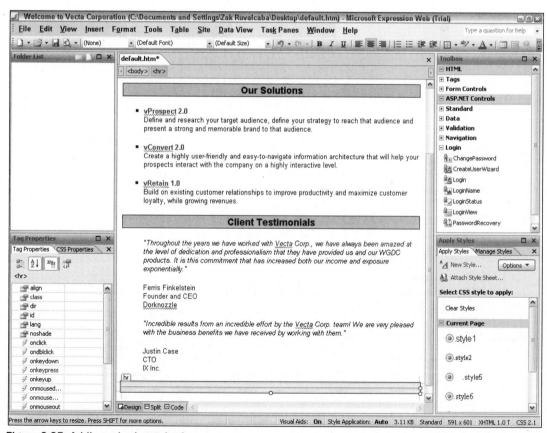

Figure 2-25: Adding a horizontal rule

To access the horizontal rule's Properties dialog box, select the horizontal rule, and then select the "Show tag properties" icon located fourth from the left within the Tag Properties Task Pane. The Horizontal Line Properties dialog box appears (see Figure 2-26).

As you can see from Figure 2-26, the Horizontal Line Properties dialog box allows you to set the width (in pixels or percent), height, alignment, and color of the horizontal line, and whether or not to enable shading. For this example, enter a width of 500 and choose the Pixels radio button. Additionally, check the "Solid line (no shading)" checkbox and click OK. Immediately, you'll notice that the horizontal rule's width and shading changes to reflect the change made within the Horizontal Line Properties dialog box.

Figure 2-26: Horizontal Line
Properties dialog box

As you saw in this example, the "Show tag properties" icon opens a dialog box that enables visual property modification of a selected element. Regardless of the element you have selected, the dialog that shows will always display properties that relate to the selected element. Keep this in mind as the chapters progress. While the list of Tag Properties is always an option, the visual dialog box that opens when you click the "List tag properties" icon is a nice alternative for those who aren't familiar with the values that the particular properties listed within the Tag Properties list support.

Checking the Spelling of a Web Page

One of the last things that you should do before calling a Web page finished is to check the spelling within the page. Expression Web integrates a spell-checking engine that functions in exactly the same manner as the spell-checking engines found in many Office applications. You've probably noticed the small, red, squiggly underlines that appear under some of the text elements within the Web page. These red, squiggly underlines are Expression Web's spell-checking engine at work. Expression Web is alerting you to the fact that the text elements for Vecta, vProspect, vConvert, vRetain, and Dorknozzle aren't found within Expression Web's dictionary. While you know that these words are spelled correctly, because they're uncommon and pertain specifically to the fictitious Vecta Corp. company, Expression Web is alerting you to the fact that these text elements may need special attention. These words should be part of the Vecta Corp. vocabulary, so add them to Expression Web's dictionary.

To do this, right-click on a word that has the red line underneath it to access the context menu. As you can see from Figure 2-27, Expression Web suggests words to replace the word it thinks is misspelled.

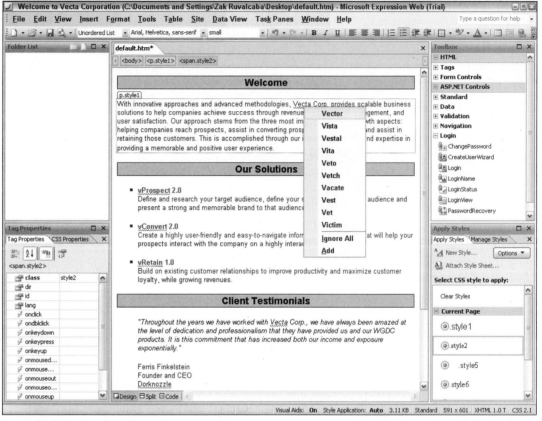

Figure 2-27: Word suggestions

If you know that the word is misspelled, you can easily select an option from this list to quickly replace the misspelled word. Additionally, notice that toward the bottom of the context menu, one option exists for ignoring all instances of that word, and a second option for adding the word to Expression Web's dictionary. Choose the Add option now.

Immediately, the context menu closes and the red, squiggly lines that used to appear underneath the instances of that word disappear. From here on out, whenever you type the word "Vecta" within a Web page, Expression Web will recognize it as a legitimate word. Even better, if you type the word "Vecta" within any other Office applications, those Office applications will also recognize the word!

> **Words that you add to the dictionary aren't actually stored by Expression Web specifically. They're actually stored in a shared text-based file called** `CUSTOM.DIC`. **This file, which resides at** `C:\Documents and Settings\<computername>\ Application Data\Microsoft\Proof`, **is shared and accessible by all Office applications, including Expression Web.**

Now, let's assume that you have a lengthy document that you want to begin spell-checking on. You can access the Spelling dialog in an effort to scan the entire page and access options such as ignoring instances of a word, ignoring all instances of a word, adding a word to the dictionary, and more.

To access the Spelling dialog, simply choose Tools ⇨ Spelling ⇨ Spelling. The Spelling dialog will appear, similar to Figure 2-28.

As you can see from Figure 2-28, the Spelling dialog includes the following functionality:

❑   *Not in Dictionary* — As Expression Web scans your document, words that are not found within the dictionary are listed here one at a time.

❑   *Change to / Suggestions* — Once a word has been located that is not found within the dictionary, suggestions are made. You can select a word from this list and click the Change button to change to the word highlighted within the "Change to" text box.

❑   *Ignore* — Ignores and skips over the selected word. This is valid for the current Web page only. Choosing this option will not add the item to the dictionary.

❑   *Ignore All* — Ignores and skips over all instances of a selected word. This is valid for the current Web page only. Choosing this option will not add the item to the dictionary.

❑   *Change* — Changes the word within the page to the suggested word.

❑   *Change All* — Changes all instances of a selected word.

❑   *Add* — You can add a word to the dictionary so that Expression Web doesn't ever detect it as a misspelled word.

❑   *Suggest* — Click this button to re-populate the Suggestions list with words that Expression Web believes should replace the misspelled word.

❑   *Options* — Click this button to launch the Spelling Options dialog box. It is within this dialog box that you are able to set various properties for how the spell-checker should function. Options for ignoring uppercase words, ignoring words that contain numbers, ignoring Internet and file addresses, flagging repeated words, and more, are all listed within this dialog box. More important, you may also access the spelling dictionary here. Doing so would allow you to visually add, modify, and delete words from the Office dictionary (CUSTOM.DIC). Furthermore, you can also disable the spell-checker while you type.

Figure 2-28: Spelling dialog

When you're finished with the spell-checker, simply close the dialog box either by clicking the Cancel button, or by choosing the small Close button (represented by the small red X icon) that appears near the top-right corner of the dialog box.

Previewing Your Web Page in the Browser

Once you're finished with your Web page, you'll no doubt want to see what it looks like within the browser. After all, your users will eventually be viewing your Web pages through a browser anyway so it only makes sense that you at least see what your page will look like within a browser before calling the page finished. Doing this affords you the opportunity to correct errors, should they appear before uploading the final version to a Web hosting provider (discussed in Chapter 3).

The most obvious way to open your Web page within a browser is to save the file, minimize Expression Web, and then double-click the file to open it within the default browser on your computer. While this method is perfectly acceptable, there is an easier way.

Built into Expression Web is the ability to preview your Web page directly within a browser window without having to exit or minimize the program. With one click of a button, you could easily open the page you are working on, at any time, within a browser window instance. Even better, Expression Web doesn't limit you to a particular browser type; instead it gives you the opportunity to set up various browsers to use for previewing within Expression Web. To demonstrate how to preview a Web page in the browser, choose File ⇨ Preview in Browser. As you can see from Figure 2-29, a list of browsers is displayed within the menu.

Following are a few interesting points to mention about this menu:

❑ Expression Web automatically scans and includes the browsers that are pre-installed on your computer within this list.

❑ Expression Web doesn't limit you from previewing your browser in one particular size. As you'll notice, Expression Web includes three predefined browser sizes of 640 x 480, 800 x 600, and 1024 x 768. Choosing the browser type along with the given size will open your Web page within that particular browser and automatically resize the browser window to accommodate the size that you've selected.

❑ The default browser on your computer is displayed with the F12 shortcut key. This enables one-button access for Web page previewing.

❑ You're not limited to previewing your Web page one browser at a time. If you want to compare how your Web page looks in multiple browsers at the same time, simply choose the Preview in Multiple Browsers option.

One of the final items within this menu that warrants mentioning is the Edit Browser List option. Selecting this option would enable you to add other browser types to this list that have been installed after Expression Web. To demonstrate how to add other, third-party browsers to this list, choose File ⇨ Preview in Browser ⇨ Edit Browser List. The Edit Browser List dialog box appears, similar to Figure 2-30.

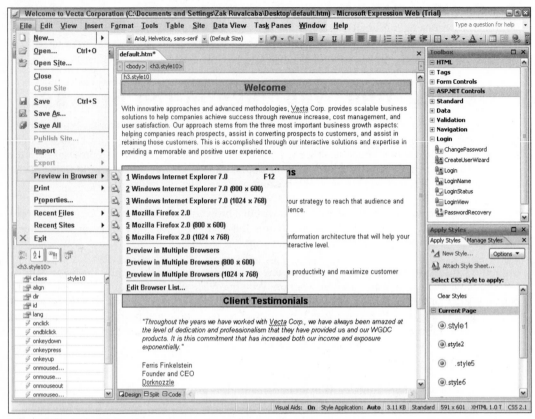

Figure 2-29: List of browsers

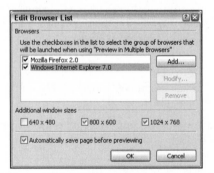

Figure 2-30: Edit Browser List dialog box

As you can see from Figure 2-30, the following features are offered within this dialog:

❑ *Browsers* — Displays a list of added browsers that are available. Upon installation, Expression Web includes the browsers that are preinstalled on your computer within this list. If you'd prefer to disable a particular browser, simply clear the checkbox.

❑ *Add* — Facilitates the addition of a particular browser type. Clicking this button launches the "Add browser" dialog box, which allows you to browse for and name a third-party browser to use within Expression Web. Once you've added the browser, it appears within the Browsers list (mentioned earlier) unchecked. To enable it within the Preview in Browser menu, simply check the corresponding checkbox.

❑ *Modify* — Allows you to edit a particular browser type. Clicking this button launches the Edit Browser dialog, which closely resembles the Add Browser dialog. If you want to change the name of the browser or path to the browser, this dialog box facilitates that process.

❑ *Remove* — Removes a browser from the Browsers list.

❑ *Additional window sizes* — Allows you to check and uncheck particular browser sizes that should appear within the Preview in Browser list.

❑ *Automatically save page before previewing* — Clicking this checkbox forces Expression Web to save the Web page before it is previewed in the browser. If this checkbox is left unchecked, Expression Web uses a temporary (.tmp) file to preview the browser instead.

Once you're comfortable with your browser list, you can click OK to accept the changes. The Edit Browser List will close, and the changes will be reflected within the Preview in Browser window. Now, to see the results of the page you've been building throughout the chapter, click F12 (or the shortcut key for the default browser on your computer). As you can see from Figure 2-31, the page in the browser mirrors the design in Expression Web closely.

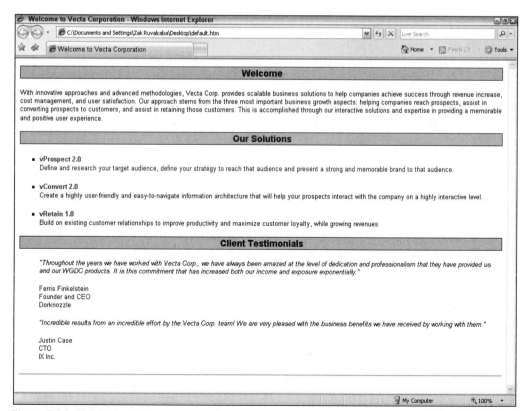

Figure 2-31: Finished page

Take a good look at this page because you'll be building an exact replica of this page for your Chapter 2 exercise.

Summary

As you have seen, building a Web page in Expression Web is extremely intuitive and easy to learn. Flanked by key Task Panes and toolbars, building simple, text-based Web pages in Expression Web is merely a matter of typing onto the development area and then specifying various formatting attributes using either the Tag Properties Task Pane or the Common/Formatting toolbars. This introductory chapter opened a whole new world to some important features within Expression Web and should serve as a foundation for future development. The next few chapters step away from development for a bit and discuss arguably one of the most important topics as it relates to Expression Web: site management.

As you'll see, Chapter 3 will begin to prepare you for working with defined Web sites. In that chapter, you'll learn how to define a Web site, as well as identify and connect to a Web hosting provider. Doing so allows you to easily and effortlessly upload your completed work for the world to see.

Exercise

In this exercise, you build the main page for the fictitious Vecta Corp. Web site. All of the files that you'll need for this exercise are available from the Wrox Web site (www.wrox.com), including the completed versions for your review. When building the Web page in this exercise, you should perform the following steps:

1. Build the main page of the Vecta Corp. Web site using some basic formatting techniques, available within the Common toolbar.

2. Start by creating a new HTML page and immediately save your document.

3. Copy and paste the text available within the external content.txt file located within the Assets folder into the new page.

4. Add paragraph and line breaks where applicable to get the page laid out section by section.

5. Format the page using a variety of techniques available within the Common toolbar. You should set headings, the font face, a font size, alignments, text styles, lists, and text colors.

6. Preview your work in the browser, and compare it with the final version, also included with the chapter files.

Working with Web Sites

Chapter 2 discussed how easy it is to build a simple, text-based Web page using Expression Web. With the many toolbars, Task Panes, and a full-featured development area, Expression Web offers the simplicity of development that many of its sibling Office applications do.

The reality, however, is that very few Web developers build simple, text-based Web pages anymore. Instead, modern Web developers are accustomed to working in Web environments where images, hyperlinks, media elements, and dynamic forms are common. Web developers are now more likely to work within an environment where all of the developer's assets (text-based content, images, media elements, and so on) are contained and managed within a single folder, otherwise known as a *Web site*.

In this chapter, you learn about the many features included within Expression Web for working with Web sites. Specifically, you will do the following:

- ❑ Gain an understanding of the importance of working with Web sites
- ❑ Create a new Web site
- ❑ Manage the Web site using the Folder List Task Pane
- ❑ Modify site settings
- ❑ Use the Publish Web Site dialog to configure a remote Web hosting provider
- ❑ Gain an understanding of the differences between FrontPage Server Extensions, Web-based Distributed Authoring and Versioning (WebDAV), File Transfer Protocol (FTP), and the File System
- ❑ See how the Copy Web Site window allows you to effortlessly drag and drop files from your local development machine over to your Web hosting provider
- ❑ See how Personal Web Packages can simplify the process of transporting large amounts of files

By the end of this chapter, you'll have a solid understanding of what it takes to configure and manage a Web site within Expression Web. You'll learn how to create a new Web site; how to create and add files, images, folders, and media elements to that Web site; and, most important, how to upload the Web site to a remote Web hosting provider with minimal effort. Let's get started!

The Importance of Working with Web Sites

As Internet users, we find ourselves accustomed to browsing what we know as Web pages and Web sites on a regular basis, and, in most cases, are probably totally unaware of the differences between the two. In Chapter 2, you saw how a Web page functions, and, for the most part, there was nothing to it. You added some content to the page, formatted it, saved it to your computer, and then previewed it in the browser to test the results. That simple Web page worked, primarily because there wasn't much else to the page. Enter Web sites.

A Web site is a set of interconnected Web pages, usually including a home page that is maintained by an individual or organization on a Web server. I'll explain a Web server in a moment; for now, imagine adding more Web pages in addition to the simple text-based home page that you built for the fictitious Vecta Corp in Chapter 2. Also imagine that within those Web pages, you've included images, media elements, and even links between the different Web pages.

Because all of your Web pages will ultimately use paths that point to the references that they include, it makes much more sense to include everything (images, media elements, and so on) within a single folder than to keep it scattered throughout your computer. In order for the world to see your creative genius, you'll need to upload all of your Web pages and associated dependencies to a special computer, equipped with a Web server. As you learn later in this chapter, a Web server is equipped with special software that allows the millions of potential visitors to browse your Web pages. If all of your Web pages, images, media elements, and so on were scattered throughout your computer, uploading all of these files to the remote Web server would be a daunting task.

Instead, you can conveniently organize all of your files within a single folder, defined within Expression Web as a Web site, on your computer. Ultimately, this would allow you to reference all of our images, media elements, and other Web pages when creating links easily because everything is contained within a single folder. Even better, it makes uploading all of the files to the remote Web server as easy as a button click.

Beyond the simplicity of organization lies special functionality offered by Expression Web within a Web site. When you define a Web site within Expression Web, Expression Web can include special folders (otherwise known as *extensions*) that contain special sub-applications and metadata that facilitate the updating of links within Expression Web when you move, rename, or delete files and folders within the Folder List. These sub-applications and metadata also come in handy when managing your Web sites within teams because they allow you to delegate permissions among members of that team. Furthermore, these sub-applications and metadata allow you to effortlessly add Web-based searches, hit counters, photo galleries, and more to your Web pages without your needing to know complex server-side programming languages.

Specifically, these extensions and metadata allow for the following:

❑ *Clean organization* — Managing a site within Expression Web begins with creating a new site (discussed in the next section). Once you've created a new site, Expression Web cleanly organizes your files within the Folder List Task Pane. The Folder List Task Pane can organize and allow you to manage assets, images, media files, scripts, includes, templates, and Web pages. In Chapter 2, you didn't work with a Web site. Instead, you had to navigate the entire directory structure to work with a particular file. By creating a new Web site, Expression Web conveniently isolates the folder referenced when the site is created within the Folder List Task Pane.

❑ *Maintaining link integrity* — Once you've created a new site, a reference is established between Expression Web and the files on your computer. If changes are made to the overall structure of your Web site (perhaps one that breaks links between Web pages), Expression Web can automatically detect the changes, alert you to them, and then fix them, if you so choose.

❑ *Quick transfer of your files to a remote Web hosting provider via a built-in FTP client* — One of the most common questions asked by beginning developers is, "Once I've finished developing my Web pages, how do I upload them to my Web hosting provider so that everyone can see them?" The answer to this question is simple. Expression Web provides a built-in File Transfer Protocol (FTP) client that you can use to easily drag and drop files from your local computer (the computer that you do your work on) to your remote Web hosting provider.

❑ *A centralized client for managing files within teams* — As you'll see later in the book, Expression Web's support for working within teams is unparalleled. Facilitated by a defined site, collaborative teams can manage sites in Expression Web through a variety of channels, including Check In/Check Out, site reports, WebDAV, and more.

❑ *The ability to generate site reports* — From an organizational management perspective, defining a site within Expression Web offers the ability to generate site reports. Workflow statistics about files that are checked out and recently modified can be generated. Additionally, you can create HTML reports that include an analysis of various accessibility and usability flaws within your Web pages or Web site.

❑ *Quick site synchronization using the site synchronization utility* — Site synchronization is the process of synchronizing numerous local instances to one remote instance. Assume for a moment that you work on your Web site at home and at work. Expression Web allows you to synchronize files between your local computer at work and the remote Web hosting provider. This way, when you get home, you're able to synchronize your home computer with the Web hosting provider, essentially overwriting old files with newer ones that were worked on throughout the day at work. This synchronization process maintains a consistently updated Web site, regardless of development location.

While there are certainly more features to be examined as the chapter unfolds, this list of features should start getting you excited about what's to come. Now that you have an idea as to why creating and working with Web sites in Expression Web is important, let's actually create one.

> Because of this book's size constraints, topics such as Web site planning, including industry standard document structures and more, are not covered. For the sake of simplicity, all of the files that you'll be using throughout the book can be downloaded from the Wrox Web site (www.wrox.com). These are the files that I'll reference as we progress through the chapters in the book.

Creating a New Web Site

Creating a new Web site within Expression Web begins with the Web Site tab within the New dialog box. You can open the New dialog box by choosing File ➪ New ➪ Web Site. The New dialog box appears with the Web Site tab automatically selected, as you can see in Figure 3-1.

As you can see from Figure 3-1, the basic structure outlined by the New Web Site dialog box mimics the functionality offered by the New Page dialog (discussed in Chapter 2) in that you have the following similar features available to you:

❑ *Categories List* — Allows you to choose between General or Template-based Web sites. You learn more about these options in future chapters of this book. For now, focus on the General category.

❑ *Web Site Type List* — Displays a custom list of Web site templates based on the selection made within the Categories list. When the General category is selected, options for creating new One Page Web sites (as well as Empty Web sites) become available. You also have the option to choose the Import Web Site Wizard (discussed later), which you can use to import a previously created Web site into Expression Web.

❑ *Description* — Provides a simple text-based explanation for the selection made within the Web Site Type List.

❑ *Preview* — Available when browsing the Templates category. You can use the Preview window to see an iconic representation of what the various templates will look like before you commit to using them by clicking OK.

❑ *Options* — Offers checkboxes that allow you to browse to and merge the content contained in one Web site with the content of one that you may already have open. The second checkbox, Use Encrypted Connection (SSL), forces Expression Web to connect to and transfer files from the remote Web hosting provider using a secure and encrypted connection. In order for this feature to work, the remote Web server must support SSL.

❑ *Location* — Specifies the location where the files should be stored on your local computer.

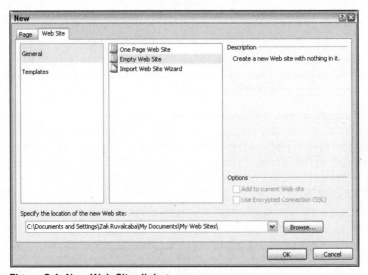

Figure 3-1: New Web Site dialog

To create a new Web site for use with the fictitious Vecta Corp, choose the General category, and then select the Empty Web Site option. In the next step, you'll need to define a location where the files should be stored on your local computer. You can initiate this process by selecting the Browse button. Doing so launches the New Web Site Location dialog box, similar to Figure 3-2.

As you'll notice from Figure 3-2, the New Web Site Location dialog box offers numerous features, including the ability to browse to a particular folder and even create a new folder (which will become the Web site) within the one you've just browsed to. For the sake of simplicity, browse to the My Web Sites folder located within the My Documents folder. Next, click the New Folder icon (it's the second icon from the right near the top right of the dialog box), enter the name Vecta Corp, and click OK. The new Vecta Corp folder is created within your My Web Sites folder. You'll also notice that Expression Web automatically opens the newly created Vecta Corp folder.

Now, click the Open button to close the New Web Site Location dialog box and return to the New Web Site dialog box. You'll immediately notice that the Location text box is pre-populated with the full path to your newly created folder. Finally, click OK to close the New Web Site dialog. A new folder (your Web site) will appear within the Folder List Task Pane.

To see what Expression Web just did, and, more important, to see how Windows treats the folder, minimize Expression Web and manually browse to the newly created Vecta Corp Web site located within your My Web Sites folder. As you can see from Figure 3-3, Expression Web adds the extensions mentioned earlier within two special folders (_vti_cnf and _vti_pvt) at the root of the Vecta Corp Web site.

Windows recognizes that these two folders exist, changes the icon of the traditional folder, and replaces it with that of a folder with a small globe in the center. This is a traditional Windows icon that represents a Web site.

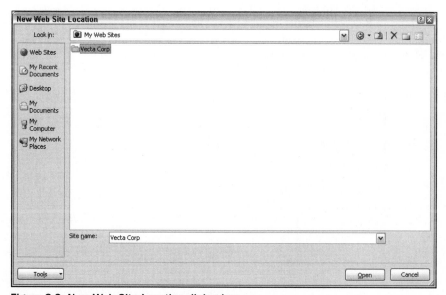

Figure 3-2: New Web Site Location dialog box

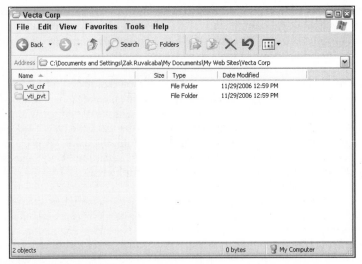

Figure 3-3: Special folders

Working with the Folder List Task Pane

As mentioned in the previous sections, a Web site isn't a Web site unless you have Web pages and elements residing within the folder that makes up the Web site. A bit later in this chapter, you'll copy pre-built files (including the file that you built in Chapter 2) into the newly created Web site. For now, however, it's important that you understand some basic file-based concepts related to the Folder List Task Pane.

If you haven't noticed, the Folder List Task Pane looks and functions much like Windows Explorer. You can create new folders and pages directly within the Folder List Task Pane and you can rename and delete folders and files once you've created them. You can even set the home page of your Web site directly from the Task Pane, and, more important, you can access the Copy Web Site (FTP) utility that's integrated into the program directly from this Task Pane as well.

While the latter will certainly be covered throughout this chapter, let's take this time to cover some introductory concepts as they relate to the Folder List Task Pane. Specifically, you will do the following:

❑ Create new folders and pages

❑ Copy content into the newly created folders

❑ Set the home page for your Web site

❑ Rename and delete folders and files

By the end of the next few sections, you'll have a solid understanding of just how intuitive and easy to use the Folder List Task Pane is. You'll also understand how important it is to make changes and modifications directly from the Folder List Task Pane, instead of from Windows Explorer.

Creating New Folders and Pages

As you've noticed, the Folder List Task Pane looks very similar to that of Windows Explorer without the many icons, task bars, menus, and the common task bar. Many of the simple file-based operations that you could expect to perform within Windows Explorer can be performed conveniently within the Folder List Task Pane. For example, during the first few introductory chapters, you will work with, create, and maintain three different folders within the Vecta Corp Web site to store files such as text-based documents, images, and even media elements (such as those created within Microsoft Expression Blend or Adobe Flash). To get started, create three new folders, naming them `Assets`, `Images`, and `Media`.

> Technically, you can give your folders any name that you like. It's simply considered standard in the Web development industry that the `Assets` folders contains files that will be used within your Web site but not directly referenced (files such as DOC, TXT, and so on); `Images` will contain JPEG and GIF files (files that are directly referenced by your Web pages); and the `Media` folder will contain animated GIFs and perhaps even animated movies that you create within programs such as Microsoft Expression Blend or Adobe Flash.

You have two options available to you when it comes to creating new folders within the folder list. Possibly the easiest method is to choose the small folder icon that exists within the title bar of the Folder List Task Pane. Selecting this icon immediately creates a new folder within the Vecta Corp Web site. Name it **Assets**. The second method for creating new folders within the Folder List Task Pane is to right-click onto the root `Vecta Corp Web Site` folder within the Folder List Task Pane to access the context menu, and choose New ⇨ Folder. Name this one **Images**. When you've finished, your Folder List Task Pane will resemble Figure 3-4.

You'll walk through the process of copying content into the newly created folders shortly. Before you do, however, it's important to walk through the process of creating new pages directly within the Folder List Task Pane.

In most cases, you'll create a new page, add some content to the page, and then save the file directly within the defined Web site. In some instances, however, you may find that creating all of your files before adding content helps you to visualize the overall navigation structure for your site. If this is the case, you can easily create new files within the Folder List Task Pane by choosing the New Page icon that appears within the Folder list title bar just to the right of the New Folder icon that you used earlier. Selecting this icon immediately creates a new HTML page at the root of your Web site, similar to Figure 3-5.

> It's important to note that when you click the New Page icon in the Folder List Task Pane, the new page is created as `default.htm`. If you select File ⇨ New ⇨ HTML to create a new file, the new page is created as `Untitled_1.htm`.

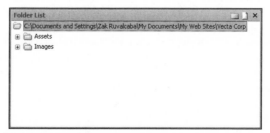

Figure 3-4: Folder List Task Pane

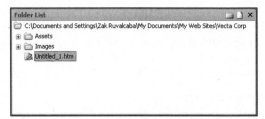

Figure 3-5: HTML page at the root of the Web site

If you don't have files open, Expression Web displays the Web Site window by default. The Web Site window, like the Folder List Task Pane, displays the folder and file structure of your Web site. Even better, the Web Site window displays much more detailed information about the files contained within the Web site.

As in Windows Explorer, the Web Site window displays file view columns that list the name of the folder or file, the size of the file, the type of file it is, the date the file was last modified, and the user who last modified the file. You'll also notice that the status bar of the Web Site window displays buttons that allow for quick access to features such as the Copy Web Site utility, site reports, and the Hyperlinks validation utility. Also note that any task that you may want to perform within the Folder List Task Pane may also be performed within the Web Site window. For example, you can create, rename, and delete folders and pages directly from this window.

Now that you have a basic understanding of how folders and files are created within the Folder List Task Pane, let's add the content that you'll use throughout some of these introductory chapters. Once you've downloaded the chapter files and opened the folder within Windows Explorer, you'll immediately notice the text file, fourteen image files, and two Web pages that the `Files` folder contains. These are the elements that you'll be adding to the Vecta Corp Web site for use within this chapter.

To add these files to their respective folders, simply select the element(s) and physically drag it from the folder within Windows Explorer and into the specific folder within the Folder List Task Pane. As you can see from Figure 3-6, once expanded, the folders within the Folder List Task Pane will display the newly added files.

More important, the files that you've just copied into the folders within the Folder List Task Pane will also reside within the `Vecta Corp Web Site` folder located within the My Web Sites folder. Remember that the folder structure outlined within the Folder List Task Pane is merely a reference to the Vecta Corp Web Site folder contained on your computer.

> **In this chapter, you manually created a new Web site, added folders to that Web site, and then practiced copying the elements that you'll use with the Web site from Windows Explorer into the folders visible within the Folder List Task Pane. To avoid unnecessary repetition, future chapters will have the Web site and files contained within the Web site already predefined. When you begin future chapters, you'll need only to copy the files from the Wrox Web site onto your computer, and then choose the Open Site option available from the File menu.**

Figure 3-6: Newly added files

Setting the Home Page

One of the advantages of working with Expression Web is the many sub-utilities that are built into the program. For example, in the previous section, you saw that the Web Site window contains buttons for launching the site reports, navigation, and hyperlinks utilities. These are but a few of the many utilities included within Expression Web to aid you in building sound, structurally well-built Web sites.

While these utilities are certainly examined as the chapter and book progress, it's important to understand that these features are worthless without a clearly defined home page. A home page, as defined by Expression Web, is the main Web page for your Web site. It's the page that all users will automatically go to when they browse to your Web site for the first time. The page that you created in Chapter 2, for example (`default.htm`), could be considered your main page because it includes various text-based elements such as the welcome text, client testimonials, a list of the company's solutions, and more that are usually placed within a home page. Expression Web uses the home page as a baseline for the overall structure of your Web site. As you'll see throughout the book, it allows features that rely on a home page (such as site reports, navigation, and hyperlinks utilities) to work.

You probably noticed that one of the files you copied over is named `main.htm`. Let's assume that `main.htm` is the home page of your site and is functionally equivalent to the `default.htm` page that you created in Chapter 2. To set `main.htm` as your home page, simply right-click onto the file within the Folder List Task Pane to access the context menu and choose the "Set as Home Page" option. Immediately, Expression Web converts the file to `default.htm` and places the small house icon next to the filename. This house icon is a symbolic representation for home page.

> **Depending on the names of the files that you copy over, Expression Web is smart enough to detect files with the names** `default.htm`, `home.htm`, `index.htm`, `welcome.htm`, **and so on, and automatically give them the Home Page status.**

Now that the home page is set, all utilities that rely on a home page will work. More important, when users browse to your site for the first time, this is the page that they will be redirected to automatically.

Renaming and Deleting Files

Just as you can rename and delete files within Windows Explorer, the Folder List Task Pane also allows you to rename and delete files. For example, the Untitled_1.htm file was created in a previous section. Obviously, that name isn't very intuitive because it doesn't tell you much about what the file contains. Instead, you might think about renaming it to something that's more descriptive of what the file contains or may contain.

To rename the file, simply right-click the file within the Folder List Task Pane and choose the Rename option. Immediately, the file changes to allow you to rename it. Enter another name (perhaps solutions .htm), remembering to keep the .htm file extension. When you've finished renaming the file, click Enter to commit the change.

Deleting files within the Folder List Task Pane is just as easy as renaming files. To delete a file within the Folder List Task Pane, simply select the file (perhaps the newly created solutions.htm), and click the Delete key on your keyboard. You can also delete a file by right-clicking the file within the Folder List Task Pane to access the context menu and choosing the Delete option. Either method causes the Confirm Delete dialog to appear. Click Yes to confirm the deletion of the file.

Modifying Site Settings

Now that the new Web site has been created and content has been added to the folders contained within the Web site, you may want to think about configuring site-specific settings in Expression Web. Available by choosing Site ➪ Site Settings, the Site Settings dialog box offers configurable properties for enabling or disabling the hidden metadata files that are automatically added to your site, enabling team collaboration via check-in and check-out, utilizing the ASP.NET development server when previewing pages in the browser, setting the default encoding type for Web pages that you create within the site, and more. In all, five tabs represent various types of site-specific functionality and operations:

- ❑ General settings
- ❑ Preview in browser settings
- ❑ Advanced settings
- ❑ Language settings
- ❑ Database settings

In most cases, the default site settings will work just fine for the majority of your sites. There may be sites that you develop, however, where Expression Web's hidden metadata files aren't needed. Furthermore, as you learn in the second half of the book, there may be sites where you'll want to configure a database to use for various dynamic pages within your site. Should these scenarios arise, the Site Settings dialog box facilitates these processes and is available on a per-site basis by accessing the Site Settings option from the Site menu.

General Settings

The General tab offers basic options for the Web site. It's within this tab that you can change the Web site name, view the full path to the Web site on your computer (for reference purposes only), enable or disable the hidden metadata files that are stored within the Web site, and enable or disable document check-in and check-out when working in collaborative teams. The General tab offers the following options:

❑ *Web name* — Displays the current Web site name. You're free to change the Web site name here and click either OK or Apply to commit the change. Changing the Web site name here also changes the folder name for the Web site within Windows Explorer.

> **It's important to understand that when changing the name of the Web site/folder in Expression Web, you're merely changing the local representation of the site. There is absolutely no correlation here between the Web site/folder name in Expression Web and the real world URL for the published site.**

❑ *File location* — Displays the full path to the location of the Web site on your computer. This is a read-only label and is meant for reference purposes only.

❑ *Manage the Web site using hidden metadata files* — Enables or disables the use of the hidden metadata folders on your Web site. The metadata folders, represented first by the `_vti_cnf` folder, contain information about every file within your Web site (such as which links are within each file). The second `_vti_pvt` folder is responsible for storing configuration information for the Web site as a whole. It's important to note that if you disable the use of the hidden metadata files within your site, many features such as automatic hyperlink validation and dynamic Web templates won't be available to you. In our case, since you've already defined the site, these two folders were placed into your Web site. Since this is the case, the "Manage the Web site using hidden metadata files" checkbox becomes disabled.

❑ *Use document check-in and check-out* — Enabling this checkbox allows you to work with the built in check-in and check-out features in Expression Web. This is especially useful when working in collaborative teams where the potential exists for many developers to work on the same file.

Preview in Browser Settings

The Preview tab offers options for defining how your Web pages will be previewed in the browser should you decide to use the "Preview in Browser" feature. The Preview tab offers the following options:

❑ *Preview using Web site URL* — By default, Expression Web uses its own methods for previewing Web pages in a browser. For example, static HTML pages are launched within a browser using the full path to the location of the Web site. For instance, the Vecta Corp Web site would be previewed using the path `C:\Documents and Settings\<computername>\My Documents\ Vecta Corp`. For dynamic pages, Expression Web uses the built-in ASP.NET development server because dynamic pages will not run otherwise. If you prefer to use the built-in ASP.NET development server for the previewing of all of your Web sites, regardless of the whether they are static or dynamic, you can simply choose the Use Microsoft ASP.NET Development Server checkbox, and then click the "For all Web pages" radio button. Because the ASP.NET development server is not needed for static HTML Web pages, the "For only ASP.NET Web pages" radio button would suffice and, more important, make the previewing of pages in your browser run much faster.

❑ *Preview using custom URL for this Web site* — The final option for previewing pages in the browser is to simply provide your own custom URL. You can do this by choosing the "Preview using custom URL for this Web site" radio button and then specifying the URL for your Web site. This option becomes especially useful in cases where you have a unique IP address and perhaps even a port number that needs to be used to view the particular Web site. For example, the default Web port number to access a Web site on a Web server is port 80. In some cases, a system administrator may lock that port number down as it becomes too obvious and vulnerable to attackers. The system administrator may, instead, provide access to another, not so obvious port number that you'd need to use to access your Web files. Since Expression Web assumes that all Web sites are accessible via port 80, you'd need to supply the custom URL here to have Expression Web bypass that. A common URL within this dialog box may resemble `http://70.37.66.24:8081/main.htm`. In this case, you're forcing Expression Web to use a custom IP address, followed by the port number 8081, to access the Web page `main.htm`.

Advanced Settings

You can use the Advanced tab to set the default client-side validation language to use for your Web pages when working with ASP.NET, enable or disable hidden files and folders within your Web site, and delete temporary files. The Advanced tab provides the following options:

❑ *Default validation script language* — ASP.NET includes a dynamic set of validation controls that you can use to perform common client-side validation tasks for your ASP.NET pages. Choose an option from this menu to set the default client-side scripting language that should be used in conjunction with these validation controls. Options include VBScript and JavaScript. These options only apply when working with server-side technologies such as ASP.NET in Expression Web.

❑ *Options* — Earlier, I discussed the `vti_` folders that Expression Web creates for you. By default, Expression Web adds these folders (and the files within these folders) to your Web site as hidden. If you prefer to make these folders/files (as well as other hidden folders/files) visible, enable this checkbox. If you prefer to keep these folder/files hidden, disable this checkbox.

❑ *Temporary files* — Click the Delete Files button to delete any and all temporary files that Expression Web creates within your Web site.

Language Settings

You can use the Language tab to set the default language that will appear when messages are displayed on the server. Options in this tab also include the ability to set the default page encoding. The Language tab offers the following options:

❑ *Server message location* — Sets the language that should be used when server messages are displayed in the browser. As of this writing, English (U.S.) is the only language supported.

❑ *Default page encoding* — Sets the default encoding type for Web pages within your Web site. In summation, *encoding* is the byte (or sequence of bytes) representing each character in an HTML or plain text file. Because Unicode (UTF-8) is able to represent any universal character in the Unicode standard, and is backward-compatible with ASCII, it is steadily becoming the preferred encoding for e-mail and Web pages. Expression Web uses Unicode (UTF-8) as the default encoding for all Web pages.

Database Settings

As discussed later in the book, Expression Web allows you to build dynamic Web sites that can integrate directly with databases. For the most part, when you create dynamic pages (ASP.NET), you can specify connections to databases on a per-page basis. However, you can use the Database tab as a way of setting global databases that should be offered to all Web pages within your Web site. Again, this is covered in much more detail later in the book.

Publishing Your Web Site

One of the benefits of using a visual editor such as Expression Web is that, aside from being a feature-rich and robust Web page editor, it also fronts as an easy-to-use client that you can use to upload your files to a remote Web hosting provider. Regardless of whether your Web hosting provider is on a remote computer or on your local network, Expression Web can easily connect to and facilitate the transfer of your files using a variety of protocols.

The next few sections examine the features built into Expression Web that facilitate the process of establishing a connection, connecting to, and then transferring files to a remote Web hosting provider. Specifically, you learn about the following:

- ❑ The Publish Web Site dialog
- ❑ Connecting to a server equipped with FrontPage server extensions
- ❑ Connecting to a server equipped with WebDAV
- ❑ Connecting to a server using the File Transfer Protocol (FTP)
- ❑ Connecting to a server on your local network using the file system
- ❑ Dragging and dropping files from your local computer to the remote Web hosting provider using the Copy Web Site window
- ❑ Site synchronization

The next few sections provide step-by-step instruction on topics involving establishing a connection to a Web hosting provider. The discussion also explains how you can connect to and transfer files from your local computer to the remote Web hosting provider using a variety of methods.

One of the topics receiving the most attention is that of FTP. If you're using FTP as the method for transferring files from your local computer to a remote Web hosting provider, I assume that you've already found and created an account with a particular Web hosting provider. If you'd like direction in terms of which Web hosting provider to use, you can browse to the Vecta Corp site at www.vectacorp.com to see which Web hosting provider I recommend.

The Publish Web Site Dialog

Uploading files to your remote Web hosting provider starts with defining properties for connecting to the remote server. Once you've defined how Expression Web should connect to the remote server, you can use the Copy Web Site window to facilitate the file transfer. To define the properties that Expression Web should use to connect to the remote server, open the Remote Web Site Properties dialog, accessible by selecting File ➪ Publish Site. The Remote Web Site Properties dialog will appear, similar to Figure 3-7.

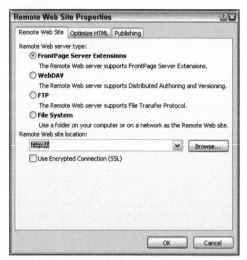

Figure 3-7: Remote Web Site Properties dialog

You can also open the Remote Web Site Properties dialog by choosing the Copy Web Site button that appears near the bottom of the Web Site window.

As you can see from Figure 3-7, the Remote Web Site Properties dialog is split up into three different tabs, each representing properties that you may want to customize either before publishing or while publishing your files to the remote server. Specifically, these tabs include the following:

❑   *Remote Web Site* — Use the options in this tab to set the remote server type. Once the remote server type has been set, you can further customize the location of the remote server within the Remote Web site location text box.

❑   *Optimize HTML* — Use the options in this tab to optionally optimize various aspects of your HTML files before publishing. Certain properties that you may consider for optimization include removing comments, HTML whitespace, Expression Web tracing images, and more.

❑   *Publishing* — Use the options offered in this tab to set how and what gets published to the remote server. For example, you can set preferences within this tab that forces Expression Web to publish all files to the remote server, effectively overwriting previous versions of the files on the remote server. You can also set preferences that allow Expression Web to make a determination on which files need to be published by comparing changes for files on both the remote server and local computer. Other options include the ability to write publishing information to, or read from, a log file.

Setting the Remote Server Type

While this book covers the Optimize HTML and Publishing options available within the Remote Web Site Properties dialog, for now, let's turn our attention to defining the remote server type and, more important, defining the location of remote Web server. Setting these options now will allow you to connect to and transfer files using the Copy Web Site window later.

As you saw in Figure 3-7, Expression Web allows you to connect to a Web hosting provider and transfer files to that Web hosting provider using a variety of methods, including the following:

❑   A Web server running FrontPage Server Extensions

❑   A Web server that supports WebDAV

❑   A Web server using the File Transfer Protocol (FTP)

❑   A Web server running on your local network/file system

FrontPage Server Extensions

Expression Web goes a long way in terms of providing a simple and feature-rich environment for Web authoring, managing, and serving tasks. However, to take full advantage of the powerful features offered by Expression Web, you need FrontPage Server Extensions. Introduced to work hand-in-hand with Expression Web's predecessor FrontPage, FrontPage Server Extensions are a collection of software components (ISAPI DLLs and CGI executables) created by Microsoft to install in addition to the Web server software. FrontPage Server Extensions work by telling the Web server how it should respond to commands generated by Expression Web and, more important, visitors of the Web site.

So, what benefits do FrontPage Server Extensions provide you and the visitors to your Web site? Specifically, FrontPage Server Extensions offer the following:

❑   From a development perspective, they allow Expression Web to communicate with the Web server, allowing direct uploads and downloads of files using a more common protocol in HTTP as opposed to FTP.

❑   From a Web site visitor's perspective, they let the Web server provide Expression Web-specific features to the Web site visitor's browser, without requiring any extra programming or scripting on the part of the Web page designer.

As you'll see in the next section, the traditional approach to uploading and downloading files to and from the Web server is FTP. To this day, FTP is the most common approach simply because it's platform-agnostic. With FrontPage Server Extensions, however, uploads and downloads occur using HTTP, much like the way WebDAV works. What this means for the developer is that no additional ports need to be opened on the firewall to allow access to the Web server as is the case with FTP. Additionally, FrontPage Server Extensions provide the Expression Web user with added benefits in terms of configuration and management.

As you'll see throughout the book, FrontPage Server Extensions allow Expression Web to present detailed information regarding hyperlinks, navigation, and folders that exist on the Web server without Expression Web ever having to download any files. Furthermore, FrontPage Server Extensions allow administrators to retrieve site-specific information such as Web settings or security configurations through the direct upload/download structure.

Your Web site visitors, on the other hand, could care less about the added benefits that FrontPage Server Extensions provide the developer. They're simply interested in browsing your Web site to retrieve the information that they came to see in the first place. FrontPage Server Extensions allow you to include numerous features that improve the overall user experience — features that would have otherwise required complex server-side programming or scripting had they not been designed to work with Expression Web and FrontPage Server Extensions.

As you'll see in Chapter 8, "Adding Interactivity with Behaviors," Web Components offer dozens of added features that you can include within your Web pages that ease the development process on your end and, more important, improve the user experience on your visitor's end. Features such as dynamic effects (marquees and interactive buttons), an integrated Web search, hit counters, photo galleries, rotating banners/pictures, and more are all available to you providing you install FrontPage Server Extensions on the Web server and, more important, set up Expression Web to connect to the FrontPage Server Extensions-enabled Web server.

Try It Out   Installing FrontPage Server Extensions

Now that you have a basic understanding as to how FrontPage Server Extensions can improve your experience with Expression Web and, more important, how FrontPage Server Extensions facilitate an enhanced browsing experience for your Web site's visitors, let's walk through the process of actually installing FrontPage Server Extensions on your Web server.

1. Assuming your Web server runs on a Windows Server 2003 environment, start by selecting Start ⇨ Control Panel ⇨ Add or Remove Programs.

2. Next, choose the Add/Remove Windows Components button.

3. Select the Application Server option within the Components list and click the Details button.

4. Now choose the Internet Information Services (IIS) option within the "Subcomponents of Application Server" list and click the Details button.

5. If the FrontPage 2002 Server Extensions option is checked within the "Subcomponents of Internet Information Services (IIS)" list, then FrontPage Server Extensions are installed and ready to go on your Web server. If it's unchecked, however, check it now and click OK.

6. You'll next progress through the installation wizard. Accept all of the defaults until FrontPage Server Extensions are installed on your Web server. Once you've finished, exit out of all of the dialogs.

FrontPage Server Extensions will now be installed and ready to go on the Web server. The next step is to connect to the FrontPage Server Extensions-enabled Web server through Expression Web. This can be done by following these steps:

1. Within the Remote Web Site Properties dialog box, click the FrontPage Server Extensions radio button.

2. Next, enter the path to the remote Web site location by entering either a file system path or a valid URL within the Remote Web site location dialog box. If your FrontPage Server Extensions-enabled server resides on your network, you can browse to its location to retrieve the file system path by clicking the Browse button. The configured dialog box should resemble Figure 3-8.

> **Remember that the path that you see in the screenshot is for example purposes only. Should you decide to use the FrontPage Server Extensions option, it's up to you to find a remote Web hosting provider that supports it. Once you've identified a Web hosting provider, your domain name will technically be the Remote Web site location — just like** `http://www.vectacorp.com/vc` **is mine.**

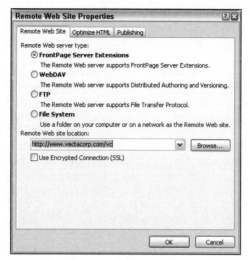

Figure 3-8: Configured dialog box

3. If your remote Web server supports encrypted connections via SSL, you can optionally enable the Use Encrypted Connection (SSL) checkbox.

4. Click OK to close the Remote Web Site Properties dialog box.

5. You're next presented with the "Connect to" dialog box. Enter the User name and Password in the provided text boxes and click OK.

If you've entered the valid credentials, Expression Web will connect to your Web server successfully. You're now ready to connect to and begin transferring files to a remote FrontPage Server Extensions-enabled Web server.

> **Because of the added benefits and features offered by FrontPage Server Extensions, this is the option that I'll use throughout the book. If your organization or Web hosting provider doesn't support FrontPage Server Extensions, you can still follow along with the book using the FTP option covered next. Roughly 90 percent of what is covered in this book can be accomplished and transferred to your Web hosting provider using the methods outlined in the next three sections.**

File Transfer Protocol

As you'll notice, most of the examples covered in this book use the first remote Web server type of FrontPage Server Extensions to connect to and transfer files between the local computer and the remote server. While the overall process will be somewhat transparent to you, the reason for choosing FrontPage Server Extensions is simple. Expression Web includes numerous components that you may optionally use within your Web sites to extend the functionality offered by your Web pages and ultimately provide a better user experience for the visitors to your Web sites. These components, however, rely on FrontPage

Server Extensions being installed on the remote Web server. While the book's examples use the Front-Page Server Extensions method, you're completely free to use whichever method you find best suits your organization.

One such method, File Transfer Protocol (FTP), is arguably the most popular and widely used method for connecting to and transferring files to a remote server — so much so, in fact, that Web hosting providers automatically send their users FTP-specific information for connecting to their Web sites when they sign up for an account, assuming that will be the method you'll use to connect to their Web server.

From a client's perspective, nothing needs to be done in terms of installation to begin working with FTP. You'd simply configure Expression Web by supplying it with the remote FTP server path, a username, and a password and you're set to go. From a server standpoint, configuration can become an arduous task, requiring the FTP software to be installed, directories to be added, permissions to be set, and, more important, a port or ports to be opened on the firewall. While I won't bother you with the administrative details, suffice it to say that FTP can become a chore to configure and operate.

With that said, it's still the most commonly used protocol for connecting to and transferring files from a local computer to a remote Web server. To configure Expression Web to connect to a remote Web server using FTP, follow these steps:

1. Open the Remote Web Site Properties dialog box by choosing Site ⇨ Remote Web Site. Now select the Remote Web Site Properties button located in the upper-right corner of the window. The Remote Web Site Properties dialog box will appear. With the Remote Web Site Properties dialog box open, choose the FTP radio button.

2. Enter the path to the remote Web server by entering a valid URL within the "Remote Web site location" dialog box.

> If you've connected to a particular FTP site before, Windows is smart enough to store that FTP path within your My Network Places list. To access this list of sites, simply click the Browse button. The New Publish Location dialog box will appear. Choose either the Web Sites category or the My Network Places category on the left side. If the FTP site is listed, select it, and click Open to automatically fill in the "Remote Web site location" text box with the FTP path.

3. In some cases, your Web server may have different subfolders residing at the root of the main FTP site. For example, the Vecta Corp FTP site has two subfolders within the FTP root, one called `databases` and one called `webroot`. Technically, the content within the `webroot` directory is what's shown to a user in the browser. The `databases` folder is used specifically to store databases that the site may use and, for security reasons, is kept out of the `webroot` directory. Because this is the case, the FTP directory would be `webroot`. Enter that within the "FTP directory" text box, as shown in Figure 3-9.

> In my case, I also have subsites set up within the `webroot` folder for the various projects I'm involved with. For the Vecta Corp site, I have a folder called `vc`. I can append the folder name `vc` to the `webroot` directory name.

4. Click OK to close the Remote Web Site Properties dialog box.

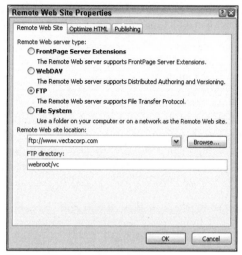

Figure 3-9: Entering the FTP directory

With the information you've provided, you are now ready to connect to and begin transferring files to a remote Web server using FTP.

WebDAV

The preceding section discussed FTP as a viable method for transferring files from the local computer to the remote server. What many developers don't realize, however, is that FTP has its disadvantages, such as the following:

❑ Using FTP requires that you open additional ports on your firewall (usually port 21), which can increase the attack surface of your network and make it more susceptible to penetration by attackers.

❑ FTP has no file-locking mechanism, so it's possible for two users to upload different versions of the same file simultaneously, causing one to be overwritten.

❑ The FTP approach means you have to edit your content locally on the client. In other words, to edit a page already on the Web server, you would have to download it to the client, edit it there, and then upload it again to the remote server once the changes have been made. As you can imagine, this can become a time-consuming and inefficient approach to managing content.

The solution to these problems is Web-based Distributed Authoring and Versioning (WebDAV). WebDAV allows teams to collaboratively edit and manage files on remote Web servers. WebDAV includes numerous versioning and control features such as file locking (which prevents authors from overwriting each other's changes), remote file management, versioning, and more. Because WebDAV is merely an extension of the HTTP/1.1 protocol, WebDAV overcomes the three issues just described because of the following:

❑ WebDAV uses port 80, the same port used by HTTP for Web access. So, using WebDAV means you don't have to open any extra ports on your firewall.

❑ WebDAV lets only one user modify a file at a time, while allowing multiple users to read it. This allows files to be locked while they are being edited, preventing unexpected changes from occurring.

❑ WebDAV enables you to edit files on the server instead of your having to download them first to the client. Editing files remotely using WebDAV is as easy as if they were locally present, which makes the process transparent to the content producer.

Aside from the benefits listed here, WebDAV is easy to configure and easy to begin working with. While this discussion doesn't cover installation of WebDAV on the remote Web server (I'll assume that your network administrator is handling this), it will discuss how to configure and then connect to a remote Web server using WebDAV within Expression Web. Before you begin configuring Expression Web to use WebDAV, you'll want to do two things on the Web server.

First, you want to make sure WebDAV is enabled. If you don't have access to the remote WebDAV installation, check with your system administrator. Second, you want to create a new virtual directory within IIS so that you can publish files to it using WebDAV.

> **Again, if you're walking through this process, I'll assume that you have some working knowledge in terms of using a Web server such as IIS. If you've never used a Web server like IIS, don't worry. These topics and more will be covered in the second half of the book.**

Assuming you're using Windows Server 2003, let's walk through this process now:

1. Open IIS on your Web server [Start ⇨ Settings ⇨ Control Panel ⇨ Administrative Tools ⇨ Internet Information Services (IIS) Manager], expand the computer name node, and select the Web Service Extensions option.

2. Make sure that the WebDAV option is listed and allowed. If it's prohibited, click the Allow button (see Figure 3-10).

3. Now, expand the Web Sites tree node, right-click onto the Default Web Site node, and choose the Virtual Directory option available from the New submenu, as you can see in Figure 3-11.

4. When the Virtual Directory Creation Wizard appears, click Next.

5. Enter the alias name **Vecta Corp** and click Next.

6. Browse to the Vecta Corp path on the server (assuming it exists) and click OK. Click Next.

7. Enable the Read, Run, Write, and Browse options, similar to Figure 3-12, and click Next.

8. Click Finish to close the Virtual Directory Creation Wizard.

The new virtual directory will now be created in IIS, similar to Figure 3-13. This is the new WebDAV-enabled directory that you'll now be able to publish to.

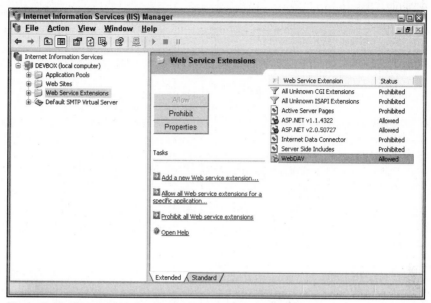

Figure 3-10: The dialog box after you've clicked the Allow button

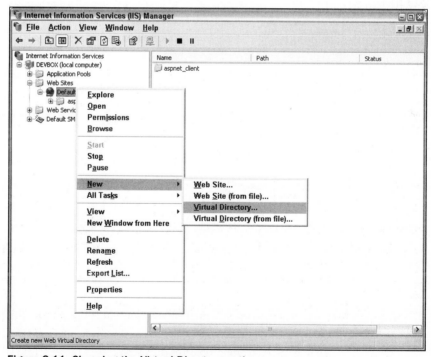

Figure 3-11: Choosing the Virtual Directory option

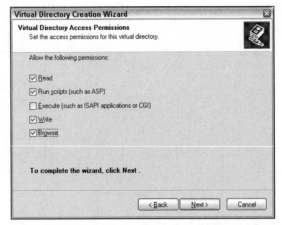

Figure 3-12: Enabling the Read, Run, Write, and Browse options

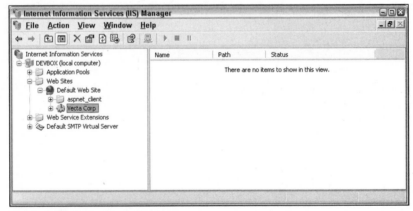

Figure 3-13: New virtual directory

With the server configured to use WebDAV, you're now ready to configure Expression Web to connect to it. You can configure Expression Web to use WebDAV by following these steps:

1. Within the Remote Web Site Properties dialog box, click the WebDAV radio button.

2. Enter the path to the remote Web site location by entering either a file system path or a valid URL within the "Remote Web site location" dialog box. If your WebDAV-enabled server resides on your network, you can browse to its location to retrieve the file system path by clicking the Browse button.

3. If your remote Web server supports encrypted connections via SSL, you can optionally enable the Use Encrypted Connection (SSL) checkbox.

4. Click OK to close the Remote Web Site Properties dialog box.

With the information provided, you are now ready to connect to and begin transferring files to a remote Web server using WebDAV.

The File System

The final method that you may decide to use to connect to a Web server is the file system option. Typically, you'd use this option when the Web server that you'd like to connect to resides on the same network that your development computer is on.

For example, if the UNC share on your network is VC (short for Vecta Corp), you would simply type **\\VC** within the Remote Web site location text box. Furthermore, you would append the name of the Web folder that contains all of the Web files on the Web server to that path. A more realistic path would resemble \\VC\Web.

> **In Microsoft and Novell-based networks, the Universal Naming Convention (UNC) is a way to identify a shared file in a computer without having to specify or know the storage device it is on. In the instance mentioned here, the UNC for the Web server is VC, which is short for Vecta Corp. Using this UNC, Expression Web can easily connect to the Web server using the File System option.**

Optimize HTML Options

While developing your Web pages within Expression Web, take into account that, in certain instances, Expression Web adds special markup that you may decide to remove before publishing your files to your remote Web hosting provider. Known as *HTML optimization* in Expression Web, you can have that special markup (or certain instances of markup) automatically removed by setting various preferences available from the Optimize HTML tab, which is in the Remote Web Site Properties dialog box, shown in Figure 3-14.

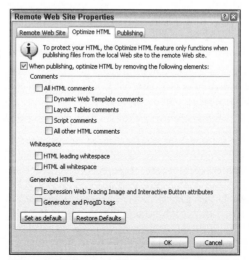

Figure 3-14: Remote Web Site Properties dialog box

As you can see from Figure 3-14, Expression Web allows you to remove various types of elements by first checking the "When publishing, optimize HTML by removing the following elements" checkbox. Once that checkbox is enabled, the following types of elements can be removed:

❑ *Comments* — Comments are a developer's way of including browser-ignored lines of text within code to help explain or clarify a certain portion of that code. Developers comment code as a way of referencing and re-referencing code that was written perhaps months or years in the past. By reading comments that may have been included at the time the code was written, the developers are then able to re-familiarize themselves with what they were trying to accomplish. Additionally, Expression Web adds comments to various types of elements, including Dynamic Web Templates, Layout Tables, and Scripts. You can have Expression Web automatically remove these automatically generated comments, or comments that you may have manually written, by selecting the checkbox that coincides with the specific comment you want removed. In certain scenarios, you may find yourself writing your own comments. If this is the case, you may decide to remove these comments by checking the "All other HTML comments" checkbox. This would effectively strip out comments that you write, or comments that were generated by other visual editors and/or third-party software. Alternatively, you may just decide to remove all comments altogether. If this is the case, choose the "All HTML comments" checkbox.

❑ *Whitespace* — As you develop Web pages visually, Expression Web automatically formats the code that is rendered by the browser for you. Depending on the tags that are included in the code, indents, tabs, and more may be used for code formatting purposes. While this automatic formatting of the code in the background is extremely useful for a developer when trying to read code line-by-line, the whitespace that is produced as a result may end up bogging down the browser during the rendering process. While the performance impact is rather minimal, it is a performance loss nonetheless. If you'd prefer to remove this automatically generated whitespace, simply choose either one or both of the Whitespace checkboxes.

❑ *Generated HTML* — Optionally, you may decide to automatically strip out Tracing Images and Interactive Button attributes that are generated by Expression Web. If this is the case, select the "Expression Web Tracing Image and Interactive Button attributes" checkbox. Additionally, Expression Web is known to automatically include two metatags, used for tracking purposes. These two tags, `Generator` and `ProgId`, can be removed without ill effects by selecting the "Generator and ProgID tags" checkbox.

> It's important to note that when you optimize HTML, the particular elements are removed from the files that are transferred to the remote Web hosting provider. The local files, on the other hand, remain intact.

Publishing Options

The final set of options included within the Remote Web Site Properties dialog box are those that allow you to customize how Expression Web publishes your Web pages to the remote Web server. Split into two categories (General and Logging) and visible in Figure 3-15, the Publishing tab within the Remote Web Site Properties dialog box allows you to set what and how Web pages get published to the Web server, how Expression Web should determine which pages to send to the Web server, and whether or not Expression Web should maintain a log file of the publishing process.

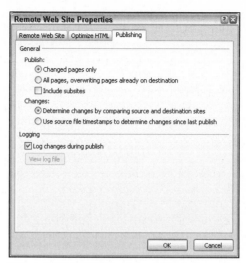

Figure 3-15: Publishing tab split into two categories

As you can see from Figure 3-15, the Publishing tab offers the following options:

❑ *Publish* — Use the radio buttons offered within the Publish group to set which pages get published to the remote Web server. Selecting the "Changed pages only" radio button guarantees that only pages that have changed locally get published to the remote Web server. If, on the other hand, you prefer to simply overwrite all of the files on the remote Web server, you can choose the "All pages, overwriting pages already on destination" radio button. Selecting this option prevents Expression Web from attempting to compare changed files on the local computer with those on the remote Web server. You may also decide to include any subsites created within the root of the primary Web site by enabling the "Include subsites" checkbox.

❑ *Changes* — Use the options offered within the Changes radio group to set how Expression Web determines what files should be uploaded to or downloaded from the remote Web server. For example, if you choose the "Determine changes by comparing source and destination sites" radio button, Expression Web will manually scan and compare all of the Web pages within your local Web site with those on the remote Web site. The downside to this method is performance because Expression Web must scan each and every file to make the determination. With large sites, you can expect to wait minutes. The second option, "Use source file timestamps to determine changes since last publish," forces Expression Web to add a timestamp to each and every Web page on the remote Web server. The advantage to this method is speed. Expression Web doesn't have to scan all of the source code from either the local computer or remote Web server to determine which files need to be changed. Instead, Expression Web reads one line, the timestamp included within each file. The only downside to this approach is that you end up with a small line of code within every Web page in your Web site.

❑ *Logging* — Enable the "Log changes during publish" checkbox to force Expression Web to record changes as they are made during the publishing process. If, for any reason, you ever need to see the text-based log file, simply click the "View log file" button.

Using the Copy Web Site Window

Once you've established a connection to the remote Web server, the next step is to use the Copy Web Site window to get your files from your local computer over to your remote Web server, and vice versa. Aside from simply being able to copy your files to and from the remote Web server, the Copy Web Site window, shown in Figure 3-16, facilitates site synchronization, allows you to customize how and what you see within the Local and Remote Web site panes, displays a status of files published, and more.

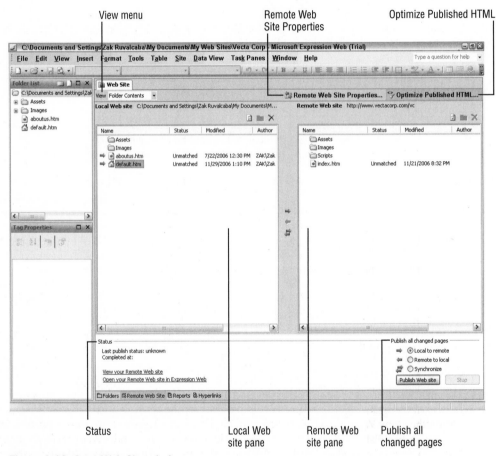

Figure 3-16: Copy Web Site window

As you can see from Figure 3-16, the Copy Web Site window offers the following functionality:

❑   *View* — The View menu customizes what you see within the Copy Web Site window. Selecting the Folder Contents option causes the Copy Web Site window to display the standard folder structure of both the local computer and remote Web server. As you can see from Figure 3-16, the structure that is displayed in both the Local and Remote Web site panes mimics the look of Windows Explorer. Select the "Files to Publish" option when you want to customize the Local Web site pane to show only files that have been changed locally and that need to be published to the remote Web server. The opposite of the "Files to Publish" option is the "Files not to Publish" option. Selecting this option customizes the panes to display a list of files that match on both the local computer and remote Web server. The fourth and final item within the list is the "Files in Conflict" option. Selecting this option displays a list of files that either don't match up on both the local computer and remote Web server, or files that Expression Web simply can't figure out on its own and is asking you to make the determination.

❑ *Remote Web Site Properties* — Launches the Remote Web Site Properties dialog box with the Remote Web Site tab selected. You'd select this option if you need to make changes to the properties used for connecting to the remote Web server.

❑ *Optimize Published HTML* — Launches the Remote Web Site Properties dialog box with the Optimize HTML tab selected. You'd select this option if you need to set HTML optimization options for files to be published.

❑ *Local Web site pane* — Displays the list of files on your local computer associated with your defined Web site. The Local Web site pane displays a series of file view columns, including the following:

❑ *Name* — Displays the name of the folder or file within your Web site.

❑ *Status* — Displays the status of a particular file in relation to its match on the remote Web server. Possible values include Changed, Unchanged, and Conflict.

❑ *Modified* — Displays the last modified date and time of the file.

❑ *Author* — Used when working in a collaborative team to display the username of the person who last made the change.

❑ *Type* — Displays the type of file.

❑ *Size* — Displays the size of the file in kilobytes.

❑ *Remote Web site pane* — Displays the list of files on your remote computer associated with your defined Web site. The Remote Web site pane displays a series of file view columns similar to those within the Local Web site pane.

❑ *Status* — Displays status labels for current operations being performed on pages within your Web site. Depending on the type of connection you're making to the remote Web server, the Status area also displays hyperlinks for viewing the remote Web site within a browser, and also launching the remote Web site within a new instance of Expression Web.

❑ *Publish all changed pages* — Use this group of radio buttons to set how files should be transferred within the Copy Web Site window, should you decide to simply publish the entire site. For example, to publish the Web site from the local computer to the remote Web server, choose the "Local to remote" option and click the "Publish Web site" button. To transfer files from the remote Web server to the local computer, choose the "Remote to local" option and click the "Publish Web site" button. To simply perform a synchronization of files on the local computer with those on the remote Web server, choose the Synchronize radio button and click the "Publish Web site" button.

Transferring Files to and from the Remote Server

Now that you have an idea as to how the Copy Web Site window operates, let's review the process of transferring files from the local computer to the remote Web server. Regardless of which method you're using to connect to the remote Web server, the process of transferring files is a simple matter of drag and drop.

For example, in Figure 3-16, you saw the files `aboutus.htm` and `default.htm` within the Local Web site pane. You probably noticed that the status of the two files read Unmatched. The reason for this is simple — they don't exist on the server. Because they don't exist on the Web server, Expression Web displays the status as Unmatched and also displays a small arrow icon (pointing to the right) just to the left of the file. Now, because they don't exist on the server, you might think about manually selecting the files and dragging them over to the remote.

To do this, you'd simply hold the Ctrl key and select both files. With both files selected, you could either drag and drop the files onto the remote, or you could choose the "Publish Selected Files from the Local Web site to the Remote Web site" icon located in the toolbar, between the Local and Remote Web site panes. Either method you choose causes the Copying Files dialog to display the status of the transfer. Once the Copying Files dialog closes, you'll notice that the two files will be listed within the Remote Web site pane, and more important, their status changes to read Unchanged, as you see in Figure 3-17.

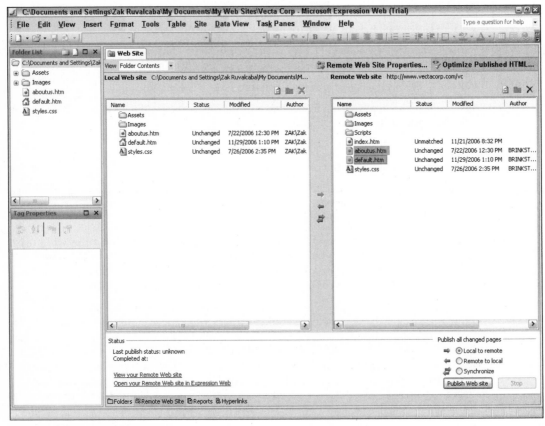

Figure 3-17: Unchanged status

The reverse process, copying files from the remote Web server to the local computer, can be accomplished using the same process. You'd simply select the files on the remote Web server and then drag and drop them onto the Local Web site pane. Additionally, you could also choose the "Publish Selected Files from the Remote Web site to the Local Web site" icon located in the toolbar, between the Local and Remote Web site panes.

As you can see, the manual process of dragging and dropping files onto the remote Web server and vice versa is fairly simple. In some cases, however, the size of your Web site may make it somewhat time-consuming to select each and every changed file before dragging to the remote Web server. This is where the "Publish all changed pages" set of radio buttons comes in. If you'd prefer to allow Expression Web to automatically choose and copy over all of the changed files from the local computer to the remote Web server, you can simply check the "Local to remote" radio button and click the "Publish Web site" button. As soon as you click the button, Expression Web displays the status of the connection within the status label, and then displays a progress indicator similar to the one shown in Figure 3-18, indicating the progress of the file transfer.

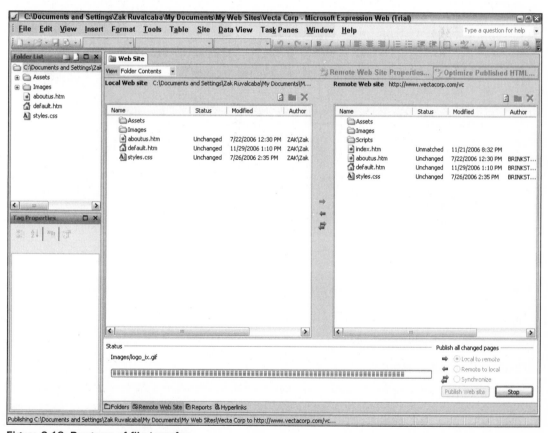

Figure 3-18: Progress of file transfer

When the progress indicator finishes, the Status labels change to display the status of the transfer and the date and time the transfer completed. You'll also notice that a "View your publish log file" link appears. Select this link and the HTML-based Publish Log appears, as you see in Figure 3-19.

As you can see, the Publish Log displays detailed information about the file transfer — such as the time it took to transfer the files, the local and remote paths that the files used during the transfer process, and a series of filters within the "Show only" menu that allows you to customize what you see within the log.

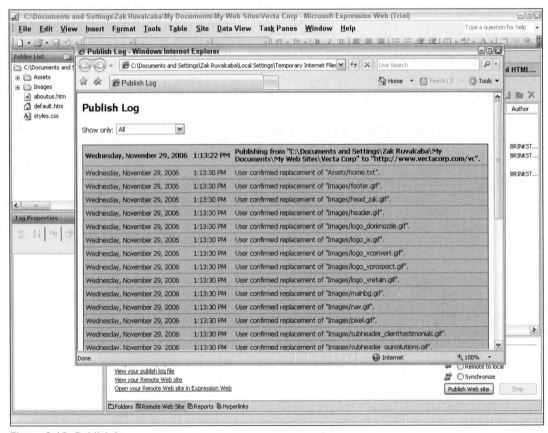

Figure 3-19: Publish Log

Site Synchronization

Although it's great to be able to transfer files from your local computer to the remote Web server by simply dragging and dropping files to and from, the truth is that most people work in an environment where a local computer can actually be represented by two different instances. In this scenario, keeping accurate folder and file structures between two local computers can be extremely difficult.

For example, assume you do work at home and at the office. While you'd still publish your Web sites to a remote Web server installation, technically, the home and office computers represent two local Web sites. Figure 3-20 clearly illustrates this model.

In this model, you could potentially do work on your Web site from home, upload your files to the remote server, go to the office, do some more work, and then accidentally upload over files that you had modified from home. To prevent any such disasters from occurring, you could use the Synchronize option available from within the "Publish all changed pages" radio group. When you select this option and click the "Publish Web site" button, Expression Web figures out which files are out of sync on both the local computer and remote Web server, and overwrites the older copies with the newer, regardless of which computer the older files reside on. This feature conveniently allows you to do work at the office, upload your files to the remote, and then synchronize your home files with the files that have changed on the remote Web server, and vice versa.

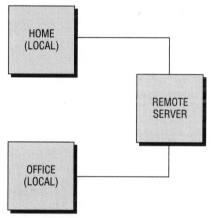

Figure 3-20: Two local Web sites

Deploying Web Sites with Personal Web Packages

One of the many issues facing developers is that of deployment. From a Windows development perspective, there is no problem. In most cases, you need only to compile your application into an executable, and you're done. In some instances, when icons, databases, third-party assemblies, configuration files, and more need to be packaged along with the executable, a utility is used that packages up all of the files nicely and creates an installer.

From a Web development standpoint, you have no such utilities. For the most part, you either have to publish your files to the remote server, or, in some cases, you can use a compression utility to package all of the files into a single ZIP file that you can then store for later use. While these options have been around for quite some time, there is a better way in Expression Web in what are known as *Personal Web Packages*.

A Personal Web Package is a self-contained file that can contain all of the Web files and their dependencies for your Web site. When you create a Personal Web Package, you get to pick (or you can let Expression Web pick) which files (including their dependencies), get packaged together into the self-contained .fwp file. Then, when you're ready to un-package the Personal Web Package (perhaps at a new development location), you only need to conveniently import the Personal Web Package directly from within Expression Web.

Creating Personal Web Packages is encouraged for two reasons. First, it's a handy way to back up your files, and second, it's a clever way of compressing only the files you need for your Web site to operate into a self-contained package that can be transported to a Web server that maybe doesn't have FrontPage Server Extensions or the FTP software installed.

To create a new Personal Web Package, start by selecting File ⇨ Export ⇨ Personal Web Package. The Export Web Package dialog appears, as you can see in Figure 3-21.

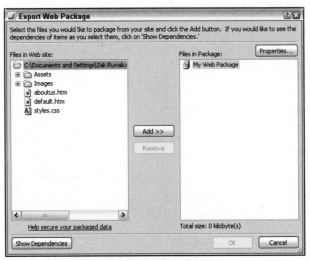

Figure 3-21: Export Web Package dialog

As you can see from Figure 3-21, the Export Web Package offers the following options:

❑ *Files in Web Site pane* — Displays a complete list of files currently in your local Web site.

❑ *Files in Package pane* — Displays a list of files in your Web Package as you add them from the "Files in Web site" pane.

❑ *Properties* — Click the Properties button to launch the Web Package Properties dialog box, similar to what you see in Figure 3-22. In this dialog box, you can set the title of the Web package, add a description, add the author name and company name, view the size of the package in kilobytes, and see a list of external dependencies for the Web package. As you can see from Figure 3-22, new values are set for Title, Description, Author, and Company.

❑ *Add/Remove* — Adds to or removes files from the "Files in Package" pane.

❑ *Total size* — Displays the total package size in kilobytes as you add and remove files from the package.

❑ *Show Dependencies* — Selecting a file from the "Files in Web site" pane and then choosing the Show Dependencies button displays a list of files that the selected file is dependent on. As you can see from Figure 3-23, I selected the default.htm file and then clicked the Show Dependencies button. Because my copy of default.htm includes images, those images are listed as dependencies. From a deployment standpoint, including only dependent files is critical in keeping the size of the package at a minimum.

Once you've finished adding files to your Web Package and you've configured the optional properties on the Web Package, you can click OK to launch the File Save dialog box. It's within this dialog that you're able to navigate to the location on your computer where you'd like the Web Package saved to. For the sake of simplicity, save it within the Vecta Corp Web site root.

When you're ready to deploy your Web Package, simply choose File ⇨ Import ⇨ Personal Web Package, browse to the Web Package, and click Open to launch the Import Web Package dialog box, shown in Figure 3-24.

Figure 3-22: Web Package Properties dialog box

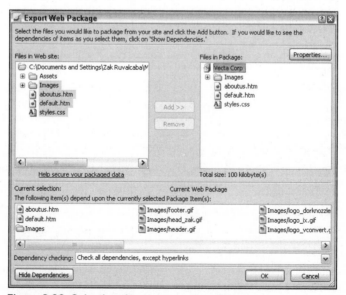

Figure 3-23: Selecting the `default.htm` file

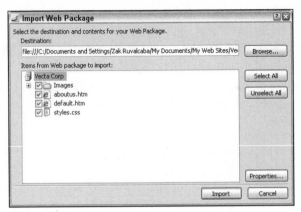

Figure 3-24: Import Web Package dialog

You can use the Import Web Package dialog box as a way of selecting and/or deselecting files that you'd like to deploy. Click OK to deploy the files to your Web site.

Summary

As you have seen throughout this chapter, Expression Web offers an intuitive approach for defining Web sites. You also saw how easy it is to connect to and publish pages from your local development computer to your remote Web server using a variety of options, including FrontPage Server Extensions, FTP, WebDAV, and the file system. Once you've defined your connection, the Copy Web Site window facilitates a smooth and easy approach to file transfer. Whether you drag and drop files, allow Expression Web to upload automatically, or decide to take advantage of the Synchronization feature, it's easy to see that the components used in Expression Web for defining, connecting, and transferring Web sites to a remote Web server are painless and easy-to-use.

Chapter 4 moves you forward in your development efforts. You'll begin to add images and media elements, and even explore the concept of linking to other Web pages within your newly defined Vecta Corp Web site.

Exercise

In this exercise, you'll be defining the new Vecta Corp Web site. All of the files that you'll need for this exercise are available from the Wrox Web site, including the completed versions for your review. When building the Web page in this exercise, you should perform the following steps:

1. Create a new Web site for the Vecta Corp Web site.

2. Select the text, image, and Web page files included with the chapter download, and place them within their appropriate folders in the Web site.

3. If you haven't done so already, choose a Web hosting provider. As mentioned earlier in the chapter, a Web hosting provider that I recommend can be found on the fictitious Vecta Corp Web site by visiting www.vectacorp.com.

4. Once you've selected a Web hosting provider, obtain the remote path, your username, and password, and configure the Remote Web Site Properties dialog for your Web site that you may connect to and begin transferring files.

5. Open the Copy Web Site window and practice copying your files to and from the remote Web server. Also, practice making changes to local files and try your hand at the Synchronize feature.

6. Open a browser window and navigate to your site. Make sure that changes that you made locally appear when you browse to your Web site.

Working with Images, Media, and Hyperlinks

In Chapter 2, "Building a Web Page," you saw just how easy it is to build a simple, text-based Web page in Expression Web. You explored helpful features that allowed you to easily paste in copied text within the development area. You also looked at various formatting features such as line breaks, paragraph breaks, headings, colors, font faces, sizes, and more — essentially, tasks that allowed you to manipulate the text within the development area.

While the foundation for future development was laid in Chapter 2, the reality remains that most Web developers expect more from their Web pages than simple text-based documents. Realistically, Web developers expect to include imagery, multimedia elements, and even some level of interactivity that allow users to browse various Web pages within a Web site. If this sounds like you, then this chapter will be right up your alley.

In this chapter, you go beyond the simplicities of simple text-based Web development and move into the interactive and visual realm. Specifically, you will do the following:

- ❑ Understand the importance of including images within your Web pages
- ❑ Add images to your Web pages
- ❑ Manipulate image properties directly from Expression Web
- ❑ Examine hyperlinking

By the end of this chapter, you'll have built on the introductory concepts introduced in Chapter 2. You'll understand how images are added and modified directly from within Expression Web, you'll see how interactive media elements are added, and most important, how links can be created for text and images within Expression Web. You'll see how including images, interactive elements, and hyperlinks can greatly improve the user experience of the fictitious Vecta Corp Web site.

Inserting Images into Your Web Page

As you saw in Chapter 2, building Web pages is somewhat limiting. You're limited in font faces, sizes, and, to a certain extent, you're limited to certain color choices, as well. Unfortunately, the topic of images is fairly limiting as well. While print designers have always had a plethora of image types to choose from (EPS, TIF, JPEG, BMP, PCX, PICT, and PNG), Web developers are limited to a select three (GIF, JPEG, and PNG). Even worse, because you're dealing with the Web, bandwidth becomes an issue. For this reason, images must usually remain small, which results in degradation of quality and loss of color variation. While print publishers aren't typically limited by size, Web developers, on the other hand, must use special tools to optimize images before they're ready for use within Web sites.

It's safe to say that working with images is one of the most complex topics in Web development. Knowing what types of images to use and knowing when to use them are huge factors when designing for the Web. To help you navigate through this complexity, the following file types should be used, as described here:

❑   *Graphical Interchange Format (GIF)* — GIF is used for images or graphics with fewer colors and for graphics without much tonal range. Because GIFs read color in a horizontal line, the more color encountered when reading, the larger the file size. Also, because GIFs read color in a horizontal line, too much color gradation can result in *banding* (which is the process of gradients being broken up into bands representing a lower dimension of color variation). GIFs also have a color table attached to them that dictates to the graphic how many colors and which color can be used in the artwork. More colors in the color table yield larger file sizes. GIFs can also store transparencies and animations but are ideal when used for flat, low-color graphics.

❑   *Joint Photographic Experts Group (JPEG)* — JPEG is a lossy compression standard used on graphics with high tonal ranges such as photographs. This compression standard removes pixels from an image to reduce the file size. Too much compression can result in artifacts, which causes the image to look blurry and unclear. As a good rule of thumb, use the JPEG file format when adding pictures to your Web sites that contain a lot of gradation such as family photos, scenic photographs, and so on.

❑   *Portable Network Graphics (PNG)* — PNG was introduced as a replacement to GIF some time ago. PNG holds a few advantages over GIF: First, color features are greater in that PNG supports alpha transparencies. What this means is that you can have 256 levels of transparency instead of just on and off as with GIF, cross-platform control of image brightness, and two-dimensional interlacing (a method of progressive display that is similar to JPG). Also, PNG compresses 5–25 percent better than GIF, making this an attractive format for Web developers. Unfortunately, the downside to using PNG on the Web is that browser support (or, more specifically, down-level browser support) for PNG is simply not up to par. Even the newer versions of Internet Explorer don't support the transparency features in PNG just yet.

As a rule of thumb, if you're working with flat, solid images (text, line art, clip art), use GIF. If, however, you're working with images with a lot of color gradation such as artwork or photographs, use JPEG.

As you've probably noticed, the images used on the Vecta Corp Web site (located within the Images folder) are all GIF. The reasons for this are simple. First, for this Web site, you want the maximum number of potential visitors to be able to access the site without having to wait for large images to load. Because of this, you want to use images that support lower color depths in an effort to keep the file size small. Second, most of the images used by the Vecta Corp Web site have little color in them anyway. As you'll see, most of the images fall within the 256-color spectrum. This makes them good candidates for the smaller and faster-loading GIF file format.

Now that you have a basic understanding of the various types of files that you can work with on the Web, let's actually add a few to a Web page within Expression Web.

Try It Out   Inserting an Image into a Web Page

You can add images to a Web page using a variety of techniques in Expression Web. To help you understand these techniques, follow these steps:

1. If you haven't done so already, open the Vecta Corp Web site files for this chapter within Expression Web. Immediately open the `default.htm` file. You'll notice that the `default.htm` file is basically the page built in Chapter 2, only slightly modified (the subheaders have all been removed).

2. With the Folder List Task Pane open near the left of the Document Window, expand the `Images` folder and locate the file called `header.gif`. Select it and drag it into the `<p>` tag area located at the top of the Web page. The result of the image addition will look something like Figure 4-1.

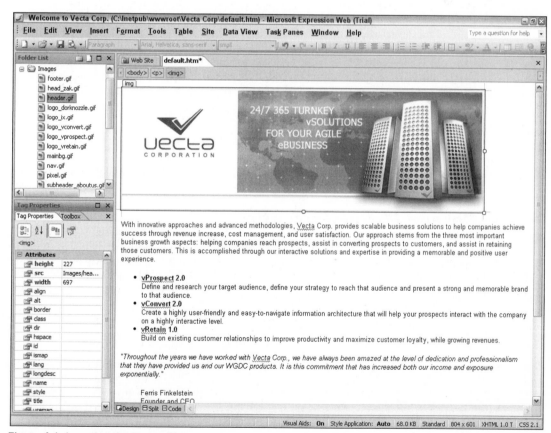

Figure 4-1: Inserting the image file

You'll notice that as you add the image to the page, the Accessibility Properties dialog box automatically opens. While accessibility is covered with more detail in Chapter 16, "Building Accessible and Standards-Compliant Web Sites," for now, you can prevent this dialog from appearing automatically by choosing Tools ⇨ Page Editor Options. When the Page Editor Options dialog box appears, uncheck the Prompt for accessibility properties when inserting images check box. Click OK to close the dialog box.

3. Dragging and dropping images from the Folder List Task Pane is certainly easy, but there are still other ways to include images within your Web page. This time, place your cursor in the <p> tag area, located in between the word "experience" and the first bullet point for vProspect 2.0. This is the spot to insert the subheader image that represents Vecta Corp's solutions. To insert the image, choose Insert ⇨ Picture ⇨ From File. Choosing this method launches the Picture dialog box, which allows you to browse to and select the file called subheader_oursolutions.gif, again located within the Images folder. With this image now selected, choose Insert. The image appears within the Web page.

4. The final method for inserting an image into your Web page is slightly more complex and involves selecting and configuring the Image Placeholder within the Toolbox Task Pane. To use this method, locate the Toolbox Task Pane. (If it isn't open, choose Task Panes ⇨ Toolbox.) Now, expand the HTML set of tools. Once the HTML set has been expanded, you'll notice two sets: Tags and Form Controls. Expand the Tags set. Locate the Image option, select it, and drag it into your Web page, preferably into the <p> tag area between the first client testimonial and the last bullet point for "Our Solutions." You'll immediately notice a small Image icon that appears within the <p> tag. What you want to do now is to configure the path to the image file.

    To do this, locate the src property located within the Tag Properties Task Pane. Place your cursor in the text box just to the right of the property until a small button with three dots appears. Click that small button to launch the Select File dialog box. Just as you did in the previous step, browse to and select the file called subheader_clienttestimonials .gif and click Open. Immediately, the dialog box closes and the new subheader image appears where the small image icon used to reside, similar to Figure 4-2.

Setting General Picture Properties

As is the case with text, and as you'll see with other elements that you'll include within your Web pages, images have various properties that you can manipulate. For example, you may decide to set properties that define how text should wrap around an image, how much spacing to include around the image, or whether or not the image should have a border, or you may even decide to set simple properties such as the width and height for the image.

In general, Expression Web figures out the default width and height of an image by reading the width and height values stored as part of the binary file. While Expression Web doesn't directly support the ability to change these dimensions (otherwise known as *resampling*), it does allow you to temporarily change how the browser should interpret the width and height through a process known as *stretching*.

> To stretch an image, you would simply grab the small white endpoints of the image (once the image had been selected) and drag until the image is smaller or bigger than you want it. You'll immediately notice that the quality of the image is greatly reduced. A better way of changing the physical dimensions of an image would be to resample the image using a program intended for that purpose. Microsoft Expression Design or the built-in Microsoft Office Picture Manager are both well-suited for tasks such as these.

Three different methods exist for manipulating the various types of properties associated with images:

❑ *Picture Properties* — You can use the Picture Properties dialog box (outlined in this section) to set basic image properties visually. Properties within this dialog box include the ability to set the path to the image, alternate text that should be associated with the image, a hyperlink for the image, and various appearance properties such as text wrapping, alignments, border thickness, margins, and more.

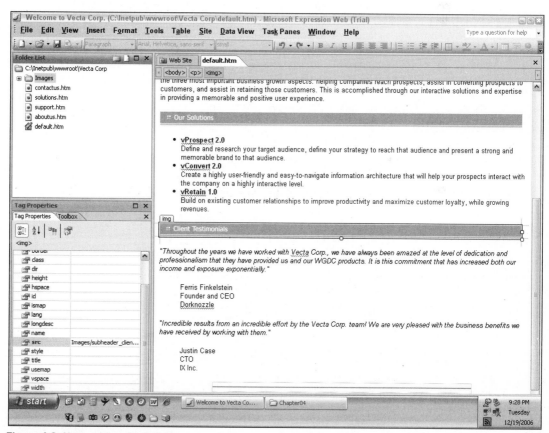

Figure 4-2: New subheader image

❑   *Tag Properties Task Pane* — Remember that every element that you add to your Web page is ultimately represented by an HTML tag of some sort. Images are no different. Because of this, you can use the Tag Properties Task Pane to visually manipulate all of the properties associated with the image in one convenient list. As you saw in Chapter 2, Tag Properties don't extend to just images. All elements, including text, have properties that you can manipulate within the Tag Properties Task Pane.

❑   *Image Toolbar* — For the most part, you'll want to perform major image-editing tasks such as resampling, brightness and contrast changes, cropping, and opacity changes in programs that are suited for these operations such as Microsoft Expression Design or Microsoft Office Picture Manager. However, if access to Graphic Designer is not possible, you can use Expression Web to quickly and easily perform simple editing tasks such as changing the brightness and contrast, rotating an image, cropping, and more.

While the Tag Properties Task Pane and the Image Toolbar are definitely covered in the next few sections, let's take this time to discuss the Picture Properties dialog box. As mentioned in the preceding list, the Picture Properties dialog box allows you to manipulate various properties for an image visually. To access the Picture Properties dialog box, simply right-click onto the image that you want to change properties for, and choose the Picture Properties option from the context menu that appears. The Picture Properties dialog box appears, as shown in Figure 4-3.

As you can see from Figure 4-3, the Picture Properties dialog box reveals two different tabs (the General tab is shown by default), each allowing you to visually manipulate different types of properties for an image:

❑   General Properties

❑   Appearance Properties

Let's discuss the interface within each tab in greater detail.

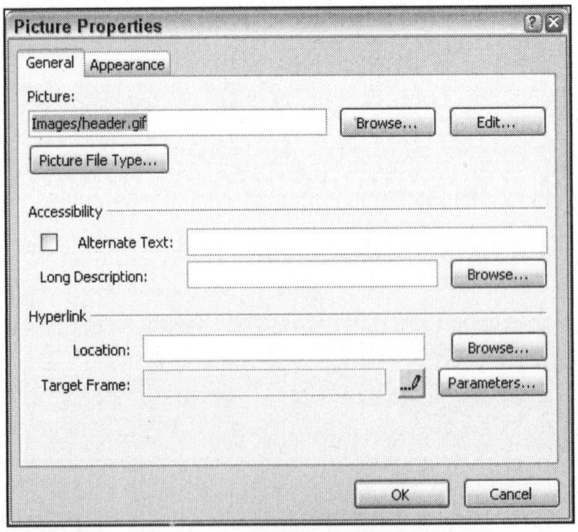

Figure 4-3: Picture Properties dialog box

General Properties

You can use the properties outlined in the General tab to visually set basic aspects of the image. As you can see from Figure 4-3, the properties offered within this tab are separated into three groups:

❑ *Picture* — Use the properties within this group to change the path to the source of the image file. Options within this group also include the ability to quickly open the image and edit it within the included Microsoft Office Picture Manager, and the ability to change the file type. A detailed overview of Microsoft Office Picture Manager and changing the file type is provided later in this chapter.

❑ *Accessibility* — Use the options offered within the Accessibility group to set the alternate text and long description properties for the image. Accessibility is covered with more detail in Chapter 16, "Building Accessible and Standards-Compliant Web Sites."

> For accessibility reasons, developers should specify the alternate text for an image. This text should be a descriptive representation of the image and is used by text-to-speech readers to describe the image to a user with visual disabilities. If the description of the image becomes too long, you may decide to break it out into a separate text or HTML file. When this is the case, simply supply the path to that file within the Long Description text box. The text-to-speech reader, recognizing that this property is set, gives the disabled user the option to read both the alternate text for the image and/or the long description associated with the image.

❑ *Hyperlink* — Use the options in the Hyperlink group to associate a path that the browser should redirect to when the user clicks the image. Simply specify the path within the Location text box (the target frame is optional) and the image will instantly be clickable within the browser. A detailed overview on linking and target frames is provided later in this chapter.

Appearance Properties

You can use the properties outlined by the Appearance tab (shown in Figure 4-4) to visually set how the image, and, more important, how elements that surround the image, will look within the browser. For example, you may decide to set how text wraps around an image, set the alignment of an image, set whether or not the image should have a border, specify spacing around an image (otherwise known as *margins*), and even stretch the image by defining new width and height values.

As you can see from Figure 4-4, the properties in this tab are separated into three groups:

❑ *Wrapping style* — Use the properties in the "Wrapping style" group to set how text and other elements should wrap around the image. Possible values include None (text will not freely wrap around the image), Left (the image will be aligned left and text will wrap around the right side of the image), and Right (the image will be aligned right and text will wrap around the left side of the image).

❑ *Layout* — Use the properties outlined within the Layout group to set the alignment of the image, set a border for the image, and to set vertical and horizontal margins for the image. While the values for border thickness and margins are represented by numeric values, possible values for alignment include Baseline, Sub, Super, Top, Text-top, Middle, Bottom, and Text-bottom.

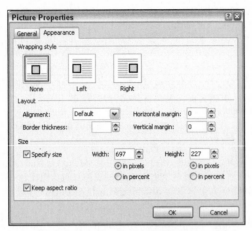

Figure 4-4: Properties in the Appearance tab

❑   *Size* — Use the options outlined within the Size group to change the default width and height for the image using either pixels or percentage values. Remember that when you change the width and height values here, you're simply telling the browser to render different width and height values than what are stored as part of the binary makeup of the image. This process is known as *stretching* and doesn't necessarily result in the best quality image.

Stretching the image is easy. You'd simply enter new numeric values within the Width and/or Height text boxes and then choose the unit type of either pixels or percent. You may even decide to maintain the aspect ratio for the image when stretching (represented by the "Keep aspect ratio" checkbox) — That is, when either the width or height is adjusted, a value is entered automatically by Expression Web for the opposing value to keep either the height and/or width ratio from appearing stretched too much horizontally or vertically. If you prefer not to include the width and height attributes and attribute values as part of the image tag in code, simply clear the "Specify size" checkbox.

Using the Tag Properties Task Pane to Modify Image Properties

While the Picture Properties dialog box is a great option for beginning developers who know little about HTML and prefer a more visual approach to the modification of properties associated with images, it's far from complete in the properties that it outlines. For example, you can't uniquely identify an image from the Picture Properties dialog box. You also can't apply a CSS class to an image, associate an image map for the image, or even specify a client-side function that should be called when the image is clicked. While most of these properties don't relate to anything being discussed in this chapter and are generally considered more advanced concepts, the point remains that the Picture Properties dialog box, while great for quick and visual property modification, lacks a complete set of modifiable properties for images. If you have experience with HTML and are aware of the complete set of properties and possible values that images support, maybe the Tag Properties Task Pane is better suited for your needs.

As mentioned earlier in the chapter, the Tag Properties Task Pane (available in the left third of Expression Web, under the Folder List Task Pane) reveals a complete list of properties available for any element that you happen to be working with within the development area. For example, if you're working with a <p> element, the Tag Properties Task Pane changes to reflect properties that can be customized for the <p> tag. If you happen to be working with tables, the Tag Properties Task Pane tailors itself to display a list of modifiable properties for tables, table rows, and cells. In this case, because you are working with images, selecting an image reveals a complete list of properties that you may choose to configure for images (shown in Figure 4-5). More important, this list is much more complete than the properties that were available to you within the Picture Properties dialog box.

Right away, you'll notice some interesting features available within the Tag Properties Task Pane (highlighted by the callouts in Figure 4-5), including the following:

❑ *Show categorized list* — Clicking this button causes the Tag Properties list to organize properties into two groups: Attributes and Events.

❑ *Show alphabetized list* — Clicking this button removes the categorized display and instead shows all of the properties in one complete list organized alphabetically.

❑ *Show set properties on top* — Clicking this button displays properties that have values associated with them at the top of the list.

❑ *Show tag properties* — This launches the tag properties dialog box associated with the currently selected element. Because you currently have an image selected, clicking this button would cause the Picture Properties dialog box to open.

❑ *Current tag* — Displays the currently selected tag within the development area.

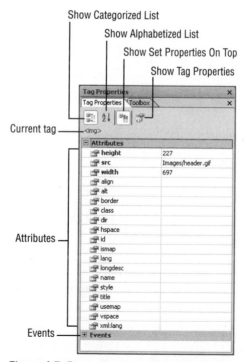

Figure 4-5: Properties to configure for images

❏ *Attributes* — When the "Show categorized" list is enabled, this category displays a list of properties (otherwise known as *attributes*) associated with the currently selected tag. Attributes appear in the left column, while attribute values appear in the right column. A complete list of attributes associated with images (<img> tag) is outlined later in this section.

❏ *Events* — When the "Show categorized" list is enabled, this category displays a complete set of events that you may use to associate with your image. As you'll learn in Chapter 8, "Adding Interactivity with Behaviors," events are used in conjunction with functions to associate client-side interactivity (usually in the form of JavaScript) with your images.

As you may have guessed, the only downside to using the list of properties that are available from the Tag Properties Task Pane is that a certain level of experience in HTML is required to use them. If you aren't familiar with HTML, however, don't worry, because the following list describes each of the properties that are available in the list with some level of detail:

❏ align — Specifies how elements should align themselves around the image. Possible values include absbottom, absmiddle, baseline, bottom, left, middle, right, texttop, and top.

❏ alt — Specifies the alternate text that should be associated with the image.

❏ border — Adds a border to your image based on the numeric value that you specify here.

❏ class — Associates a CSS class with your image. For information on classes, see Chapter 5, "Page Formatting Using Cascading Style Sheets."

❏ dir — Sets the reading order of the image. Possible values include ltr (content flows left to right) and rtl (content flows right to left).

❏ height — Specifies the height of the image in pixels. Again, this doesn't change the dimensions of the image as defined by its binary makeup. It merely stretches the image so that the browser reads the new value and temporarily changes the height of the image in the browser.

❏ hspace — Defines spacing (defined as a numeric pixel value) above and below the image.

❏ id — Uniquely identifies the image. The id attribute can be manipulated through both client- and server-side technologies.

❏ ismap — Sets whether the image is a server-side image map.

❏ lang — Sets what language the browser should use to display language-specific choices for the image.

❏ longdesc — As mentioned earlier in the chapter, the longdesc attribute (which is short for "Long Description") should be used in situations where accessibility is crucial. You can set this property in an effort to provide text-to-speech readers the option of reading a more detailed version of alternate text for an image. This value would accept a URL pointing to the long description file represented as either a text or HTML file.

❏ name — Uniquely names the image. The name attribute is functionally equivalent to id but can be manipulated dynamically only through client-side technologies.

❏ src — Defines the path to the image. This is the location that the browser will use to grab the image and display it within the browser.

❏ style — Allows you to specify an inline style that should be associated with the image. This is covered with more detail in Chapter 5, "Page Formatting Using Cascading Style Sheets."

❑   title — Sets the text-based ToolTip that will appear when the user's mouse hovers over the image.

❑   usemap — Specifies the client-side image map that should be associated with the image. Image maps are covered with more detail later in this chapter.

❑   vspace — Defines spacing (defined as a numeric pixel value) to the left and right of the image.

❑   width — Specifies the width of the image in pixels. Again, this doesn't change the dimensions of the image as it's defined by its binary makeup. It merely stretches the image so that the browser reads the new value and temporarily changes the width of the image in the browser.

❑   xml:lang — Another crucial accessibility property is xml:lang. While the alt attribute defines the text that should appear for text-to-speech readers, the xml:lang property defines which language that text should be displayed in.

As you can see, the complete list of properties that you may choose to customize for images is extensive. In most cases, the properties covered in the Picture Properties dialog box are all you'll ever need access to. If and when your HTML skills improve, the Tag Properties Task Pane is a handy and convenient way of quickly and easily manipulating properties for elements within the development area.

Using the Pictures Toolbar to Modify Image Properties

As mentioned earlier, Expression Web includes limited functionality that allows you to effortlessly make quick edits to your images without having to fall back on other programs such as Expression Design or Microsoft Office Picture Manager. Available from the Pictures toolbar, Expression Web allows you to add text to your images, rotate your images, set the stacking order, adjust brightness and contrast, crop an image, and more. To open the Pictures toolbar, choose View ➪ Toolbars ➪ Pictures. The Pictures toolbar will appear as shown in Figure 4-6.

Figure 4-6: Pictures toolbar

As you can see from Figure 4-6, the Pictures toolbar surprisingly includes a rich set of image-editing features that can be used directly within Expression Web. Specifically, these features include the following (moving left to right in the toolbar):

❑   *From File* — Launches the Select Picture dialog box. It's within this dialog box that you can browse to and select an image to add to your Web page. This method is simply an iconic representation of the Insert ➪ Picture ➪ From File method.

❑   *Auto Thumbnail* — Click this button to convert your image into a thumbnail.

❑   *Bring Forward and Send Backward* — Use these buttons to bring an image forward or to send an image backward. These features are especially useful when your images are contained within <div> tags that have an associated z-index. If your images aren't contained within a <div> tag that uses a z-index, clicking one of these buttons attaches an inline style to the image with the z-index set. More information on <div> tags and the z-index is provided in Chapter 7, "Advanced Page Structuring Techniques Using CSS."

❑   *Rotate Left and Rotate Right* — Click either of these buttons to rotate your image either to the left or to the right.

❏ *Flip Horizontal and Flip Vertical* — Click either of these buttons to flip your image either horizontally or vertically. Choosing this option causes Expression Web to open a Save dialog box. The Save dialog box displays the modified image, asking you to save it before the page can be saved successfully.

❏ *More and Less Contrast* — Click either of these buttons to add or reduce contrast from the image.

❏ *More Brightness and Less Brightness* — Click either of these buttons to add or reduce the brightness of the image.

❏ *Crop* — Click this button to create a cropping marquee within your image. You can then position the cropping marquee around an area within your image and click the Crop icon again within the Pictures toolbar to crop that particular section from the image.

❏ *Set Transparent Color* — Clicking this button and then choosing a color within your image will convert the selected color within the image into a transparency. This option is ideal when you have an over-abundance of a color within your image that matches the background color of the Web page. Because the color of the image matches the color of the Web page background, you can greatly reduce the file size of the image by converting that color within the image into a transparency. The background color of the Web page ends up showing through the transparency and it appears as if the image were never changed. This option only works with images that support transparency such as GIF.

❏ *Color* — Click this button to reveal the color submenu. From this menu, you may choose options for converting the color of your image. Options include the ability to convert your image to grayscale, or black and white (if your image were a bitmap), or give your image a washed-out effect.

❏ *Bevel* — Click this button to add a simple bevel effect to your image. This effect is ideal for use with buttons that you may create within an image-editing program as the bevel would add dimension to the button. The more you click the bevel button the darker the bevel becomes.

❏ *Resample* — When Expression Design is installed on your computer, this button becomes enabled. You can then click this button to initiate the process of resampling your image. Again, *resampling* is the process of the image-editing program that reduces pixels from the image in an effort to change the physical dimensions of the image. Resampling provides the best quality when changing the physical makeup of the image.

❏ *Hotspot Tools* — As you'll see later in this chapter, you can create multiple links within a single image, also known as an *image map*. To create these links within the image, you would define what are known as *hotspots*. The idea is that a user browsing your page could select one of these hotspots and then be instantly redirected to the page that you define as the path for the hotspot. These hotspots can be created using the buttons available within this group in the Pictures toolbar.

❏ *Restore* — Click this button to restore the image back to its original state.

One of the unique benefits of using some of these built-in image editing features in Expression Web is that you can try out some of the effects and, if you don't like them, simply click the Restore button to convert the image back to its original state. Even better, assume that you may or may not like a change that you've made on an image. Perhaps you added a bevel and maybe you need approval from someone else before you commit to the new change. When the bevel is added, Expression Web doesn't actually change the physical makeup of the image at that moment. Instead, Expression Web gives you the option of either replacing the image that the rotation has been performed on, or gives you the option of saving the rotated image as a copy. This option is provided to you within the Save Embedded Files dialog box at the instant that you save your Web page.

Editing an Image Using the Pictures Toolbar

To give you an idea of how images can be edited using the Pictures toolbar and, more important, how you can use the Save Embedded Files dialog box to save a copy of the image, follow these steps:

1. Select the header image within the Web page and click the Bevel button within the Pictures toolbar. Instantly, dimension is added to your header image.

2. To see that the original image has not been affected by the bevel addition, choose File ⇨ Save. Rather than allowing you to perform the save operation, Expression Web, recognizing that an image modification has been performed, launches the Save Embedded Files dialog box, shown in Figure 4-7.

3. You'll notice that the Save Embedded Files dialog box provides numerous options that you may decide to choose from before actually saving your image. This is discussed next. For now, ensure that the `header.gif` image is listed within the "Embedded files to save" list box. Select it and choose the Rename button.

4. Now, replace the name for `header.gif` with the name `header_copy.gif`. The Action for the image should change from Overwrite to Save.

5. Click OK to commit to the saving of both your new image and the Web page. Now, to see that Expression Web did indeed create a copy of the image that you just applied a bevel to, select the `Images` folder within the Folder List Task Pane and choose View ⇨ Refresh or click F5. You'll notice that you now have `header.gif` and `header_copy.gif` listed within the Task Pane. What this means is that if you change your mind on the beveled image, simply delete it from the page (and optionally from the Folder List Task Pane), and then drag the original image (`header.gif`) back into the Web page.

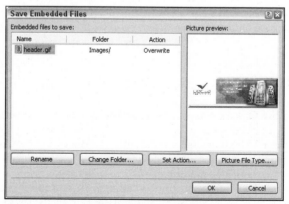

Figure 4-7: Save Embedded Files dialog box

As you may have noticed from Figure 4-7, the Save Embedded Files dialog box offers numerous options that are worth further explanation, including the following:

❑ *Embedded files to save* — Displays a list of modified images within your Web page. Whenever you attempt to save a Web page that contains images that have been modified using the Pictures tool-bar, any images that have been affected will be listed here. The list provides the name of the file, the folder in which the file resides on your computer, and the action that will be performed on the file once you click OK. Options include Overwrite (default), Save, and Use Existing.

❑ *Picture preview* — Displays a thumbnail size version of your modified image for previewing purposes.

❑ *Rename* — Click this button to rename the image selected within the "Embedded files to save" list.

❑ *Change Folder* — Launches the Change Folder dialog box. You can use this dialog box to browse to and select a different folder to save the image into. When you choose a different folder, the Action of the image within the list changes to Save.

❑ *Set Action* — Launches the Set Action dialog box. It's within this dialog box that you are able to set the action that will be performed on the image. For example, if you want to overwrite the existing image on your computer within the newly modified image, keep the "Overwrite existing file" radio button selected. If you prefer not to use the modified version of the image, choose the "Don't overwrite the existing file" radio button and click OK.

❑ *Picture File Type* — If you prefer to change the file type associated with the image, click the Picture File Type button. This is covered in more detail later in this chapter.

Editing an Image with Microsoft Office Picture Manager

For most of us, common computer-based tasks such as writing a letter, managing a spreadsheet, or building a presentation is simply a matter of opening Word, Excel, or PowerPoint. As a Windows-based user, you've become accustomed to using these programs and others included within the Office suite for performing common day-to-day tasks such as the ones mentioned. What most Office users don't realize, however, is that Office also comes with a suite of tools that can better improve your user experience with the Office set of products. These tools, also known as Microsoft Office Tools, are installed automatically when you install or update Office. While a dozen or so tools exist to aid in the Office user experience, one specific tool can better improve the way you work with Expression Web. This tool is Microsoft Office Picture Manager.

Microsoft Office Picture Manager (available by choosing Start ➪ Programs ➪ Microsoft Office ➪ Microsoft Office Tools ➪ Microsoft Office Picture Manager) is a simple, Office-centric utility that you can use to manage picture assets for your Office products. Because Picture Manager reads the images contained within your `My Pictures` folder located within your `My Documents` folder by default, centralized organization and management of picture-based assets for your Office products become easy.

Beyond organization and management, however, Picture Manager also provides options for image editing. Red-eye removal, brightness and contrast adjustments, cropping, image rotating, image optimization, image resampling, and more are all available within Picture Manager. What this means is that if you don't have access to more powerful, image-editing–specific programs such as Microsoft Expression Design, at the very least, Office Picture Manager is available and ready for you to use. Even better, Expression Web integrates directly with Picture Manager. The benefit for you is that you don't have to leave Expression Web to work in Picture Manager. Instead, you can launch an instance of Picture Manager directly from Expression Web, make modifications to your image, and then click a "Save and Close" button to close Picture Manager and return to Expression Web.

Try It Out   Editing an Image Using Office Picture Manager

To see how images can be edited using Office Picture Manager directly from Expression Web, follow these steps:

1. Start by finding the image head_zak.gif located within the Images folder of the defined Vecta Corp Web site. Once you've identified the image within the Folder List Task Pane, select it and drag it onto the page, preferably at the beginning of the welcome text, just under the main header image. You'll immediately notice that the image is too big for that area and must be resized. Sure, you could launch the Picture Properties dialog box, switch over to the Appearance tab, and change the width and height dimensions that way. Remember, however, that that would be stretching the image, not resampling it, and would result in poor quality. Instead, use Office Picture Manager to resize the image the right way.

2. To launch the image within Picture Manager, right-click the image and choose Picture Properties. The Picture Properties dialog box will appear. Now click the Edit button. Immediately, the image is opened within Office Picture Manager also shown in Figure 4-8. If your image opens in a program

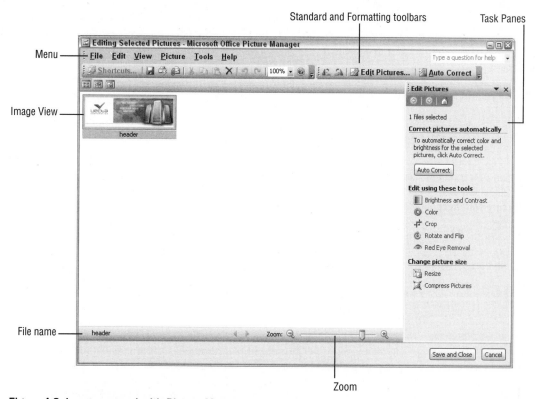

Figure 4-8: Image opened with Picture Manager

other than Office Picture Manager, you'll have to manually open Office Picture Manager by choose Start ⇨ Programs ⇨ Microsoft Office ⇨ Microsoft Office Tools ⇨ Microsoft Office Picture Manager. With Office Picture Manager now open, you can browse to the image file by choosing File ⇨ Add Picture Shortcut, then browsing to and selecting the folder that contains your image. This way, not only will your image appear, but so, too, will all of the images used in the Vecta Corp site.

3. As you can see, Picture Manager is a relatively simple looking program and contains few features for editing, formatting, and organizing the images within your site. While these features are examined in more detail in just a bit, for now, choose the Resize option located within the Task Pane. The Task Pane changes to accommodate image resizing.

4. You'll notice that the Resize Task Pane is split into two categories: "Resize settings" and "Size setting summary." From the "Resize settings" category, choose the "Custom width x height" radio button and enter the new values of **75** and **65**, respectively, within the width and height text boxes and click OK. Picture Manager changes the image size, but, more important, to accommodate aspect ration, automatically changes the 75-pixel value that you entered to 73.

5. Click the "Save and Close" button to save the image (overwriting the old version). Close Office Picture Manager, and return to Expression Web. Finally, to see the changes reflected in Expression Web, right-click the image that you just modified, and choose the Reset Size option from the context menu. You'll notice that the image changes to reflect the width and height change.

6. As you learned earlier in the chapter, you can format the text around the image by right-clicking onto the image and choosing Picture Properties. When the Picture Properties dialog appears, switch to the Appearance tab and click the Left option from the Wrapping style group. Click OK. You'll notice that the text now wraps around the right side of your image.

As you've seen, Picture Manager is fairly simple to use. As you can see from the callouts in Figure 4-8, Picture Manager includes the following features:

❏ *Menu* — Similar to all Office products, the menu bar offers access to all operations that can be performed within Picture Manager.

❏ *Standard and Formatting Toolbars* — Unlike Expression Web (which includes numerous toolbars), Picture Manager includes two toolbars: the Standard and Formatting toolbars. You can use these toolbars to visually access commonly used operations such as Save, Copy, Cut, Paste, Undo, Redo, Rotate, and more.

❏ *Image View* — Displays the image(s) to be edited. If you have multiple images open, you may decide to change how Picture Manager displays the image. This can be done by choosing either of the icons located just above the image view. Options include Thumbnail, Filmstrip, and Single picture views.

❏ *File name* — This is a simple text-based label that displays the name of the file to be edited.

❏ *Zoom* — Move the slider up and down to zoom in or out of the image.

❏ *Task Panes* — At the heart of Picture Manager are the Task Panes. Whether you're resizing an image, cropping an image, or performing some other image editing task, the Task Panes will always change to accommodate the task about to be performed.

As you can see, numerous options exist within Picture Manager for making quick and simple modifications to your images. You should explore these features as they'll no doubt improve your experience with Expression Web.

Changing the Picture File Type

As you've seen, you can accomplish basic image-editing tasks from both the Pictures toolbar and from Expression Web's integration with Microsoft Office Picture Manager. However, other tasks (such as quickly converting an image from one file type to another) can't be accomplished using these methods. While you could certainly use Microsoft Expression Design, Expression Web includes an easier and transparent way via the Picture File Type dialog box.

Accessible by right-clicking an image and selecting the Change Picture File Type option from the context menu that appears, the Picture File Type dialog box (shown in Figure 4-9) allows you to quickly and effortlessly convert an image's file type to another type.

As you can see from Figure 4-9, the Picture File Type dialog box offers the following features:

❑ *Original file* — Displays the filename for the image before the conversion.

❑ *Original size* — Displays the file size for the image before the conversion.

❑ *Changed file* — Displays the filename for the image after it's been converted.

❑ *Changed size* — Displays the file size for the image after it's been converted.

❑ *File types* — Displays a radio button list of available image types that you may convert your image to. Expression Web recognizes the existing file type and automatically selects that radio button. For a detailed explanation of the file types listed here, refer to the beginning of this chapter.

❑ *Settings* — Displays more advanced settings for the GIF and JPEG file format. When GIF is selected, you're provided with interlacing and transparency options. When JPEG is selected, the options displayed here allow you to set the quality of the image, as well as how many progressive passes should be used by the browser when loading the image.

To convert your image from one file type to another, you simply select the new file type from the file types list, optionally manipulate some of the advanced settings, and click OK. The image's file type will be visible and identifiable by its new file extension within the Folder List Task Pane.

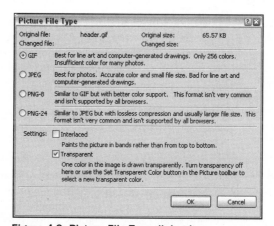

Figure 4-9: Picture File Type dialog box

Linking Pages Within Your Web Site

One of the basic premises behind working with the Web is that you can create pages that link between each other. This concept (known as *hyperlinking*) is the foundation behind the HyperText Markup Language (HTML). By simply adding text to the page and then associating a link with that text, you can allow your users to interact with multiple pages within a Web site, as opposed to being confined to a single page. Of course, like so many other features included within Expression Web, Expression Web has excellent support for creating and working with the following types of links:

❑ Text links

❑ Image links

❑ Image maps (multiple links within one image)

❑ Named anchors (multiple links within the same page)

Before you jump directly into linking, however, it's important to discuss paths and targets. Creating a hyperlink is merely the process of assigning a path to the hyperlink reference (`href`) of text, images, hotspots within image maps, or anchors. When you assign a path to one of these elements, you are making a link available from your linked element to the endpoint via the path. When it comes to paths, you have three to work with:

❑ *Document Relative* — Possibly the easiest type of path to work with, Document Relative paths require little more than the path from the current file to the target file. For example, if you were working with a file located in the folder `Vecta Corp\Departments\Marketing\Press Releases\` and you needed to link to a file called `marketing.htm` within the `Marketing` folder, you would simply use `../../marketing.htm` as your path. The `../` essentially forces the browser to back out of the current folder. The same holds true if you were working with a file within the same `Press Releases` folder and you needed to reference an image within the `Images` folder located within the `Press Releases` folder. In that case, your path would resemble `Images/file.gif`. Simple enough, right? The downside to working with Document Relative paths is that you can back out of only so many folders, two before it becomes impractical. If you are working within a lengthy folder structure, the Site Root Relative path might be your answer.

❑ *Site Root Relative* — The downside to working with Document Relative paths is that once you go beyond two folders deep in a folder structure, using Document Relative paths becomes impractical. This is where Site Root Relative paths become useful. Because Site Root Relative paths have no limit to folder depth, they become handy when you're dealing with a large and complex folder structure within your site. For instance, the example in the Document Relative path description references the path `Vecta Corp\Departments\Marketing\Press Releases`. If you were working with a file within the `Press Releases` folder and needed to link to the file `default.htm` within the `Vecta Corp` folder root, you could use a Site Root Relative path to simply reference the `path /default.htm`. The `/` instructs the browser to find the site root and then retrieve `default.htm`.

❑ *Absolute* — You can use Absolute paths when referencing files located in paths that don't (and, more than likely, never will) change. For example, the domain names `http://www.vectacorp.com` and `http://www.modulemedia.com` will never change. These are said to be *absolute* so you could assign these domain names as your absolute paths. Furthermore, you could also use a specific folder within that domain. For example, if you wanted to reference an image within the Images folder of the www.vectacorp.com site, you could reference its absolute path as http://www.vectacorp.com/Images/image.gif.

Once you've assigned a path to an element within your Web page to create a link, you may also want to declare a target. A target exists as a way of instructing the browser how to open the path. For example, the following four targets can be assigned when working with hyperlinks in Expression Web:

❑ self — Opens the path within the same browser window as the original page. This target is the default.

❑ blank — Forces the browser to open the path within a new browser window instance. This keeps the original page in the background.

❑ parent — When working with frames, choose this option to load the linked document in the parent frame or parent window of the frame that contains the link. If the frame containing the link is not nested, then the linked document loads in the full browser window.

❑ top — When working with framesets, choose this option when you want to load a linked document in a full browser window, thereby removing all frames.

The coming sections take the simplicities of paths and targets to the next level by introducing you to how Expression Web facilitates working with hyperlinks, otherwise known as just *links*. Specifically, you'll learn how to create links within text, images, multiple links within an image, and multiple links within the same page, and how to use Interactive Buttons to smooth the process of working with large amounts of links within your site.

Linking Text and Images to an Existing Web Page

While Expression Web supports linking for images, multiple areas within an image, multiple areas within a page, and more, quite possibly one of the most widely used type of link is the text-based link. Text-based links are easy to create and maintain with Expression Web, and involve nothing more than typing text into your Web page, highlighting the text, and then associating a path using the Insert Hyperlink dialog box. Once you've associated a path to a text element, the text element becomes linked to the page provided within the path, and the text element's color turns blue and underlined (the Internet standard for a hyperlink).

Try It Out   Inserting a Text-Based Link in Your Web Page

You'll notice that the downloaded chapter files include some pre-built Web pages (aboutus.htm, solutions.htm, support.htm, and contactus.htm). Unfortunately, a user has no way of navigating to these pages from the main Vecta Corp Web page. To see just how easy it is to add and maintain text-based links within your Web page, you will build a simple text-based navigation menu on the main Vecta Corp Web page default.htm that allows users to easily browse to the other pages in the Vecta Corp site. To do this, simply follow these steps:

1. Open the main Vecta Corp page, default.htm, if it isn't open already.

2. Once you open the page, you'll notice that there's no way to allow a user to link from the main page to the other Vecta Corp Web pages that have been pre-built and included for you within

the chapter downloads. To remedy this, you need to construct a text-based navigation menu just under the header that you added earlier in the chapter and before the main introductory text. Place your cursor just before the headshot image and click Enter. This creates a new paragraph break in between the header and the introductory text. Now create a text-based navigation menu with the text **Home | About Us | Solutions | Support | Contact Us**.

3. Highlight the About Us text element within the newly created navigation bar.

4. To associate a path to this text element, thus creating a link, choose Insert ⇨ Hyperlink. The Insert Hyperlink dialog box appears. You can also right-click the text element and choose the Hyperlink option from the context menu to open the Insert Hyperlink dialog box.

5. You'll notice that the Insert Hyperlink dialog box includes numerous features for working with different types of links, as well as features for extending the links that you create. For now, find the `aboutus.htm` file within the list, select it, and click OK.

6. The Insert Hyperlink dialog box will close and, more important, the About Us text element turns blue and is underlined. Unless you've never visited a Web page before, you should know this to be the standard color and style for hyperlinks. To finish up the navigation menu, repeat Steps 3–5, associating Home with `default.htm`, Solutions with `solutions.htm`, Support with `support .htm`, and Contact Us with `contactus.htm`. Once you've finished, the page should resemble Figure 4-10.

7. Save your work and preview the results in the browser by pressing F12. Try selecting any of the links within the navigation menu. You should now be able to link from one page to the next.

As you can see, working with text-based links is simple. For the most part, you simply highlight the text that you want to create the link for, choose Insert ⇨ Hyperlink, and then associate a file from the Insert Hyperlink dialog box to create the link. In most cases, the Insert Hyperlink dialog box is straightforward, and when working with text-based links, is simply a matter of choosing the file to associate with the new hyperlink. However, the Insert Hyperlink dialog box also provided other useful features for extending the functionality of your links. For example, you may decide to link to an area within the page, or to create a new document to link to, or to link to an e-mail address. All of this, and more, is conveniently available from the Insert Hyperlink dialog box. As you saw, the Insert Hyperlink dialog box offers the following options:

❑ *Link to* — Choose an option from this category when you want to link to an existing file or Web page located within your currently defined Web site, link to a place (bookmark) within an existing document, create a new document from scratch to link to, or link to an e-mail address. Depending on which category you select from this list, the Insert Hyperlink dialog box changes to accommodate the particular functionality.

❑ *Text to display* — You can quickly change or make edits to the text on your Web page within this text box. For example, if you'd prefer the text to read "About the Company" as opposed to "About Us," you can quickly make the change here without having to cancel out of the dialog box to make the change within the Web page.

❑ *ScreenTip* — Click this button to launch the Set Hyperlink ScreenTip dialog box. You can then enter a text value within the text box. The text value that you enter here is the value that appears in the small, yellow ToolTip when the user's cursor rolls over a hyperlink.

❑ *Look in* — Expand the drop-down menu to browse your computer for a particular file to link to. You can also click the Up One Folder icon to back out of the folder that appears within the Site directory list box.

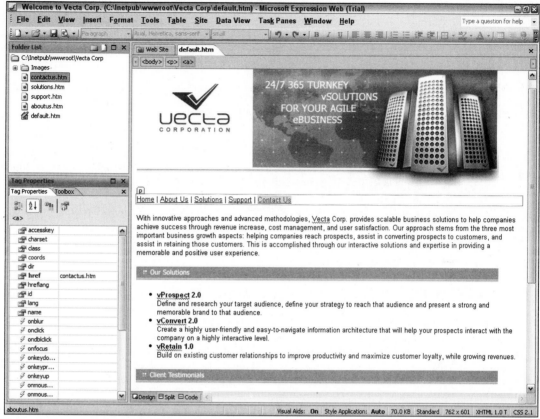

Figure 4-10: Associating the hyperlinks

❑ *Browse the Web / Browse for File* — Click the Browse the Web button to open a browser window. This allows you to browse and link to a Web site, thus creating an absolute path for your link. You may also launch the Select File dialog box by clicking the Browse for File button. Because the Select File dialog box is built specifically around searching for files within your computer, it's a bit easier to use when looking for a particular file to link to.

❑ *Site directory* — This list box contains the complete structure of your defined site (Current Folder). Like Windows Explorer, you can click into and back out of folders within your site directly from this list. You can also view a list of pages you recently browsed to (Browsed Pages) or files that you have recently opened (Recent Files) directly from this view.

❑ *Address* — This is the path that will be associated with your link. In this case, because you selected the aboutus.htm file, aboutus.htm is shown within this text box. Depending on where you are within your site's structure and what link you're trying to establish for a particular file, this text box may change to display site root relative paths (the default when working with links in Expression Web).

❑ *Bookmark* — As you'll see in the coming sections, you can create links to a particular section within a page, otherwise known as bookmarks. Once you have these bookmarks set up within the page, click this button to view the list.

❑ *Target Frame* — As you learned in the introductory section for links, targets are a way of opening links within the same page, new blank page, and so on. You can set a target for your link by clicking this button. Doing so launches the Target Frame dialog box. From this dialog box you can choose from Page Default (which is equivalent to _self), Same Frame (_self), Whole Page (_top), New Window (_blank), or Parent Frame (_parent).

❑ *Parameters* — You can set up optional parameters to pass along the address bar by setting those parameters up within the Parameters dialog box that appears when you click this button. As you'll see in a few sections, you can also pass parameters for e-mail links. Doing so would allow you to pre-populate the Subject line, Body, and more for an e-mail client when working with e-mail links.

❑ *Remove Link* — Once you've established a link, the Insert Hyperlink dialog box changes to the Edit Hyperlink dialog box. When you're in the Edit Hyperlink dialog box, this button becomes visible. You can click this button to remove the hyperlink association for a text or image element.

You can establish a hyperlink for an image in exactly the same fashion as for text elements. If you'd prefer to link an image, simply select the image, choose Insert ⇨ Hyperlink, and then associate a particular path for the image within the Insert Hyperlink dialog box. In the browser, the user would be able to click the image to link to the particular page.

Linking to a Bookmark within a Web Page

Similar to the process of creating links to individual pages is the process of creating links within sections of a page. To understand how bookmarks function, imagine having a page that contained so much information that you had to create a separate navigation menu to link users to portions of that page. For example, the page solutions.htm contains an overwhelming amount of content (done intentionally for this lesson) that's relevant to the solutions that Vecta Corp provides. Rather than forcing the user to scroll from the top of the page down, you'll manually add bookmarks within each of the three sections in the page. Then, you'll create a sub-navigation menu, not unlike the one on the main page, that when each navigation item is clicked, automatically redirects the user to that particular section on the page.

Try It Out   Inserting and Linking to Bookmarks

In this section, you learn how to use bookmarks. Specifically, you learn how to add a bookmark. Then, you create a link that points to a bookmark within a page. To accomplish this, follow these steps:

1. Open the page solutions.htm.

2. Browse to the first solution (vProspect 2.0) represented by the text-based heading, place your cursor next to the heading, and choose Insert ⇨ Bookmark. The Bookmark dialog will appear.

3. Type the text **vProspect** within the Bookmark name text box and click OK.

4. Initially, you won't notice a change to the page. The bookmark is considered a formatting mark and won't actually be visible to you on the page until you decide to switch on formatting marks. You can do this by choosing View ⇨ Formatting Marks ⇨ Show. Immediately, a small flag icon appears where your cursor was positioned to insert the bookmark, as shown in Figure 4-11.

5. Repeat Steps 2–4, adding bookmarks for the other solutions, vConvert and vRetain. When you've finished, save the page.

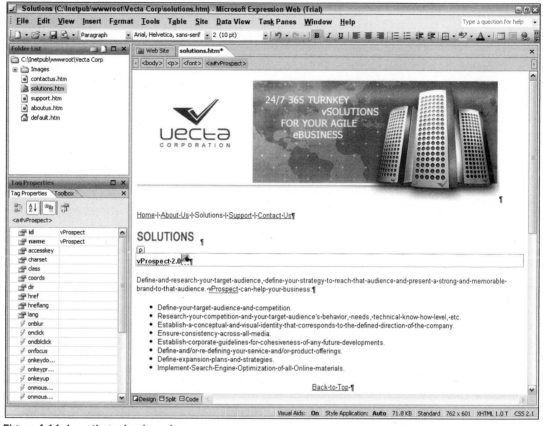

Figure 4-11: Inserting a bookmark

6. Now that the three bookmarks have been created within the page, you can create links to them. On the main Vecta Corp Web page (default.htm), you have a bulleted list of solutions. Let's assume that you wanted to make those three solution headings links to the bookmarks within the solutions.htm page. This would provide your users a quick method for browsing to the particular section within the solutions.htm page that was representative of what they selected on the main page. To do this, start by opening default.htm.

7. Highlight the first heading within the Our Solutions section titled "vProspect 2.0" and choose Insert ⇨ Hyperlink. The Insert Hyperlink dialog box appears.

8. From the Site directory list, choose the solutions.htm page. This time, however, click the Bookmark button located just to the right of the dialog box. The" Select Place in Document" dialog appears, as shown in Figure 4-12.

9. Choose the vProspect bookmark and click OK. The Address text box is populated with the full path to that bookmark, specifically solutions.htm#vProspect. Click OK to set the link.

Figure 4-12: The Select Place in Document dialog

10. Repeat Steps 7–9 until all three of your headings point to their respective bookmarks within the oursolutions.htm page.

11. Once you've finished, save your work and test the results in the browser by choosing F12. When the page appears in the browser, click on a link. You should instantly be redirected to the solutions.htm page. More important, however, the browser should drop you down to the particular section represented by the link that you clicked.

As you can see, bookmarks are a powerful linking technique that can improve the user experience when dealing with links in a site. Of course, you could extend this functionality by adding a submenu within the solutions.htm page that resembles that of the main page. This would allow your users to select an item within the submenu to link down to the particular section in the same page. Furthermore, you might think about adding a bookmark at the top of the page called top. Then, you can include a hyperlink at the end of each section called Back to Top. The idea is to associate the Back to Top links with the bookmark on the page called top so when users are finished reading the content within the section, they simply need to click the Back to Top link to be redirected back up to the top of the page.

Linking to an E-mail Address

Yet another type of link that you might think about using is a link to an e-mail address. This common type of link allows a user to click on what resembles a hyperlink to another page within the site. In this case, however, rather than the user linking to another Web page, the user's e-mail client is launched and the To and Subject fields are pre-populated.

Try It Out   Inserting an E-mail Link

To see how e-mail links are created within Expression Web, you'll use the support.htm page to create an e-mail link to customer support. This enables current Vecta Corp clients to send questions and inquiries to the Vecta Corp client support team by simply clicking a hyperlink. To create the e-mail link, follow these steps:

1. Open the page support.htm.

2. Find the text that reads "Email a Question" and highlight it.

3. Choose Insert ⇨ Hyperlink. The Insert Hyperlink dialog box appears.

4. This time, from the "Link to category" selection menu, choose E-mail Address. The Insert Hyperlink dialog box's interface changes to accommodate an insertion of an e-mail address and subject.

5. Within the "E-mail address" text box, enter the e-mail address **support@vectacorp.com**. You'll notice that Expression Web automatically prefixes "mailto:" to your e-mail address. This is how the browser is instructed to open the user's default e-mail client. Within the Subject text box, enter the text **General Question**. When you're finished, the Insert Hyperlink dialog box resembles Figure 4-13. Also notice the "Recently used e-mail addresses" list box. This list box simply provides a quick way of browsing and selecting from a list of e-mail addresses that you may have recently used.

6. Click OK to close the Insert Hyperlink dialog box and return to the Web page.

7. Save your work and preview the results in the browser by pressing F12. When the page appears, click the link. You'll notice that the default e-mail client that you may have set up automatically opens, as shown in Figure 4-14. More important, the To and Subject fields are automatically populated within the e-mail.

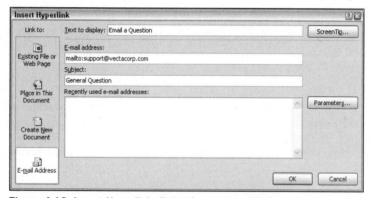

Figure 4-13: Insert Hyperlink dialog for an e-mail link

Creating Multiple Links Within an Image

In certain situations, you may find that creating multiple text-based links or links from a single image will simply not get the job done. You may find that instead of linking a single image to a page, creating multiple links within the image or even linking just a portion of the image is more along the lines of what you need.

If this is the case, Expression Web allows you to work with what are known as image maps. An *image map* is a code-based collection of hotspots within an image that, when clicked, can link the user to a particular page. For example, the fictitious Vecta Corp Web site includes a header image that spans across the top of every page. Near the top left of the header image is the Vecta Corp logo. Typically, this area is reserved as a link that, when clicked, redirects the user back to the main page.

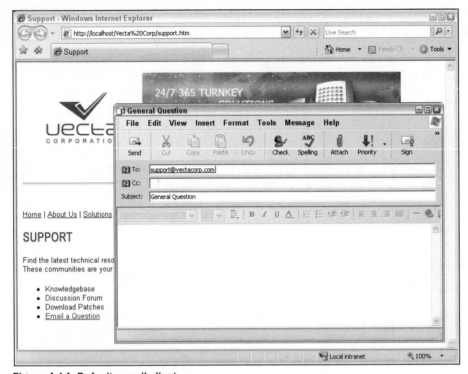

Figure 4-14: Default e-mail client

Rather than linking the entire header image (a process you learned how to accomplish earlier in this chapter), you might think about establishing a smaller, more refined link, around just the logo. The link area that would surround the logo would become the hotspot. When the user views this page in the browser, the only clickable area within the image would be the area defined as the hotspot, or more specifically, the area that surrounds the image.

Try It Out   Creating a Link Hotspot Within an Image

To give you an idea as to how hotspots are created within an image, simply follow these steps:

1. Open the page `aboutus.htm`.

2. Ensure that the Pictures toolbar is open. If it's not open, you can open it by choosing View ➪ Toolbars ➪ Pictures. Initially, the Pictures toolbar will be disabled. To enable it, select the header image (`header.gif`) within the Web page.

3. The last five or so buttons within the Pictures toolbar exist for creating hotspots. To see how these are created within an image, select the Rectangular Hotspot button.

4. Draw a rectangle to surround the Vecta Corp logo within the header image, as shown in Figure 4-15. As soon as you let go of the mouse button, the Insert Hyperlink dialog box appears.

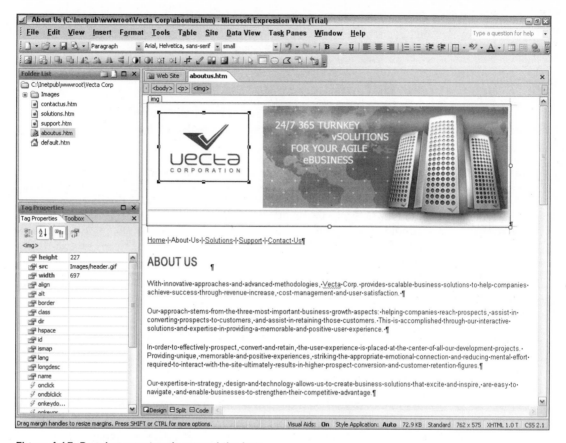

Figure 4-15: Drawing a rectangle around the logo

5. If you've followed the book section by section, the "Link to category selection" menu will have the E-mail Address button selected. Choose the "Existing File or Web Page" option. Within the Site directory list, find `default.htm` and click OK. The Insert Hyperlink dialog box closes.

6. The area (hotspot) that surrounds the Vecta Corp logo is now treated as a link. To see the link in action, save your work and preview the results in the browser by pressing F12. You'll notice that rolling over the image does nothing. It isn't until you roll over the area that you defined as a hotspot that the cursor changes, allowing you to click the link. Doing so redirects you back to the `default.htm` page, as intended.

Of course, you're not limited to just one hotspot within an image. If you feel creative, you might think about creating your entire navigation menu as an image, using icons and fonts of your choice, and then establishing hotspots for every link item within the image to create a purely image-based navigation menu. Additionally, you could customize the image that the hotspot was created for.

As is the case with all elements in Expression Web, an image that has a hotspot association can have its properties modified within the Tag Properties Task Pane. One property that you might want to customize right off the bat is `border`. You probably noticed a small, 1-pixel border that surrounded the header image within the browser. You can disable this border by entering a value of 0 within the `border` property in the Tag Properties Task Pane when the header image is selected.

Using Interactive Buttons

One of the biggest time-savers included in Expression Web is Interactive Buttons. Interactive Buttons are a set of pre-built yet customizable images, made to look like buttons, that you can use with your Web sites in Expression Web.

So, why would you use Interactive Buttons over your own buttons? The answer is simple. You probably wouldn't, in most cases. However, for those who have never used complex image-editing programs, and wouldn't know where to start when it comes to creating and customizing their own image-based buttons, Interactive Buttons are a life-saver. Additionally, Interactive Buttons are great for those who do understand image-editing programs, but require a feature that allows them to quickly and effortlessly build simple buttons for use within their Web sites without their having to rely on costly third-party tools to get the job done.

Try It Out   Re-Creating the Navigation Menu Using Interactive Buttons

To experience how Interactive Buttons can slice time away from your development tasks, you rebuild the navigation menu that you've been working with on the main Vecta Corp Web page, `default.htm`. You can do this on your own by following these steps:

1. Open the page `default.htm` if it's not already open.

2. Highlight the entire navigation menu beginning with "home" and dragging over to Contact Us until the whole menu is highlighted. Click Delete to remove it.

3. With your cursor blinking within the <p> tag, select Insert ⇨ Interactive Button. The Interactive Buttons dialog box appears.

4. You'll immediately notice that the dialog box is split up into three tabs, each representing a certain level of customization that you may decide to make on an Interactive Button. For now, simply select a button style from the Buttons list. For the sake of simplicity, choose "Border Left 6" because it matches up somewhat to the Vecta Corp design.

5. Because this is the first button that you're creating, it will represent the first item in your navigation menu, or Home. Because this is the case, add the text **Home** within the Text text box.

6. Click the Browse button located next to the Link text box and browse to the file `default.htm`. Because this Interactive Button represents the Home link, technically, it should also link to that page when clicked. Once you've finished customizing the Button tab, your customizations should resemble those shown in Figure 4-16.

7. Click OK to create the new Interactive Button. You'll notice the new button, complete with customized text and the hyperlink, is added to the page where your old text-based navigation menu used to reside.

8. To finish up the navigation menu, repeat Steps 3–7, adding the same Interactive Button style, but customizing the text and links so that you have new buttons for About Us, Solutions, Support, and Contact Us. When you've finished creating the navigation menu, your page should resemble Figure 4-17.

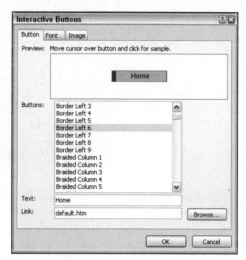

Figure 4-16: Customized Button tab

9. Save your work. The Save Embedded Files dialog should appear because you'll need to save the images that Expression Web creates for the functionality of the Interactive Buttons. Accept the defaults and click OK to finish saving the document. Finally, test the results in the browser by pressing F12. Your new image-based navigation menu, built using Interactive Buttons, should display within the browser. Even better, you should be able to click each item to link to the respective page.

    While the process of creating an Interactive Button is easy enough, there are a fair number of customizations that you're able to make. For example, maybe you decide to choose a different font other than Arial, and perhaps even change the size from the default of 10 pixels. If this is the case, you'd simply switch over the Font tab and make the necessary changes. Perhaps you'd like to make simple changes to the style of the button. If that's the case, you'd switch over to the Image tab and make fine-tuned changes to the width, height, and so on, for the button.

As mentioned, there are three tabs within the Interactive Buttons dialog box, each performing a specific customization task on the Interactive Button. In summation, the following properties are revealed by the Button tab, also visible in Figure 4-18:

❑   *Preview* — Provides a simple preview of the button selected within the Buttons list.

❑   *Buttons* — Provides a list of more than 100 different button styles to choose from. Select a style from this list to see what it looks like within the Preview pane.

❑   *Text* — Enter the text that should be displayed on the button here.

❑   *Link* — Enter the link that should be associated with the button here. If you don't know the file name, you can browse to it by choosing the Browse button.

Switching over to the Font tab reveals a complete set of properties used for modifying the font face, size, style, color, and alignment of the text that will be displayed on the button. The Font tab resembles Figure 4-18.

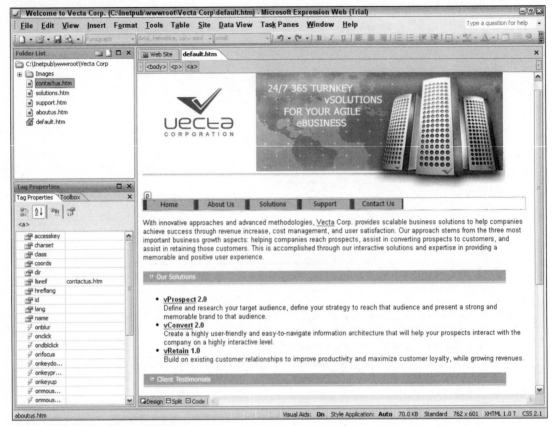

Figure 4-17: Page with navigation menu

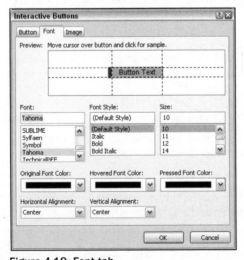

Figure 4-18: Font tab

The Font tab offers the following options:

❑ *Preview* — Provides a simple preview of the text as it's customized for the button.

❑ *Font* — Offers a list box of fonts (from your computer) that you may use to customize the font face for the text displayed on your button. Unlike font faces in HTML, you're not regulated by the types of fonts that you're able to use. Because Interactive Buttons are saved as images, you are free to use any font you choose.

❑ *Font Style* — Provides a list of style options for the text. Options include Italic, Bold, and Bold Italic.

❑ *Size* — Displays a list of font sizes in pixels that you may decide to use for the text. If a size isn't listed, feel free to add it yourself within the Size text box that appears above the list box.

❑ *Original Font Color* — The basic premise behind Interactive Buttons is that they are really three separate images that interact because of client-side scripting in conjunction with the user's mouse behavior. In reality, Interactive Buttons consist of three images: the *original image* (the image that appears when the image hasn't been selected or the user's mouse hasn't hovered over it), the *hover image* (the image that appears once the user's mouse hovers or rolls into the image), and the *pressed image* (the image that appears once the user physically clicks on the image). The color that you choose within this menu is the color that is used for the font before it has been hovered into or pressed on.

❑ *Hovered Font Color* — The color that you choose within this menu is the color that is used for the font when the user's mouse hovers or rolls over the image.

❑ *Pressed Font Color* — The color that you choose within this menu is the color that is used for the font when the user's mouse presses the image.

❑ *Horizontal and Vertical Alignment* — Set the horizontal and/or vertical alignment of the text within the button.

Finally, the Image tab reveals a complete set of properties used for modifying the width and height of the image and whether or not Expression Web should create the various hover and pressed states. Other options, including whether or not to create code that preloads the images, are also included within this tab. The Image tab resembles Figure 4-19.

In detail, the Image tab outlines the following properties:

❑ *Preview* — Provides a simple preview of the button as it's customized.

❑ *Width and Height* — Sets the width and height of the button in pixels.

❑ *Maintain proportions* — Click this checkbox to maintain the button proportions (aspect ratio) of the button as the width and height are adjusted.

❑ *Create hover image* — Click the checkbox to instruct Expression Web to automatically create the hover state of the button.

❑ *Create pressed image* — Click the checkbox to instruct Expression Web to automatically create the pressed state of the button.

❑ *Preload button images* — Instructs Expression Web to add client-side code that forces the browser to preload the three different button states before any one of the states loads.

Figure 4-19: Image tab

❑ *Make the button a JPEG image and use this background color* — Click this radio button to instruct Expression Web to create the Interactive Button as a series of JPEG images. If this option is selected, a background color must be supplied. If none is selected, white is used.

❑ *Make the button a GIF image and use a transparent background* — Click this radio button to instruct Expression Web to create the Interactive Button as a series of GIF images. When this option is selected, no background color is used for the three different button states. Instead, the background is transparent.

Managing Web Site Hyperlinks

One of the last tasks that you perform on your Web site before calling it done is checking for broken links. Again, in this case, managing links within the fictitious Vecta Corp Web site was easy. You're only dealing with five pages and maybe a dozen or so links.

Remember that not all of the Web sites you build are going to be this simple. Chances are that pages within your Web sites will grow in number. That growth will undoubtedly bring complexity in the hierarchy you decide to employ for your navigational structure. And, of course, that complexity also brings a higher chance of having broken links appear within your site. To check for broken links, Expression Web conveniently features a link-checking utility. Using this utility, you can easily have Expression Web search for and centrally display all of the broken links within your site and, more important, give you a chance to fix them.

Try It Out   **Checking for Broken Links**

So that you have a chance to see how Expression Web scans and presents broken links within your Web site, follow these steps:

1. Throughout the development of the fictitious Vecta Corp Web site, you've been careful to create links that have valid paths. Thus, running the link-checking utility will do little good. Before you run the link-checking utility, create a link that points to a file that doesn't exist, thus creating a broken link. To do this, start by opening `default.htm`, if it's not open already.

2. Place your cursor next to the Contact Us link, and type **Careers**.

3. Highlight the text and choose Insert ➪ Hyperlink. The Insert Hyperlink dialog box appears. Add the path `careers.htm` within the Address text box and click OK. The new link will be created for the Careers text. Obviously, because `careers.htm` doesn't exist, this will be considered a broken link. You know that because you've purposely created it. Now, imagine having hundreds of pages in your site and not knowing whether or not any of those pages have broken links. You can check for these broken links by choosing Site ➪ Reports ➪ Problems ➪ Hyperlinks. Immediately, the Web Site window displays, complete with your broken link to `careers.htm`, as shown in Figure 4-20.

4. To fix the broken link, right-click the item and choose the Edit Hyperlink option that appears from the context menu. The Edit Hyperlink dialog box appears, as shown in Figure 4-21.

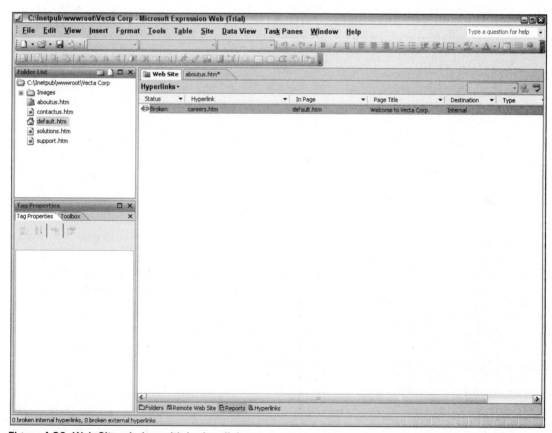

Figure 4-20: Web Site window with broken link

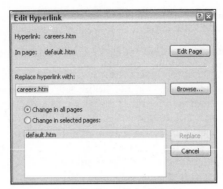

Figure 4-21: Edit Hyperlink dialog box

5. Within the "Replace hyperlink with" text box, click the Browse button to launch a secondary Edit Hyperlink dialog box to search for and select a file to replace the broken path. Because you have career information within the About Us page, choose the `aboutus.htm` file and click OK. The secondary dialog closes and the primary Edit Hyperlink dialog is displayed again, this time with the new `aboutus.htm` path within the "Replace hyperlink with" text box.

6. The next step is to replace the link instance within the particular page where the link appears. Because you've added it only within `default.htm`, that is the only file that appears within the file list. Click the "Change in all pages" radio button and click the Replace button. The Edit Hyperlink dialog closes and the broken link reference is removed from the Hyperlinks list within the Web Site window.

As you might imagine, this could prove to be one of the biggest time-saving features built into the product. No longer do you have to wait for your users to e-mail you about broken links within the site. With this utility, you can do all the work within Expression Web before publishing the site to the remote Web server.

Summary

In this chapter, you learned how to work with images, media elements, and hyperlinks. You learned about the three types of images that you can use on the Web: GIF, JPG, and PNG. You saw how easy it is to insert and customize various properties for images within your Web pages, and how easy it is to make simple edits for your images within Office products such as Microsoft Office Picture Manager.

Additionally, you learned about hyperlinking, including the three types of paths used when working with links and the types of targets that you may use when linking to pages within your Web site. Finally, you learned how to work with text-based links, image-based links, multiple links within an image, and targeting bookmarks within a page.

With the basics under your belt, let's now focus on more advanced Web development concepts. Beginning in Chapter 5, the focus shifts to page formatting concepts using Cascading Style Sheets. As the book progresses, you'll learn more advanced page structuring techniques using tables and later, page structuring techniques using CSS.

Exercise

In this exercise, you'll rebuild the simple Vecta Corp Web site, this time incorporating images. Furthermore, you'll incorporate hyperlinks to allow the user to link between the various pages within the Web site. All of the files that you'll need for this exercise are available from the Wrox Web site (www.wrox.com), including the completed versions for your review. When building the Web page in this exercise, you should perform the following steps:

1. Create a new Web site for the Vecta Corp project.

2. Create new pages for the main Home page, the About Us page, the Solutions page, the Support page, and the Contact Us page.

3. Create a new navigation menu for the site.

4. Copy the text from each text file located within the Assets folder and paste it into its respective Web page.

5. Add the header image to the top of each page. The main Home page should also incorporate the three subheading images for Our Solutions and Client Testimonials.

6. Add the navigation menu under the header image within every page of your site.

Page Formatting Using Cascading Style Sheets

As you have seen, HTML is extremely restrictive when it comes to Web page formatting. But this is by no means a fault of the language, as HTML was created as a means of formatting documents for the sole purpose of sending them along sparse networks in the smallest and fastest way possible. Unfortunately, many beginning Web designers who are experts in the print industry jump to Web development thinking that visual editors function the same way as popular print design programs do. They think visually rather than practically, which results in "hacked" code, mediocre page structures, and, in general, poorly designed pages that leave many people with a sour attitude toward Web development and HTML in general.

A better solution is available. Cascading Style Sheets (CSS) provides what many designers and developers have asked for over the years: more control, more flexibility, and more pizzazz to the overall look of their pages. How? CSS has endless support for font styles, sizes, and weights. It supports tracking, leading, text indenting, and paragraph spacing. Form elements can contain background colors, borders, and styles. With CSS, you can now use your own custom images for bullets. Additionally, you can control the structure of your Web pages using various positioning attributes offered through CSS. All of this, combined with various features for customizing your cursor, and with increasing browser support for the newest CSS specifications, makes CSS the hottest trend for creating and formatting Web pages now and in the future.

This chapter progresses beyond the confines of HTML formatting. Specifically, you will do the following:

- ❑ Learn what CSS is and how it differs from HTML
- ❑ Create style rules using the New Style Sheet dialog box
- ❑ Define classes within an external style sheet
- ❑ Explore font, block, background, border, box, position, layout, list, and table formatting options that can be applied to your Web pages via a style sheet
- ❑ Apply styles using both the Apply Styles Task Pane and Style toolbar

- ❏ Manage style properties using both the CSS Properties and Manage Styles Task Panes
- ❏ Attach style sheets to Web pages that have already been built
- ❏ Check for style usage and errors using CSS reports

By the end of this chapter, you'll have gained some valuable insight into one of the hottest topics for Web developers today in CSS. While this chapter is primarily limited to using CSS for page-formatting purposes, as you'll see in Chapter 7, "Advanced Page Structuring Techniques by Using Layers and CSS," CSS can and will be used as a means to structure pages.

Introduction to Cascading Style Sheets

Imagine for a moment that the fictitious Vecta Corp Web site used the same font face, color, and size consistently throughout the site. Also imagine for one moment that the Vecta Corp site consists of 300 pages and you needed to change the fonts from Arial to Verdana, and from a color of black to gray throughout the site. You can imagine how frustrating it would be to open every single one of those 300 pages and manually change every place that you had a font applied to a section of text. CSS solves this dilemma. With CSS you can create one file (maybe call it `styles.css`) and apply style rules within that CSS file that dictate how the text within your Web site should look. If the time ever came to change the font properties, you would do it in that one CSS file and your changes would instantly appear throughout the entire site.

Style sheets are usually contained within an external CSS file (but they don't have to be) and are linked in to every Web page that you are working with using the `<link>` tag. Therefore, any and all styles from that CSS file can be applied to the Web pages that you are working with, ultimately providing you with the flexibility to quickly and easily modify one CSS file that propagates changes to all Web pages that share the CSS file in your Web site.

While this chapter mentions one way to create style sheets (through an external CSS file), there are, in fact, three different ways to create them:

- ❏ *External file* — Arguably the most popular and time-efficient way to create style sheets is using an external CSS file. By creating an external style sheet file, you can link this file to any and all of your Web pages using the `<link>` tag. Later, when the time comes to make changes to the appearance or structure of your Web site, you make modifications on the one CSS file, and all of the pages of your Web site will instantly change to reflect the changes made within the CSS file.

- ❏ *Document wide* — Another efficient way to create styles is to simply add them straight to your Web page using the `<style>` tag (and then placing the `<style>` tag within the `<head>` tag of your Web page). Using a document-wide style sheet doesn't afford you a global repository for styles within your site, but it does allow you to create styles that can be used throughout the Web page.

- ❏ *Inline* — Inline styles allow for quick additions of styles within a tag. An inline style could look similar to this: `<input type="text" style="border-style:groove" />`. In this case, a text box's border style is set to appear with a beveled (otherwise known as *grooved*) border.

Now that you have an idea about how you create style sheets, let's take a look at how styles are defined within style sheets. A CSS file consists of numerous parts working together to form rules in an effort to enhance the look of your Web pages. These rules can consist of font properties, positioning properties, border properties, and much more. Figure 5-1 shows the makeup of a typical style rule.

Selectors (Tag Redefinition, Class, and ID)

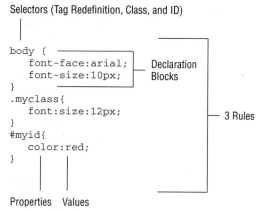

Figure 5-1: Typical style rule

As you can see from the callouts in Figure 5-1, a typical style rule contains selectors, declaration blocks, properties, and values, all organized to form the style rule. These rules are typically structured within an external file or document-wide `<style>` tag to form a style sheet.

There are three ways to define styles in Expression Web:

❑ *Classes* — Arguably the most popular way of defining styles within a style sheet, classes allow you to set up a custom style and use the class name as an attribute value later in the tag. For example, if you were to set up a class named `.myclass` and give it the appropriate properties and values, you could later add the class as a style reference to a paragraph of text as follows:

```
<html>
<head>
<style type="text/css">
.myclass {font-family:Arial;}
</style>
</head>

<body>
<p class="myclass">Vecta Corporation</p>
</body>
</html>
```

In this case, the rule is defined (as a document-wide style sheet) so that a class is set with the `font` property and the value of that property is set to `Arial`. The `<p>` tag uses the class, accessing it with the `class` attribute, and renders the text "Vecta Corporation" as Arial within the browser.

❑ *ID* — Generally used in cases when you need to stylize an element, as well as manipulate the element using client-side scripting. For example, if you were to create an ID named `#myclass` and give it the appropriate properties, you can later add the ID to your code and have it referenced within a client-side scripting language as follows:

```
<html>
<head>
<script>
```

```
function alertme() {
    window.alert(document.form1.mytextbox.value);
}
</script>

<style>
#mytextbox {background-color:silver;}
</style>
</head>

<body>
<form name="form1">
<input type="text" id="mytextbox" />
<input type="button" id="btnSubmit"
    value="Click Me"
    onClick="alertme()" />
</form>
</body>
</html>
```

This example creates a text box with an ID named `mytextbox`. While this uniquely identifies the element, it also allows you to set its style using the # identifier within the document-wide style sheet. Even better, you can reference the same ID within your client-side script to extract the value and present it within a message box when the button is clicked.

> You probably noticed the # identifier used here, whereas the previous example used the . identifier. For the most part, Expression Web handles all of this visually. But just be aware that, in code, classes are prefixed with the . identifier while IDs are prefixed with the # identifier.

❑ *Tag redefinitions* — Tag redefinitions are an excellent way to redefine the properties of HTML tags as they are defined within the browser. For example, Heading 1, represented by the `<h1>` tag, is generally defined by the browser as having a font size of about 32px, a font face of Times New Roman (depending on user settings within the browser), and a color of black. You can change the way the tag appears in the browser by redefining the tag using a CSS tag redefinition as follows:

```
<html>
<head>
<style>
h1 {font-family:arial;font-size:12px;color:red;}
</style>
</head>

<body>
<h1>Welcome to the Vecta Corp. Web site!</h1>
</body>
</html>
```

In this scenario, the `<h1>` tag redefinition is defined with properties of Arial for the font, 12 pixels for the size, and red for the color. In the body, you do little more than wrap the text element with the `<h1>` tag. In the browser, your text is defined with the properties you set in the document-wide CSS style sheet.

As you can see, the power of CSS is virtually limitless. With three methods for creating style sheets and three methods for defining styles within those style sheets, you now have an opportunity to greatly improve the look and general feel of your Web site using a flexible and robust environment. But you may still be in the dark as to the differences between HTML and CSS. The next section dissects the differences.

CSS Versus HTML

While CSS properties can create the same types of presentation effects as HTML tags and attributes, in reality, CSS styles go far beyond the restrictive aspects of HTML, enabling you to create stunning effects that ordinarily wouldn't be able to be created using HTML. Beyond simple text effects, CSS styles can also be used to lay out the entire page, entirely avoiding the use of HTML structuring techniques such as tables (covered in Chapter 6). This allows HTML to be used for its primary purpose of conveying the structure of the content, while the style sheet defines the presentation and overall "look." A detailed list of differences appears in the following table.

Element	HTML	CSS
Font face	Limited to common font faces with slight variations for families.	Limited to common font faces with slight variations for families.
Font size	Limited to absolute sizes of 1–7 and relative sizes of +1–+7 and -1 – -7.	Virtually limitless. You can use pixels, points, picas, inches, centimeters, metric, and so on. Even better, the size is limited only by the space available on your page. Therefore, you can use 11.25 points, 2.25 inches, and so on.
Color	Standards-compliancy dictates 256 Web-safe colors.	Standards-compliancy dictates 256 Web-safe colors.
Font weight	Limited to <strong> and <em>.	Options include Bold, Bolder, Normal, Light, Lighter, and various numeric weight values.
Case	No automatic conversion to uppercase or lowercase.	Supports automatic conversion of uppercase and lowercase, or even the ability to capitalize the first letter in the word.
Text decoration	Supports underline and strikethrough.	Supports underline, strikethrough, and over-line, and can even remove underlines from links using the None property.
Link rollovers	Not supported.	Using contextual selectors such as Hover, you can have links within the page that change color when a user rolls over them.

Continued

Element	HTML	CSS
Background color and images	Can set the background color of the page, tables, cells, and layers. Unfortunately, background images will always tile.	Supports background color for the page, tables, cells, layers, and even text. You can limit tiling to just vertically or horizontally, or you can prevent tiling entirely.
Block formatting	Limited to non-breaking spaces, paragraph breaks, and line breaks. Text indenting is limited to the `<blockquote>` tag.	Properties exist to control word spacing, letter spacing, vertical alignments, text indenting using pixel spacing, and so on.
Table formatting	Cell padding and cell spacing must be defined for the entire table. Thus, padding and spacing appears around all edges of the table and cell.	Cell padding and cell spacing can be adjusted on each side of the table independent of other sides. This means that the left edge of all tables and cells can have a spacing and padding of 0, while other sides can have a spacing or padding of 5.
Borders	Tables, layers, images, and cells can contain simple borders. Sizes are controlled by pixel, and the color is limited depending on element type.	All elements (including text) can have borders. Even better, border styles can be set; widths can be set in pixels, percentages, inches, and so on; and the color can be customized as well.
Lists	Lists are limited to bullets, squares, numbers, and Roman numerals.	All options available in HTML are relevant in CSS, including the ability to customize your own image to use with the list item and also to control the positioning of the image within the list item.
Positioning	Limited to HTML-based techniques to control the placement of elements on the page.	CSS positioning properties in conjunction with the `<div>` HTML tag offer functionality for creating draggable and precisely positioned elements on your Web page and, ultimately, the browser. This feature set mimics the functionality of print design programs closely.
Cursor customization	Not supported in HTML. Can be set using JavaScript.	Cursor can be customized to 14 different cursor types.

This chapter merely scratches the surface in the comparison of HTML and CSS, but, at the very least, you will begin to see the overall benefits that CSS has over HTML. While this examination sheds some light on the differences between HTML and CSS formatting, the real comparison will be made by you as the chapter unfolds. And, while you are not expected to master the concepts that you've learned thus far, the idea is that you at least have a solid foundation for these important concepts as you review Expression Web's CSS integration. Most of the concepts that you've learned are covered throughout the many dialog boxes, toolbars, and Task Panes in Expression Web. For this reason, it's important to get these introductory topics out of the way early.

Working with CSS in Expression Web

Now that you have a basic idea about the underpinnings of CSS, let's dive right into Expression Web's integration with CSS. As you'll learn throughout the rest of the chapter, Expression Web offers a vast array of toolbars, Task Panes, and dialog boxes that facilitate working with external, document-wide, and inline style sheets. Furthermore, these toolbars, Task Panes, and dialog boxes aid in the implementation of classes, IDs, and tag redefinitions within your Web pages. Specifically, you will do the following:

❑ Define how Expression Web should create and subsequently apply CSS to your Web pages using the Style Application toolbar

❑ Create your first style rule using the New Style dialog box to create an external style sheet

❑ Explore the many property modification possibilities that CSS offers in font, block, background, border, box, position, layout, list, and table options

❑ Learn how to apply styles once they've been created using both the Apply Styles Task Pane and the Style toolbar

❑ Understand how to manage styles using both the Style Properties and Manage Styles Task Panes

❑ Create a style rule by redefining an HTML tag

❑ Attach previously built style sheets to existing Web pages

Defining How CSS Is Created and Applied Within Expression Web

The assumption here is that most beginning Expression Web users won't actually care about CSS concepts or how Expression Web creates and applies styles to elements within Web pages. If you fall into this mold, you're probably just eager to begin creating Web pages and don't actually care about what Expression Web is doing "under the hood."

While this is certainly fine, the fact remains that CSS integration is abundant in Expression Web and is arguably the single greatest integration asset within Expression Web apart from HTML. If you've read the introductory sections in this chapter, then you'll no doubt understand that CSS has limitless possibilities. Furthermore, because of external style sheets, Expression Web now has the power to set the appearance of elements on your Web pages globally.

Many beginning Web designers ignore this fact because they simply want to build pages without carefully considering the long-term management perspective. When you're working with CSS in Expression Web, should styles be created inline automatically for you? Should you have document-wide styles created automatically for you instead? After all, document-wide styles would give you the ability to change properties for the entire page easily. Or, does it benefit you down the road, as your site grows, to create one external style sheet file, add your style rules to the style sheet file, and then apply them manually to elements within your Web pages, essentially preventing Expression Web from doing anything automatically for you?

These are questions you'll want to answer before you begin adding styles to your Web pages. Choosing the inline or document-wide route would allow you to create Web pages faster because Expression Web does most of the work for you automatically. Choosing the external route means that properties must be created manually for every element within your Web page. While the upside to this approach is easier management down the road as your site grows, the downside is careful planning initially, which results in slower development of pages at first.

While you'll learn the benefits to each approach with experience, in the meantime, Expression Web offers a toolbar that allows you to customize how Expression Web should create and ultimately apply styles within your Web pages. Available by selecting View ⇨ Toolbars ⇨ Style Application and visible in Figure 5-2, the Style Application toolbar allows you to set whether to allow Expression Web to automatically create styles for you, or choose whether you want them to be created manually. If you go the manual route, Expression Web allows you to choose whether to force Expression Web to automatically create inline or document-wide styles as you apply properties to elements within your page. Additionally, you can choose to bypass the inline or document-wide options and have an external style sheet created instead.

Figure 5-2: Style Application toolbar

The Style Application toolbar offers the following options:

❑ *Style Application* — Options within this list include Auto and Manual. When you choose the Auto option, the rest of the options within the Style Application toolbar are disabled. What this means is that if you select an element within your Web page and then apply the Arial font to it from within the Common toolbar, for example, Expression Web automatically creates a class within a document-wide style sheet and associates that class to the selected element within the page. As you add properties to elements on your page, Expression Web simply adds to the existing document-wide style sheet on the page. While this is the simplest option available, it's far from flexible to the intermediate-advanced user and is nowhere near global to the Web site.

When you choose the Manual option, the rest of the toolbar becomes enabled. This option allows you to choose how Expression Web should create and subsequently apply styles to elements within your Web page. Should they be created inline, as part of a document-wide style sheet, or will you simply override these options and create an external style sheet file on your own? Whichever option you choose, it's available within the Target Rule menu.

❑ *Target Rule* — If you've selected the Manual option from the Style Application menu, you're next task is to choose how Expression Web should create styles. As you'll see by expanding the menu, options include New Inline Style, New Auto Class, or Apply New Style. If you choose the New Inline Style option, Expression Web creates a new inline style rule for the selected element on the page. For example, if you select a paragraph of text and apply the Arial font to that element, Expression Web adds the style rule inline to the `<p>` tag. The result would resemble `<p style="font-family:Arial, Helvetica, sans-serif">`.

If, however, you decide to choose the New Auto Class option, Expression Web closely mimics the functionality that would be applied had you chosen the Auto option from the Style Application menu. For example, if you select a paragraph of text and apply the Arial font, Expression Web would automatically create a class within a document-wide style sheet. Then it would apply the class reference using the class attribute for the `<p>` tag as follows: `<p class="style1">`. The downside to this approach is that you don't have control over the names of the classes. By default, classes are created as `.style1`, `.style2`, `.style3`, and so on. This is not very intuitive when you want to apply a particular class to an element and the only differentiation between the many classes is a meaningless numeric value.

The final option, and by far the most flexible, is the Apply New Style option. Selecting this option launches the New Style dialog box. It is within this dialog box that you're able to use the options mentioned previously (inline or document-wide), or deviate from these options and choose the more global and site-wide manageable external style sheet option.

❑ *Reuse Properties* — From an efficiency standpoint, select the Reuse Properties button to force Expression Web to figure out whether the style selected in the Target Rule menu contains or doesn't already contain a declaration for the element you format on the Web page. If a declaration already exists, Expression Web simply uses the previously created declaration. If it doesn't, however, Expression Web creates a new one.

For example, let's say you select an element and choose the Arial font from the Common toolbar. Depending on what option you have selected in the Target Rule menu, Expression Web creates a rule (`.style1` by default) and applies it to the selected element. Now, let's say you select a second element and apply the Arial font to that element as well. Expression Web, recognizing that this property has already been established within the `.style1` class, doesn't create a new rule; but uses the `.style1` class on the new element instead. If this button were disabled, Expression Web would simply create a new class (`.style2`) for the second element even though the declaration of both rules is the same.

❑ *Show Overlay* — Click this button to display a dotted box in Design view around content that uses the style that is selected in the Target Rule box. In general, this is purely a visual enhancement setting.

Depending on your Web site's needs, you'll probably be switching back and forth between opening and closing this toolbar. In general, keep the following matrix in mind when making a decision as to which options should be selected within the Style Application toolbar:

Scenario	Style Application
Beginning-Intermediate user looking to create a simple Web site as fast and easily as possible.	Auto
Small Web site where the appearance of the page and elements within those pages varies greatly.	Manual, Target Rule: Inline Styles
Small to medium–sized Web site. The appearance of Web pages and elements within those pages remains somewhat consistent throughout.	Manual, Target Rule: Auto Classes
Medium to large–sized Web site. The appearance of Web pages and elements within those pages remains mostly consistent throughout the site with little to no variation from page to page.	External Style Sheets

As you can see, the options that you decide to enable within the Style Application toolbar can vary greatly, depending on your needs. You should explore all of these options at your leisure. For the purposes of the Vecta Corp site, and to prepare you to work with large sites, let's explore the external style sheet option. This option and tools for working with this option are discussed in the next few sections.

Defining Classes Within an External Style Sheet — Creating a Style Rule

As you've learned so far, external style sheets are by far the most flexible and manageable methods site-wide for working with CSS in your Web sites. Unless you're building simple pages with little to no formatting, you should strive to use external style sheets whenever possible. Initially, it takes a bit more planning, but in the long term, it can reduce redundant property modifications greatly.

As you've seen, Expression Web can create styles for you automatically. You'd simply select an element within your Web page, choose formatting options from the various toolbars, and instantly Expression Web creates rules using either an inline or document-wide style sheet. Other times, however, you'll want to build your own style sheet and pre-set your own formatting options within an external style sheet file. When this is the case, you need to use the New Style dialog box.

Try It Out   **Building a Style Rule Within an External Style Sheet by Using the New Style Dialog Box**

To help you better understand the process of creating a new style rule, let's build a simple class using the New Style dialog box for the three solutions (vProspect, vConvert, and vRetain). To do this, follow these steps:

1. If you haven't done so already, open the Vecta Corp Web site files for this chapter within Expression Web. Immediately, open the `default.htm` file. You'll notice that the `default.htm` file is basically the page that you built in the previous chapters, but slightly modified to accommodate the lessons covered in this chapter.

2. With the Style Application toolbar open, choose Manual from the Style Application menu and choose Apply New Style from the Target Rule menu. Immediately, the New Style dialog box will appear, similar to Figure 5-3.

3. As you can see from Figure 5-3, the New Style dialog box looks like a program in itself! For now, choose the "New style sheet" option from the "Define in" menu.

4. Enter the text **.solutionText** within the Selector text box (don't forget the dot). Remember that you're creating a class here. You can manually enter the class name of your choice within the Selector text box. If you were redefining a tag, you could select the tag from this menu instead.

5. Select the "small" option from the "font-size" menu, "bold" from the "font-weight" menu, and a dark blue color from the "color" menu, and clear the "Apply new style to document selection" checkbox. Click OK.

6. Expression Web asks if you want to attach the style sheet that will be created to the page that you're currently working with (`default.htm`). Choose Yes.

7. You'll notice that a new file is added to the tabbed file chooser called `Untitled_1.css`. Select it. As you can see from Figure 5-4, the new style rule is created within the style sheet file. The name ".solutionText" appears as the class name and the two properties for `font-size` and `color` are declared within the braces (this makes up the declaration). Go ahead and save the file to the root of your Web site as `styles.css`. Once you've saved the file, you're free to close it. Also, notice that the `styles.css` file will appear within the Folder List Task Pane.

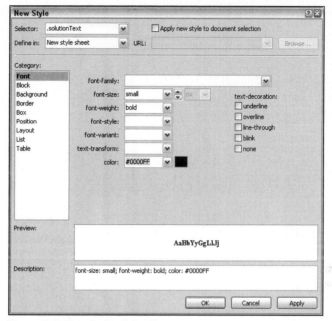

Figure 5-3: New Style dialog box

8. Now, switch back over to default.htm. To see the reference that Expression Web creates to the style sheet file, switch over to the Code view. As you can see from the shaded code in Figure 5-5, Expression Web adds the <link> tag to reference the styles.css file.

9. Finally, switch back over to the Design view and save the default.htm page.

As you can see, creating an external style sheet isn't very difficult. What this does now is allow you to build a site-wide set of styles that, once created, can be applied to elements throughout your site. In the coming sections, you learn how to apply those styles to the elements within the page. For now, however, let's review some of the other features available within the New Style dialog box. As you can see from Figure 5-3, the New Style dialog box offers the following options:

❑ *Selector* — Allows you to freely enter the selector name when working with classes or IDs. If you're working with tag redefinitions, however, you can choose from a list of HTML tags that may be redefined from this list instead.

❑ *Define in* — Allows you to define how the style sheet should be created. Choose the "Current page" option if you want Expression Web to create a document-wide style sheet. Choose the "New style sheet" option when you want to create a new, external style sheet file from scratch (this is the route that you took). Finally, choose "Existing style sheet" when you already have a style sheet created and you'd like Expression Web to place the selector that you're working with into that style sheet file. When this option is selected, the URL text box becomes enabled.

❑ *Apply new style to document selection* — Enable this checkbox if you'd like Expression Web to automatically apply the selector and its properties to the last element that you selected within the Web page before opening the New Style dialog box.

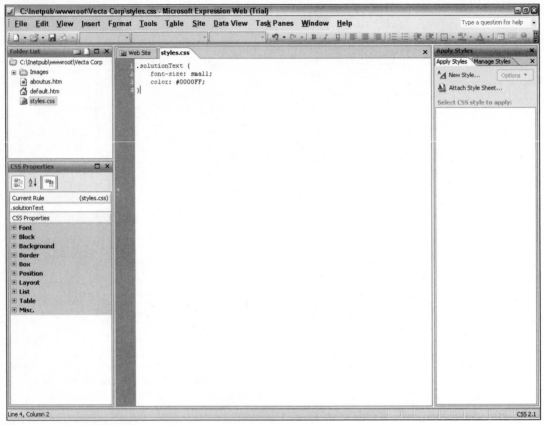

Figure 5-4: New style rule is created within the style sheet file.

❑ *URL* — Select the "Existing style sheet" option from the "Define in" menu to enable this text box. Once the text box is enabled, enter or browse to the style sheet file that you want to place the selector into. If the style sheet hasn't been linked into the existing page, Expression Web gives you the opportunity to do so once you click OK within the New Style dialog box.

❑ *Category* — Lists a collection of specific categories for working with CSS. Depending on the option that you select within this list, the Properties pane tailors itself to accommodate the category-specific properties. If you'd like to create properties for fonts, select the Font category. If you want to make changes to the background of an element, choose the Background category, and so forth.

❑ *Properties* — Displays category-specific properties based on the option that you select within the Category list. These properties are covered with great detail in the remainder of the chapter.

❑ *Preview* — As you manipulate properties, Expression Web gives you an idea how your element will look in the Web page by displaying the preview here.

❑ *Description* — As you manipulate properties, Expression Web outlines the rule declaration, property by property, here.

As you can see, the features offered by the New Style dialog box are fairly straightforward once you understand what each does. What really drives the style rules that you create and ultimately how your elements look in your Web pages are the properties that you choose to customize within the Category list and Properties pane. As you can see, there are nine categories to choose from; each customizes the view of the Properties pane to support property-specific settings for your elements. The next few sections dissect the following categories and their properties:

- ❑ Font options
- ❑ Block options
- ❑ Background options
- ❑ Border options
- ❑ Box options
- ❑ Position options
- ❑ Layout options
- ❑ List options
- ❑ Table options

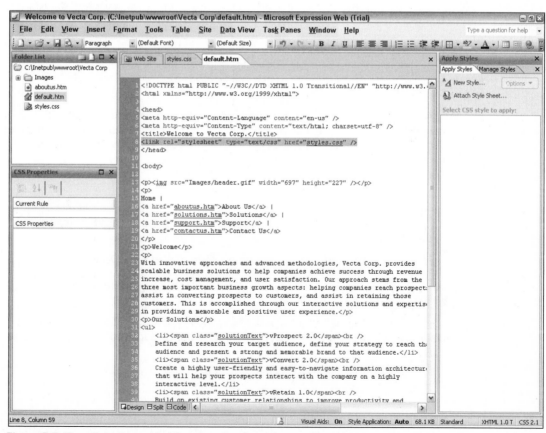

Figure 5-5: The <link> tag added to reference the styles.css file

Font Options

The Font category, shown in Figure 5-3, provides you with the ability to format text-level elements, including their face, size, decoration, weight, color, and so on. The following is a detailed list of properties available in the Font category:

❑ *font-family* — Use this menu to select from four available font families, including Arial, Times New Roman, Courier New, and Algerian. If you're working within an intranet environment, you may even decide to pick from a list of fonts installed on your computer. These are all listed below the four standard font families.

❑ *font-size* — Allows you to select from a list of preset values. You can also enter any number you choose, and then select from the menu to the right to select a measurement type. Options include pixels, points, inches, centimeters, millimeters, picas, European metric system, and so on.

❑ *font-weight* — This menu includes numerous options for controlling the weight of text on the page. Options include various bold properties, as well as numeric weight values from 100 to 900.

❑ *font-style* — Choose from any of the options within this menu to control the style of text on your page. Options include normal, italic, and oblique.

❑ *font-variant* — Choose from one of two options in this menu to set the variant on text to either normal or small-caps.

❑ *text-transform* — Choose an option from this menu to capitalize the first letter of each word in the selection, or to change all selected text to uppercase or lowercase.

❑ *color* — Use the color picker to choose from a palette of 216 Web-safe colors, including colors from your operating system's color palette.

❑ *text-decoration* — Choose options from this checkbox group to underline text, create a line above text (overline), create strikethrough text, or cause text to blink. The blink property is supported only by older Netscape browsers. The default option for text is None, whereas the default option for links is Underline.

Block Options

The Block category of the New Style dialog box, shown in Figure 5-6, provides you with the ability to define spacing and alignment settings for elements within your Web pages.

The following is a detailed list of properties available in the Block category:

❑ *line-height* — Traditionally referred to as *leading*, enter a value here to set the height of spacing that appears in between each line of text.

❑ *vertical-alignment* — Select an option from this menu to specify the vertical alignment of an element on your Web page. Options include baseline, bottom, middle, sub, super, text-bottom, text-top, and top.

❑ *text-align* — Sets the alignment of text on the page to left, right, center, or justify.

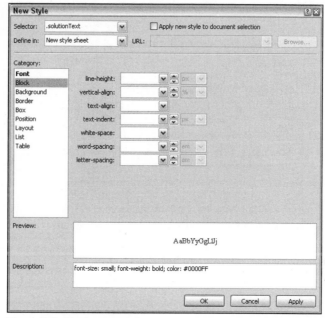

Figure 5-6: Block category

❑ *text-indent* — Enter a value within this text box to have the first line of text in your paragraph indent. You can also enter a negative number to outdent, but the appearance of the indentation depends on the browser.

❑ *white-space* — Select an option from this menu to specify how whitespace within the selected element is handled. Options within this menu include normal, nowrap, pre, pre-line, and pre-wrap. Choose normal to collapse whitespace, pre to retain all whitespace (including spaces, tabs, and returns), nowrap to specify that text wraps only when a line break (<br>) is encountered, and so on.

❑ *word-spacing* — Enter a value within this text box to set the spacing between words. Once you've entered a value, you can choose one of the measurement options from the menu just to the right. Negative numbers are also allowed, but the appearance depends on the browser.

❑ *letter-spacing* — Enter a value within this text box to increase (represented by a positive value) or decrease (represented by a negative value) space between letters or characters.

Background Options

The Background category of the New Style dialog box, shown in Figure 5-7, provides you with the ability to customize backgrounds for your elements within the page. Additionally, you may even decide to set the background of the page from this menu. Modifying these values gives you control over the color, image, repetition of an image, and so on.

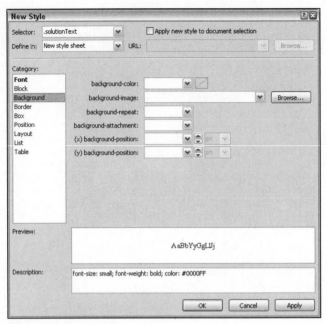

Figure 5-7: Background category

The following is a detailed list of properties available in the Background category:

❑ *background-color* — Use the color picker to choose from a palette of 216 Web-safe colors, including colors from your operating system's color palette. This option effectively sets the background color of the element (including the page, if you decide to apply the selector to the page).

❑ *background-image* — Use the Browse button to browse to and select an image within your site to use as the background image for the element (including the page, if you decide to apply the selector to the page).

❑ *background-repeat* — Select an option from this menu to set the tiling of the background image. Options include no-repeat, repeat, repeat-x, and repeat-y. The default value is repeat. The no-repeat option places the image as the background to the element, but will prevent it from repeating horizontally and vertically. The repeat-x option will repeat horizontally only, while the repeat-y option causes the image to repeat vertically.

❑ *background-attachment* — Use the attachment option to force a background image to its fixed position, or to allow it to scroll along with the content. The scroll option is supported by Internet Explorer, but not Netscape.

❑ *x and y background-position* — Use options offered in these menus to specify the initial position of the background image in relation to the element it's attached to. This can be used to align a background image to the center of the page, both vertically and horizontally. Again, this property is supported by Internet Explorer, but not Netscape.

Border Options

The Border category of the New Style dialog box, shown in Figure 5-8, provides you with the ability to make changes to borders. This feature will work only on items that accept borders for attributes such as text boxes, tables, layers, and so on.

The following is a detailed list of properties available in the Border category:

❑ *border-style* — Use this group of options to specify the style of the border. Options include dashed, dotted, double, groove, hidden, inset, none, outset, ridge, and solid.

❑ *border-width* — Select or enter a value within this text box to set the width of the border. Selectable options include thin, medium, and thick. Of course, you can also enter your own numeric value, followed by the measurement type.

❑ *border-color* — Use the color picker to select from a palette of 216 Web-safe colors. Unlike HTML where border colors are limited depending on the element used, border colors for all elements that support borders can be set independent of one another here.

If you remember from the opening paragraph of this chapter, CSS allows you to finely customize which side of an element should have a border. For example, if you were to attach a border to an element in HTML, you would be forced to apply the border to all four sides of the image. CSS allows you to not only set borders to all four sides of the element, but to also choose just to have a border on one particular side. Or, you may decide to make one side bigger than the others. Perhaps you make all four sides a different style, width, and size. All of this and more is possible in CSS. If you prefer to make all four sides the same, simply choose the "Same for all" checkbox. Doing this forces all four sides of the element for which you are applying the border to accept the properties that you set in the top area.

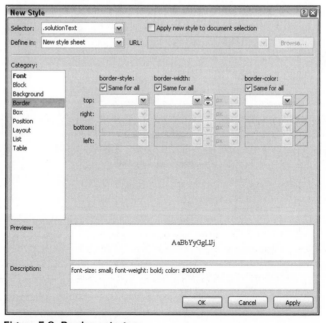

Figure 5-8: Border category

Box Options

The Box category of the New Style dialog box, shown in Figure 5-9, provides you with the ability to change and customize attributes within box-level elements. For example, tables, text boxes, and the Web page itself are examples of box-level elements and support the box model. Options within this category include the ability to set padding and margins (spacing) for box-level elements.

The following properties are available in the Box category:

❑ *padding* — Use this group of options to specify the amount of space that should be added in between an element and the element's border. Unlike HTML, which forces you to enter one value for all sides, you can enter separate values followed by the measurement independently of other sides. As was the case with the Border category, if you'd like to use the same value for all sides of the element, check the "Same for all" checkbox.

❑ *margin* — Use this group of options to specify the amount of space that should be added between elements such as cells within a table or the margins for the entire page. Unlike HTML, which forces you to enter one value for all sides, you can enter separate values followed by the measurement independently of other sides. As with the Border category, if you'd like to use the same value for all sides of the element, check the "Same for all" checkbox.

You'll also notice that Expression Web provides you with an iconic representation of the box model. This reference is especially handy when you need to quickly choose between setting borders, padding, or margins.

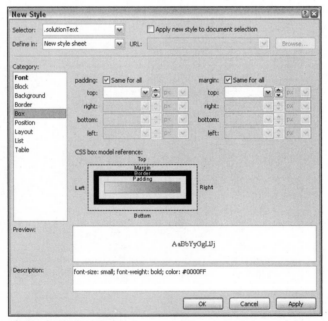

Figure 5-9: Box category

Position Options

The Position category of the New Style dialog box, shown in Figure 5-10, provides you with options that allow you to position `<div>` and `<span>` tags freely on the Web page. Setting these properties allows for pinpoint accurate movement and placement of various elements within your Web pages.

The following is a list of properties available in the Position category:

❑ *position* — Choose one of the four options in this menu to set the type of positioning the element should have in the browser. Options include absolute, relative, static, and fixed.

❑ Setting the type to absolute guarantees that the element's positioning is governed by the top-left corner of the page (the elements positioning should be set using the top, right, bottom, and left text boxes).

❑ Choose relative when you want to position an element relative to another element's flow within the page.

❑ Choose static when you want to place the element in a fixed position within the text flow (left and top properties should not be set).

❑ Fixed positioning is a subcategory of absolute positioning. The only difference is that for a fixed positioned box, the containing block is established by the viewing area. Have you ever scrolled down a page and seen a fixed navigation menu on the page that doesn't seem to scroll away as you scroll down? Chances are that that navigation area is contained within a `<div>` tag and CSS has been applied, with the fixed positioning property set. This prevents that area from moving along with the viewing area's position.

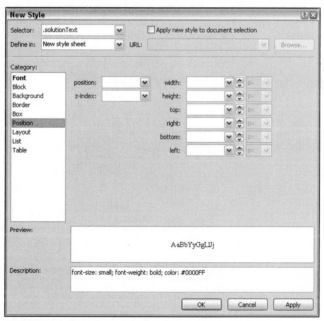

Figure 5-10: Position category

❑ *z-index* — One interesting aspect of using CSS positioning is that elements have the potential to be stacked and overlapped. Use the `z-index` property to set the stacking order of elements when working with CSS positioning. Higher z-indexed elements appear above lower z-indexed elements.

❑ *width and height* — Sets the width and height of the `<div>` or `<span>` tag (which encapsulates the positioned element) based on a value you enter and a measurement you select.

❑ *top, right, bottom, and left* — Enter values within these text boxes to set the physical location of the element on the page. While the default measurement is represented by pixels, you can also choose to use picas, points, inches, millimeters, centimeters, percentages, and European metric system by selecting the appropriate option from the measurement menu.

This category is discussed in much more detail in Chapter 7, "Advanced Page Structuring Techniques by Using Layers and CSS."

Layout Options

The Layout category of the New Style dialog box, shown in Figure 5-11, provides you with the ability to customize how elements are treated within box-level formatting elements such as the `<div>` and `<span>` tags. For instance, you can add a `<div>` tag to your Web page, insert a paragraph of text into the `<div>` tag, and then apply properties from the Layout category to set how the text should be treated within the `<div>` tag.

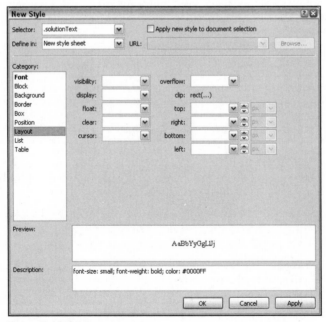

Figure 5-11: Layout category

The following is a list of properties available in the Layout category:

❑ *visibility* — Choose an option from this menu to set the display condition of the element within the page. Options include inherit, visible, hidden, and collapse.

❑ Inherit guarantees that a nested element will inherit the visibility properties of its parent element. If it has no parent element, the visibility will default to visible.

❑ Choose the visible option when you want to show the element regardless of the parent value.

❑ Choose the hidden option when you want to hide the element regardless of the parent value.

❑ Choose the collapse option when working with table rows and columns. Collapse essentially removes the row or column entirely from a table, but does not recalculate the widths and heights of the `<td>` tags in the other rows.

❑ *display* — Choose an option from this menu to specify whether an element is displayed, and if so, how it is displayed. For example, you can mimic the look and functionality of a table by using various properties offered within this menu such as `table`, `table-column`, `table-row`, `table-cell`, and so on.

❑ *float* — Choose an option from this menu to set which side elements (such as text, `<div>`, tables, and so on) will float around an element.

❑ *clear* — Use the options offered in this menu in conjunction with float. Specifically, options within this menu set the sides of an element where other floating elements are not allowed. Options include left (no floating elements allowed to the left side), right (no floating elements allowed to the right side), both (no floating elements allowed to either the right or left side), and none (allows floating elements on either side).

❑ *cursor* — Choose an option from this menu to change the pointer image when the pointer is over the element controlled by the style. There are 17 different cursor options to choose from.

❑ *overflow* — Choose an option from this menu to set how content within the `<div>` tag should be treated if it exceeds the width and/or height of the `<div>`. Options include visible, hidden, scroll, and auto.

❑ Choose visible when you want the `<div>` to automatically resize if the content exceeds the width and/or height of the `<div>`.

❑ Choose hidden when you want the content within the `<div>` to appear hidden if it exceeds the width and/or height of the `<div>`.

❑ Alternatively, you can choose scroll to automatically have scroll bars appear to the right and bottom of the `<div>`, enabling you to scroll the content within the `<div>`. This option will display scroll bars even if the content doesn't exceed the width and/or height.

❑ Choose auto when you want to display scroll bars within the `<div>` only when the content exceeds the width and/or height of the `<div>`.

❑ *clip top, right, bottom, and left* — Enter numeric values within this series of text boxes to define the part of the `<div>` that is visible.

List Options

The List category of the New Style dialog box, shown in Figure 5-12, provides you with the ability to customize the way lists are created within Expression Web. You can customize options for bullets and numbers, even providing your own custom image to use as a bullet.

The following is a detailed list of properties available in the List category:

❑ *list-style-type* — Choose from one of the options in this list to identify the type of list that should be applied to the selected element. Options include disc, circle, square, decimal, lower-roman, upper-roman, lower-alpha, upper-alpha, and more.

❑ *list-style-image* — Use the Browse to button to select a custom image to use in place of the standard black circular bullets that the browser renders.

❑ *list-style-position* — Select an option from this menu to set whether list item text wraps indents (outside) or whether the text wraps to the left margin (inside).

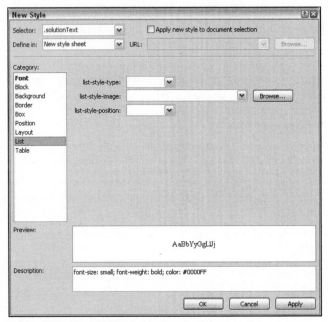

Figure 5-12: List category

Table Options

The Table category of the New Style dialog box, shown in Figure 5-13, offers properties for working with tables specifically in CSS. In CSS 1.0, properties didn't exist for working with tables and the content within the tables directly. Developers, looking to reduce the amount of code used in their Web pages, were still hamstrung by the volume of code that had to be generated by the <table>, <tr>, <th>, and <td>

tags (covered with more detail in Chapter 6). Even worse, numerous attributes for captioning, spacing, padding, and so on, made the use of tables monotonous in their implementation, and really defeated the purpose of what CSS was trying to eliminate: redundant code. In CSS 2.0, thought was given to tables and their implementation. You now have properties that address tables directly.

The following is a list of properties available in the Table category:

❑ *table-layout* — Options within this menu allow you to define the display behavior of tables, specifically the width of table cells defined by the CSS property `width`. Large tables can be displayed more quickly if the browser doesn't have to "read" the entire table and all its contents in order to display the correct widths.

❑ *border-collapse* — Choose one of the two options from this menu to set whether borders of neighboring table cells should be combined to form a single border. Options include collapse (join and create a single border) or separate (do not join but instead remain as two separate borders).

❑ *border-spacing* — Enter a numeric value within this text box to define the distance between cell borders within the table.

❑ *empty-cells* — Choose from one of the two options in this menu to set whether a table's cell should display its border (`show`) even if no content exists within the cell. If you'd prefer to hide the table border, choose the `hide` option.

❑ *caption-side* — You can define a table caption in HTML by using the caption element. The menu of options outlined here allows you to define the position of that caption either at the top or at the bottom of the table.

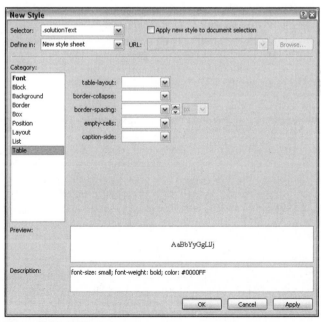

Figure 5-13: Table category

Applying Styles by Using the Apply Styles Task Pane and Style Toolbar

As you've seen, creating styles is a relatively simple process that involves little more than deciding what type of style sheet to create and then figuring out what type of selector to use. Once you have that squared away, it's merely a matter of creating your style rule using the New Style dialog box. So, now what? The external style sheet has been created and a style rule (.solutionText) has been defined within the style sheet. The next logical step is to apply the .solutionText class to an element (preferably a text element) within the page.

Applying styles to elements within Expression Web is much easier than actually creating the style rule. In fact, Expression Web supports numerous methods for accomplishing this task. For example, you may decide to use the full-featured Apply Styles Task Pane, the simple-to-use Style toolbar, the code-centric Tag Properties Task Pane, or, if you consider yourself more of a technical person and prefer to dive into the code, you might switch over to the Code view and apply the class to particular element manually. While all of these options are certainly viable, let's explore the most common next.

Try It Out   Apply Styles to Elements in Your Web Page

To help you understand how Expression Web facilitates style application to elements on your page, let's explore three methods for applying the newly created .solutionText class to the three solution text elements: vProspect, vConvert, and vRetain. To do this, follow these steps:

1. Open the default.htm page if it's not already open.

2. The first method that you'll use to apply a class to an element is the Tag Properties Task Pane. If this pane isn't already open, open it now by choosing Task Panes ⇨ Tag Properties. Now, highlight the first solution element vProspect 2.0 and choose the solutionText option from the "class" property menu within the Tag Properties Task Pane, as shown in Figure 5-14. You'll notice that the heading element turns blue and is bolded (properties that you specified when you created the class).

3. As you can see, the Tag Properties method for attaching classes to elements is fairly simple. Another simple method that you can use to apply styles to elements on your Web pages is the Style toolbar. To open the Style toolbar, choose View ⇨ Toolbars ⇨ Style. The Style toolbar appears. As you can see from Figure 5-15, the toolbar allows you to apply a class or ID to an element on the page. It also allows you to open and create new styles via the New Style dialog box. Last, it facilitates the attachment of a previously built style sheet (covered in a later section) by simply choosing the Attach Style Sheet button. For your purposes, select the solution element vConvert 2.0 and then select the solutionText class from the Class menu within the Style toolbar, shown in Figure 5-15. Again, you'll notice that the solution text element changes to reflect the style properties outlined within the class.

4. The final method that you may decide to implement is to attach the style class using the Apply Style Task Pane. Because this Task Pane is the most flexible when working with styles sheets, it is explored in greater detail later. For now, ensure that the Task Pane is open by choosing Task Panes ⇨ Apply Styles. As you can see from Figure 5-16, the Task Pane lists the .solutionText class and, more important, displays a preview of what the class will look like when applied. To apply the class, highlight the solution element vRetain 1.0 and then simply click the class within the Apply Styles Task Pane, shown in Figure 5-16. Once again, you'll see the solution element's physical properties change to match those outlined within the class.

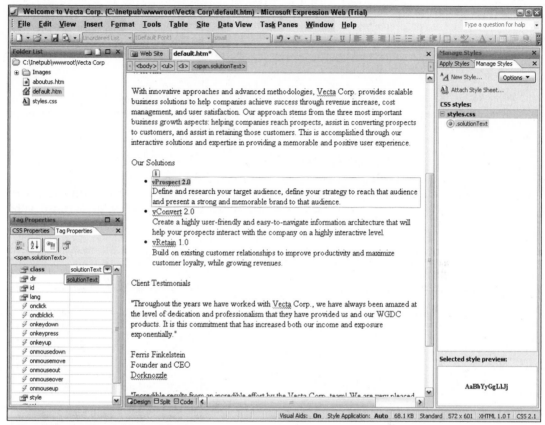

Figure 5-14: Tag Properties Task Pane

As you've seen, applying styles to elements within your Web pages is fairly easy and straightforward. However, if your goal is to use the Apply Styles Task Pane, then you should be aware of other options that the Task Pane offers. The Apply Styles Task Pane is by far the most versatile and feature-rich method for applying style rules to elements within your page. From this Apply Styles Task Pane you have the ability to not only apply styles, but also to create new styles, attach existing style sheets, categorize the view of styles by style application, delete styles, rename style rules, modify styles, and much more. As shown in Figure 5-16, the Apply Styles Task Pane supports the following functionality:

❑ *New Style* — Click this link to open the New Style dialog box and begin creating a new style rule.

❑ *Attach Style Sheet* — Click this link to open the Attach Style Sheet dialog box. As you'll see in a few sections, you can use this dialog box in an effort to link existing, pre-built style sheets into your Web pages.

❑ *Options* — Click this button to expand a menu of options that you can select from to customize the look and, more important, how you interact with the Apply Styles Task Pane. Options include the ability to categorize styles within the Style Selection List by order or by type. You may decide to show all styles, show only styles that are used in the page that you have open, or show only styles that are used on the current selection. Finally, the option menu allows you to customize the background color for a class listed within the Style Selection List.

❏ *Style Selection List* — Style rules that can be applied to elements within your Web page appear in this list. If you prefer to clear a style that may be attached to a particular element, simply select the element and click the Clear Styles option within this list. Rolling over the `solutionText` class reveals a submenu that you can expand. This submenu and the options that it offers are covered in greater detail next.

As you read in the preceding list, the Style Selection List outlines all styles that can be applied to elements within your Web pages. If you roll your cursor over a style within this list, you'll notice an expander arrow that appears, allowing you to access a separate submenu of the following options:

❏ *Apply Style* — Simply applies the selected style to an element on the page.

❏ *Go To Code* — Opens the style sheet file and highlights the style rule that the class belongs to within code. If your style is contained within a document-wide style sheet, Expression Web switches the development area into Code view and highlights the style rule contained within the `<head>` tag of the Web page.

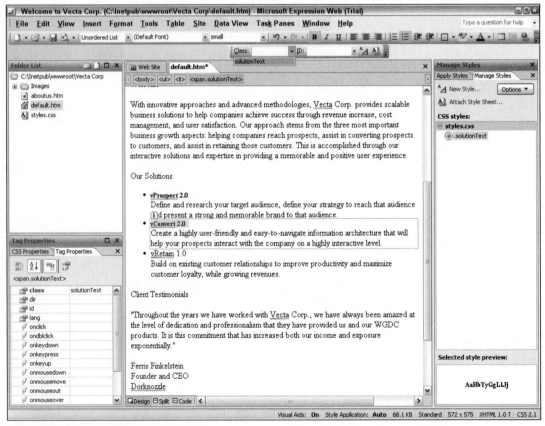

Figure 5-15: Style toolbar

❑ *Select Instances* — Select this option to highlight all of the element instances on your Web page that use the selected style rule. If you selected this option now, vProspect 2.0, vConvert 2.0, and vRetain 1.0 would all be highlighted. This would allow you to quickly apply a different class to all three elements.

❑ *New Style* — Choosing this option opens the New Style dialog box so you can begin creating a new style rule.

❑ *New Style Copy* — Allows you to create a new style based on properties that you've specified in the selected style. Selecting this option launches the New Style dialog box, but copies the style properties of the selected style and pre-populates the New Style dialog box based on those properties.

❑ *Modify Style* — Launches the Modify Style dialog box. Although it has a different name, the Modify Style dialog box is the same as the New Style dialog box. The only difference is that the Modify Style dialog box pre-populates the properties that were originally set for the style rule.

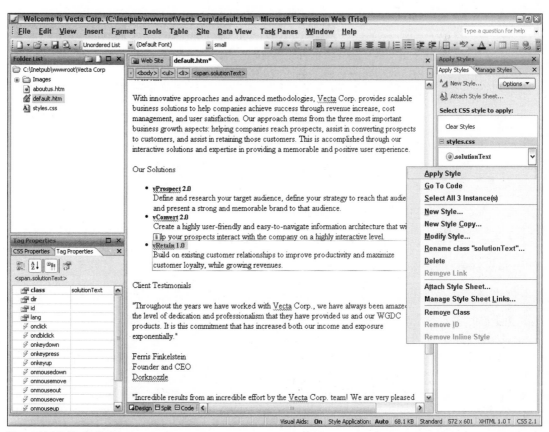

Figure 5-16: Task Pane

❑ *Rename* — Opens the Rename Class dialog box. Use this dialog box to rename the class. Expression Web will automatically scan and detect Web pages that contain elements that link to the class and automatically correct them with the new name.

❑ *Delete* — Deletes the selected style and removes its linkage to elements in your site.

❑ *Remove Link* — Select this option to completely remove the style sheet linkage for the open Web page.

❑ *Attach Style Sheet* — Choosing this option opens the Attach Style Sheet dialog box. As you'll see later in the chapter, you can use this dialog box in an effort to link existing, prebuilt style sheets into your Web pages.

❑ *Manage Style Sheet Links* — Select this option to launch the Link Style Sheet dialog box. It is from this dialog box that you're able to centrally manage all of your linked style sheets. From this dialog box you're able to add style sheets, edit existing style sheets, remove style sheet linkages, and even move up or down style sheet references on particular Web pages.

❑ *Remove Class* — Removes the class reference from the element on the Web page.

❑ *Remove ID* — Removes the ID reference from the element on the Web page.

❑ *Remove Inline Style* — Removes the inline style reference from the element on the Web page.

One other subtle feature offered by the Apply Styles dialog box is the colored dots that appear next to the style rule within the list. In this case, you'll notice a green dot outlined with a black circle just to the left of the solutionText class. A green dot represents a class, while a black circle surrounding the dot means that the class is being used on the current page. In general, there are six icons that will appear next to the style rules that you create. The following table provides some insight into each.

Icon	Description
Red dot	Appears next to ID-based styles.
Green dot	Appears next to class-based styles.
Blue dot	Appears next to tag redefinitions.
Yellow dot	Appears next to inline styles.
Black circle surrounding dot	Surrounds dots whose styles are used within the current page.
@	Appears next to imported external style sheets. (Note: Imported style sheets are different than linked style sheets. While linked style sheets use the <link> HTML tag to include an external style sheet, imported style sheets rely on the @Import statement and are primarily used to hide particular styles from older browsers such as Netscape 4.)

Now that you have a general idea as to how CSS styles are applied to elements on your page, let's look at managing styles that you create.

Managing Styles with the CSS Properties and Manage Styles Task Panes

So far in your project, you've created and applied only one style rule. Imagine having a site that contained hundreds of Web pages, each containing dozens of classes, IDs, and/or tag redefinitions. Managing all of those styles centrally could prove to be a tough task. Fortunately, Expression Web includes a Manage Styles Task Pane, shown in Figure 5-17, which displays a list of classes, IDs, and tag redefinitions used and unused throughout your entire Web site. Because all style rules are centrally displayed within this list, managing the styles now becomes a snap.

As you can see from Figure 5-17, the Manage Styles Task Pane, available by choosing Task Panes ➪ Manage Styles, displays a core set of functionality that closely resembles that of the Apply Styles Task Pane. The Manage Styles Task Pane differs from the Apply Styles Task Pane in that the following functionality is outlined (which is not included in the Apply Styles Task Pane):

❑ *CSS Style List* — Displays a complete list of styles that you've created for your Web site. You can right-click a style within this list to access a menu of options that closely resembles the options outlined in the previous section. For example, from the context menu that appears, you can apply styles to elements on the page, go to the style rule within code, select all instances of the rules usage within the page, create a new style by launching the New Style dialog box, copy an existing style, modify a style, rename a style, delete a style, remove the linkage to a style sheet, attach a style sheet via the Attach Style Sheet dialog box, and manage style sheet links.

❑ *Selected Style Preview* — Visually displays what the selected style within the CSS Style List will look like.

Functionally, the Manage Styles Task Pane functions similar to the Apply Styles Task Pane. Visually, it provides an alternative for managing large volumes of styles for your Web site. While the Manage Styles Task Pane offers up an alternative option for managing styles, the CSS Properties Task Pane is useful when you want to make quick additions or modifications to existing styles without having to re-launch the New/Modify Styles dialog box. Shown in Figure 5-18, the CSS Properties Task Pane outlines every possible CSS property that you may choose to modify, and even outlines rules that may be applied to a selected element on the page.

Figure 5-17: Manage Styles Task Pane

Show Categorized List

Show Alphabetized List

Show Set Properties on Top

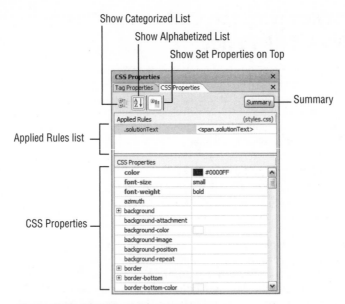

Applied Rules list

CSS Properties

Summary

Figure 5-18: CSS Properties Task Pane

As you can see from Figure 5-18, one of the solution elements has been selected. The Applied Rules list displays how the style is applied and, more important, what selector type was used. You can decipher from the list that the vProspect 2.0 text element on the page was wrapped with a <span> tag. That <span> tag uses the class attribute to make reference to the .solutionText class. The benefit to using this Task Pane is that you can quickly manipulate style rules by adding, removing, or modifying properties for the style rules.

Try It Out   Adding Properties to a Style Rule by Using the CSS Properties Task Pane

To see how the CSS Properties Task Pane allows you to quickly make changes to style rules, follow these steps:

1. Highlight one of the solution elements that has the .solutionText class associated with it.

2. Click the "Show categorized list" icon located first from the left within the CSS Properties Task Pane.

3. Expand the Font category.

4. With the Font category expanded, find the font-weight property and choose the bold option from the menu that appears when you select your cursor in the value column.

You'll quickly notice that the bold property isn't applied only to the highlighted solution element, but rather it's applied to every element that uses the .solutionText class. This is the beauty in CSS. You don't have to select every element to make a property modification. You simply modify the class, and every element that uses the class adopts the new change. It becomes even more impressive when you're dealing with hundreds of pages that contain numerous references to the particular style rule.

As you can see from the callouts in Figure 5-18, the CSS Properties Task Pane offers functionality that warrants mentioning. Specifically, this functionality includes:

❑ *Show categorized list* — Click this button to display a categorized list of CSS properties within the CSS Properties list. The properties are split up into groups that include Font, Block, Background, Border, Box, Position, Layout, List, Table, and Miscellaneous.

❑ *Show alphabetized list* — Click this button to display an alphabetized list of CSS properties within the CSS Properties list.

❑ *Show set properties on top* — Click this button to group properties that you've previously set at the top of the CSS Properties list.

❑ *Summary* — Click this button to configure the CSS Properties list to show only a summary of properties that are applied to the selected element within the page.

❑ *Applied Rules list* — Displays a list of rules that are applied to the selected element within the page. The column on the left displays the selector type, whereas the column on the right displays how the selector type is referenced by the selected element.

❑ *CSS Properties* — Displays a complete list of CSS properties that can be modified for your style rules. The list will display as either a categorized or alphabetized list, depending on which option is selected. The column on the left of this list displays the CSS property, whereas the column on the right displays the property value.

Now that you have a general idea as to how CSS rules are defined and managed using the various toolbars and Task Panes in Expression Web, let's actually build some more styles. In the next couple of sections you'll branch out beyond simple class-based style development, actually work with redefining HTML tags, and even work with contextual selectors to build rollover effects for the hyperlinks in the navigation menu.

Designing Styles by Redefining HTML Tags

Up to this point, you've seen how to create new style rules using the class selector type specifically. A second method for defining styles, as you learned at the beginning of this chapter, is to simply redefine HTML tags.

Redefining HTML tags is the process of overriding, through the use of CSS, how the browser renders the appearance of a particular HTML element. A perfect example of a tag redefinition (and one that will be explored in more detail) is redefining the `<body>` tag. By default, the browser renders content on the page to use the default font face and font color that the user has customized in the browser (usually Times New Roman and black). Furthermore, unless margins are specified, the browser renders the page with margins at the top, left, bottom, and right side of the page. Through the use of CSS, you can redefine the look of the `<body>` tag (the tag that's responsible for the properties mentioned previously) to render margins that you specify, and even employ the Arial font to all content in the page and ultimately the site.

Redefining an HTML Tag

To better understand how to redefine HTML tags using CSS in Expression Web, follow these steps:

1. Open the New Style dialog box. You can do this by clicking the New Style link within either the Apply Styles or Manage Styles Task Panes. Either method you choose will launch the New Style dialog box.

2. Ensure that the "Existing style sheet" option is selected within the "Define in" menu and that `styles.css` is selected within the URL menu. From the Selector menu, choose the body option. This is the `<body>` tag that you will redefine now.

3. In the Font category, select the Arial, Helvetica, sans-serif option from the font-family menu.

4. Also, select the small option from the font-size menu.

5. Switch over to the Box category, clear the "Same for all" checkbox for margin and enter the value **25** for left. This adds 25 pixels of spacing to the left side of the page.

6. Click OK to close the New Style dialog box. Immediately, the page changes to accommodate the properties that you've redefined for the `<body>` tag. Furthermore, notice that the body tag redefinition is listed within the CSS styles list in the Manage Styles Task Pane, as shown in Figure 5-19. Finally, notice that the icon preceding the tag redefinition is blue, whereas the icon preceding the `solutionText` class above the redefinition is green. Remember that the green icon represents a class, whereas the blue icon represents a tag redefinition. The black circle surrounding the icon means that the style is applied to the current page.

So, you're probably wondering how Expression Web automatically applied the style to the page. Remember that you redefined properties for an HTML tag. You are essentially instructing the browser to take what it knows of how the `<body>` tag should be displayed and completely disregard it. Instead, it should render the properties that you define. Because the `<body>` tag is included in every HTML page, the properties appear automatically without your having to do anything!

Using Contextual Selectors

Other rules, such as *contextual selectors*, exist for creating CSS styles for certain tag states. The difference between normal selectors (such as classes, IDs, and tag redefinitions) and contextual selectors is that contextual selectors must be associated with an already defined selector, and are defined based on the context of usage within the page. For example, let's assume that you've defined a class to set the link state of your navigation menu. The class may resemble the following:

```
.navlink {
    font-size:16px;
    color:red;
}
```

In this simple example, you are defining a class called `.navlink` with a font size of 16 pixels and a color of red. You could then apply this class to each item within your navigation menu in an effort to physically change the characteristics of the elements within the Web page. You could then create a style that forces the links characteristics to change once the user's cursor rolls over each of the navigation items. This is where contextual selectors come in. In general, there are four contextual selectors, defined as follows:

❑   a:link — The styling given to all links.

❑   a:visited — The styling given to all links that have been clicked.

❑   a:hover — The styling given to all links when the cursor rolls over them.

❑   a:active — The styling given to all currently selected links.

By their definition, contextual selectors are associated with the <a> tag. That's not to say that they have to be used specifically with the <a> tag. Instead, you may decide to use a contextual selector in conjunction with the .navlink class. The addition to the code would look something like this:

```
.navlink {
    font-size:16px;
    color:red;
}
.navlink:hover {
    color:blue;
}
```

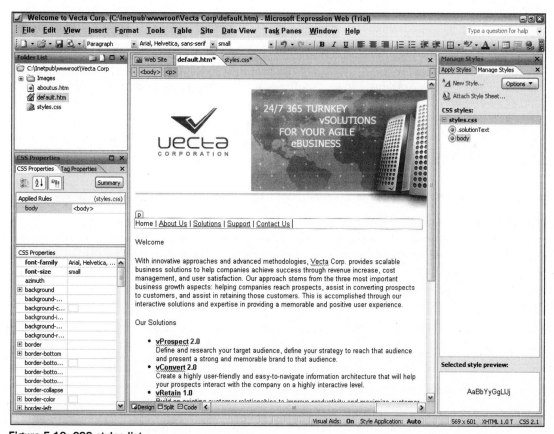

Figure 5-19: CSS styles list

As you can see, you don't remove the existing `.navlink` class; instead, you append to it. By using the contextual selector hover, you can define how the text should appear when the cursor's mouse rolls over the element that has the `.navlink` class associated with it. In this scenario, you're essentially telling the browser to handle the rollover state of just the elements that have the `.navlink` class associated with them. Of course, you could also use the standard `<a>` tag redefinition to redefine all links within your Web page. This code would resemble the following:

```
a:link {
    font-size:16px;
    color:red;
}
a:hover {
    color:blue;
}
```

In this case, all links appear as 16 pixels and red. Additionally, when the user's cursor rolls over a link within the page, the color of that link changes to blue.

Try It Out   Working with Contextual Selectors

Now that you have a general idea as to what contextual selectors are and when they are to be used, let's take this time to build a new class for the navigation menu. Then, you'll work with the hover contextual selector to set the color that navigation menu links should change to when the user's cursor rolls over them. To do this, follow these steps:

1. Open the New Style dialog box. You can do this by clicking the New Style link within either the Apply Styles or Manage Styles Task Panes. Either method you choose will launch the New Style dialog box.

2. Ensure that the "Existing style sheet" option is selected within the "Define in" menu and that `styles.css` is selected within the URL menu. Within the Selector text box enter the class name **.navlink**.

3. In the Font category, select the "small" option from the "font-size" menu.

4. Choose the "bold" option from the "font-weight" menu.

5. Check the "none" checkbox within the "text-decoration" checkbox group.

6. Choose a blue color that matches the color scheme of the Vecta Corp Web site from the color selector. Don't forget that you can also sample colors from elements (such as images) on the page.

7. Click OK to close the New Style dialog box. Notice the new `.navlink` class that appears within the Apply Styles Task Pane just underneath the existing `.solutionText` class.

8. Select an element from the navigation menu such as About Us and apply the `.navlink` class to it by selecting it within the Apply Styles Task Pane. Repeat this process until all four navigation items have the class applied to them. Don't worry about the Home item. This is where the user currently is, so you don't want that to have the same style as the other navigation items. The result of the class association will resemble Figure 5-20.

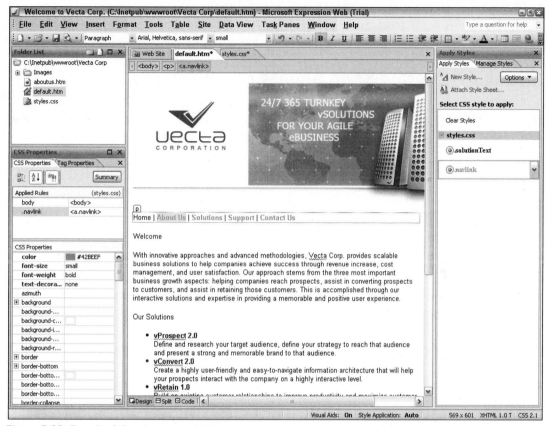

Figure 5-20: Result of the class association

Now that the class has been created, you'll next want to create the contextual selector. You can do this by following these steps:

1. Open the New Style dialog box. You can open the dialog box by clicking the New Style link within either the Apply Styles or Manage Styles dialog box. The New Style dialog box appears.

2. Ensure that the Existing style sheet option is selected within the "Define in" menu and that styles.css is selected within the URL menu. Within the Selector text box, choose the option a:hover. However, before you do anything further, replace the a with .navlink.

3. Pick a color from the color menu that you want to appear when the user's cursor rolls over the navigation menu item. Sample the red color from the Vecta Corp logo within the header image.

4. That's all you need to do. Click OK to close the New Style dialog box.

Now, if you have the Apply Styles dialog box open, you won't notice anything different. This selector doesn't appear within the list because it's not a selector that you apply to elements. Technically, it's part of the .navlink, but is used only within the context of the hover state, hence the name "contextual selector." To see the style, switch over to the Manage Styles Task Pane. In this view, you can see the style listed. To see the fruits of your labor, press F12 to preview the result in the browser. As you'll see, rolling over any navigation item causes the item's color to change from blue to red.

Attaching Existing Style Sheets to Web Pages

In certain situations, you'll find yourself working with legacy Web sites that were created using pure HTML formatting techniques. As you might imagine, if the Web site is a legacy site, chances are that numerous files are going to exist, making it difficult (if not impossible) to build and apply styles to each and every element. In cases such as this, maybe building a CSS file and then attaching the file to each and every page within the Web site makes more sense. While you'll still need to apply classes to elements on the page, at the very least, certain tag redefinitions (such as the <body> tag) can be redefined to improve the look of the legacy site.

Try It Out   Attaching a Style Sheet

Attaching a style sheet to an existing Web page is easy and can be accomplished in just a few simple steps. To attach a style sheet to a Web page, follow these steps:

1. Open the included `aboutus.htm` file. So far, you've been applying styles to the main `default.htm`, leaving `aboutus.htm` out of the CSS loop. Because you'll want to style that page like the main page, it's the perfect candidate to apply a style sheet to.

2. Click the Attach Style Sheet link from either the Apply Styles or Manage Styles Task Panes. Either method you choose will cause the Attach Style Sheet dialog box to appear, as shown in Figure 5-21.

3. As you can see from Figure 5-21, the dialog box features a text box and Browse button so you can browse to and include the path to the style sheet that you want to attach. Also included is an "Attach to" radio group that allows you to determine how you want to attach the file either to all of the pages within the site, selected pages within the Folder List, or to the page that you currently have open. Finally, an "Attach as" radio group allows you to specify whether to link the file in using the <link> tag or to use the @Import statement. For our purposes, browse to and select the `styles.css` file. Choose the "All HTML pages" option and ensure that the Link radio button is selected. Click OK.

4. Immediately, the dialog box closes and the style sheet is attached to `aboutus.htm`. Even better, the style sheet is attached to `solutions.htm`, `support.htm`, and `contactus.htm`, all in one shot! Save your work.

As you can see, attaching a style sheet is a powerful operation that has the potential to save you a lot of time and energy when trying to work with prebuilt style sheets for a Web site. While you'll still need to apply classes to elements that require them, at the very least, the foundation level styles (such as the <body> tag redefinition, for example), will already be done for you.

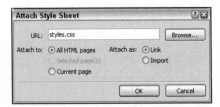

Figure 5-21: Attach Style Sheet dialog box

Working with CSS Reports

One of the last operations that you'll want to perform on a CSS-formatted Web site before calling it done is to conduct CSS usage and error reports. Doing so allows you to check one last time for unused styles, undefined classes, mismatched case, and more. Correcting these types of errors now will ultimately enhance your user's experience on your site and reflect much more positively toward the professionalism of your organization.

Conducting CSS reports is a fairly easy operation and involves little more than the CSS Reports dialog box, available by choosing Tools ➪ CSS Reports. As you can see from Figure 5-22, the CSS Reports dialog box is split up into two types of reporting features: Errors and Usage.

The CSS Reports dialog box allows you to conduct error and usage reports. These two tabs offer the following functionality:

❑   *Errors* — Configure options within this tab to check for general CSS errors within your entire site, open Web pages, selected pages within the Folder List, or the current page. This operation will search for unused styles, undefined classes, and/or mismatched case.

❑   *Usage* — Configure options within this tab to check for class, ID, and tag redefinition usage within your entire site, open Web pages, selected pages within the Folder List, or the current page.

Figure 5-22: CSS Reports dialog box

Try It Out   **Conducting a CSS Report**

To better understand how to conduct CSS usage and error reports, follow these steps:

1.   Open `default.htm` if it's not already open.

2.   So that errors are produced when you conduct your CSS error report, let's purposely associate an element within the page to an undefined class. To do this, highlight the "Welcome" text and enter a fictitious class name such as **myHeading** within the class property in the Tag Properties Task Pane.

3.   Open the CSS Reports dialog box by choosing Tools ➪ CSS Reports.

4.   Within the Errors tab, choose the Current page radio button and ensure that all three checkboxes are selected. Click Check.

5.   Notice that as soon as you click Check, the CSS Reports dialog box closes and the CSS Reports results Task Pane appears, as shown in Figure 5-23.

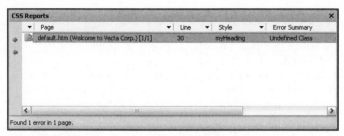

Figure 5-23: CSS Reports results Task Pane

As you can see from Figure 5-23, the line that appears within the Task Pane alerts you to the fact that there's an undefined class reference on line 30 within `default.htm`. You can right-click the error that's produced within the Task Pane and select the Go To Page option. Expression Web immediately opens the page that contains the error in Code view and highlights the class reference, making it easy for you to make the quick fix.

Summary

This chapter provided information about what Cascading Style Sheets is and what it can provide to your Web sites. You learned about the three ways to create styles sheets in external, document-wide, and inline. Furthermore, you learned about the three different ways to create selectors in classes, IDs, and tag redefinitions. As the chapter progressed, you looked at the different methods for creating, applying, and managing styles within Expression Web. Specifically, you looked at the Style and Style Application toolbars, the New Style dialog box, and the Apply Styles, Manage Styles, and CSS Properties Task Panes. You learned how to create rollover effects for your linked elements by using contextual selectors, how to attach style sheets to existing Web pages, and how to run CSS reports.

Chapter 6 deviates a bit from CSS and begins discussing page structuring techniques using tables. The discussion then jumps right back into CSS by discussing alternatives to table-based structuring techniques by looking at page structuring techniques using CSS-P.

Exercise

In this exercise, you style the Vecta Corp Web site by building a style sheet for it. Within the style sheet, you integrate classes and tag redefinitions to create style rules for the body tag of the page, the navigation menu at the top of each page, the subheadings, and the solution links. When building the Web page in this exercise, you should perform the following steps:

1.   Create a new external style sheet for the Vecta Corp Web site called `styles.css`.

2.   Within the style sheet, redefine the `<body>` tag so that you change the font, size, and margins for the Web pages. The selector should reside within the external style sheet.

3.   Create a class for each of the three subheadings: Welcome, Our Solutions, and Client Testimonials. The selector should reside within the external style sheet.

4. Use the contextual selectors `a:link`, `a:visited`, and `a:hover` to define the style for the navigation menu. Again, the selector should reside within the external style sheet.

5. Create a separate class for each of the three solution links within the Our Solutions sections. This class should reside within a document-wide style sheet because it relates to the main page only.

6. Use the Attach Style Sheet feature to apply the newly created style sheet to the rest of the pages within the site.

Web Page Structuring Techniques by Using Tables

One of the biggest complaints that graphics designers have when moving from print design to Web design is that HTML is so finicky. More specifically, the placement of elements within your Web pages is limited because of the lack of tools available to control the organization of the media elements within the page. While this may be true to a certain extent, HTML is, in fact, extremely flexible and offers many rich elements that can be used to control the organization of content within your Web pages. As this book unfolds, you learn about various elements and technologies that Expression Web supports to control the placement of elements on your page with pinpoint accuracy. Technologies such as Cascading Style Sheets (CSS), and elements such as layers and tables, can be used by Web developers who strive for the fluid look that print design programs have offered for years. The trick, of course, is learning the intricacies of the elements and how Expression Web allows you to work with them within its framework.

In this chapter, you begin to move from the simplicities of inserting and modifying elements on the page to a richer topic that involves structuring and placement of elements on the page using HTML tables. As you'll begin to see, tables offer a flexible and simple alternative (to basic formatting techniques covered thus far) for controlling the placement of elements within your Web pages. Specifically, you will do the following:

- ❑ Learn to insert a table within Expression Web
- ❑ Select table elements
- ❑ Quickly format a table using Table AutoFormat
- ❑ Modify table properties, including adding and removing rows, columns, and cells
- ❑ Modify cell properties, including splitting and merging cells
- ❑ Understand the concept behind nested tables
- ❑ Work with Layout Tables, including drawing tables and cells directly within your Web page

By the end of this chapter, you'll have gained some valuable insight into one of the most powerful HTML structuring techniques in tables. You'll have learned how to construct and modify tables, as well as how tables can be used to structure and organize all of the elements of the Vecta Corp Web site to create a fluid design that closely mimics a print collateral piece.

Inserting and Working with Tables

If you remember from Chapter 2, "Building a Web Page," the development of the Vecta Corp Web site was severely limited visually to inserting text within a vertically linear fashion. Elements on the page were organized such that you inserted text, followed by a line break, more text, and then repeated the process until the page looked somewhat presentable. While this process may work for simple Web pages, it does little in terms of allowing you to create aesthetically pleasing and eye-catching Web pages. Even in Chapter 4, "Working with Images, Media, and Hyperlinks," while you were able to incorporate some level of interactive content to increase the appeal of the site, the reality remains that the design of the Web pages was hampered by the fact that elements, regardless of text, image, or media element, were structured in a vertical fashion, where placement of elements with pinpoint accuracy was impossible to achieve.

As your Web pages become more intricate and complex, structuring your Web pages using elements such as tables becomes more of an essential and viable alternative (see Figure 6-1).

As you can see from this Vecta Corp prototype, the design is slightly more complex in its structure than the designs covered in previous chapters. You'll notice that the same header appears near the top, but, in this case, a color band (that marks the navigation area) stretches vertically from the header down to another footer graphic near the bottom of the prototype. A white area to the right of the navigation area is reserved for the content of the site.

As you can see from the graphic, the complexity of the design warrants a structuring technique beyond the simplicities of normal paragraph and line breaks. This is where tables come in. You can use tables to structure this relatively more complex design such that the header and footer areas are fixed at the top and bottom, but more important, so that the navigation area can reside in the same relative location as the content (Welcome, Our Solutions, and Client Testimonials) for the site. Before jumping right into using tables to structure the site, however, let's dissect some of the basic features and functionality available for working with tables in Expression Web.

Let's begin by inserting a simple table. Not only will this help you understand all of the features available for working with tables in Expression Web, but it will show you how the design drawbacks mentioned previously can be overcome by using tables to structure your designs.

Try It Out   Inserting a Table

To insert a table within Expression Web, follow these steps:

1. If you haven't done so already, open the Vecta Corp Web site files for this chapter within Expression Web. Immediately open the `default.htm` file. You'll notice that the file is empty save for the fact that the beginnings of a style sheet file have been created for you. To get you started, the style sheet has been created and the `<body>` tag has been redefined with default font face, font size, alignment, background color, and page margin values. The structure of the site however, will be built throughout the chapter.

Figure 6-1: Using tables to structure a Web page

2. Place your cursor within the page and insert a new table by choosing Table ➪ Insert Table. The Insert Table dialog appears, as shown in Figure 6-2.

3. As you can see from Figure 6-2, the Insert Table dialog box offers more than a dozen features, all aimed at providing you with a rich set of tools for structuring elements within your Web pages. While the discussion will certainly cover all of these features in depth, for now, let's focus on getting a table within the Web page. Customize the Insert Table dialog box so that it resembles Figure 6-2. Specifically, within the Size set of options, add **2** rows and **3** columns.

4. Within the Layout set of options, select the Left option from the Alignment menu, enter values of **0** for both "Cell padding" and "Cell spacing," click the "Specify width" checkbox and enter a value of **697** pixels within the width text box. (Don't forget to choose the "In pixels" radio button.)

> While the width doesn't have to be set here, it certainly doesn't hurt. So, why 697? If you look at Figure 6-1, the biggest graphic in the design is `header.gif`. The graphic `header.gif` is **697** pixels wide. Because this is the largest graphic associated with the site, it would be safe to assume that your table could also be the same width.

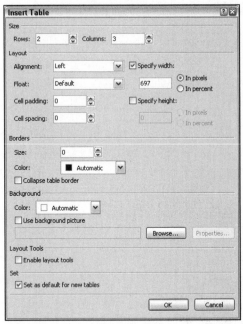

Figure 6-2: Insert Table dialog

5. Now, within the Borders set of options, enter a value of **0** in the Size text box.

6. For now, leave the rest of the options at their defaults. Click OK to close the Insert Table dialog box. The new table appears within the Web page, as shown in Figure 6-3.

As you can see from Figure 6-3, the new table appears centered within your Web page.

> It's not centered on the page because of properties that you set within the Insert Table dialog box. It's centered because `text-align` property was preset for you within the pre-built `styles.css` file. The `styles.css` file, which was already linked into the `default.htm` file when you opened it, redefined the `<body>` tag to display everything on the page as centered. For more information on CSS, refer to Chapter 5, "Page Formatting Using Cascading Style Sheets."

Another interesting aspect of the table is the fact that a new style was created and automatically applied to the table. Within the Apply/Manage Styles Task Panes, the `.style1` class was created within a document-wide style sheet. As you can see in Figure 6-4, the style is also added in code in an effort to set the border width, border color, and alignment of text within the table.

You'll also notice that the class reference is added to the `<table>` tag. Of course, this is all completely normal. World Wide Web Consortium (W3C) standards dictate that properties for HTML elements should be set using CSS whenever possible. Expression Web, trying to adhere to these standards, automatically generates styles for properties that traditionally could've been set as HTML attributes and values within the tag.

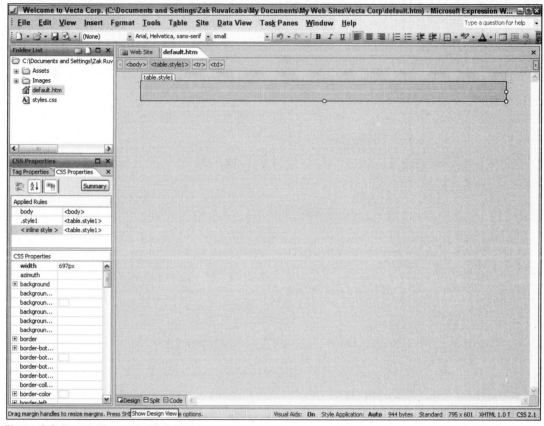

Figure 6-3: New table within Web page

As the chapter progresses, you'll work with the various properties that Expression Web offers for selecting, adding, and modifying rows and cells within the table. For now, let's review the options that you saw within the Insert Table dialog box. As you can see from Figure 6-2, the following options were available for configuration:

❑ *Rows* — Specifies the number of rows that the table will contain.

❑ *Columns* — Specifies the number of columns that the table will contain.

❑ *Alignment* — Select an option from this menu to set the default alignment of text within the cells of the table. Options include Left, Right, and Center. You'll also notice a Default option. Choosing this option forces the alignment of the cells to be set according to the *parent value*. The parent to the table, in this case, is the page. And, because you set the `text-align` property of the `<body>` tag to center within the external style sheet file, the table, recognizing this, also set the alignment of text to center. To override this, you manually set the alignment of text to left align.

❑ *Float* — Specifies how text and images will wrap around the table. Options include Right (table is aligned right and elements wrap around the left side) and Left (table is aligned left and elements wrap around the right side).

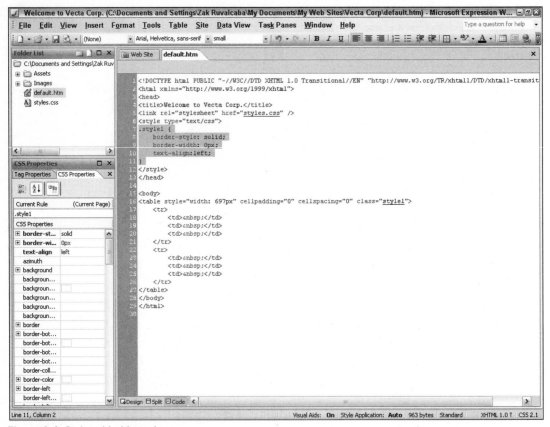

Figure 6-4: Style added in code

❏ *Cell padding* — Enter a number within this text box to set the amount of spacing between the contents of a cell and the cell border.

❏ *Cell spacing* — Enter a number within this text box to set the amount of spacing between cells.

❏ *Width* — Click the "Specify width" checkbox, and then enter a numeric value within the associated text box to set the width in either pixels or percent for the table.

❏ *Height* — Click the "Specify height" checkbox, and then enter a numeric value within the associated text box to set the height in either pixels or percent for the table. Height is rendered correctly only in Internet Explorer.

❏ *Border Size* — Enter a numeric value within this text box to set the thickness of the table border in pixels.

❏ *Bolder Color* — Select a color from the color selection menu to set the color of the border, if one is specified within the Border Size text box. If the Border Size is set to 0, selecting a color choice from this menu automatically changes the Border Size to 1 pixel.

❏ *Collapse table border* — Select this checkbox to set the CSS border-collapse property for the table to collapse. If you recall from Chapter 5, this property sets whether borders of neighboring table cells should be combined to form a single border. The "collapse" option joins and creates a single border around the table. Leaving this option unchecked forces all cells within the table to have borders.

❑ *Background Color* — Select a color from the color selection menu to set the background color of the table.

❑ *Background Picture* — Click the "Use background picture" checkbox, and then browse to and select an image to use as the background picture for your table.

❑ *Layout Tools* — Click this checkbox to enable Layout Tables mode for the table. This option is covered in more detail later in the chapter.

❑ *Set* — Click this checkbox to set the properties that you've configured as defaults for future table insertions.

As you can see, the set of properties offered by the Insert Table dialog box is extensive. Ultimately, these properties are geared toward providing you with a rich set of customizable properties that you can apply to your tables to create a fluid structure for elements on your Web page. You still have a lot to accomplish to get your design exactly the way you want it. For now, however, the foundation is set. Before you begin adding images and text to cells within the tables, let's review some important aspects of how to select tables, rows, and cells.

Selecting Table Elements

Before you begin adding elements to the newly created table, it's crucial that you understand some important concepts, including a topic as simple as selecting the table and elements such as rows and cells within the table. As your table-based designs become more and more complex, you'll begin to work with numerous tables within a page, including tables within table cells, also known as *nested tables*. When that time comes, the skill of selecting tables and rows, columns, and cells within a table become invaluable. There are numerous ways to select a table, including the following:

❑ Select the table by clicking anywhere within the page, holding the cursor, and then dragging it into the table.

❑ You can roll your cursor over the outer border of the table until your cursor changes to a Move cursor. Now, click to select the table.

❑ You can place your cursor within any cell in the table, at which point the Tag Chooser appears within the development area. Simply select the `<table.stlye1>` tag to select the table.

❑ You can select the table by first placing your cursor within one of the table's cells and choosing Table ➪ Select ➪ Table.

Regardless of which of the four methods you choose, the same result is produced: the table is selected. Selecting rows and columns within the table is just as easy. To select a row or column within the table, choose from one of the following three methods:

❑ The easiest method for selecting a row or column within a table is to click within a table's cell, hold your cursor down, and then drag across or down the table row or column until the desired number of cells within the row or column is selected. Doing this allows you to select a specific number of cells within the row/column or the entire row/column itself.

- ❏ Place your cursor within a cell in the table and choose the `<tr>` tag from the Tag Chooser that appears. You'll notice that as soon as you roll your cursor into the `<tr>` tag, the row your cursor is in is highlighted in blue. Unfortunately, tables don't contain tags that represent the columns within a table. Because of this, the same method can't be used to select columns.

- ❏ Place your cursor within a cell in the table and choose Table ⇨ Select ⇨ Row. This selects the entire row. To select a column, choose Table ⇨ Select ⇨ Column.

Regardless of the method you choose, the result is the same. The row or column within the table is selected. Selecting cells within a table works similarly. To select cells within a table, choose from one of the following four methods:

- ❏ The easiest method for selecting a cell within a table is to place your cursor in a cell within the table and click the `<td>` tag that surrounds your cursor. You'll notice that as you move your cursor into the `<td>` tag, your cursor changes into a Move cursor not unlike the one that appeared when you selected the table.

- ❏ Place your cursor within a cell in the table and choose the `<td>` tag from the Tag Chooser that appears. You'll notice that as soon as you roll your cursor into the `<td>` tag, the cell your cursor is in is highlighted blue.

- ❏ Place your cursor within a cell in the table and choose Table ⇨ Select ⇨ Cell.

- ❏ You may decide to select multiple cells at once. When this is the case, hold down the Ctrl key and then freely click the desired cells within the table. This allows you to select various cells at once, and even allows you to select cells that may not be next to each other.

As you can see, options for selecting tables or rows, columns, and cells within the table are abundant. While the topic may seem trivial initially, the rationale for selecting these elements will become obvious as the complexity of your table-based designs increases.

Modifying Table Properties

Now that your table is on the page, chances are that you'll want some way of manipulating some of the many properties associated with it. Maybe you'd like to add a border, add rows and columns, perhaps even change the background color of the table after you've inserted it. If this is the case, don't worry. You don't have to start over because you've already closed the Insert Table dialog box. Instead, you can access and modify properties of the table via the Modify Table dialog box.

You can access the Modify Table dialog box by selecting and then right-clicking the table and choosing the Table Properties option from the context menu that appears. You can also place your cursor in a cell within the table and choose Table ⇨ Table Properties ⇨ Table. Either method you choose launches the Modify Table dialog box, which closely resembles (it's actually the same dialog box) the Insert Table dialog box you saw in Figure 6-2. It's within this dialog box that you're given another opportunity to modify properties of the table (rows, columns, alignment, width, height, cell padding, cell spacing, and so on) that you may have overlooked when inserting the table initially.

While the Modify Table dialog box is responsible for handling some of the generic properties offered by the table, in reality, CSS styles are being generated under the hood. As you saw in Figure 6-4, Expression

Web automatically generates document-wide styles to control the look of the table and rows, columns, and cells within the table. What this should tell you is that more accurate property modifications can be accomplished via the CSS Properties Task Pane. As you can see from Figure 6-5, placing the cursor within the table reveals a complete set of CSS properties that have been set or can be set for the table within the CSS Properties Task Pane.

Realistically, most (if not all) of the properties that you'll need to modify for a table exist within the Insert/Modify Table dialog box. What really drives the look of a table is how many rows and columns the table contains. Furthermore, how you want your content organized within the design will govern how many rows or columns need to be added or removed from the initial insertion of the table, whether or not cells need to be merged or split, and so on.

The next few sections expand beyond the simplicities of inserting and formatting table properties. Specifically, you'll learn about the following:

- ❑ Adding and removing rows, columns, and cells
- ❑ Splitting and merging cells
- ❑ Inserting content into cells
- ❑ Modifying cell properties
- ❑ Inserting nested tables

The next few sections will really orchestrate the structure of the table-based Vecta Corp Web site. Let's move forward.

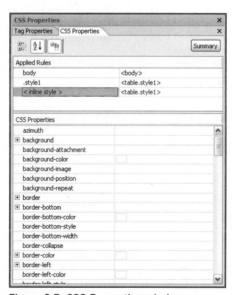

Figure 6-5: CSS Properties window

Adding and Removing Rows, Columns, and Cells

In most cases, you'll insert a table based on some preconceived idea of what the structure of your Web page should look like. Maybe you even have a prototype not unlike the one visible in Figure 6-1 that you can play around with in an effort to visualize the row and column structure for your table-based design. Looking further at Figure 6-1, can you visualize how many rows and columns the table that will structure the site should have? No? Try looking at Figure 6-6 and see if your idea matches that figure.

As you can see from the lines drawn across the graphic, the beginnings of the table-based design begin to materialize. You can clearly see a table where the structure of the table is set at three rows and two columns. You can see that you'll need one solid row across the top of the table to fit the header into (you'll need to merge cells to accomplish this). You'll also need to add and manipulate some of the cell properties for the navigation area (you can configure a background image for the blue bar that tiles down the page). Furthermore, you'll need to add the footer across the bottom of the table (you'll need to merge cells to accomplish this, as well). Finally, and probably the most complex, you'll need to add a nested table within the content area that will outline the structure for the Welcome, Our Solutions, and Client Testimonials text.

Figure 6-6: Visualizing the number of rows and columns

As you can see from Figure 6-6, the ideal structure of the table should be three rows and two columns. The table that you've inserted up to this point is two rows and three columns. You obviously need to add a row and delete a column from the existing table.

Try It Out   Add and Remove Rows and Columns

To insert and remove rows and columns from a table, follow these steps:

1. Again, the current table's structure is incorrect. To get the table so that it will work with your design, you'll need to add a row and remove a column from the existing table. To add a row to the structure of the table, you can do one of a few things. Possibly the easiest method for adding a row is to place your cursor within the last cell of the table and press Tab. Instantly, a new row appears below the table. Another option is to place your cursor in a cell within the table and choose either Table ➪ Insert ➪ Row Above or Table ➪ Insert ➪ Row Below. Either one of these options will insert a new blank row above or below the table. Finally, you can right-click within a cell and choose the Insert ➪ Row Above or Insert ➪ Row Below option from the context menu that appears. Either one of the three methods will produce the same result. You should now have three rows in your table.

2. You'll need to remove one of the columns within the table. The easiest method for removing a column is to click, hold, and drag from the first cell down to the last cell within the column and press the Backspace key. Doing this deletes the column from the table. Another option is to place your cursor in a cell within the table's column that you want to delete and choose Table ➪ Delete ➪ Columns. Finally, you can right-click within a cell and choose the Delete ➪ Columns option from the context menu that appears. Either one of the three methods will produce the same result. You should now have two columns in your table.

In reality, the methods outlined in the previous steps are but one way of adding and removing columns. For example, the Table ➪ Delete submenu offers you the ability to not only delete columns, but also to delete the entire table, delete a row, or even delete a particular cell within the table. Additionally, the context menu's set of options offers the same features. You can use the Table ➪ Insert submenu to insert rows above or below the position of your cursor within the table, and you can also use the options within this menu to insert columns to the left or right, cells to the left or right, or even a caption to include as part of the table.

> Captioning a table is good practice when attempting to outline a general summary of the contents of the table. From a user experience standpoint, it allows the user to read the caption, find out a bit about what the table contains, and then decide as to whether or not to read all of the content within the table instead.

While these methods summarize ways of inserting and removing individual rows, columns, and cells for a table, the reality is that certain situations will call for you to add multiple rows and/or columns to the structure of a table. When this is the case, you may decide to use the Insert Rows or Columns dialog box instead. Available by choosing Table ➪ Insert ➪ Rows or Columns, and visible in Figure 6-7, the Insert Rows or Columns dialog box allows you to insert multiple rows or columns above or below the position of your cursor within the table at once.

Figure 6-7: Insert Rows or Columns dialog box

This option is an excellent alternative to methods covered previously for inserting numerous rows and/or columns at once.

> Of course, if you want to completely change the structure (rows and columns) of your table in one shot, you can always access the Modify Table dialog box. As you saw in Figure 6-2, the Insert/Modify Table dialog box allows you to manipulate the row and column structure of the table quickly using a convenient interface.

By now, your table should have three rows and two columns, the ideal structure for the table-based Vecta Corp Web page. With the core structure of the table set, you can now focus on manipulating the cell structure so that you may then begin adding content such as images and text to cells within the table.

Splitting and Merging Cells

Looking at the table now, it's clear that you are close to being able to add images and text to it. However, there's still one thing left to do. If you recall, the header image (`header.gif`) is 697 pixels wide, too big to fit in one of the two cells within the first row of the table without altering the structure of the table and receiving undesirable results. The same is true for the footer image. Instead, merge the two cells in the first and third rows. This will combine both the first and second cells together into one cell that spans 697 pixels across the table. Because both the header (`header.gif`) and footer (`footer.gif`) images are 697 pixels wide, they'll fit perfectly within their respective cells (first and third rows).

While you will merge the first and second cells together within the first and third rows, you'll leave the second row as is. This allows you to cleanly separate the navigation area (the first cell of the second row) with the main content area (the second cell of the second row). Figure 6-8 illustrates what you need to do next to allow the header, footer, navigation, and main content areas to coexist without error.

To merge cells within a table, simply click, hold, and drag to select both cells within the first row. Alternatively, you can also hold down the Ctrl key and click each one of the two cells within the first row and then choose Table ⇨ Modify ⇨ Merge Cells. You'll immediately notice that the two cells within the first row become one 697-pixel-wide cell. Repeat this process for the third row (footer) in the table. When you've finished, the table will have one cell in the first row, two cells in the second row, and one cell in the third row. The table is now ready for images and text.

Remember that most of the operations that you are performing can also be accessed via the context menu. The Modify submenu of options is also available by right-clicking onto the table once you've selected the cells to merge.

Splitting cells within a table can be accomplished in much the same way. Simply place your cursor into the cell that you want to split, and choose Table ⇨ Modify ⇨ Split Cells. The Split Cells dialog box appears, similar to Figure 6-9.

As you can see from Figure 6-9, the dialog box allows you to pick whether to split the cell into columns or rows, and allows you to choose the number of columns/rows to split the cells into. You'll notice that the default value within the "Number of columns" text box is 2. Expression Web automatically figures out that the natural flow of the table is two columns. Because of this, it presents the value 2 within the text box.

Figure 6-8: Allowing header, footer, navigation, and main content to coexist

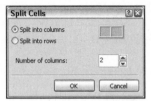

Figure 6-9: Split Cells dialog box

Inserting Content into Cells

With the header and footer cells in the table now merged, you are ready to begin adding and formatting the elements that will make up the table-based Vecta Corp Web page. As you'll see, the images and text that you insert into the cells within the table will really hammer home the point of table-based structuring.

Try It Out   **Inserting Content into Cells of a Table**

To add images and text within cells of the newly created table, follow these steps:

1. Start by inserting the most obvious of images, the `header.gif` image. You can insert this image by expanding the `Images` folder within the Folder List Task Pane, selecting the `header.gif` image, and then dragging it into the cell within the first row of the table.

2. Insert the footer image. Again, select the `footer.gif` image from the Folder List Task Pane and drag it into the cell in the third row. The result should resemble the design shown in Figure 6-10.

3. Just by adding these two images, you can begin to see the benefit of working with table-based structuring techniques. The header and footer images will eventually surround the navigation and main content areas of the page, giving the design a fluid, print-like look. If you're not seeing it yet, don't worry. You still have a lot to do. Now that you understand how to insert images within cells of a table, let's begin to add the content that will make up the navigation and main content areas. To add content within the navigation area, place your cursor within the first cell in the second row and enter the text **Home**, followed by a line break (press Enter), **About Us**, line break, **Solutions**, line break, **Support**, line break, and finally **Contact Us**.

4. Create the links for these navigation items. Highlight the Home text, choose Insert ➪ Hyperlink. The Insert Hyperlink dialog box appears. Select the `default.htm` file and click OK to close the Insert Hyperlink dialog box and apply the link to the Home text. Repeat this process for the rest of the text elements, linking About Us to `aboutus.htm`, Solutions to `solutions.htm`, Support to `support.htm`, and Contact Us to `contactus.htm`.

> **You'll note that** `aboutus.htm`, `solutions.htm`, `support.htm`, **and** `contactus.htm` **don't yet exist. That's OK. All you should care about at this point is creating the links within the navigation bar. Eventually, you'll create these pages. Since that's the case, for now, simply type the page name (**`aboutus.htm`, `solutions.htm`, `support.htm`, **and** `contactus.htm`**) within the Address text box in the Insert Hyperlink dialog box.**

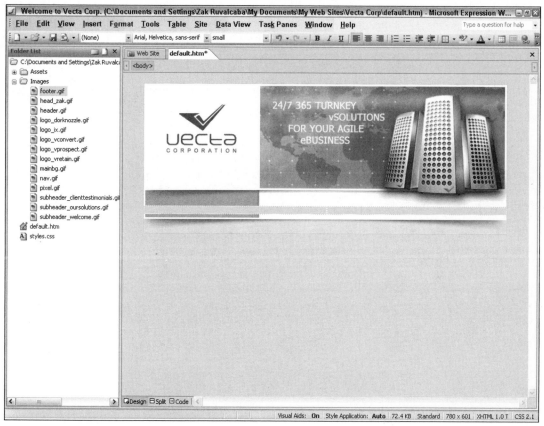

Figure 6-10: Inserting the header and footer image

5. Apply styles to these navigation items. You'll notice within the Apply Styles Task Pane, a class called `.navlink` (a class based conceptually on what you built in Chapter 5) has been included. Select each individual link within the navigation menu and apply this class. You'll notice that the navigation item turns red and, more important, indents (because of a left padding of 50 pixels that you specified within the class) from the left edge of the table border. The result will resemble Figure 6-11.

> **Don't highlight all of the links at once and apply the style. This will prevent the hover contextual selector from working. Instead, select each individual link and apply the class.**

6. The final few steps involve adding some of the content that will appear within the second cell of the second row in the table. To add this content, begin by selecting the `subheader_welcome.gif` image (located within the `Images` folder in the Folder List Task Pane) and dragging it into the second cell in the second row.

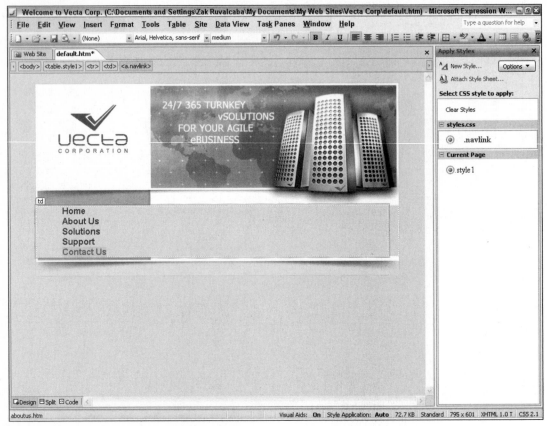

Figure 6-11: Applying styles to navigation items

7. Open the text file that contains the Welcome text (`home.txt`). If you remember from earlier chapters, the `Assets` folder within the Folder List Task Pane contains these files. Expression Web has an integrated text editor and will allow you to open the file directly within its framework by simply double-clicking the file. Once open, highlight only the first paragraph of text (if word wrapping is turned off, it will be the first line of text), copy it, close the document, and paste the text into the same cell that you dragged the small Welcome subheader image into. You will need to add two line breaks (created by pressing Enter) after the Welcome subheader image to separate the text away from the image and force it onto the next line. The result will resemble Figure 6-12.

While there is still some work to perform on both of the navigation and main content cells, the basic structure of the site is coming together nicely. In the next section, you'll see that with some simple cell formatting techniques, you can set the width of each cell, background of each cell, vertical alignment of the cells, and more. Let's move forward.

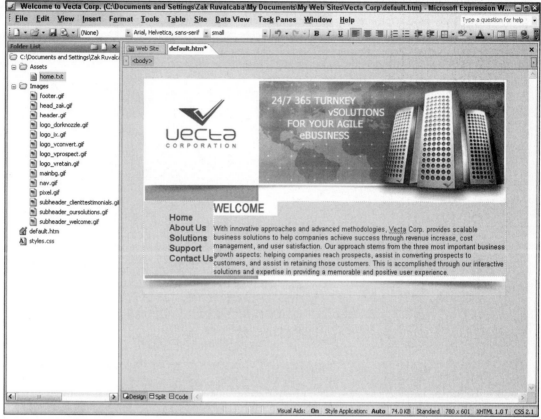

Figure 6-12: Formatting the Welcome text

Modifying Cell Properties

Up to this point, you've managed to insert some form of element within each cell of the table. The header and footer images consume the first and third cells of the table. The navigation menu consumes the first cell within the second row while the Welcome content makes up the second and final cell within the second row of the table. While the header and footer fit nicely within their respective cells, you can clearly see that the navigation and content areas are misaligned, and, in general, the cells that make up the structure that contains the content seem to run into each other. Furthermore, the navigation and content area's lack of a background color/image make the cells appear not to fit very well within the overall design aesthetic.

Of course, you can remedy this situation by manipulating properties for the cells within the table. Just as you modified table properties earlier in the chapter, each cell within a table also supports specific property modifications. For example, you may decide to adjust the cell's width, background color, background image, vertical alignment, and more.

You access cell properties in much the same way as you access table properties. You simply place your cursor within the cell whose properties you want to modify and choose Table ⇨ Table Properties ⇨ Cell. You may also choose to access cell properties by right-clicking directly within the cell and choosing the Cell Properties option from the context menu that appears. Regardless of the method that you choose for modifying cell properties, the result is the same. The Cell Properties dialog box appears, similar to Figure 6-13.

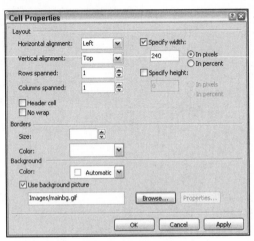

Figure 6-13: Cell Properties dialog

As you can see from Figure 6-13, the Cell Properties dialog box offers the following functionality:

❑ *Horizontal alignment* — Select an option from this menu to horizontally align content within the cell. Options include Left, Right, Center, and Justify.

❑ *Vertical alignment* — Select an option from this menu to vertically align content within the cell. Options include Top, Middle, Baseline, and Bottom. Choose Baseline specifically when you have two different types of elements (an image and text, for example) and need to align both to the bottom of the cell by their baseline (the absolute bottom of both elements).

❑ *Rows spanned* — Determines the number of table rows spanned by the cell. This property is usually set automatically for you.

❑ *Columns spanned* — Determines the number of table columns spanned by the cell. As is the case with "Rows spanned," this property is usually set automatically for you.

❑ *Header cell* — Converts the <td> tag used by the cell into a <th> tag representing a table header. From an efficiency standpoint, the <th> tag automatically bolds and centers content within the cell, effectively streamlining the generated code.

❑ *No wrap* — Prevents content within the cell from wrapping. If a width is associated with a cell where "No wrap" is enabled, and the content exceeds that width, the cell is automatically stretched to accommodate the excess content.

❑ *Width* — Click the "Specify width" checkbox, and then enter a numeric value within the associated text box to set the width in either pixels or percent for the cell.

❑ *Height* — Click the "Specify height" checkbox, and then enter a numeric value within the associated text box to set the height in either pixels or percent for the cell. Height is rendered correctly in Internet Explorer only.

❑ *Border Size* — Specify a numeric value within this text box to set the size, in pixels, for the border that should surround the cell.

❑ *Border Color* — Select a color from the color selection menu to set the color of the inner border for the cell.

❑ *Background Color* — Select a color from the color selection menu to set the background color of the cell.

❑ *Background Picture* — Click the "Use background picture" checkbox, and then browse to and select an image to use as the background picture for your cell.

Now that you understand how cell properties are accessed, and, more important, what properties can actually be set for cells, let's push forward and actually manipulate the properties for the two navigation and content cells within the table-based design.

Try It Out   Modifying Cell Properties

To modify properties for the navigation and content cells, follow these steps:

1. Right-click the navigation cell (first cell in the second row) and choose the Cell Properties option from the context menu that appears. The Cell Properties dialog box appears.

2. Within the Cell Properties dialog box, choose the "Specify width" checkbox and enter a numeric value of **240** pixels. This provides some space in the navigation area and will prevent the welcome text in the content cell from running into and overlapping the navigation cell.

3. Choose the Top option from the "Vertical alignment" menu.

4. Click the "Use background picture" checkbox, and browse to and select the `mainbg.gif` image located within the `Images` folder of the Vecta Corp Web site. The result will resemble Figure 6-13. Click OK to close the Cell Properties dialog box.

5. The next step is to customize the content cell. Again, right-click the content cell (second cell in the second row) and choose the Cell Properties option from the context menu that appears. The Cell Properties dialog box will appear.

6. Within the Cell Properties dialog box, choose the "Specify width" checkbox and enter a numeric value of **457** pixels, which is the total width of the table (697) minus the width of the navigation cell (240).

7. Choose the Top option from the "Vertical alignment" menu.

8. Choose a white color from the Background Color selection menu. Click OK to close the Cell Properties dialog box.

Once you've closed the Cell Properties dialog box, the design will start coming together. Specifically, the content within the navigation and content cells now fits perfectly within the flow of the design.

While the design appears complete, in reality, there's still some work left to be done. The two columns that will house the Our Solutions and Client Testimonials content still need to be created underneath the main Welcome text that you just formatted. To format the Our Solutions and Client Testimonials text within the content cell, you need to use nested tables.

Inserting Nested Tables

With the basic structure of the table-based Vecta Corp Web site complete, you can focus on other, more advanced concepts. One of these concepts involves using tables to structure content within the cell of another table, otherwise known as *nested tables*. Nested tables should be used when you need to further structure content, such as the Our Solutions and Client Testimonials text, so that the design you want to achieve can't be done without the use of more tables. Figure 6-14 provides an example.

As you can see from the outlines in the figure, the three-column text structure wouldn't be able to be created without the use of nested tables. The use of nested tables in this case will further enhance the design by structuring important text within columns, giving the appearance of a well-structured print collateral piece.

Figure 6-14: Using nested tables

Try It Out   **Inserting a Nested Table**

An understanding of how nested tables work is important to table-based Web design. As the complexity of your Web sites grow, so too will be the number of nested tables that you'll employ. So that you understand how to work with nested tables within Expression Web, follow these steps:

1.   Place your cursor at the end of the Welcome text and add two new line breaks (by pressing Enter) so that you have space to add your new nested table.

2.   Select Table ➪ Insert Table. The Insert Table dialog box appears.

3.   Configure the dialog box so that you have **3** rows and **3** columns, set the width to **457** pixels (the width of the cell that the nested table will reside in), and set the cell padding, cell spacing, and border sizes to **0** pixels. Click OK to close the Insert Table dialog box. The new nested table will appear within the content cell, similar to Figure 6-15.

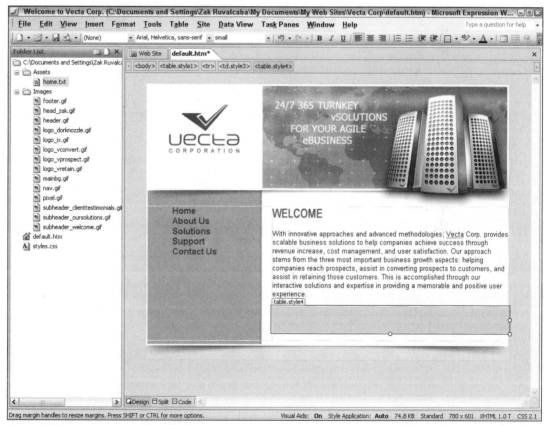

Figure 6-15: New nested table within the content cell

4. Add both the subheader_oursolutions.gif and subheader_clienttestimonials.gif images to the first cell and third cell of the first row, respectively.

5. Now you'll need to set the spacing of the center column. This will prevent the Our Solution text from running over and into the Client Testimonials text. To do that, right-click within the center cell in the first row and choose the Cell Properties option from the context menu that appears. When the Cell Properties dialog box appears, click the "Specify width" checkbox and enter a value of **17** pixels. Click OK to close the Cell Properties dialog box. The width is now set for the center column.

6. Add the Our Solutions and Client Testimonials text to their respective cells. Open the home.txt file once again and copy the Solution text. Switch back over to the default.htm file and paste the text within the first cell in the third row (the second row is used purely for spacing, similar in concept to the center column). Now switch back over to the home.txt file, copy the Client Testimonials text, switch back over to the default.htm file, and paste the text into the third cell of the third row.

7. To force the text within the cells to align to the top of their respective cell, it would probably be a good idea to format the vertical alignment property for each cell. You can this by right-clicking within the cell and choosing the Cell Properties option from the context menu that appears. When the Cell Properties dialog box appears, choose the Top option from the "Vertical alignment" menu and click OK. When you've finished, the result of the page will resemble Figure 6-16.

Of course, this is just the beginning. You can further enhance the look of the content within the nested table by adding the three logo images for vProspect (logo_vprospect.gif), vConvert (logo_vconvert.gif), and vRetain (logo_vretain.gif) to their respective positions within the Solutions text. As you did earlier in the book, you can also link the Solution headings to the solutions.htm page. Additionally, you might think about italicizing the client quotes. With the formatting skills that you've learned up to this point, the possibilities are seemingly endless.

Formatting Tables Using Table AutoFormat

One handy feature that you may want to take advantage of when working with table-based designs in Expression Web is Table AutoFormat. Rather than spending time configuring a color scheme for your tables and cells within your tables, you can simply use the Table AutoFormat feature to automatically add professional-looking styles to your tables with a couple of short clicks. Even better, if down the road you decide that you don't like a particular table's color scheme, simply attach another with a couple of short clicks.

> While the Table AutoFormat feature automatically creates a color scheme for your tables, it's important to note that table formatting can also be accomplished by you manually through CSS. As you learned in Chapter 5, you could easily create a class selector that outlines formatting properties for the table, and then associate that class selector with the table.

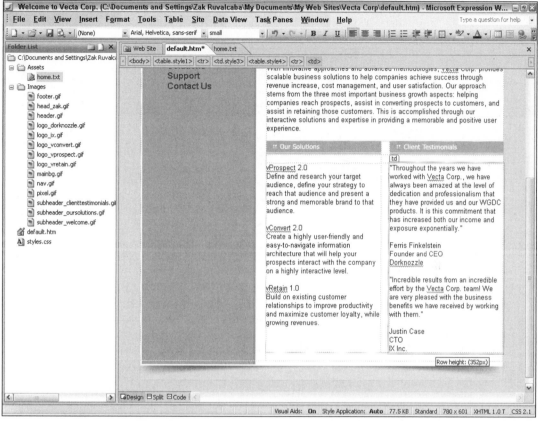

Figure 6-16: Inserting a nested table

Try It Out   Using Table AutoFormat

Expression Web's Table AutoFormat feature is a time-saver that you'll undoubtedly want to take advantage of within your designs. To learn how to format tables using Table AutoFormat, follow these steps:

1. Create a new page on which to practice the Table AutoFormat feature. You can do this by choosing File ➪ New ➪ HTML. Immediately save the file as autoformat.htm.

2. You'll want to insert a table to apply the AutoFormat feature to. To create the new table, choose Table ➪ Insert Table. When the Insert Table dialog appears, enter **10** rows and **3** columns and click OK to close the Insert Table dialog box. The new table appears on the page.

3. Place your cursor within the table and choose Table ➪ Modify ➪ Table AutoFormat. The Table AutoFormat dialog box will appear, similar to Figure 6-17.

4. As you can see from Figure 6-17, the dialog box allows you to set a particular color scheme from the Formats list. Once a format is chosen, you can further configure how and what part of the table will have the color scheme applied to it. Find a color scheme within the Formats list that you like and click OK to see the color scheme applied to your table.

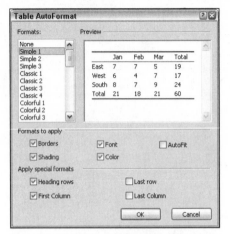

Figure 6-17: Table AutoFormat dialog box

You probably also noticed that the Table AutoFormat dialog, shown in Figure 6-17, outlines various properties for controlling how and what is configured by the formatting of the color scheme for the table. Specifically, the following features are offered by the dialog box:

❑ *Formats* — Choose 1 of 38 different colors schemes from this list to apply to your tables.

❑ *Preview* — Provides a preview of what the selected color scheme from the Formats list will look like when applied to your table.

❑ *Formats to apply* — Allows you to specify whether or not the color scheme should apply border, shading, font, color, and AutoFit properties to the table.

❑ *Apply special formats* — Allows you to specify whether or not the color scheme should be applied to row headings, the first column within the table, the last row within the table, or the last column within the table.

As you can see, the Table AutoFormat feature has the potential to free you from tedious color tinkering when working with tables. If you're a developer who doesn't put a lot of stock in the subtleties of a table's color scheme, yet still want the table to look somewhat presentable, then the Table AutoFormat feature is perfect for you.

Inserting and Working with Layout Tables

As you've seen, tables offer a flexible structuring alternative to conventional Web page formatting techniques. These techniques (which you learned throughout the first five chapters) limit your creativity by forcing you to organize your Web page's content in a boring, linear fashion. In this chapter, you saw how tables allow you to deviate from the unexciting world of line breaks and paragraph breaks by offering an elegant approach to page structuring that, when done correctly, allows you to organize content within a Web page to closely mirror that of a print collateral piece.

If there were a downside to using tables (aside from the fact that standards are moving away from tables and into CSS), it would be that figuring out the structuring (rows and columns) of the table initially can be a matter of trial and error. Many times, you'll find yourself inserting a table with a certain number of rows and columns, only to find that structure changes many times over throughout the development life-cycle of the Web page. As the specifications for the structure of the table change, so, too, will your frustration level toward the tedious process of inserting, removing, merging, and splitting rows, columns, and cells.

To ease your development of table-based designs, Expression Web introduces a unique, visual approach to table-based structuring known as *Layout Tables*. Layout Tables work similarly to many popular print design programs in that tables and cells within the tables are manually drawn on the page. Rather than opening the Insert Table dialog box, trying to figure out the initial structure of the table-based design, and then fumbling with inserting, removing, merging, and splitting areas within the table, Layout Tables, and the tools within Expression Web that support working with Layout Tables, take a more visual and interactive approach.

With Layout Tables, you now have the freedom to physically draw a table to the width and height specifications that you think your table-based layout will need. Later, if that specification changes, simply click, hold, and drag the resize handles to expand or contract the size of the Layout Table. Need areas to place content into within the Layout Table? Not a problem. Layout Cells can be drawn and resized just as easily within a Layout Table to act as the content areas within the Layout Table that you'll eventually insert your elements into.

The next few sections focus entirely on Layout Tables and the content areas within Layout Tables, also known as *Layout Cells*. You'll rebuild a separate version of the main Vecta Corp Web page primarily by drawing and manipulating Layout Tables and Cells. If you thought working with tables (and the Insert Tables dialog box) was easy, wait until you finish these next few sections.

Drawing Tables

Working with Layout Tables in Expression Web is easy! You'd simply create a new HTML page and then begin drawing. What really drives the simplicity of Layout Tables within Expression Web, however, are the toolbar, menu items, and the Task Pane used to work with Layout Tables. As you'll learn, Expression Web offers a "Layout Tables and Cells" Task Pane and a Tables toolbar to facilitate the development of Layout Table–based designs. Before dissecting the toolbar and Task Pane used when working with Layout Tables, let's dive right in and begin reconstructing the main Vecta Corp Web page using Layout Tables. Then, before discussing Layout Cells, let's dissect the toolbar and Task Pane to provide a comprehensive understanding of what these tools can provide to you while working with Layout Tables and Cells.

Try It Out   Drawing a Layout Table

Layout Table–based Web designs begin with drawing a Layout Table. To see how easy it really is to draw a table within a Web page, follow these steps:

1. Start by creating a new page to practice Layout Tables on. You can do this by choosing File ⇨ New ⇨ HTML. Immediately save the page as `layouttables.htm`.

2. Now choose Task Panes ⇨ Layout Tables. The Layout Tables Task Pane appears, similar to Figure 6-18.

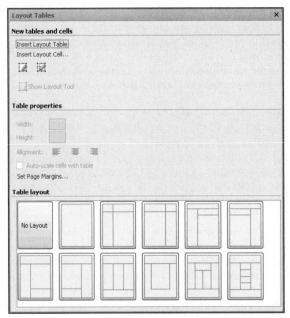

Figure 6-18: Layout Tables and Cells dialog box

3. Within the Layout Tables Task Pane, click the Draw Layout Table icon (it's the first icon from the left within the "New tables and cells" subcategory in the Task Pane). Your cursor will immediately change to a pencil.

4. Click, hold, and drag from the top-left corner of the Web page down and to the right within the Web page to draw a new table.

5. Within the Layout Tables Task Pane find the Width and Height text boxes and enter values of **697** and **500** for the width and height, respectively. The result of the new Layout Table will appear, similar to Figure 6-19.

With the Layout Table now on the page, you'll immediately notice some interesting things related to how the table is shown and, more important, how you're able to interact with the table. First and foremost, resizing the table is easily done using the small blue squares that appear along the perimeter of the Layout Table. To resize the table, simply click, hold, and drag the Layout Table to contract or expand the size of the Layout Table. Furthermore, the Layout Table offers a small size (in pixels) box near the vertical and horizontal center of each side of the Layout Table. Aside from simply showing you the width and height of the table, each one of these size boxes also offers a submenu of options, available by clicking the small expander arrow icon located just to the right of each size. Clicking this submenu reveals the following options:

❑ *Change Column Width/Change Row Height* — Click either one of these options to launch the Column/ Row Properties dialog box. The dialog box simply offers another alternative for setting the width/ height of the table, setting whether to make the column/row autostretch, whether or not to use a column/row spacer image, and whether or not to force Expression Web to clear contradicting widths/heights. Contradicting widths and heights occur when you set the width/height of a Layout Table, but the sum of the widths/heights of the cells within the table don't equal the width/height of the table.

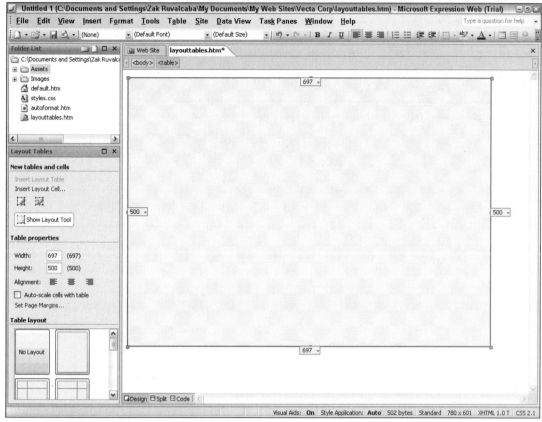

Figure 6-19: Result of the new Layout Table

❑ *Make Column Autostretch/Make Row Autostretch* — Functionally equivalent to setting the width/ height to 100 percent versus a fixed pixel width/height. When a column or row is set to auto-stretch, the table's width/height always consumes 100 percent of the browser's width/height even if the user resizes the browser window manually.

❑ *Use Column Spacer Image* — Spacer images are used to control spacing in Layout Tables. A *spacer image* is a single-pixel transparent image that is stretched out to be a specified number of pixels wide. Because a browser can't draw a table column narrower than the widest image contained in a cell in that column, placing a spacer image in a table column forces browsers to keep the column at least as wide as the image. Of course, you don't have to create the spacer image when you select this option. Instead, Expression Web makes reference to a preinstalled spacer image on a FrontPage Server Extensions–enabled site.

As you can see, drawing a table within a Web page is simple. Unfortunately, the Layout Table alone does nothing for you. It isn't until you add Layout Cells within the Layout Table, that you're able to structure content on the page. Before getting too far ahead of myself, however, let's dissect some of the features available within the Layout Tables Task Pane, including two that you've just used. Once you understand what options are offered in the Layout Tables Task Pane, and how they're used, creating

Layout Table-based designs is a snap. Specifically, the features offered by the Layout Tables dialog box include the following:

❑ *Insert Layout Table* — Click this link to quickly create a 450 pixel by 450 pixel Layout Table within your Web page.

❑ *Insert Layout Cell* — Click this link to launch the Insert Layout Cell dialog box. As you'll see in the next section, you can use this dialog box to quickly format dimensions for a Layout Cell, and then insert that cell within the Layout Table.

❑ *Draw Layout Table* — As you saw in Step 3 in the introductory discussion for this section, choosing this icon causes your cursor to change to a pencil. You then clicked, held, and dragged within the page and drew a Layout Table.

❑ *Draw Layout Cell* — Choose this icon to change your cursor to a Layout Cell-based cursor. Then click, hold, and drag within a Layout Table to draw a Layout Cell within the table.

❑ *Show Layout Tool* — Select this icon to display a table (drawn or not) in Layout mode. Deselect this icon to disable most of the options within the Layout Tables Task Pane, and show the table within the Web page using the standard view shown throughout the chapter. Properties for the table must be set using either the Tag or CSS Properties Task Panes, or the Tables toolbar (covered later).

❑ *Width and Height* — As you saw in Step 5 of the introduction to this section, you can enter numeric values within these two text boxes to set the width and/or height of the table in pixels.

❑ *Alignment* — Choose from one of the three icons offered within this icon set to change the alignment of the table within the page. Options include Left, Center, and Right align.

❑ *Auto-scale cells with table* — Click this checkbox to have Layout Cells drawn within a Layout Table automatically resize and scale when the parent table is resized and scaled.

❑ *Set Page Margins* — Click this link to launch the Page Properties dialog box with the Advanced tab selected. You can then enter numeric values within the Top, Left, Bottom, and Right margin text boxes to set the physical margins of the Web page in pixels.

❑ *Table Layout* — Choose from a set of pre-built table layouts within this list. As soon as you click one of these options, the layout (similar to the representative icon) is instantly created within the Web page.

As you can see, the Layout Tables Task Pane offers numerous options for helping you work with Layout Tables and, as you'll see in the next section, Layout Cells. For the most part, this Task Pane is all you really need to get going with drawing and customizing Layout Tables and Cells. However, if you prefer to work with the many toolbars that Expression Web offers, then maybe the Tables toolbar is for you. Available by selecting View ➪ Toolbars ➪ Tables, the Tables toolbar shown in Figure 6-20 is a button-based toolbar that allows you to draw tables, insert Layout Tables and Cells, show the Layout Tool, and more, using visual icons.

Figure 6-20: The Tables toolbar

As mentioned throughout the book, toolbars simply offer an alternative to most Task Panes by relieving you of important real estate that is crucial when working with extra-wide Web pages within Expression Web. The Tables toolbar is no different. As you can see from Figure 6-20, the Tables toolbar offers the following options:

- ❑ *Column to the Left/Column to the Right* — When a table is on the page, click one of these two icons to insert a column either to the left or right of the column where your cursor is positioned.

- ❑ *Row Above/Row Below* — When a table is on the page, click one of these two icons to insert a row either above or below the row where your cursor is positioned.

- ❑ *Delete Cells* — Click this icon to delete a selected cell within a table.

- ❑ *Merge Cells/Split Cells* — Click one of these two icons to either merge selected cells, or split a cell into one or more rows or columns.

- ❑ *Align* — Click one of these three icons to align content within the cells of your table either to the top, center, or bottom of the specific cell.

- ❑ *Distribute Rows Evenly/Distribute Columns Evenly* — Click one of these two icons to distribute multiple rows/columns within the table evenly. To give you a better idea as to how this feature works, assume for a moment that you have a table that is 400 pixels wide. Also assume that you have two cells within the table (with no physical dimensions set). Clicking the Distribute Columns Evenly button, for example, would automatically set each cell within the table to 200 pixels. Because you have two cells, 2×200 would equal 400, or, more specifically, the total width of the table.

- ❑ *AutoFit to Contents* — Click this icon to automatically have Expression Web resize the table to the dimensions of the widest element (image, text, and so on) within a cell of the table.

- ❑ *Fill Color* — Choose a color from the selection menu that appears to set the background color of the table.

- ❑ *Table AutoFormat* — Click the Table AutoFormat icon to launch the Table AutoFormat dialog box. As you saw earlier in the chapter, the Table AutoFormat dialog box produces a list of pre-built color schemes that you may associate with your tables. If you prefer not to set border, shading, font, color, and so on, simply pick a format from the Table AutoFormat list to quickly format the look of the table without having to launch the Table AutoFormat dialog box. If you know what color scheme that you'd like to apply and prefer not to launch the Table AutoFormat dialog box, simply select the color scheme name from the drop-down menu that appears just to the left of the Table AutoFormat icon instead.

- ❑ *Show Layout Tool* — Click this icon to display a table (drawn or not) in Layout mode.

- ❑ *Draw Layout Table* — Choose this icon to change your cursor to a pencil. Then click, hold, and drag within your page to draw a Layout Table.

- ❑ *Draw Layout Cell* — Choose this icon to change your cursor. Then click, hold, and drag within a Layout Table to draw a Layout Cell within the table.

Now that the basic structure of the table has been drawn within the Web page, you can focus on drawing Layout Cells. As you'll see, Layout Cells become the content areas within the Layout Table. This is where all of your images and text elements will end up going.

Drawing Cells

With the foundation to the Layout Table–based structure complete, you're now ready to add the sections that will serve as the content areas for the design. If you recall, earlier in the chapter, you added a table using the Insert Table dialog box. Within the dialog box, you were given the opportunity to specify the number of rows and columns that you wanted your table to have. As soon as you clicked OK within the Insert Table dialog box, the table, complete with rows and columns, was added to the page.

Layout Tables work slightly differently. With Layout Tables, you're responsible for not only drawing the Layout Table onto the page, but also the Layout Cells within the Layout Table, as well. Once the Layout Cells are drawn within the Layout Table, you can begin adding, organizing, and formatting your image and text elements in an effort to create the structure that you compiled earlier on in the chapter.

Try It Out	Drawing Layout Cells

Layout Cells act as the content areas within Layout Tables. Without Layout Cells, the Layout Table is useless. To see how Layout Cells are added within Layout Tables, follow these steps:

1. Within the Layout Tables Task Pane, click the Draw Layout Cell icon. You cursor will change to accommodate drawing Layout Cells within Layout Tables. Alternatively, you can also choose the Draw Layout Cell link within the Tables toolbar.

2. Click within the upper-left corner of the Layout Table, hold the cursor down, and drag down and to the right until you span the entire width of the Layout Table. As you drag your cursor down, keep in mind that you'll need a height of 227 pixels. While this is difficult to gauge while drawing, try to drag the Layout Cell so that the height of the Layout Cell is at least in that range.

3. Now, right-click on the newly drawn cell and choose the Cell Properties option from the context menu that appears. The Cell Properties dialog box will appear. Within the dialog box, enter a height value of **227** pixels and click OK. The dialog box will close and the drawn Layout Cell will change to accommodate the modified height value. So far, the design should resemble Figure 6-21.

4. You need to draw the footer cell. Again, click the Draw Layout Cell icon within the Layout Tables Task Pane. Once your cursor changes, draw a cell that spans the entire width of the table near the bottom of the Layout Table. The height should be roughly 35 pixels, although you'll change this within the Cell Properties dialog box.

5. Again, right-click on the newly drawn cell and choose the Cell Properties option from the context menu that appears. The Cell Properties dialog box will appear. Within the dialog box, enter a height value of **35** pixels and click OK. The dialog box will close and the drawn Layout Cell will change to accommodate the modified height value.

6. The next step is to draw Layout Cells for the navigation and content areas within the Layout Table. To do this, choose the Draw Layout Cell icon within the Layout Tables Task Pane and immediately draw a cell that spans the entire height of the remaining Layout Table's real estate (237 pixels), but this time, it should span a width of only 240 pixels. To adjust the width accurately, right-click on the cell and choose the Cell Properties option from the context menu that appears. The Cell Properties dialog box will appear. Within the dialog box, enter a width value of **237** pixels and click OK. The dialog box will close and the drawn Layout Cell will change to accommodate the modified width value.

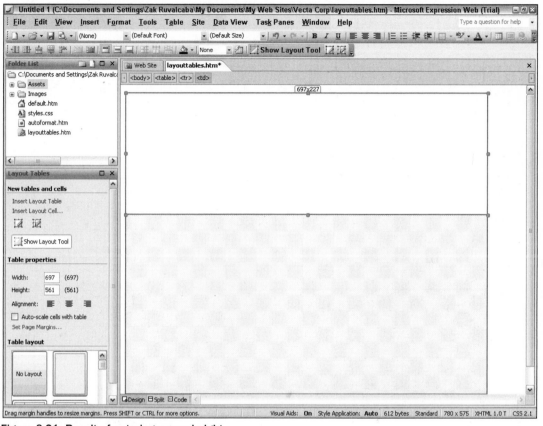

Figure 6-21: Result of entering a new height

7. Draw the content cell within the remaining area. If all of your Layout Cells were drawn correctly, the final Layout Cell should span a width of 457 pixels and should have a height of 237 pixels. The result of the design should resemble Figure 6-22.

8. Although you can still add images and content to cells while in Layout mode, for now, click the Show Layout Tool icon within the Tables toolbar to see what the finished table looks like in its normal state. You'll notice that the design that is shown closely resembles what you would have created using a more traditional approach in the Insert Table dialog box.

To finish off the design, open the Folder List Task Pane and drag the `header.gif` and `footer.gif` images into their respective cells. You should also right-click within the navigation cell, choose the Cell Properties option, and browse to and select the `mainbg.gif` image to use as the background image for that cell. Additionally, you should add the Navigation and Welcome text that will reside in the main content area. When you're finished, the design should closely resemble what you completed earlier in the chapter.

As you've seen, drawing Layout Tables and Layout Cells is easy. It completely streamlines working with table-based Web design by providing a flexible and feature-rich alternative to dialog boxes and wizards.

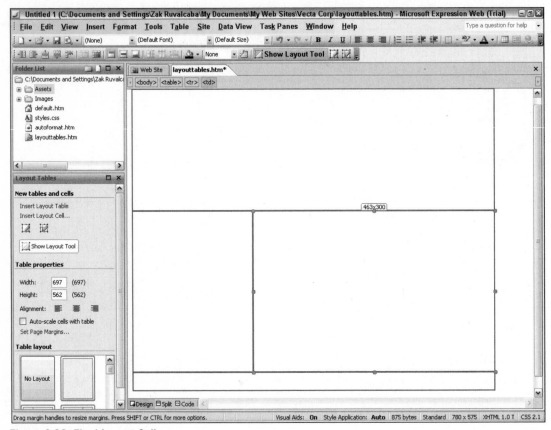

Figure 6-22: Final Layout Cell

Summary

It's hard to argue with the fact that tables offer a feature-rich and robust alternative for structuring elements within your Web pages. Whether you need to incorporate images, text, interactive media elements, or a combination of the three, tables open the door to a whole new world of Web page design.

As you learned in this chapter, tables, when used correctly, offer the designer a graceful alternative to creating rich designs that closely mirror those of print collateral pieces. Whether you're using tables purely to structure data elements within your Web pages, or you're using tables to structure the design of your entire Web site, Expression Web offers an extensive toolset for working with and managing tables within your Web pages.

In this chapter, you explored tables as an alternative Web page structuring technique. Specifically you learned how to insert tables onto a Web page using the Insert Table dialog box. You learned how to select rows, columns, and cells within the table. You also saw how the Modify Table dialog box, the Table menu, and CSS Properties Task Pane can be used to format elements of the table, including inserting, removing, splitting, and merging columns, rows, and cells. Additionally, you learned how to quickly format a table using the Table AutoFormat feature. Toward the end of the chapter, you explored an easier technique for working with table-based Web pages in Layout Tables and Layout Cells.

While tables are an excellent alternative to Web page structuring, the fact remains that Web standards discourage their usage, opting for the more standards-compliant alternative in CSS. As you'll see in Chapter 7, CSS, or more specifically, CSS-P (Positioning), offers even more benefits to pinpoint precise structuring techniques.

Exercise

In this exercise, you completely rebuild the Vecta Corp Web site using tables. When rebuilding the Web site in this exercise, you should perform the following steps:

1. Create new pages for each of the five Vecta Corp Web pages.

2. Within each page, attach the provided `styles.css` file. This will give you access to the redefined <body> tag (which sets the alignment of elements on the page, and sets the margins, background color, font, and font size) and `.navlink` classes.

3. Insert a new 3-row by 2-column table on the page, giving it a width of 697 pixels.

4. Add the header and footer images to their respective cells of the table (the first and third cells).

5. Add a navigation menu within the first cell in the second row. Create links for each navigation item that points to its respective page. Apply the `.navlink` class to each link within the navigation menu. Format the properties of this cell so that the cell has the `mainbg.gif` image attached as the background. Furthermore, set the width of the cell to 240 pixels.

6. Add the content (for each page) to the content cell (cell next to the navigation menu). Customize the cell width to 457 pixels. Add subheader images above the content within the cell.

7. On the main page, add a nested table to control the structure of the Our Solutions and Client Testimonials content.

Advanced Page Structuring Techniques by Using Layers and CSS

In Chapter 6, "Web Page Structuring Techniques by Using Tables," you learned that using HTML tables to structure the content of elements on your Web pages is not only easy, but, when done correctly, extremely flexible. Unfortunately, you probably also noticed that the more complex the site became, the process of getting the tables perfectly adjusted and getting the content exactly where you want it to be was hit-or-miss at best. After working with adding and removing rows and columns, merging and splitting cells, and setting table and cell properties, and having experimented with horizontal and vertical spacing, you might be thinking that there must be a better way to structure your site. This is where layers and CSS positioning come in.

Layers (and more specifically, the CSS positioning properties that drive how layers are created and positioned within the page) allow for what designers have been clamoring at for years, better pinpoint control over their Web designs. After all, print designers have had the luxury of working with programs that allow for text and image boxes that can be freely dragged and positioned anywhere within the development environment for years. Why isn't this functionality also available for Web designers?

Now it is — in layers and CSS. Layers, not unlike text and image boxes in popular print design programs, allow Web designers to freely add elements to the development area, and then freely drag and position those elements anywhere within the development area that they choose. If you need to change the placement, simply drag the layer to another location. The placement of the layers within the Web page is handled using CSS (specifically, positioning properties).

For the developer, positioning within the development area is seamless because the developer needs only to click, hold, and drag a layer (complete with the contents it contains) within the development area to create a Web design with very little hassle. From a browser's standpoint, the design is irrelevant. The browser parses out the positioning properties that are associated within the layer to present a fluid design alternative to basic formatting and table-based formatting techniques.

This chapter represents a major shift in how you design and work with Web pages in Expression Web. Specifically, you will do the following:

❑ Learn about alternative page structuring techniques using layers and CSS

❑ Understand how to insert, draw, nest, and delete layers

❑ Modify layer properties using the Positioning toolbar and Layers Task Pane

❑ Redesign the Vecta Corp Web site using layers and CSS

Throughout this chapter, you learn some slightly more advanced structuring concepts that may seem foreign at first. While some of the concepts may seem frustrating initially, rest assured that the more you use the concepts that you'll learn in this chapter, the less likely you'll be to revert back to using antiquated and deprecated structuring techniques learned thus far.

Introduction to Layers

When you think of layers, if the first thing that comes to mind is digital imaging programs — stop. Although a stacking order is associated with layers, they're better known for alternative Web page design options than they are for creating collages and masking effects.

Layers in the world of Web design mean freedom from messy table workarounds and total control of content layout. To achieve this, layers offer CSS positioning properties for precise placement of elements on the page. Even better, layers offer a third dimension, much like their name suggests. This dimension is called *z-index*, ripped from geometric practices based on x, y, and z coordinates. The higher a layer's z-index value, the closer it appears to the front of the screen. The lower the z-index value, the further away it seems, resulting in an item closer to the background.

And the functionality doesn't stop there. As you'll learn throughout the chapter, layers not only offer methods for positioning and stacking, but also offer properties for showing and hiding layers (also known as *visibility*), for setting the borders and shading, for setting background colors, and much more.

Before I get too far ahead of myself, however, let's backtrack a bit to an introduction and discussion of the evolution of layers. In the late 1990s, the World Wide Web Consortium (W3C) established a new HTML 4.0 specification that introduced radical changes to the way developers could write HTML, and even better, format that HTML using a new and more robust CSS specification. Combined with JavaScript, the phenomenon was coined Dynamic HTML (DHTML) and, thus, introduced designers and developers to a whole new way of working with Web pages.

The idea was simple. DHTML was the harmonious combination of HTML, CSS, and JavaScript. Among other things, DHTML would allow developers to change the style declarations of an HTML element by means of JavaScript. Even better, through the use of "layers," elements on the page could be precisely positioned in the browser window using absolute or relative positioning properties. As part of this transition, browsers scrambled to support what was touted as the next "big thing" in Web development.

As a result of the browser wars of the time, the two major browsers, Netscape and Internet Explorer, ended up supporting very different extensions to the original specification. For example, the HTML 4.0 specification brought about two tags used to generate and work with layers: the `<div>` and `<span>` tags. While

Internet Explorer supported these tags, Netscape 4.0 did not (in terms of creating layers), instead opting for the proprietary <layer> and <ilayer> tags. To make a long story short, the dust settled, and a major shift in the browser industry saw users preferring Internet Explorer over Netscape version browsers and, therefore, the trend moved to support the more popular and much more flexible <div> and <span> tags. Newer versions of Netscape, Firefox, Opera, Safari, and Internet Explorer now fully support the use of <div> and <span> tags, while the <layer> and <ilayer> tags have since been deprecated.

Throughout this chapter, you'll learn about the two tags used when working with layers (the <div> tag much more so than the <span> tag). As you'll see, Expression Web facilitates much of the complex development for you, adding <div> tags automatically for you and, more important, attaching positioning properties to the <div> tags as well. If you feel that you need to manipulate properties for the layers (positioning, stacking, visibility, and so on) manually, the Positioning toolbar and Layers Task Pane are always available and ready for quick property modification.

Working with Layers

Now that you've had a formal introduction to the power of layers, let's actually insert and work with them in Expression Web. In the following sections, you'll learn about the various techniques for working with layers and, more specifically, the CSS properties that support using layers to build table-less Web pages in Expression Web. Specifically, you'll learn to do the following:

- ❑ Insert layers
- ❑ Insert content into layers
- ❑ Modify layer properties via the Positioning toolbar and Layers Task Pane
- ❑ Draw a layer
- ❑ Nest a layer within a layer
- ❑ Add border and shading properties to layers
- ❑ Delete a layer
- ❑ Build a table-less Web page using layers and CSS

Inserting a Layer

There are a couple of options for inserting layers into a Web page. The method you use depends on your needs and skill set. By far, the easiest method for inserting a layer is to use the Layer option located within the HTML set of options when clicking the Insert menu. To use this method, follow these steps:

1. If you haven't done so already, browse to the Wrox Web site and download the files needed for this chapter. Specifically, you'll use the default.htm page; the styles.css file, which contains starter rules for your site; and the images associated with the Vecta Corp Web site. For the purposes of this discussion, open default.htm. You'll notice that, for the most part, the file is blank. Aside from margins, text, and background color properties being set, the page is a blank canvas for you to practice layers on.

2. Place your cursor within the page and select Insert ⟹ HTML ⟹ Layer. The new layer appears on the page, as shown in Figure 7-1.

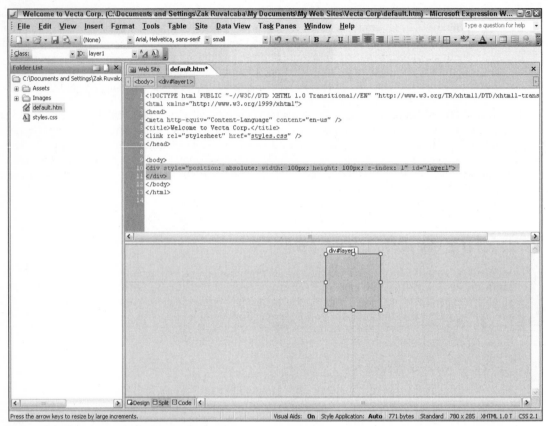

Figure 7-1: New layer appearing on the page

As you can see from Figure 7-1, the layer doesn't look like anything other than a small 100-pixel by 100-pixel box with a 1-pixel border surrounding it. (This border is a visual aid and won't actually render in the browser unless you specifically set a border in CSS.) Rest assured, however, that this small box will offer a whole new world of functionality to you. As you'll see, this new layer can house text and image elements, it can be resized according to its content's dimensions, and more important, it can be accurately positioned anywhere on the page that you wish, altogether making it the most flexible and robust design option within Expression Web.

As you'll also notice from Figure 7-1, Expression Web adds the layer to the page visually, while the majority of the work is performed under the hood in code. As you can see from the code that's added, a layer is nothing more than a `<div>` tag with a unique ID and some inline CSS properties to control the width, height, positioning, and stacking order of the layer. In the coming paragraphs, you'll learn that a layer can be freely positioned anywhere you want on that page. Once you position the layer where you want it, Expression Web also adds the positioning properties `left` and `top` to the inline style rule.

Exploring the layer further, you'll notice some interesting aspects regarding its look within the Design view. To select the layer, simply roll your cursor over the border of the layer until your cursor turns into the Move icon. Now, simply click to select the layer. Notice that the layer highlights and displays small white squares (otherwise known as *resize handles*) at each point and in the middle of each line. Also notice that a handle appears in the top-left corner of the layer (also shown in Figure 7-1) that displays the tag (<div> or <span>) as well as the unique ID associated with the layer.

Ultimately, you can use the small white resize handles to click, hold, and drag out to resize the layer vertically, horizontally, or both. Additionally, you might want to reposition the layer on the page. To do this, you simply select the layer by either its handle or by clicking within the border of the layer, hold the cursor down, and then drag the layer to another part of the development area. You'll also notice that as you drag the layer around, your layer is maintained in the center of a blue crosshair. This visual aid allows you to accurately see where (in pixels) your layer will reside within the context of the browser. This becomes even more helpful when you have rulers shown as it allows you to see where the absolute center of the layer will be positioned vertically and horizontally with the page.

The other method for inserting a layer is to physically draw it onto the page, much like the method that you used for drawing Layout Tables. This method is covered in more detail later in the chapter.

Inserting Content into Layers

Inserting content into a layer is just as easy as it is to insert content into the cell of a table. Obviously, the only major difference is that once you've added content to a layer, it can be freely positioned anywhere you want on the page. To demonstrate this, let's insert text into the layer that you added in the previous section. Then, to demonstrate how to add images to a layer, you'll create a new layer and then drag an image into the layer from the Images folder within the Folder List Task Pane.

Try It Out   **Inserting Content into Layers**

Inserting content into layers is just as easy as inserting content into cells of a table. Follow these steps to learn how:

1.   To insert text into the first layer (the layer you created in the previous section (layer1)), start by opening the home.txt file located within the Assets folder within the Folder List Task Pane. Locate the vProspect 2.0 text within the file, highlight it, and copy it. Once you've copied the text, close the home.txt file.

2.   With the text copied place your cursor within the layer and click Edit ➪ Paste, or press Ctrl+V. The text should now appear within the layer.

> You'll notice that the text is centered within the layer. The reason for this is simple. The styles.css file that is automatically linked into the default.htm file defines the text-align property as centered. The layer, recognizing this, inherits those same properties, and also aligns the text to the center within the layer. To override this, highlight the text within the layer and click the Left Align icon within the Common toolbar. Your text will now be aligned to the left, while text outside of the layer will still be centered on the page.

3.   Create a second layer to insert an image into. You can do this by clicking somewhere outside of the existing layer, preferably within the page. This deselects the layer and prevents a nested

layer from being created instead. Choose Insert ⇨ HTML ⇨ Layer. The second layer (layer2) appears in the development area.

4.   To add the image to the layer, expand the `Images` folder within the Folder List Task Pane, select the `logo_vprospect.gif` image, and drag it into the second, newly created layer. The result will resemble Figure 7-2.

While the layers seem to fit perfectly around their respective elements, you'll probably notice that the text and the image on your design are slightly undersized compared to the size of the layers. To resize the layers to correspond with their content, simply click, hold, and drag the resize handle located in the bottom-right of each layer. Alternatively, you can also double-click within a resize handle to have the layer automatically resize to fit snugly around the content within the layer.

To see how to freely move layers around on the page, move the layer that contains the logo (layer2) and place it just to the left of the text layer (layer1), also shown in Figure 7-2. You'll begin to notice the flexibility that layers offer. Adding them to the page is easy, moving them is easy, and resizing them respective to the content within them is easy. The next few sections discuss the various properties you can set for layers using both the Positioning toolbar and Layers Task Pane.

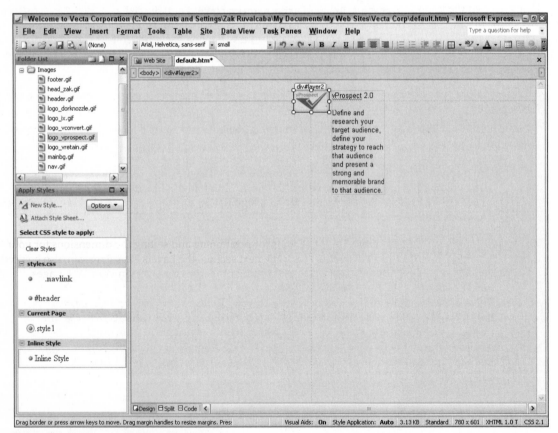

Figure 7-2: Adding an image to the layer

Modifying Layer Properties with the Positioning Toolbar

In most cases, dragging a layer on the page to position it within your Web page will be enough. In other cases, however, you'll need finer control to precisely position a layer within the Web page. Perhaps you require a layer's positioning to be set at exactly 50 pixels from the top of the browser and 50 pixels from the left side of the browser. Dragging a layer to that exact position could pose a problem. Even though you could try and drag it, or even select the layer and click the arrow keys to position the layer, exact positioning will still be tough using these methods. Instead, you may decide to use the Positioning toolbar. As shown in Figure 7-3, the Positioning toolbar (available by choosing View ➪ Toolbars ➪ Positioning) offers visual options for setting positioning, width and height, z-index, and more for a layer.

Figure 7-3: Positioning toolbar

As you can see from Figure 7-3, the Positioning toolbar offers the following properties:

- ❑ *Positioning Type* — Select from this submenu to set the positioning type for a layer. Options include absolute (default), fixed, relative, and static. These options are discussed in much more detail in Chapter 5, "Page Formatting Using Cascading Style Sheets."

- ❑ *Left, Top, Right, and Bottom* — Enter numeric values within these text boxes to set the positioning of the layer from the left, top, right, and/or bottom of the browser window.

- ❑ *Width and Height* — Enter numeric values within these text boxes to set the width and/or height of the layer. By default, these values are represented in pixels (px). To use percents, simply substitute the px value with the % symbol.

- ❑ *Z-Index* — Enter a numeric value within this text box to set the z-index (stacking order) of the layer. Remember that the higher the z-index, the higher in the stacking order the layer is. The lower the z-index, the lower in the stacking order the layer is.

- ❑ *Bring Forward and Send Backward* — Click either the Bring Forward or Send Backward buttons within the Positioning toolbar to either increase or decrease the z-index for a layer by 1.

While this toolbar offers the most precise options for positioning and setting the dimensions for your layers, it isn't the only method. As you'll see in the next section, the Layers Task Pane can also be used as a visual alternative to centrally managing and setting properties for layers in your Web pages.

Modifying Layer Properties with the Layers Task Pane

Another option for customizing layer properties is the Layers Task Pane. You can use the Layers Task Pane as a way to set a layer's ID, visibility properties, z-index, and more. The Layers Task Pane (shown in Figure 7-4) can be opened by choosing Task Panes ➪ Layers. Alternatively, you can right-click a layer's border to access the context menu and choose the Layer Properties option to open the Layers Task Pane.

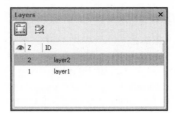

Figure 7-4: Layers Task Pane

With the Layers Task Pane open, you'll immediately notice that the style and overall appearance of the Task Pane is strikingly familiar, looking much like a Layers Task Pane would in an image-editing program. For example, you can drag layers above or below other layers (effectively changing the z-index of the layers on the page), or you can change the visibility of the layer by clicking within the visibility column (represented by the eyeball) to show or hide the layer. You can even double-click on the layer within the Layers Task Pane to manually change the ID for the layer. All this and more is possible through the Layers Task Pane. As you can see from Figure 7-4, the following features are available from the Layers Task Pane:

❑   *Insert Layer* — Click this button to insert a 100-pixel by 100-pixel layer onto your Web page. This option is functionally equivalent to choosing Insert ➪ HTML ➪ Layer.

❑   *Draw Layer* — As you'll see in the next section, clicking this button allows you to manually draw a layer onto the Web page with the dimensions that you want. Rather than being forced to insert a layer with 100-pixel by 100-pixel dimensions, this option gives you total control over how big or small the layer should be by allowing you to draw it onto the Web page.

❑   *Visibility* — You can click in this column for a particular layer to change the visibility property for a layer. Icons include a closed eye (Hidden), an open eye (Visible), and no eye, the default (which represents Inherit).

❑   *Z* — You can double-click the layer in this column to change the z-index (stacking order) for the specific layer. Of course, you can also drag and drop layers above or below other layers in the Layers Task Pane to accomplish the same task. Remember that the higher the z-index, the higher in the stacking order the layer is. The lower the z-index of the layer, the lower in the stacking order the layer is.

❑   *ID* — You can double-click the layer in this column to change the layer's unique identifier (ID). For a `<div>` tag to be considered a layer by Expression Web, it must have an ID.

While the features outlined in the previous bullet points seem relatively obvious, the true power in the Layers Task Pane begins to reveal itself when you right-click a layer within the Layers Task Pane. As you can see from Figure 7-5, right-clicking a layer reveals properties that allow you to cut, copy, and paste a layer, change the layer's visibility, modify a layer's ID and z-index, apply borders and shading, and even manipulate the positioning of the layer.

In detail, the context menu for a layer offers the following customizable properties:

❑   *Cut, Copy, and Paste* — Click one of these three options to cut, copy, and/or paste the layer within a Web page.

❑   *Visibility* — Select from one of the options here to change the visibility property for a layer to either Visible, Hidden, or Default.

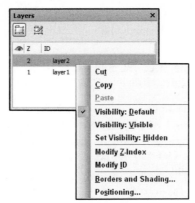

Figure 7-5: Right-clicking a layer to
reveal properties

❑   *Modify Z-Index* — Select this option to change the z-index for a layer. This is functionally equivalent to double-clicking within the Z column for a layer.

❑   *Modify ID* — Select this option to change the ID for a layer. This is functionally equivalent to double-clicking within the ID column for a layer.

❑   *Borders and Shading* — Click this option to launch the Borders and Shading dialog box. You can use this dialog box to add borders and shading properties to your layer. This option is covered with more detail later in this chapter.

❑   *Positioning* — Click this option to launch the Position dialog box. You can use this dialog box to set the wrapping style, positioning style, location, and size of the layer. These options are also available within the Positioning toolbar.

As you can see, the Layers Task Pane offers numerous features to make it easy for you to customize and manage layers for your Web pages. Whether you're adjusting the z-index, ID, visibility, or positioning of a layer, the Layers Task Pane offers an easy and visually intuitive interface for performing any layer-related task that you need.

Drawing a Layer

Another simple alternative to adding a layer to the page is to use the Draw Layer method. Whereas the Insert Layer button on the Layers Task Pane and the Insert ➪ HTML ➪ Layer methods produce a standard 100-pixel by 100-pixel layer, the Draw Layer method, available as the second button within the Layers Task Pane, allows you to click, hold, and drag to draw a layer within the page to the dimensions that you want.

Try It Out   **Drawing a Layer**

Follow these steps to see just how easy it is to draw a layer:

   1.   Within the Layers Task Pane click the Draw Layer button. Your cursor will change to accommodate drawing a layer.

2.   Click, hold, and drag to create a layer with the dimensions that you choose within the Web page. As soon as you let go, the new layer will be created.

3.   Of course, you can add content to a drawn layer just as easily as you added content to an inserted layer. To see this firsthand, select the `subheader_welcome.gif` image from the Folder List Task Pane and drag it into the drawn layer.

The layer is eventually created to look similar to the one created using the Insert Layer method, discussed earlier in the chapter. The only difference here is that by drawing a layer, you are able to set the initial dimensions of the layer to anything you want, as opposed to setting them at the default 100 pixels by 100 pixels. You'll use this method later in this chapter to draw layers when you build the table-less version of the Vecta Corp Web site.

Nesting Layers

Similar to the process of nesting tables within a cell of another table, layer nesting is the process of placing content in one layer that's contained (nested) within a second layer. One key benefit to nesting layers is the ability to structure content in a layer so that it's part of the flow of content of the layer that it's nested within. The main Vecta Corp Web page (`default.htm`), for example, uses the navigation menu on the left side, while the main content for the page is structured centrally on the right.

As you'll see, the design will use one layer to house the navigation items and, more important, the main content text that will appear to the right. Unfortunately, you won't be able to include both the navigation menu and the content text so that they line up in two columns using one layer. Instead, you'll create one layer that houses the navigation items, and then create a second layer, nested within the first, that contains the main content text. Using various CSS properties such as positioning type, float, and more, you'll be able to structure both the navigation items and the nested layer so that they appear to be lined up in a two-column structure. Figure 7-6 illustrates this idea with more detail.

Once you begin to rebuild the Vecta Corp Web site using layers and CSS, CSS properties yet to be introduced (such as relative positioning, the `float` property, the `text-align` property, and more) will begin to make much more sense.

Before you begin building the Vecta Corp Web site using layers and CSS, however, there are just a few more concepts to cover. Nesting layers is one of them.

Try It Out   **Creating a Nested Layer**

Understanding how to nest layers will be important when you rebuild the Vecta Corp Web site using layers and CSS. To see how Expression Web facilitates this process, follow these steps:

1.   With the page you've been working with open, ensure that the Layers Task Pane is available. If it isn't, choose Task Panes ➪ Layers. Now, click the Insert Layer button. Immediately, a new 100-pixel by 100-pixel layer is added to the page.

Figure 7-6: Nesting layers

2. With your cursor positioned in the layer, click the Insert Layer button once again. Again, a new 100-pixel by 100-pixel layer is added to the page. This time, however, the new layer is nested within the first layer. This becomes noticeable when you look at the Layers Task Pane. As you can see from Figure 7-7, the second layer (layer4) has the same z-index as the first layer (layer3), and, more important, is branched off of the first layer (layer3). In Expression Web, this represents a nested layer.

3. To remove the nesting of a layer, simply click the nested layer within the Layers Task Pane, hold, and drag it out (either up or down) of its branch tree.

4. With the layer un-nested, you can easily re-nest a layer by clicking the layer you want to nest within the Layers Task Pane, holding the cursor down, and then dragging the layer into the layer that you want to nest within.

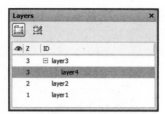

Figure 7-7: The second layer

As you can see, the process of nesting and un-nesting layers isn't all that difficult. As you'll see later in this chapter, what really drives how nested layers (and the content contained within nested layers) function, are the CSS properties that you'll use in conjunction with your nested layers.

Adding Borders and Shading to Layers

In some cases, you might find that adding certain effects to your layers will greatly enhance the appearance and, more important, the usability of layers within your Web pages for your users. Maybe you plan on using layers as a way to organize links hierarchically within your site. When a user rolls over a top-level link, perhaps a "fly-out" menu appears with sub links that are relevant to the top-level menu item. Figure 7-8 illustrates this example.

As you can see in the cropped sample from the www.msnbc.com Web site, MSNBC uses layers to organize a potentially large and complex link structure within its site in a clean, intuitive, and easy-to-find manner. When the user rolls over a top-level menu item, the "fly-out" menu is shown, complete with links that are relevant to the item the user is rolling over. Using positioning properties, the developers of the Web site can position each layer next to its respective menu item. Also, using visibility properties, the developers of the site could set the visibility property of each layer initially to hidden. Then, when the user rolls over a menu item, the particular layer that belongs to the rolled-over menu item has its visibility property change to visible. This is yet another great example of layers in use and a model that you'll replicate in Chapter 8 during the discussion of interactivity with Behaviors.

For the purposes of this section, however, examine Figure 7-8 a bit further. Notice the layer that is currently visible has a thin, 1-pixel, black border surrounding just the right side and bottom. This is where borders come in. As you saw earlier in the chapter, Expression Web offers a Borders and Shading dialog box that's conveniently available from a context menu when you right-click a layer within the Layer Task Pane. Using the Borders and Shading dialog box, you, too, could emulate this effect and more.

Try It Out   Adding a Border to a Layer

To see how the Borders and Shading dialog box can be used to add effects such as borders to a layer, follow these steps:

1. With the page you've been working with open, ensure that the Layers Task Pane is available. If it isn't, choose Task Panes ➪ Layers. Now, right-click layer1 within the Layers Task Pane and choose the Borders and Shading option from the context menu that appears. The Borders and Shading dialog box will appear, similar to Figure 7-9.

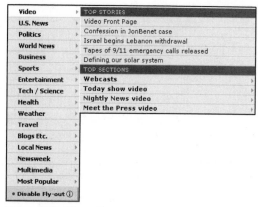

Figure 7-8: "Fly-out" menu

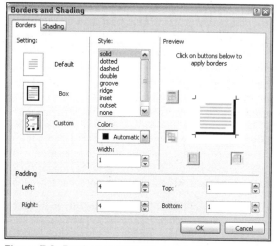

Figure 7-9: Borders and Shading dialog box

2. While the intricacies of the dialog box are discussed in detail later, for now, choose the Custom option from the Setting list.

3. Choose the "solid" option from the Style menu.

4. Deselect the icons that represent lines for the top and left side of the box within the Preview pane. The results of the options that you select are also visible in Figure 7-9.

5. Leave the rest of the options at their defaults and click OK to close the Borders and Shading dialog box. You'll notice that the new border is applied to the layer within the Web page.

6. Save your work and preview the result in the browser by pressing F12. The border should be applied to the layer on the bottom and right side of the layer, similar to Figure 7-10.

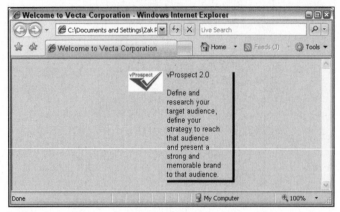

Figure 7-10: Border applied to the layer on the bottom and right side of the layer

As you can see, some of the effects that you previously thought required lines and lines of code to create can actually be created using simple-to-use and intuitive dialog boxes. In this example, you used the Borders and Shading dialog box to create a simple border that surrounded the bottom and right edge of the layer. However, you've merely scratched the surface as it relates to the dialog box. The Borders tab of the Borders and Shading dialog box offers the following functionality:

❑ *Setting* — Choose from one of these three options to set how borders should be applied to the layer. Choosing Default prevents a border from being applied to the layer. When you open the Borders and Shading dialog box for the first time on a layer, this is the option that's selected. Obviously, this is because layers don't have borders associated with them initially. If you'd like a solid border that surrounds the perimeter of the layer, choose the Box option. If you'd like to customize which sides of the layer will have borders associated with them, choose the Custom option.

❑ *Style* — Choose from a list of eight different border styles that may be applied to your layer. Options include solid, dotted, dashed, double, groove, ridge, inset, and outset. When you open the Borders and Shading dialog box for the first time on a layer, the "none" option is selected by default.

❑ *Preview* — For the most part, the Preview pane acts as an iconic representation of what the borders for your layer will look like as you apply properties to it. However, notice the small buttons that surround the top, bottom, left, and right edge of the layer within the pane. Use these buttons to add or remove a border for a particular side of the layer.

❑ *Color* — Choose from the color selection menu to set the color of the border for a layer when one is present.

❑ *Width* — Enter a numeric value within this text box to set the width in pixels for the border of the layer when one is present.

❑ *Padding* — Enter numeric values within these text boxes to set the padding in pixels for the left, right, bottom, and/or top of the layer. Similar to cell padding in tables, a *layer's padding* represents the amount of space between the content and the border of a layer.

Now, switch over to the Shading tab in the Border and Shading dialog box, as shown in Figure 7-11.

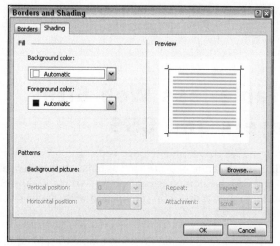

Figure 7-11: Shading tab

The following functionality is available in the Shading tab:

❏ *Fill* — Select a color from one of these color selection menus to set the background and/or foreground color of the layer. Setting the foreground color actually causes the text to change to the color that you select here.

❏ *Preview* — Displays an iconic representation of what your layer will look like as you manipulate properties within this tab.

❏ *Background picture* — Browse to and select an image to use as the background for your layer.

❏ *Vertical and Horizontal position* — When a background picture is specified, enter numeric values within these text boxes to set the vertical and/or horizontal position of the background picture within the layer. These properties are usually specified when the Repeat property is set to "no-repeat."

❏ *Repeat* — Select an option from this menu to specify whether or not the background picture that you've selected should repeat within the layer. Options include "repeat," "no-repeat," "repeat-x" (repeat horizontally only), and "repeat-y" (repeat vertically only).

❏ *Attachment* — Choose an option from this menu to specify whether or not the background picture should scroll along within the content contained within the layer, or remain at a fixed position.

As you've seen, there are numerous properties that you might think about setting for a layer. In general, most of these properties can also be set within the New Style dialog box or CSS Properties Task Pane. However, if you prefer a more direct and dialog box-friendly approach, then maybe the Borders and Shading dialog box is for you.

Deleting a Layer

If you decide that a particular layer is no longer needed, you can easily delete it using one of two methods. The easiest way to delete a layer is to select it on the page and press the Delete or Backspace key on your keyboard. This effectively removes the layer and its content from the page. Alternatively, you could select a layer from the Layers Task Pane and press the Delete or Backspace key. Either method results in the layer being removed from the page.

Designing Table-less Web Sites by Using Layers and CSS

One of the biggest trends in Web development today is designing Web sites that don't use traditional techniques for controlling the structure of a site such as tables, but rather, rely on a more forward thinking approach in layers and CSS positioning to control the layout and flow of Web pages. Known as CSS positioning (CSS-P), positioning properties (in conjunction with layers) can be used to create standards-compliant Web designs.

In the next few sections, you'll dive right into CSS positioning by rebuilding the Vecta Corp Web site using layers and CSS. Specifically, you'll learn how to do the following:

❑   Design a style sheet with page structuring properties in mind

❑   Insert <div> tags and associate them with style rules that define positioning

❑   Use relative positioning to control the flow of elements to coincide with the flow of the page

❑   Work with nested layers in a practical application

❑   Use float properties to control how content that surrounds nested layers should behave

These next few sections, more than any other covered thus far, will truly provide you with a good understanding of the world of layers and CSS for page-structuring purposes. While the topics can become complex, you should hang in there, because the world of Web development is moving more and more every day to this preferred method of content organization and structuring.

Designing Layers Using a Style Sheet

In the previous sections of this chapter, you learned how easy it is to insert layers using either the Insert ⇨ HTML ⇨ Layer option or the Draw Layer option available from the Layers Task Pane. Although these are viable options for designing a page using layers, they aren't the best choice when designing a site that contains many pages. The reason for this is simple. When you use either of these methods to insert layers on the page, Expression Web, as you saw earlier in the chapter, automatically assigns document-wide CSS positioning properties for each layer. While this method is fine for individual pages, it becomes inflexible and nearly impossible to manipulate globally when working with a site that contains many pages.

A better alternative to working with layers, especially when you're designing the structure of a site, is to create an external style sheet (which you already have for the project) and define numerous rules that define the various sections of the page. For example, you know the site will contain the following major sections based on the design you've been working with up to this point:

❑   *Header* — You know you'll have a header that resides near the top of the page. The header will have a width of 697 pixels and a height of 227 pixels. You also know that the header will contain the `header.gif` image. These will be important characteristics to consider when designing the header layer.

❑ *Navigation* — Just under and to the left of the header layer, you will have a simple navigation menu that defines the Home, About Us, Our Solutions, Support, and Contact Us links. In this scenario, you can add a layer that will serve as a container for the five navigation menu items. Even though this layer will contain the navigation menu, it will also contain a nested layer for the content. Because of this, set the width of the layer to **697** pixels and then set the height to **200** pixels. While the height doesn't much matter, it will help to set a starting point so that you may gauge the look of the site as you go.

❑ *Content* — The third section to include on the page is the content layer. Because you'll want this layer to reside next to the navigation items, you'll need to use some CSS wizardry to accomplish this task. As you'll see, you end up nesting this layer within the Navigation layer and then setting the CSS `float` property to left so that the navigation items can be positioned, without error, next to the Content layer.

❑ *Footer* — The final section of the site will define the footer of the page. The footer will have a width of 697 pixels and a height of 35 pixels. Also, the `footer.gif` image will need to reside within this section. Like the Header section, these are important characteristics to consider when designing the footer layer.

Now that I've outlined the major sections within the page, let's begin outlining the CSS rules. Because you know you'll have at least four major sections in the page (Header, Navigation, Content, and Footer), you can surmise that you'll need at least four CSS rules named `header`, `nav`, `content`, and `footer`, respectively.

Try It Out   Designing the Style Sheet for a Layer-Based Web Site

To begin creating the rules that you'll use within the new layer-based Vecta Corp Web site, follow these steps:

1. Create a new HTML page by choosing File ⇨ New ⇨ HTML. Immediately save the page as `default.htm`, overriding the previous page.

2. Attach the existing `styles.css` style sheet by opening the Manage Styles Task Pane (Task Panes ⇨ Manage Styles), selecting the Attach Style Sheet link, browsing for the `styles.css` file, and then clicking OK. Again, the `styles.css` file created for you will set the default font face for the page, the font size, background color, text alignment, and page margins.

3. Create a new CSS style rule by clicking the New Style icon within the Manage Styles Task Pane. The New Style dialog box appears.

4. Enter the selector name **#header** within the Selector text box. Remember that the pound symbol represents an ID. This is the type of selector to use for the layers moving forward.

5. Choose the "Existing style sheet" option from the "Define in" menu. Once this option is selected, the URL menu becomes enabled. Choose the `styles.css` option from that menu.

6. Switch over to the Position category. Select the "relative" option from within the "position" menu. Set the width to **697** pixels and the height to **227** pixels. The New Style dialog box should resemble Figure 7-12 so far.

7. Click OK.

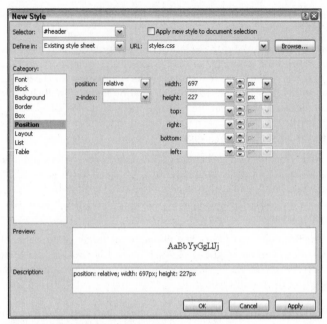

Figure 7-12: New Style dialog box

You'll notice that, in this case, you are using the "relative" positioning type as opposed to the default of "absolute." Because you want the layer to appear centered on the page, you'll need to take advantage of properties that have already been specified when the `<body>` tag was redefined. Because you specified the `text-align` property to center, you can inherit the previously created properties from that tag redefinition and also force the layer to center. To do this, you simply choose "relative" as the positioning type. It's relative to the flow of the page, and since the flow of the page is centered, so, too, will be your layer.

That's it! You'll notice that the `styles.css` file is opened as a new tab within the tabbed file chooser. Selecting it will display the new CSS rule within the code. You'll also notice the new ID appears within both the Apply and Manage Styles Task Panes. This time, however, it appears with a small red dot next to it. The red dot, as you now know, represents an ID.

So far so good. Let's now move to building the rule that will define the navigation menu and ultimately the nested content layer within the Navigation layer. To define the properties that will make up the nav layer, follow these steps:

1. Create a new CSS style rule by clicking the New Style icon within the Manage Styles Task Pane. The New Style dialog box appears.

2. Enter the selector name **#nav** within the Selector text box.

3. Choose the "Existing style sheet" option from the "Define in" menu. Once this option is selected, the URL menu becomes enabled. Choose the `styles.css` option from that menu.

4. Now, you must set the alignment of the content that will eventually appear within this layer. To do this, switch to the Block category and choose the "left" option from the text-align menu. Remember that because the `text-align` property is set to center for the `<body>` tag redefinition, all layers that you define as "relative" will also use that same property and force the contents within the layer to also be centered. To override this, simply choose a different text alignment for the selected layer. This isn't an issue for the header and footer layers because the layers are designed with the exact dimensions of the image that will reside within them. Text alignment has no impact in this case.

5. If you remember from previous versions of the Vecta Corp Web site, a background image was included that ran down the left side of the navigation menu. In Chapter 6, for example, you added this image as a background to a cell that contained the navigation menu. Of course, you can include it here as well. To do that, switch over to the Background category and browse to and select the `mainbg.gif` image from the background-image file field. Because you want this image to repeat vertically only, choose the "repeat-y" option from the Background-Repeat menu.

6. Switch over to the Position category. Select the "relative" option from within the "position" menu. Set the width to **697** pixels and the height to **200** pixels.

7. Click OK to close the New Style dialog box. The new ID will be created and visible within both the Apply and Manage Styles Task Panes.

Now, let's move to defining the properties that will eventually make up the nested content layer. To define these properties, follow these steps:

1. Create a new CSS style rule by clicking the New Style icon within the Manage Styles Task Pane. The New Style dialog box appears.

2. Enter the selector name **#content** within the Selector text box.

3. Choose the "Existing style sheet" option from the "Define in" menu. Once this option is selected, the URL menu becomes enabled. Choose the `styles.css` option from that menu.

4. Choose the Box category, clear the "Same for all" checkbox within the Padding group of options, and enter a value of **15** for left. This will give you a nice 15-pixel pad from the left band in the navigation menu.

5. Switch over to the Position category. In this case, select the "absolute" option from within the position menu. The reason for this is simple. Because the content layer will eventually be nested within the Navigation layer, you'll want to fix the layer at a specific position within the Navigation layer. To fix the layer at a specific position, choose "absolute" and then specify the top and left values. Once you've selected the absolute position type, enter values of **0** for top and **220** for left. This will force the content layer to be positioned at the top edge and 220 pixels from the left of the layer it's contained within. The 220-pixel value that you set from the left of the layer is the space needed for the actual navigation menu. Also within the Position category, set the width to **462** pixels and the height to **200** pixels. That is, 697 (the total width of the layer) minus 462 (the width of the nested layer) minus 15 (the padding from the left) equals the 220-pixel value that you'll use as spacing for the navigation menu. The Position screen should resemble Figure 7-13.

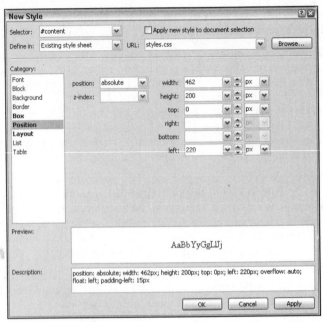

Figure 7-13: Position screen

6. Switch to the Layout category. You will next need to set the "float" property. This property is especially important when working with nested layers as it governs how other elements (the navigation menu, in this case) should wrap around the nested layer. Because you want the navigation menu to wrap around the left side of the nested layer, choose "left" from the "float" menu. Also, choose the "auto" option from the overflow menu. This will allow you to add content within this nested layer that scrolls vertically.

7 Click OK to close the New Style dialog box. The new ID will be created and visible within both the Apply and Manage Styles Task Panes.

The final step in the style sheet development process for the layer-based Web site is to define the properties that will make up the Footer layer. Similar to the Header, the Footer will simply accept a positioning type and width and height properties. To define these properties, follow these steps:

1. Create a new CSS style rule by clicking the New Style icon within the Manage Styles Task Pane. The New Style dialog box appears.

2. Enter the selector name **#footer** within the Selector text box.

3. Choose the "Existing style sheet" option from the "Define in" menu. Once this option is selected, the URL menu becomes enabled. Choose the styles.css option from that menu.

4. Switch over to the Position category. Select the "relative" option from within the "position" menu. Set the width to **697** pixels and the height to **35** pixels. The New Style dialog box should resemble Figure 7-14.

5. Click OK to close the New Style dialog box. The new ID will be created and visible within both the Apply and Manage Styles Task Panes.

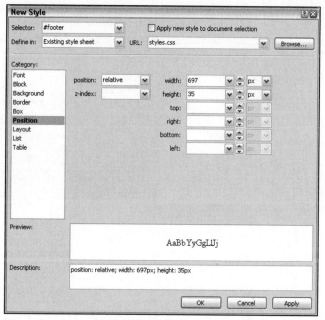

Figure 7-14: New Style dialog box

Now that I've outlined the properties for the four major sections within the site, you're ready to insert the <div> tags that will act as containers for the content. The properties outlined will serve as the formatting and positioning attributes for the <div> tags that you will add next.

Inserting DIV Tags

Now that the style rules have been defined for each section of the page, you can start adding the <div> tags that will serve as the containers for the images and text. Because you've already outlined the style rules using ID selectors in an external style sheet, you need only to insert four <div> tags (one nested) into the page and then associate those <div> tags to ID selectors using the Apply Styles Task Pane. As you'll see, once the <div> tags are inserted into the page, it's simply a matter of dragging the content into the appropriate <div> tags.

Try It Out   **Inserting DIV Tags**

Adding the <div> tags that you'll use as containers for content on your Web pages is an important next step in the layer-based structure of the Web site. To add and subsequently format the <div> tags, follow these steps:

1. With the default.htm page open, start by selecting Insert ⇨ HTML ⇨ <div>. The new <div> tag will be inserted into the Web page.

2. With the <div> tag selected, choose the #header style from the Apply Styles Task Pane. If the Apply Styles Task Pane isn't open, you can open it by choosing Task Panes ⇨ Apply Styles. The <div> tag will change to match the properties that you've specified in the last section for the Header rule.

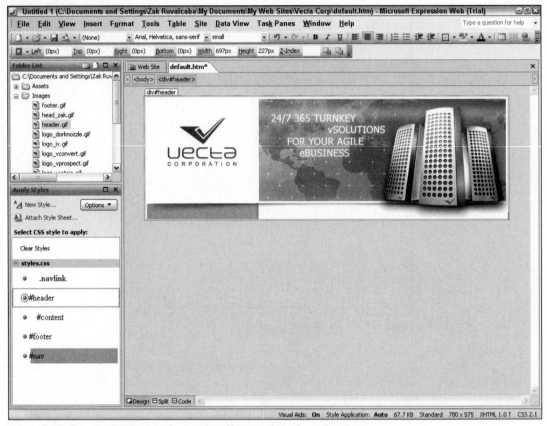

Figure 7-15: Result of dragging the header.gif image into the <div> tag

3. Open the Folder List Task Pane, expand the Images folder for your site, and select and drag the header.gif image into the <div> tag. The result will resemble Figure 7-15.

4. Repeat Steps 1–3 for the Navigation layer. Insert a <div> tag and then choose the #nav style from the Apply Styles Task Pane. In this case, the background image is already applied because you specified it as the background image when you defined the rule.

5. Again, repeat Steps 1–3 for the Footer layer. Insert a <div> tag and then choose the #footer style from the Apply Styles Task Pane. Once the layer appears on the page, select the footer.gif image and drag it into the <div> tag.

6. Before you add the nested content layer, let's build the navigation menu within the Navigation layer. Start by placing your cursor within the Navigation layer and adding the text **Home**. Highlight the text, choose Insert ➪ Hyperlink, enter the text default.htm within the Address text box, and click OK to create the new link. Place your cursor next to the Home link and click Enter to proceed to the next line. Repeat this process until all of the links About Us, Solutions, Support, and Contact Us are created. The result will resemble Figure 7-16.

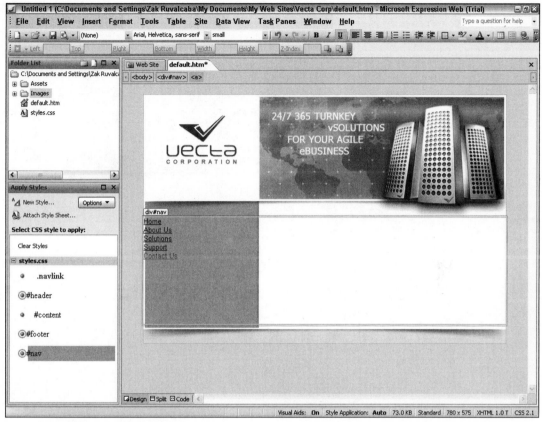

Figure 7-16: Page with links created

7. In the next section, you'll format the look for the navigation menu using contextual selectors. For now, let's insert the nested Content layer. To do this, place your cursor just after the last navigation item (Contact Us) within the Navigation layer and choose Insert ➪ HTML ➪ <div>. With the <div> tag selected, choose the content style from the Apply Styles Task Pane. You'll immediately notice that the Content layer reformats itself according to the properties that you specified when you created the rule. More important, however, the layer appears nested within the Layers Task Pane.

8. To round this out, you'll want to next insert the text that belongs in the Content layer. You can do this by dragging the `subheader_welcome.gif` image into the layer. Then, add a couple of spaces after the image, open the `home.txt` file, copy the content out of the file, and then paste it into the Content layer, just underneath the Welcome image.

9. Save your work and preview the result in the browser. As you can see from Figure 7-17, your layer-based design is right on track.

Figure 7-17: Viewing the layer-based design in the browser

The last step is to customize the look of the navigation items within the Navigation layer. Let's do that next.

Working with Contextual Selectors

The last step to perform before you call the page finished is to format the navigation items that appear within the Navigation layer. If you recall, in the last section, you inserted the navigation items with no formatting. You simply inserted the text and applied a link and left the formatting up to CSS. That CSS, or more specifically, the CSS that governs the look of the navigation items, will be created here. Technically, you could create classes that define the look of each navigation item and then apply the class to the link from within the Apply Styles Task Pane as you have been doing in previous chapters. While this method would work, it's not the most efficient when building a site purely in CSS. A more efficient way would be to use a contextual selector. By redefining the <a> tag in the context of the #nav selector, you could easily format the appearance of all links within the Navigation layer.

A *contextual selector* is a style you define that functions within the context of another style. In this case, you want to style the hyperlinks within the Navigation layer. Because you already have a style created for the Navigation layer, you can easily create a selector that styles the links the Navigation layer contains. To do this, follow these steps:

1. Create a new style by choosing the New Style link within either the Apply or Manage Styles Task Pane. The New Style dialog box will appear.

2. Enter the name of the existing Navigation layer selector (or #nav) within the Selector text box. Now, add a space just to the right of the selector name and add the text **a**. The new selector name will be #nav a. The idea is that you are redefining the <a> tag within the context of the #nav selector.

3. Choose the "Existing style sheet" option from the "Define in" menu. The URL menu will become enabled. Choose the styles.css option from this menu.

4. You'll want to define what the links will look like within the Navigation layer. To do this, choose the "medium" option from the font-size menu, click the "none" checkbox within the text-decoration set of checkboxes, choose the "bold" option from the font-weight menu, and then sample the red (#CC1C0D) color from the Vecta Corp logo from within the color selection menu.

5. Click the Apply button to see the links change on the page below the dialog box, similar to Figure 7-18.

6. The last step will be to add some padding for each element within the navigation menu. You can do this by switching to the Box category, clearing the "Same for all" checkbox, and entering a value of **30** within the left text box.

7. Click OK to close the dialog box. Instantly, your navigation menu should be formatted. Save your work and preview the result in the browser. As you can see from Figure 7-19, the table-less CSS-based Vecta Corp. Web page is complete.

Obviously, there's more that you could add here. For example, you could also create another contextual selector that defines the color that should appear for each link when the user's cursor rolls over an item. The selector name in this case would resemble #nav a:hover. That's the beauty of CSS; there are so many options at your fingertips for not only formatting and styling your pages, but also structuring them as well.

Summary

As you've seen throughout the chapter, layers offer a clean, forward-thinking alternative to developing Web pages. Using CSS in conjunction with layers (<div> tags) affords you the ability to cleanly separate positioning and formatting properties from structural code. Throughout the chapter, you learned about the various methods for working with layers, and the positioning and formatting aspects of layers in CSS. You learned how to use both the Positioning toolbar and Layers Task Pane to insert layers and modify properties offered by layers. You learned how to draw layers and add borders to layers, how to delete layers, and, more important, how to design a Web site so that structurally, it's designed in a clean, standards-compliant way using CSS.

Chapter 8 moves away from page-structuring techniques and into the world of Web page interactivity. Specifically, you learn about Behaviors. As you'll see, Behaviors can be used in conjunction with images, links, and more to create interactivity for your users such as opening browser windows, showing pop-up messages, creating those "fly-out" menus discussed in this chapter, and more.

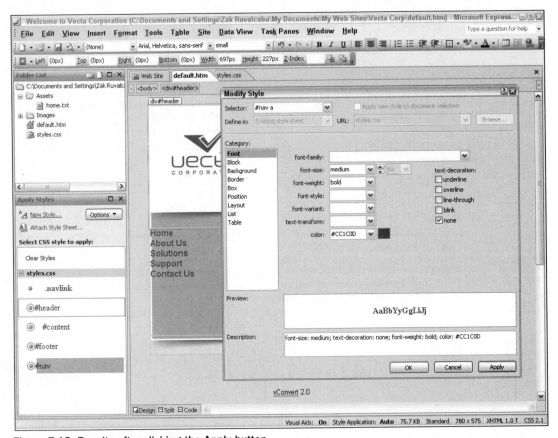

Figure 7-18: Results after clicking the Apply button

Figure 7-19: The CSS-based Vecta Corp Web page

Exercise

In this exercise, you completely rebuild the Vecta Corp Web site using layers and CSS. Follow these steps:

1. In the second half of the chapter, you rebuilt the main Vecta Corp Web page (`default.htm`) using layers and CSS. Now it's time to do it on your own. While you'll eventually create all five pages for the revamped Vecta Corp Web site, start by creating a new page for the main `default.htm` file.

2. Within the page, attach the provided `styles.css` file. This will give you access to the redefined `<body>` tag, which sets the alignment of elements, the margins, and the background color on the page, as well as the font face and font size.

3. Within the same style sheet create four new style rules (as IDs) that represent the four major areas of the Vecta Corp Web site: Header, Navigation, Content, and Footer. You can reference the dimensions, positioning type, and so on by reviewing some of the sections outlined throughout the chapter.

4. Add `<div>` tags to the page, naming them according to the area within the page that they represent. Also, associate each `<div>` tag with its corresponding style rule.

5. Add images, navigation items, and content text to each `<div>` within the page.

6. Create a new contextual selector for the Content `<div>` tag that redefines the hyperlinks within it.

7. Repeat the process for the other pages in the site.

Adding Interactivity with Behaviors

Throughout the book, you've learned some fundamental concepts as they relate to building Web sites. You've learned about functionality available within Expression Web to help you visually structure Web pages, format Web pages, style Web pages, and more. To a certain extent, all of the topics discussed thus far provided you with a generic insight into the world of client-side Web page development. "Client-side," you ask? Client-side Web development is the simple process of adding and formatting content using one, or a combination of three, technologies to structure, format, and provide interactivity for your Web pages to the client's (your audience's) browser.

At the foundation of client-side development lies the first technology: HTML. Everything you do on the Web, to a certain extent, revolves around this technology. Expression Web, by definition, is a visual tool for creating HTML pages for the Web. The second technology, discussed with detail in Chapter 5, "Page Formatting Using Cascading Style Sheets" and Chapter 7, "Advanced Page Structuring Techniques Using Layers and CSS," is, you guessed it, CSS. As you've seen, CSS controls the overall look and appearance (and, to a certain degree, the structure) of Web pages and, again, is significantly supported by Expression Web. The third and final technology, JavaScript, has yet to be discussed.

At its heart, JavaScript exists as a Web-based scripting language. While HTML defines the structure of your client-side Web pages and CSS controls the "look" of your Web pages, JavaScript exists to outline the logic that your Web pages will have in the form of a full-blown interactive scripting language similar in nature (but independent of) the object-oriented programming languages of Java, C++, or C#. For example, you may want to add functionality to your Web page that otherwise wouldn't be available through HTML or CSS, such as creating a pop-up message, a pop-up window, a pop-up menu, or even image-based rollovers for a navigation menu. Furthermore, you might want to add functionality that forces the browser to check for a specific plug-in like Flash, and have the browser react accordingly. All this and much more are possible with JavaScript.

As is true with HTML and CSS, you aren't required to know JavaScript when working in Expression Web. And as is the case with HTML and CSS, Expression Web writes all the JavaScript to make these actions happen in the form of *behaviors*. Available as canned JavaScript snippets of code and available in the Behaviors Task Pane, behaviors in Expression Web are ideal for real-world applications where time is of the essence and your JavaScript writing skills are limited.

In this chapter, you begin to deviate from the formatting, structuring, and styling features that are supported by Expression Web, and you begin to move into the world of client-side interactivity. Specifically, you will do the following:

❑ Learn about behaviors

❑ Understand how the Behaviors Task Pane facilitates the addition and management of behaviors with objects on your Web pages

❑ Use the many behaviors included within Expression Web to create pop-up messages, pop-up windows, image rollovers, and much more

Adding Client-Side Interactivity with Behaviors

To understand how behaviors in Expression Web work, you must first understand the fundamentals of JavaScript. Similar to CSS, JavaScript code is written within the `<head>` tag of your Web page. Unlike CSS, which is written within a `<style>` declaration block, JavaScript is written within a `<script>` declaration block, complete with the `language` attribute defining the language to be written within the script. A typical declaration block within a page might look something like this:

```
<html>
<head>
<title>Sample JavaScript</title>
<script language="JavaScript">

</script>
</head>

<body>

</body>
</html>
```

As you can see from the sample, the code declaration block acts as a container for the logic within the Web page. Of course, this code sample is merely a shell of the functionality. To make the page a bit more interactive, you would add three components to this example: an object, an event, and a function that represents the action you want performed. The final product might resemble something like this:

```
<html>
<head>
<title>Sample JavaScript</title>
<script language="JavaScript">
function showMessage() {
  window.alert("Hello World");
}
</script>
</head>
```

```
<body>
<input type="button" value="Click Me" onClick="showMessage();" />
</body>
</html>
```

In this case, a `Button` form object is added as a way for users to initiate the interaction between themselves and the page. Second, the `onClick` event is added as an attribute to the object. While dozens of events exist for various types of objects, the `onClick` event exists as a way of alerting the browser that, when the button is clicked, the `showMessage()` function should be called, and the code contained within the function should be executed. Finally, the function `showMessage()` is added in the code declaration block. This is where JavaScript gets complex because it represents the functionality you want performed when the user clicks the button. In this case, you want to show a pop-up message with the text "Hello World." To do this, access the built-in `alert()` method of the JavaScript `window` object and pass in the literal text "Hello World" as a parameter to the `alert()` method. When all is said and done, the user clicks the "Click Me" button on the page to receive a message, similar to Figure 8-1.

Does this pop-up message look familiar? Although this code represents an example of JavaScript in practice, it's important to remember that the example is simple. The more functionality you'll need, the more complex the JavaScript becomes. For those who don't consider themselves JavaScript wizards, behaviors, contained within the Behaviors Task Pane, are the perfect alternative to writing JavaScript by hand.

So, what was the relevance of the JavaScript example if you'll be using behaviors and the Behaviors Task Pane from here on out? The answer lies in the process outlined here. Within the code declaration block is the functionality that you need, otherwise known as an *action*. To get that action to execute, you need two things: an *object*, (represented by a `Button` form object in this example) and an *event* (represented by the `onClick` event set as an attribute within the `Button` object in this example).

The beauty in behaviors is that they contain pre-built actions bundled with a set of events. All you need to do is supply the object in the form of an HTML element such as a hyperlink, an image, a form object, or even the page as a whole. Once you've selected an object to use, you simply attach the action using the Behaviors Task Pane, pick a supported event, and you're done! Behaviors, which are essentially pre-built sets of actions bundled with various events, are attached to objects by way of the Behaviors Task Pane. To see this process in action, let's now focus on the Behaviors Task Pane.

Figure 8-1: Message after user clicks the "Click Me" button

Using the Behaviors Task Pane

The Behaviors Task Pane, available by selecting Task Panes ⇨ Behaviors, is the catalyst for attaching behaviors to objects in your Web pages. While the myriad of available behaviors certainly will be covered throughout the chapter, for now, let's walk through the process of attaching a simple behavior, similar to the one you wrote by hand in the previous section, this time using the Behaviors Task Pane.

Try It Out   **Inserting a Behavior**

Attaching behaviors to objects on your Web pages is a task that you'll find yourself performing often. Once you've learned how the process works, it's like riding a bike; you won't forget how to do it a second time. To attach a behavior to an object on the page, follow these steps:

1.   Create a new HTML page by choosing File ⇨ New ⇨ HTML. Immediately save your page as `helloworld.htm`.

2.   With your cursor now blinking in the new Web page, insert a new button form control by choosing the Input (Button) option located within the Form Controls subcategory in the Toolbox Task Pane and dragging it into the page.

> **Although Form Controls are not discussed until Chapter 9, by now you should be familiar with the Toolbox Task Pane, which was discussed in Chapter 1. The Toolbox Task Pane can be opened by choosing Task Panes ⇨ Toolbox.**

3.   With the button selected, open the Tag Properties Task Pane by choosing Task Panes ⇨ Tag Properties. As is the case with all objects in Expression Web, the Tag Properties Task Pane lists all of the properties that can be modified for an element, including your button. Locate the value property and change the value to read **Talk to Me**.

4.   If you haven't done so already, open the Behaviors Task Pane by choosing Task Panes ⇨ Behaviors. With the Task Pane open, click the Insert button to expand the Behaviors list and choose the Popup Message Behavior, similar to Figure 8-2. The Popup Message dialog box will appear.

5.   When the Popup Message dialog box appears, enter the text **Hello World** and then click OK to close the Popup Message dialog box.

6.   Save your work and test the results in the browser by pressing F12. Click the button in the browser to see the pop-up message appear, as shown in Figure 8-1.

As you can see, attaching behaviors to objects is relatively simple. You just select the object within the Web page and then choose the desired behavior from the list in the Behaviors Task Pane.

Beyond the simplicities of attaching behaviors to objects lies functionality for managing events and event views, and determining browser support. The callouts in Figure 8-3 demonstrate the selectable options offered by the Behaviors Task Pane.

Figure 8-2: Popup Message Behavior

Figure 8-3: Behaviors Task Pane

The Behaviors Task Pane offers the following features:

❑ *Events* — After you've added a behavior, the event associated with the action appears within this column. By default, Expression Web lists all events supported by the selected object. Although form objects, hyperlinks, and the page might share similar events, other objects might have different events altogether. To pick a different event for a selected object, click just to the right of the event in the event's row and choose the event from the drop-down menu, as shown in Figure 8-4.

❑ *Actions* — The action associated with the behavior appears in this column. The action cannot be changed, but can be modified by double-clicking it. Doing so opens the original dialog box associated with the behavior.

Figure 8-4: Choosing the event from the drop-down menu

❑ *Insert* — Use this submenu to pick from the list of Expression Web–supported behaviors. All of the behaviors outlined within this submenu are covered in more detail throughout the chapter.

❑ *Delete* — After you've added a behavior, you can remove it by selecting it within the list and clicking the Delete button. You may also delete a behavior by selecting it within this list and choosing the Delete key on your keyboard.

❑ *Reposition Behavior* — When you have multiple behaviors associated with a particular object, use the up and down arrows to position particular behaviors within the list. Doing this allows you to set which behaviors are called before or after others by the browser.

❑ *Tag* — Displays the tag for which the behavior either will be or is attached to. This label is meant for reference purposes only.

As you saw in Figure 8-4, an event's submenu associated with a particular behavior contains events that are relatively easy to understand just by their names. While different objects support different events, in general, there are ten that you'll use most often across the board:

❑ onclick — Event is fired and action is called when the object is clicked.

❑ ondblclick — Event is fired and action is called when the object is double-clicked.

❑ onmousedown — Event is fired and action is called while the user's left mouse click is down. This event works great when you need to call an action repeatedly while the user holds the mouse button down (dragging an object, for example).

❑ onmouseup — Event is fired and action is called when the user's left mouse button is released. This event is similar to the onclick event.

❏   onmouseover — Event is fired and action is called when the user's mouse pointer rolls over an object. This event is particularly useful when working with image-based rollovers.

❏   onmouseout — Event is fired and action is called when the user's mouse pointer rolls out of an object.

❏   onfocus — Event is fired and action is called when the object is highlighted. For example, if your cursor is in the address bar of the browser and you press Tab to highlight the next object (possibly an object in the document), the next object has focus and the address bar loses focus.

❏   onblur — Event is fired and action is called when the object loses its highlight state. For example, if your cursor is in the address bar of the browser and you press Tab to highlight the next object (possibly an object in the document), the next object has focus and the address bar loses focus. That loss of focus is the onblur event.

❏   onload — Event is fired and action is called when the page is loaded.

❏   onunload — Event is fired and action is called when the browser is closed, or a different page is loaded.

Now that you have an idea as to what behaviors are, you're familiar with the Behaviors Task Pane, you understand how behaviors are attached to objects, and you understand the fundamentals of events, let's move forward to begin outlining each behavior in detail. If you recall, clicking the Insert button within the Behaviors Task Pane reveals a set of 15 Expression Web–supported behaviors, as follows:

❏   Call Script

❏   Change Property

❏   Change Property Restore

❏   Check Browser

❏   Check Plug-in

❏   Go To URL

❏   Jump Menu

❏   Jump Menu Go

❏   Open Browser Window

❏   Play Sound

❏   Popup Message

❏   Preload Images

❏   Set Text

❏   Swap Image

❏   Swap Image Restore

Of course, choosing the appropriate behavior is really up to you. Unfortunately, trying to figure out what each behavior does can be a daunting task. For this reason, each of the rest of the behaviors will be described in detail.

The Call Script Behavior

You can use the Call Script behavior when you want to quickly write inline JavaScript for an object without having to switch to Code view. To demonstrate this behavior, let's add a button to the page, which, when clicked, attempts to close the user's browser window. From a technical perspective, when the user clicks this button, the JavaScript function `close()` is called, in which case a Close Window confirmation dialog box is displayed to the user asking if the user would like to close the browser window. Because no behavior exists for this action in Expression Web, use the Call Script behavior instead to write it yourself.

Try It Out   Using the Call Script Behavior

Follow these steps to add the Call Script behavior to an object on your page:

1. With your cursor in the page that you created in the previous section, insert a new button by dragging out the Input (Button) form control from the Toolbox Task Pane.

2. With the button selected, change the value property within the Tag Properties Task Pane to **Close Window**.

3. Next, choose the Call Script behavior from the Insert submenu within the Behaviors Task Pane. The Call Script dialog box appears.

4. Within the dialog box, enter the code **window.close();**, similar to Figure 8-5.

5. Click OK.

6. Save your work and preview the results in the browser by pressing F12. You'll notice that when you click the Close Window button in the browser window, a confirmation dialog box appears asking if you want to close the browser window (see Figure 8-6).

Click Yes here to force the browser window instance to close. Click No to keep your browser window instance open. As you can see, the Call Script behavior allows you to quickly write inline JavaScript functions that don't already exist as behaviors within Expression Web. To intermediate-advanced Expression Web users, this feature is a time-saver.

Figure 8-5: Entering the code

The Change Property and Change Property Restore Behaviors

You can use the Change Property behavior as a way of changing the physical characteristics of a particular object in response to an event. For example, assume that you wanted to set the background color of a layer when a button is clicked. Furthermore, also assume that when that same button is clicked, you want the text "Hello World" to be written within the same layer. All this and more is possible with the Change Property behavior.

Figure 8-6: Confirmation dialog box

In fact, the Change Property behavior is probably one of the most flexible and feature-rich behaviors that Expression Web offers. Not only does it allow you to set background colors and text values for layers, it also allows you to manipulate font and font spacing characteristics for text once it's been dynamically inserted. It also allows you to set the positioning of the layer, set borders for the layer, set visibility properties, and more, all with a simple click of a button.

Even better, the Change Property behavior doesn't just have to be associated with layers, it works for image and input objects as well. Perhaps you want to create a Web-based quiz where scores are dynamically tracked and written within text fields. The Change Property behavior is the perfect solution in this case, because it allows you to dynamically write the numeric score within a text field, just as the text "Hello World" could be dynamically written to a layer.

Try It Out   Using the Change Property Behavior

Again, the Change Property behavior is probably one of the most feature-rich behaviors supported by Expression Web. To give you a general idea of how the behavior has the potential for manipulating the characteristics of objects within your Web pages, let's build on the example outlined previously. Specifically, you'll add a button and a layer to the page. When the button is clicked, you'll use the Change Property behavior to set the background color of the layer, and also set the text "Hello World" dynamically within the layer. To do this, follow these steps:

1. With your cursor in the page, insert a new button by dragging out the Input (Button) form control from the Toolbox Task Pane.

2. With the button selected, change the value property within the Tag Properties Task Pane to read **Colorize and Set Text of Layer**.

3. Add a layer to the page. You can do this by choosing Insert ⇨ HTML ⇨ Layer. Once the layer has been added, freely position the layer within the page.

4. With the button selected, choose the Insert button from the Behaviors Task Pane and select the Change Property behavior. The Change Property dialog box appears.

5. While all of the specifics related to the dialog box will be examined later, for now, choose the Select Element radio button, select the div (because layers are really `div` tags) option from the Element Type menu, and then make sure that the layer's ID is selected from within the Element ID menu (layer1 by default).

6. To set the background color of the layer, click the Borders button. The Borders and Shading dialog box appears. Switch over to the Shading tab and select the red color from the "Background color selection" menu. Click OK to close the Borders and Shading dialog box.

7. You'll use the built-in JavaScript `innerText` function to dynamically write the text "Hello World" within the layer. To do this, click the Add button. The Insert Property dialog box appears. Enter the text **innerText** within the Property Name text box and the text **Hello World** within the Property Value text box. Click OK to close the Insert Property dialog box. The result of the changes made thus far should resemble Figure 8-7.

8. Click OK to close the Change Property dialog box.

9. Save your work and preview the results in the browser by pressing F12.

Within the browser, click the "Colorize and Set Text of Layer" button. Immediately, the layer becomes red and the text "Hello World" appears within the layer, similar to Figure 8-8.

While this discussion has merely covered the basics of the Change Property dialog box, you can begin to see the benefits it offers. Another example of the Change Property behavior might be to add a tooltip to the rollover state of an object. Assuming you had an object on the page that you wanted to provide more information for, you could just as easily add a layer below the object, use the Change Property behavior to change the layer's background color to yellow, set the `innerText` property of the layer so that the descriptive text is added to the layer, and then set the event of the object that calls the Change Property behavior to `onMouseOver`. This would be a practical example of the Change Property behavior's purpose.

Figure 8-7: Change Property dialog box

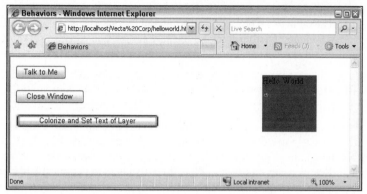

Figure 8-8: Result of clicking the "Colorize and Set Text of Layer" button

Beyond the simplicities of setting the background color and inner text properties for a layer, the Change Property dialog box supports the following functionality (also visible in Figure 8-7):

❑ *Current Element* — Click this radio button to force property changes to be made to the currently selected element. For example, if you wanted the background color and inner text properties to change for the button that's triggering the event, you would select this radio button.

❑ *Select Element* — Selecting this radio button enables the Element Type and Element ID drop-down menus. It's from these menus that you are able to select an element whose properties you want to modify:

   ❑ *Element Type* — Select from a list of Expression Web–supported elements whose properties may be changed using the Change Property behavior. Supported elements include input (text fields, hidden fields, buttons, and so on), div (layers), and images.

> Other elements are also supported in this list and will appear only when the element is added to the Web page. For the sake of simplicity, only the most popular are listed.

   ❑ *Element ID* — Once you've selected the type of element that you'd like to change properties for, choose the unique name for that element from within this list.

❑ *Property list* — As you add properties to manipulate for the selected element, Expression Web outlines the properties that will be changed, including the value for which it will change it to within this list. You'll notice that the two columns in this list outline the Property Name and Property Values, respectively.

❑ *Font* — Click this button to launch the Font dialog box. It's within this dialog box that you are able to change the font face, style, size, color, spacing, and more for text within the selected element.

❑ *Position* — Click this button to launch the Position dialog box. It's within this dialog box that you are able to set the wrapping style (float), positioning style (none, absolute, relative), location (left, right, top, bottom), size (width and height), and stacking order (z-Index) for the selected element. These properties assume that the selected element is a div (layer).

❑ *Borders* — Click this button to launch the Borders and Shading dialog box. It's within this dialog box that you are able to set borders (including the border's size, style, color, width, and padding) for a selected element. Furthermore, as you saw earlier, you can also set the background color, foreground color, and background image for the selected element from within the Shading tab.

❑ *Visibility* — Click this button to launch the Visibility dialog box. It's within this dialog box that you are able to set the visibility properties for the selected element, including Inherit, Visible, and Hidden. These properties assume that the selected element is a div (layer).

❑ *Add, Modify, and Remove* — Click the Add button to open the Insert Property dialog box. As you saw earlier, you can use this dialog box to add other properties that aren't outlined within this dialog box. The `innerText` and `innerHTML` are two such properties. Once you've added your own properties, you can modify or delete them by choosing either the Modify (which launches the Edit Property dialog box) or Delete buttons.

❑ *Restore on mouseout event* — Assuming the event that will trigger the property change on the selected element is `onmouseover`, you can force the browser to restore the properties for the selected element back to their normal state by enabling this checkbox. This effectively adds the behavior discussed next (Change Property Restore) to the `onmouseout` event for the triggering object.

Unless you're relying on the `onmouseout` event to restore the properties of an element (via the "Restore on mouseout event" checkbox), you'll no doubt want some mechanism for restoring the changed properties for an element back to their original state. This is where the Change Property Restore behavior comes in.

Try It Out   Adding the Change Property Restore Behavior

To create functionality that forces an element's properties to be restored to their normal states, follow these steps:

1. With your cursor in the page, insert a new button by dragging out the Input (Button) form control from the Toolbox Task Pane.

2. With the button selected, change the value property within the Tag Properties Task Pane to read **Restore Properties**.

3. With the button selected, choose the Insert button from the Behaviors Task Pane and select the Change Property Restore behavior. The Change Property Restore dialog box will appear, simply alerting you to the fact that the element's properties will be restored.

4. Click OK to close the Change Property Restore dialog box.

5. By default, the behavior is added to the Behaviors Task Pane with the `onmouseout` event selected. Click just to the right of the event within the Events column and choose the `onclick` event from the list that appears.

6. Save your work and test the result in the browser by pressing F12. Click the "Colorize and Set Text of Layer" button to change the properties for the layer. Next, choose the Restore Properties button to restore the layer's properties back to their original states.

The Check Browser Behavior

It's considered common practice in Web development to create pages suited for the variety of browsers currently available. The reason for this is simple. Users who visit your Web site using Internet Explorer 7.0 will have a much richer experience than those visiting your Web site using Internet Explorer for Pocket PC.

To accommodate both users, you may decide to create two different Web sites — one that includes a few images sized to the 320 × 240 pixel dimensions supported by Pocket PCs (limited in functionality, and mostly text-based), and another, a much richer design that could include CSS, JavaScript, and perhaps Flash animations suited for desktop-based browsers such as Internet Explorer, Netscape, Opera, and others. The dilemma is that you'll need some mechanism for detecting the type of browser the user could potentially use to visit your site, and then react to that discovery by displaying the appropriate content. The Check Browser behavior does just this.

Try It Out   **Using the Check Browser Behavior**

You can add the Check Browser behavior to an object on your page by following these steps:

1. With your cursor in the page, insert a new button by dragging out the Input (Button) form control from the Toolbox Task Pane.

2. With the button selected, change the value property within the Tag Properties Task Pane to read **Check Browser**.

3. With the button selected, choose the Check Browser behavior from the Insert submenu in the Behaviors Task Pane. The Check Browser dialog box appears.

4. As you'll notice, the dialog box offers features such as a browser type menu that allows you to choose from a list of common desktop browsers, a Version menu that includes a list of version numbers for the browser type you select, and a set of "Go to URL" text boxes that allow you to specify where the user should be redirected to if the user's browser version falls within the type/version number you specify. For demonstration purposes, choose the Netscape Navigator option from the browser type menu.

5. Choose the "6 and up" option from the Version menu.

6. Click both "Go to URL" checkboxes and enter the URL for the page that you are working with in the first text box (helloworld.htm) and then enter the URL **http://browser.netscape.com/ns8** (the location to download the newest Netscape browser version) in the second text box. The result of customizing the Check Browser dialog box should resemble Figure 8-9.

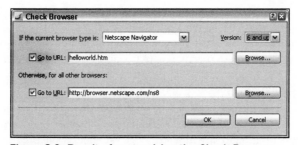

Figure 8-9: Result of customizing the Check Browser dialog box

7. Click OK to close the Check Browser dialog box.

8. Save your work and preview the page in the browser by choosing File ➪ Preview in Browser ➪ Netscape Navigator (assuming you have Netscape Navigator installed).

Assuming your installed version of Netscape Navigator is the newest 8.0 version, when you click the Check Browser button, you're kept within the `helloworld.htm` page. Of course, this is by design because you specified that if the user has Netscape Navigator 6 and up, keep the user on `helloworld.htm`. However, if you click the Check Browser button within an older version of Netscape Navigator, the user is instantly redirected to the Netscape download site.

Of course, the best way to integrate this functionality is to place it within a splash page called `index.htm` that the user doesn't ever get to see. Ideally, when `index.htm` loads, the Check Browser behavior script runs, checks the browser type, and then redirects accordingly. This would make the process much more seamless than forcing the user to click a button. Furthermore, in this example, you used Netscape Navigator as the browser to check for. You may decide to support numerous browser versions, including Internet Explorer, AOL, Opera, and so on. If this is the case, simply continue adding the Check Browser behavior until all of the desired browser types have been satisfied.

The Check Plug-in Behavior

Similar to the Check Browser behavior, the Check Plug-in behavior makes it possible to check whether your end users have a specific plug-in (such as QuickTime, Flash, Shockwave, RealPlayer, or Windows Media Player) preinstalled with their browsers. If the plug-in is detected, you can send the users to a specific page (maybe the page that uses that specific plug-in). If it's not found, however, you can direct them to an alternate page (maybe the page that directs the user to download the specific plug-in).

Try It Out   Using the Check Plug-in Behavior

Follow these steps to add the Check Plug-in behavior to an object on your page:

1. With your cursor in the page, insert a new button by dragging out the Input (Button) form control from the Toolbox Task Pane.

2. With the button selected, change the value property within the Tag Properties Task Pane to read **Check for Shockwave**.

3. Choose the Check Plug-in behavior from the Insert submenu in the Behaviors Task Pane. The Check Plug-in dialog box appears.

4. As you can see, the dialog box shows a current plug-in menu that supports five different plug-in options including Flash, QuickTime, RealPlayer, Shockwave, and Windows Media Player. Similar to the Check Browser dialog box, the Check Plug-in dialog box also offers a set of "Go to URL" text boxes that allow you to specify where the user should be redirected to if the user's browser supports or doesn't support the selected plug-in. For demonstration purposes, choose the Shockwave option from the plug-in type menu.

5. Click both "Go to URL" checkboxes and enter the URL for the page that you are working with in the first text box (`helloworld.htm`) and then enter the URL **http://www.adobe.com/shockwave/ download** (the location to download the newest Shockwave plug-in) in the second text box. Your Check Plug-in dialog box should now resemble Figure 8-10.

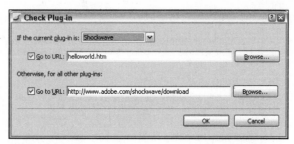

Figure 8-10: Result of customizing the Check Plug-in dialog box

6.   Click OK to close the Check Plug-in dialog box.

7.   Save your work and test the results in the browser by pressing F12.

Click the "Check for Shockwave" button. If your browser supports the Shockwave plug-in, nothing will happen. Again, this is by design because you've specified that the browser should simply stay at helloworld.htm if the plug-in is found. If your browser doesn't have the Shockwave plug-in installed, however, you should automatically be redirected to Adobe's Shockwave download page.

Again, as with the Check Browser behavior, the ideal scenario will have you creating a page that detects the plug-in and responds accordingly, essentially preventing your users from having to click a button.

The Go To URL Behavior

Possibly the easiest behavior to use aside from the Popup Message behavior is the Go To URL behavior. You can use this behavior to quickly associate a link with a form object (such as a Button). Because form objects don't support the href attribute as links do, hyperlinks for form objects must be created using JavaScript. Of course, that JavaScript is conveniently automated using the Go To URL behavior.

Try It Out   **Using the Go To URL Behavior**

Follow these steps to add the Go To URL behavior to an object on your page:

1.   With your cursor in the page, insert a new button by dragging out the Input (Button) form control from the Toolbox Task Pane.

2.   With the button selected, change the value property within the Tag Properties Task Pane to read **Visit Microsoft**.

3.   Choose the Go To URL behavior from the Insert submenu in the Behaviors Task Pane. The Go To URL dialog box appears.

4.   As you can see, the dialog box is fairly simple in concept. You can either browse to and select an existing page from your current Web site, or you can freely type an absolute path that you'd like to link to. For the purposes of this exercise, choose the latter option. Within the Go To URL text box, enter the path **http://www.microsoft.com,** similar to Figure 8-11.

Figure 8-11: Entering the path to www.microsoft.com

5. Click OK.

6. Save your work and test the results in the browser by pressing F12.

When the page loads, click the Visit Microsoft button. You should immediately be redirected to Microsoft's Web site.

The Jump Menu and Jump Menu Go Behaviors

In previous chapters, you learned how to build both text-based and image-based navigation menus. You added a text or image element, highlighted it, and then associated a hyperlink with the element to create a navigation item. When you did this for Home, About Us, Our Solutions, Support, and Contact Us, the result was a full-functioning navigation menu near the top of the Vecta Corp Web site. While this process is the most common method for creating navigation menus, it's not the only way.

The Jump Menu and Jump Menu Go behaviors exist as methods for creating a compact and centrally manageable navigation menu out of the Drop-Down Box form control. While text-based and image-based navigation menus have the potential to take up precious real estate within the Web design, the Jump Menu compacts all of the navigation menu items into a single pick-list control where only one item appears initially. It isn't until the user selects the menu that the rest of the navigation items become visible within the menu.

Try It Out   **Building a Jump Menu**

You can use the Jump Menu behavior as a way of creating a small, compact navigation menu for your Web pages. To see how this behavior works, follow these steps:

1. With your cursor in the page, insert a new drop-down menu control by dragging out the Drop-Down Box form control from the Toolbox Task Pane.

2. Choose the Jump Menu behavior from the Insert submenu in the Behaviors Task Pane. The Jump Menu dialog box appears.

3. Click the Add button. The Add Choice dialog box appears. Enter a text-based choice within the Choice text box such as **Visit Google**. Now enter the URL to Google's Web site (**http://www .google.com**) within the Value text box. The result appears, as shown in Figure 8-12.

4. Click OK to close the Add Choice dialog box.

5. You'll notice that the new choice is added within the Choices list in the Jump Menu dialog box, directly beneath a blank choice. The optional blank choice can be removed or left in place. Alternatively, you may even choose to change the blank choice to read something like "SELECT ONE."

6. Now repeat Steps 3–4, adding choices for Yahoo, Microsoft, and Vecta Corp, all the while linking the choices to their appropriate URLs.

7. Now, let's change the blank choice option so that it's a bit more intuitive to the end user. To do this, highlight the blank choice within the Choices list and click the Modify button. The Edit Choice dialog box appears. Within the Choice text box, enter the text value **SELECT ONE** and then click OK.

8. Once you've finished configuring the Jump Menu dialog box, it should resemble Figure 8-13. Click OK to close the Jump Menu dialog box.

9. Save your work and test the results in the browser by pressing F12. As you can see from Figure 8-14, the selectable menu appears within the browser.

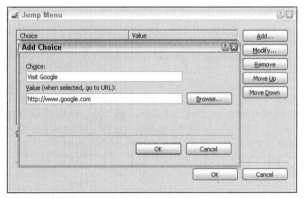

Figure 8-12: Add Choice dialog box

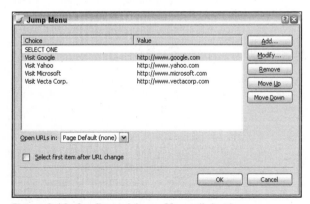

Figure 8-13: Configured Jump Menu dialog box

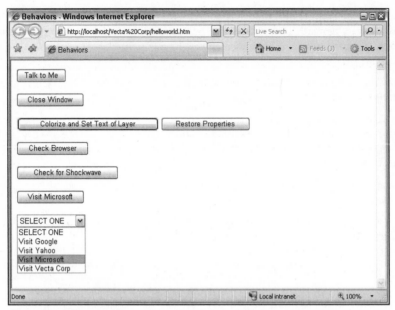

Figure 8-14: The navigation menu in the browser

Try selecting an item from the drop-down menu. Immediately, you'll be redirected to the URL associated with the choice in the menu. While you can't see the event that's created for the menu within the Behaviors Task Pane, under the hood, Expression Web uses the onchange event to detect the selection within the menu. While the process is seamless in most browsers, older browsers such as Netscape 4 or even thin-client browsers such as Internet Explorer for Pocket PC don't recognize this event.

To make this functionality as compatible as possible, you might think about adding a button form control from the Toolbox, assigning the Go value, and then associating the Jump Menu Go behavior to the button. The Go button uses the onclick event, which is understood by all browsers. When the button is clicked, the browser hands off the choice to the same function that is processed by the onchange event for the menu, and the redirection is performed.

The Open Browser Window Behavior

The next stop in this tour of Expression Web behaviors is the infamous pop-up window. Available via the Open Browser Window behavior, you can use this option as a way to open internal and external Web sites within a separate preconfigured window with specific width and height dimensions, among other functionality that you may specify. For example, you may have noticed the small secret cameras or travel advertisements that appear (in a small browser window) when you visit your favorite Web site. While you are certainly discouraged from hounding your users to buy junk, the Open Browser Window behavior certainly serves a purpose. Perhaps your Web site provides an online exam. When the user takes the exam and passes, perhaps a certificate appears within a small pop-up window. The pop-up window would make it easy for the user to print out the certificate by eliminating graphics and oddly placed text that the regular Web site might offer.

Try It Out   Using the Open Browser Window Behavior

While the online exam/certificate example is certainly useful, the Open Browser Window behavior can also be used in instances where you want to make portions of your Web site (or other Web sites) available to users within a small pop-up window. Let's use this as an example next. You can add the Open Browser Window behavior to an object on your page by following these steps:

1. With your cursor in the page, insert a new button by dragging out the Input (Button) form control from the Toolbox Task Pane.

2. With the button selected, change the value property within the Tag Properties Task Pane to read **Open Google**.

3. With the Button selected, choose the Open Browser Window behavior from the Insert submenu in the Behaviors Task Pane. The Open Browser Window dialog box appears.

4. As you can see, the Open Browser Window dialog box allows you to customize numerous properties, including the URL to display, the width and height of the window to open the URL in, and a simple name to assign to the pop-up window. You can also customize various attributes, including whether or not scrollbars should be added, whether or not to allow the user to resize the browser window once it's been opened, and so on. For the purposes of this exercise, enter the URL **http://www.google.com** within the "Go to URL" text box.

5. Assign the dimensions of **400** for "Window width" and **400** for "Window height." When you've finished, the dialog box should resemble Figure 8-15.

6. Click OK. As expected, you'll notice that the `onclick` event is assigned to the button within the Behaviors Task Pane for the action. Of course, if you really wanted to annoy your users, you could change that event to `onload`. That alteration would cause the Open Browser Window action to execute when the page is loaded, as opposed to when the user physically clicks the button. In an effort to maintain retention rates among your users, keep the `onclick` event and simply allow your users to click for themselves.

7. To preview the finished product, save your work and preview the page in the browser by pressing F12.

As you can see from Figure 8-16, clicking the button opens the Google Web site in a small 400 pixel by 400 pixel window.

Figure 8-15: Customized dialog box

Figure 8-16: Result of clicking the "Open Google" button to open the Google Web site

You'll also notice that the pop-up window is fairly plain and doesn't allow for much interaction in terms of scrolling to see all of the Web site content, or even resizing the window to make it bigger. However, if you remember, the Open Browser Window dialog box allows you to customize various attributes, including setting checkboxes for scrollbars and resize handles. In fact, the Open Browser Window dialog box supports the following functionality (accessible by double-clicking the behavior within the Behaviors Task Pane):

❑ *Go to URL* — In this text box, enter the URL of the site you'd like to display within the pop-up window.

❑ *Window name* — Enter a value within this text box to uniquely name the browser window. This value is optional.

❑ *Window width and height* — Enter the width and height (in pixels) at which you want the pop-up window to initially display within these text boxes.

❑ *Attributes* — Use these checkboxes to set whether or not you want to display the navigation toolbar, a location toolbar, a status bar, or a menu bar; enable scrollbars; or even provide resize handles. For this example, check the "Scrollbars as needed" and "Resize handles" options.

Again, save your work and preview the result in the browser by pressing F12. This time, when the pop-up window opens, you are free to resize and scroll through the pop-up window as needed.

The Play Sound Behavior

The next behavior to discuss is the Play Sound behavior. You can use this behavior as a way of playing sound files such as MP3, MIDI, WAV, and so on, within the browser window. While popular browsers such as Internet Explorer have the capability of playing most sound files directly within the browser, others may require additional software such as QuickTime to play the sound correctly. Netscape might even prompt you with a dialog box, giving you the option to choose the external audio player (QuickTime, Windows Media Player, iTunes, or RealAudio, and so on) to use.

Try It Out   **Using the Play Sound Behavior**

You can add the Play Sound behavior to an object on your page by following these steps:

1.   With your cursor in the page, insert a new button by dragging out the Input (Button) form control from the Toolbox Task Pane.

2.   With the button selected, change the value property within the Tag Properties Task Pane to read **Play Sound**.

3.   Choose the Play Sound behavior from the Insert submenu in the Behaviors Task Pane. The Play Sound dialog box appears.

4.   It's within this dialog box that you are able to browse to and select a sound file to use. A simple MIDI file called `playsound.mid` has been included within the `Media` folder for the chapter's files. Choose it.

5.   Click OK to close the Play Sound dialog box.

6.   Save your work and test the result within the browser by pressing F12.

If you're using Internet Explorer, the sound is played without the need for additional software directly within the browser when the button is clicked.

> You should be aware that a Stop Sound behavior doesn't exist. Therefore, the only way to stop the sound file from playing is to close the browser. If your users find your sound file annoying, they may be tempted to close the browser or navigate to a different page in an effort to avoid it.

The Preload Images Behavior

Typically added to image rollovers (covered later in this chapter), or when the page loads for the first time, the Preload Images behavior can be used as a way of forcing the browser to load certain elements first, before other elements on the page are rendered. This behavior is beneficial when working with image rollovers because they require two images to function correctly.

As you'll see, when the page loads, a user sees the first image. As soon as the user's cursor rolls over the image, an event (typically the `onmouseover` event) kicks in and calls necessary JavaScript code that changes the image to a second, usually different-colored image. On slower connections, the second image might appear as a broken image for a split second while it has a chance to load. To avoid showing a broken image icon (even for a split second), use the Preload Images behavior. This behavior forces the browser to load all images that are viewable on the page and to preload any images that might not be viewable on the page but must be queued for use in an effect such as a rollover. For the most part, this behavior is automatically added when working with most image-based behaviors, including rollovers in Expression Web.

The Set Text Behaviors

If you recall, earlier in the chapter you used the Change Property behavior to set the background color of a layer to red and the inner text value of the same layer to read "Hello World" when the user clicked a button. The Set Text behaviors are similar in concept to the Change Property behavior in that they allow you to dynamically set text values within not only layers, but frames, the browser's status bar, and a text field with a simple click of a button. Of course, with the numerous event and object combinations, setting text values for a layer, a frame, the browser's status bar, and a text field is not only limited to button clicks, but also to page loads, image mouseovers, and much more.

Try It Out   Using Set Text Behaviors

To give a general idea into how some of the Set Text behaviors work, let's use the Set Text of Status Bar to set the text "Hello World" within the browser's status bar when the user clicks a button. To do this, follow these steps:

1. With your cursor in the page, insert a new button by dragging out the Input (Button) form control from the Toolbox Task Pane.

2. With the button selected, change the value property within the Tag Properties Task Pane to read **Set Text of Status Bar**.

3. Choose the Set Text of Status Bar behavior located within the Set Text submenu of behaviors available by clicking the Insert button in the Behaviors Task Pane. The Set Text of Status Bar dialog box appears.

4. Within the Set Text of Status Bar dialog box, enter the message that should appear within the status bar when the user clicks the button. For this example, enter the text **Hello World**.

5. Click OK to close the Set Text of Status Bar dialog box.

6. Save your work and test the result in the browser by pressing F12.

When the page appears, click the Set Text button. Immediately, the text in the status bar changes to read "Hello World." Of course, this example demonstrates one method for setting text using the Set Text set of behaviors. If you wanted to set text for a layer, a text field, or a frame, simply pick one of the other Set Text behaviors to accomplish the task.

The Swap Image and Swap Image Restore Behaviors

For years, Web designers have strived to enhance the visual and aesthetic look of their Web pages by adding new and exciting features that push the envelope of what was previously possible on the Web. With the introduction of vector-based animation programs some years ago, Web-based, client-side scripting options for spicing up the visual appeal of Web pages fell by the wayside, giving way to more robust and flexible alternatives.

One client-side scripting technique for enhancing the visual appeal and usability of Web pages that has stood the test of time and shows no sign of ever going away is the rollover image. A *rollover image* is one that appears as a standard image within a Web page, maybe even an element within a navigation menu. It's called a rollover image because the image appears to change color when the user's mouse rolls over the image. Of course, the image isn't just magically changing color, but rather is replacing a standard image, with a second, different color image.

From a client-side scripting (JavaScript) perspective, the process is actually relatively simple. Initially, the browser loads the standard image (image1). Usually that image fits into the color scheme of the site and appears just like every other image that may belong to the group that the image surrounds. When the user's mouse rolls over the image, the onmouseover event is fired, client-side code is then executed, and the first image (image1) is dynamically replaced by a second (usually different color variation of the original image) image (image2). The process is then reversed when the user's mouse rolls out of the image. The user's mouse rolls out of the image, the onmouseout event is fired, and the original image (image1) replaces the rolled over state of the image (image2).

Of course, creating this effect is made much simpler via the Swap Image and Swap Image Restore behaviors. Rather than writing all of the tedious code to create this functionality, Expression Web conveniently includes the Swap Image behavior. And, because Expression Web assumes that you'll want to restore the image when the user's cursor rolls out of the image, it automatically adds the Swap Image Restore functionality for you as well.

Try It Out   **Creating an Image Rollover**

To see just how easy it is to create an image-based rollover, follow these steps:

1. Within the Folder List Task Pane, expand the Images folder and drag out the nav_home1.gif image so that it appears within the helloworld.htm Web pages that you've been working with.

2. Select the image and choose the Swap Image behavior from the Insert submenu in the Behaviors Task Pane. The Swap Images dialog box appears.

3. As you'll see, the dialog box includes various features outlined near the end of this section. For now, click the Browse button to browse to and find the image nav_home2.gif. This image, as you'll see, looks exactly like the original image, with one slight difference. It's a different color. Once you've found the image, the path will appear within the Swap Image URL path.

4. Make sure the Preload Images and "Restore on mouseout event" checkboxes are both checked. Once you've made your selections, the Swap Image dialog box will resemble Figure 8-17.

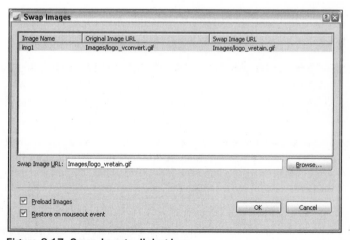

Figure 8-17: Swap Image dialog box

5. Click OK to close the Swap Image dialog box.

6. Save your work and test the results in the browser by pressing F12. As you'll see, rolling over the image causes the second, different color image to appear.

As you can see, creating rollover images is fairly simple. You include an image from the Folder List, select the image, attach the Swap Image behavior to the image, and find the image that you want to set the source to when the user's mouse rolls over the image. You may have noticed that the Swap Images dialog box outlines other functionality that you may want to be aware of. For the sake of thoroughness, the following list outlines this functionality, also visible in Figure 8-17:

❑ *Images list* — Use this list box to select the image you want to create a rollover for. Because you have only one image on the page, the image appears as the sole image in the list. It's important to note that the Swap Image behavior is attached to a single object, in this case, the Home button. Setting the source to multiple images within this dialog box would cause other images to swap states when you rolled over the Home image. If this is not the desired effect, attach a separate Swap Image behavior to each and every element that will have a rollover effect.

❑ *Swap Image URL* — Browse to and select the file you want to use as the rollover state. In this example, you found and selected the nav_home2.gif image located within the Images folder for the chapter's files.

❑ *Preload Images* — As you learned earlier in this chapter, it's important to preload images, especially when working with rollover images. Preloading images prevents a user with a slow connection from seeing a broken image for a split second while the secondary image is trying to load when the mouse rolls over an image. You should leave this option checked at all times. This checkbox prevents you from having to manually add the Preload Images behavior for your rollovers.

❑ *Restore on mouseout event* — Clearing this box causes the image to remain in its rollover state. Checking this box ensures that the rollover image returns to its original state when the user's mouse rolls out of the image. You probably noticed that the Swap Image Restore behavior is listed under the Swap Image behavior within the behaviors list. Clicking this checkbox prevents you from having to manually add this behavior for each and every image.

Summary

As you've seen throughout the chapter, behaviors, offered via the Behaviors Task Pane, offer a new level of development possibilities that require little knowledge of JavaScript. By utilizing some of the behaviors outlined in this chapter, you can offer a broad range of interactivity for your users that requires little to no development time.

This chapter introduced various concepts, including JavaScript and how JavaScript code and events are added onto the page. This provided a foundation for discussing the Behaviors Task Pane, the catalyst that drives the addition of behaviors to objects within your Web pages. As you progressed through the chapter, you looked at the various behaviors that are included within the behaviors list in Expression Web.

Chapter 9 begins a transition from client-side Web development to the world of server-side Web development. Starting with forms and form objects (which are covered in Chapter 9), server-side Web development offers developers an unprecedented (and yet complex) world of dynamic development possibilities, including working with databases, e-mail, blogs, and more.

Exercise

In this exercise, you use images provided within the Images folder of the Vecta Corp Web site to rebuild the navigation menu for the Vecta Corp Web site. Additionally, you'll use the Swap Image behavior to create rollover functionality for each navigation item in the menu. For this exercise, you should perform the following steps:

1. Open the main Vecta Corp Web page default.htm.

2. In the space provided, where the navigation menu should reside, drag each image (nav_home1.gif, nav_aboutus1.gif, nav_oursolutions1.gif, nav_support1.gif, nav_contactus1.gif) into place to create an image-based navigation menu.

3. Select each image individually and attach the Swap Image behavior. Set the source of each image's rollover state to the second image provided (nav_home2.gif, nav_aboutus2.gif, nav_oursolutions2.gif, nav_support2.gif, nav_contactus2.gif).

4. Repeat the process for the other pages in the site.

Working with HTML Forms and Form Controls

If you've used Web sites such as Amazon, Yahoo!, Google, MSN, E*TRADE Financial, eBay, and more, chances are you've used and interacted with HTML forms and may or may not have even known it. Forms are everywhere on the Web, and once you know what to look for, they're hard to ignore. Furthermore, they push development to a higher level by facilitating interaction between the client and server. Whether it's through registration forms, mailing lists, site searches, or online ordering, forms facilitate interaction between us as developers and the organization (server) we represent, and our end users (clients). Forms allow us to be "connected" with our end users by serving as a stepping stone to a whole new medium known as "Web application development." Covered in more detail beginning in Chapter 10 and moving forward, Web application development (an extremely broad and extensive topic) begins, to a certain extent, with forms.

This chapter serves as a stepping stone to a more complex, yet development rich topic known as Web application development. By the end of this chapter, you should have a deep understanding of forms and form controls; specifically, you will do the following:

❑   Understand the concept behind forms

❑   Learn the difference between forms and form controls

❑   Be able to differentiate between buttons, drop-down lists, text areas, checkboxes, radio buttons, text boxes, image fields, file fields, hidden fields, group boxes, labels, and more

An Introduction to HTML Forms

As just mentioned, forms are everywhere on the Web. They allow developers to collect and ulti-mately process data from end users. Let's take eBay as an example. As a buyer, you visit eBay in an attempt to find a sweet deal on something you probably don't need. When you visit eBay, you don't verbally tell eBay to find an item. Instead, you interact with a form containing form controls in the shape of a search text box and a Search button, similar to the one shown in Figure 9-1.

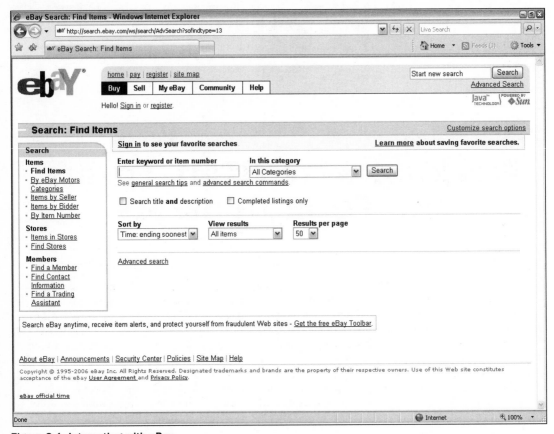

Figure 9-1: Interacting with eBay

You enter your search criteria into the text box, click the Search button, and magically the results are returned in a clean list format that you can quickly browse through. From a development standpoint, eBay uses forms and form controls to facilitate the interaction between the end user (that's you, the client) and eBay (the server). From a design standpoint, forms and form controls make it easy for users to enter the criteria that they want more information on. As a buyer, you may be familiar with this process. It's straightforward, easy to use, and, more important, intuitive.

From a seller's perspective, the process is slightly more complex, but again, involves forms and form controls. When you want to sell an item on eBay's Web site, the first step is to register as a seller. Again, this process is shown with more detail in Figure 9-2.

The point here isn't to sell eBay's services; it is to show that numerous form controls exist in an effort to collect different types of information from the seller — form controls similar to the ones you'll be using in this chapter. Text boxes, like the one used in the search form, are used to collect general information such as first name, last name, address, city, e-mail address, and so on. Drop-down lists are used to allow the user to choose from a predefined set of states and countries, and from lists of months, days, and years for birthdays. In addition, if you scroll further down the page, a checkbox is used to collect a value indicating that yes, the user accepts the user agreement when checked, or if left unchecked, no, the user does not agree with the user agreement. Finally, a button control is used to submit the information to eBay's servers for processing. (Chapter 10 discusses server-side processing of form content.)

Both models (buyer and seller) demonstrate forms and form controls used in real-world Web sites that millions of people use on a daily basis. Of course, forms and form controls aren't exclusive to eBay. Companies all over the Web use forms and form controls so that users can interact with the services they offer on their Web sites.

Even with this explanation, you still might be unclear about the differences between forms and form controls. To clear up any confusion between the two, think of the process of registering for a driver's license at your local Department of Motor Vehicles (DMV). You wait in line until your turn comes up. You tell the (usually expressionless) attendant that you'd like to register to receive a new driver's license, at which point, the attendant hands you a form.

Think about what that form contains. Paper-based forms, like the one from the DMV, contain places for you to enter your name, address, city, ZIP, phone number, car model, car type, and so on. The places on that driver's license registration form can be considered form controls. You fill out the form (that is, you fill in all the form controls, or fields) and hand it back to the attendant for processing. The Web is no different. Forms on the Web contain form controls just as the DMV's registration form contains areas for you to enter your personal information, car details, and so on.

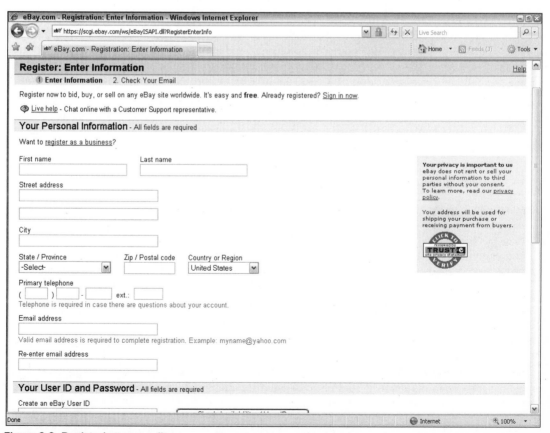

Figure 9-2: Registering as a seller

Now that you have an idea about what forms and form controls are, and when and where they are used, let's actually build them within the context of our project. The rest of the chapter dissects forms and the various types of form controls you can use when working with HTML forms in Expression Web.

Working with Forms and Form Controls

As mentioned in the previous section, the addition of form controls begins with the addition of a form. You can think of the form as the container for its form controls. When the user clicks the Submit button, the entire form (along with all the form controls in the form) is sent for processing. To this end, the form contains numerous properties that tell the browser where and how the form will be sent for processing when the Submit button is clicked. Before jumping too far ahead, however, let's add a simple form to a Web page.

Try It Out	Adding a Form to the Contact Us Page

Up to this point, you've left the `contactus.htm` page untouched. Sure, you've designed the page's structure, but the content has been purposely excluded as we hadn't discussed forms or form controls yet. Let's begin building out the page now, beginning with adding the crucial first step to dynamic Web page development: the form. To add a form to the page, follow these steps:

1. If you haven't done so already, open the Web site for this chapter within Expression Web. From the Folder List Task Pane, double-click the `contactus.htm` page to open it. As you'll see, the majority of the page structure has been completed for you. By now, I'll assume that you understand how to perform basic structuring techniques to put together a site. What is important right now is adding a form and form controls to the "contact us" page so that the potential Vecta Corp clients can easily contact the company for questions.

2. Ensure that the Form Controls node is expanded from within the Toolbox Task Pane. As you saw in Chapter 8 (when you added the `Button` control to work with behaviors), the Toolbox Task Pane can be opened by choosing Task Panes ⇨ Toolbox.

3. From the Form Controls set of objects, click, hold, and drag out the Form control so that it appears within the page just underneath the Contact Us subheader image, as shown in Figure 9-3.

Congratulations! You've just taken a giant first step toward dynamic Web development by adding the form. With the form control selected within the page (as it is in Figure 9-3), open the Tag Properties Task Pane by choosing Task Panes ⇨ Tag Properties. Like every object that you include on a Web page within Expression Web, the form control includes modifiable properties that you should be aware of. While some properties are used by all elements, others, like the form control, offer unique properties that tell the form where to send the data when the Submit button is clicked, how the data should be sent, and more.

The properties that you should be aware of include the following:

❏ name/id — Associate a value with either one of these properties to uniquely identify your form. While these values aren't specifically required, it's highly recommended that you add a value here, especially when working with client-side scripting languages such as JavaScript that rely on forms and form controls to be uniquely identified. For the purposes of this exercise, name the form "**contactusForm**."

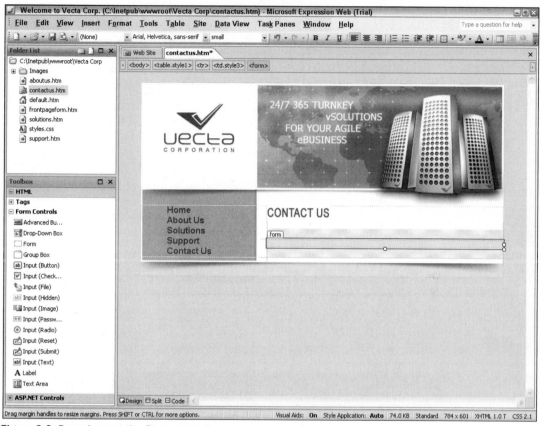

Figure 9-3: Dragging out the Form control

> name **is included for backward compatibility. According to the World Wide Web Consortium (W3C), the** name **attribute is deprecated.** ID **should be used in its place whenever possible.**

❑   action — This is by far the most important property that you can set for a form. This is where you'd enter the path to the page that will process the form when the user clicks the Submit button. While the long-winded explanations will be saved for the next few chapters, for now, know that every form's submission requires some sort of data-collection endpoint. That endpoint is generally a database, text file, XML file, or even a straight e-mail to a recipient. To get the form into that data-collection mechanism, an intermediary file (containing functions with code) must process the form and perform the insertion into the data-collection mechanism. For this chapter, that page has been created for you. The path and the value you'll want to enter into this text box is **http://www.vectacorp.com/scripts/contactus.asp**.

❑   method — Select one of the two options from this menu to set how the form should be sent to the intermediary file for processing. Two options available from this menu are post and get.

The method post, which is the Expression Web and browser default, embeds the form within HTTP headers, essentially unseen by anyone. Nine times out of ten, you'll use post in your development efforts because it's a much more secure alternative to get. However, you can use get to send the contents of all form elements within the form, appended as parameters within the URL of the page. This is beneficial when working with searches as the user can bookmark a recent search since the submitted search value is appended to the URL of the page.

Take a look at the address bar in Figure 9-4. As you can see from the lengthened URL string, eBay uses get when submitting searches for processing. If you look carefully, you can see that everything from the search value to the category of the search is included within the address bar. This allows the user (and eBay) to later bookmark/save popular searches and return to them with one click of a button.

Searches are about all you want to use the get method for. Because of the potential security vulnerability and the fact that URL strings are limited to 8,192 characters, longer forms (especially those containing sensitive data such as usernames, passwords, social security numbers, and credit card information) should be sent using the post method. For the purposes of this discussion, let's leave the form's method set to post.

Figure 9-4: Appended URL

> Even post isn't entirely secure. When using post, form data is embedded into the HTTP headers — it's not encrypted. An attacker can still compromise sensitive information using an HTPP packet sniffer. For this reason, sensitive data should always be transmitted using post over a secure connection (SSL).

❑ *enctype* — Choose an option from this menu to specify the MIME encoding type of the data submitted to the server for processing. By default, forms are sent using the application/x-www-form-urlencode type, but it's not uncommon to use the multipart/form-data type, especially when uploading files using the Input (File) form control. Even if you don't physically select an option from this menu, the form is sent using application/x-www-form-urlencode. For this reason, leave this option as is.

Although these four options aren't the only ones listed within the Tag Properties Task Pane, they are the most common for forms. As you can see, other options include *class* (for associating style classes with forms), *target* (tells the form where the intermediary file associated with the action should be opened), and others.

Now that you have an idea about how forms are inserted into the page, let's focus on inserting form controls into the form. The form controls you can insert in Expression Web include the following:

❑ Text and password fields

❑ Text area

❑ Checkbox

❑ Radio button

❑ Drop-down box

❑ Button (including Submit and Reset buttons)

Other miscellaneous form controls that are also covered here include the following:

❑ Advanced button

❑ Image field

❑ File field

❑ Hidden field

❑ Group box

❑ Label

Input (Text) and Input (Password)

Arguably, the most widely used form control is the text field, represented by the Input (Text) form control within the Toolbox Task Pane. Because text fields are so versatile, they're the perfect option when you need to create an area on your Web page into which your users can freely type plain text.

As you build Web applications, the time will come when you'll find yourself building a user-authentication Web page. As you've seen, user-authentication pages collect the username (represented by a plain text field) and a password from the user. While the username text field will always be a generic text field, for security purposes, the password text field should have some sort of mechanism for shielding wandering eyes from seeing your password as you type it in. This is where the password text field comes into play. Represented by the Input (Password) control within the Toolbox Task Pane, the password text field collects a user's password, and as the user types the password into the text field, the text is shown with asterisks instead of the plain text.

Try It Out   Adding Text Fields

Chances are you'll use the Text Field form control more than any other form control in the Toolbox Task Pane. So that you're familiar with its usage, let's add a couple of text fields to the contactus.htm page. To do this, follow these steps:

1. Place your cursor within the form you inserted in the previous section and insert a new table by choosing Table ⇨ Insert Table. When the Insert Table dialog box appears, give the new table 9 rows, 2 columns, a width of 457 pixels, and a border thickness, cell padding, and cell spacing of 0 pixels. Click OK to close the Insert Table dialog box. You'll use this newly inserted table to cleanly position text captions and form controls on the page.

2. In the first three cells of the first column, add the text **Name:**, **Phone:**, and **Email:**, respectively. You may need to reposition the table's columns so that they line up evenly.

3. Select the Input (Text) control from the Toolbox Task Pane and drag it into the first cell of the second column. The new text field will appear similar to Figure 9-5.

As was the case with the form control, the text field offers numerous text field–specific properties that you might want to be aware of. To view these properties, select the text field and open the Tag Properties Task Pane if it isn't already open. While the text field outlines numerous properties that are consistent with other HTML elements, the following are the most important:

❑ name/id — Associate a value with this property to uniquely identify the text field within the form. Although associating a value with either one of these properties isn't required, truthfully, there isn't much you can do with a text field if you don't set a value here. The application that processes the form must reference a specific text field by its unique name to grab the value it contains. For our purposes, set the id property of this text field control to **name** to correspond with the text caption in the same row.

❑ size — Associate a value with this property to set the width in characters for the text field within the form. Leaving this field blank sets the text field's character width to the default value of 20. A character width of 20 is too small for our purposes here, so enter the numeric value of **40**.

❑ `maxlength` — Associate a value with this property to set the maximum number of characters that this text field will accept. This is an excellent value to set when you want to limit a ZIP code text field to five characters or an age Text Field to three characters max. For the purposes here, leave this option as is.

❑ `value` — Associate a value with this property when you want a note or initial value to display within the text field when the page is first loaded within the browser. To see this with more detail, open eBay's Web site once more. Once you do, take a look at the search text field located within the top-right corner of the Web page. You'll notice the value "Start new search" that appears within the text field. This is the text field's initial value.

While these properties are unique to the text field, others will appear and can be set regardless of which form control you use. Some of the more important properties are as follows:

❑ `type` — In reality, checkboxes, radio buttons, text fields, password fields, text areas, file fields, image fields, hidden fields, and buttons all use the `<input>` HTML tag in code. The only unique identifier between all of these controls is the `type` attribute, represented here by the type menu. As you'll see from this menu, Expression Web offers you a quick way of changing an inserted control to any one of the controls listed by quickly selecting the specific option from the menu. Obviously, you should leave the "text" option selected here.

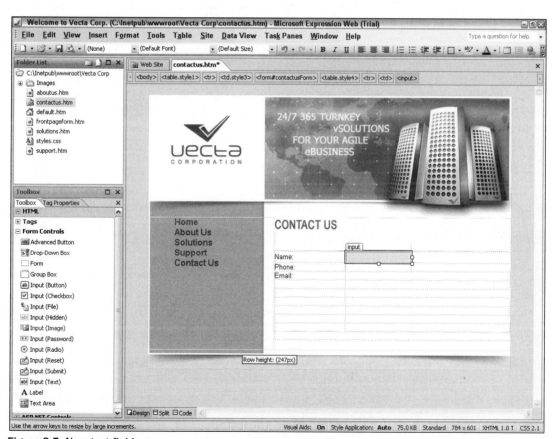

Figure 9-5: New text field

❑   `class` — When working with CSS, select a class from this menu to set the overall style of the text field. For our purposes, leave this blank.

❑   `tabindex` — Associate a numeric value with this property to set the tab order for the text field within the form. The idea here is that users should be able to tab through form objects in the browser without having to click (using their mouse). Setting the tab index for each form control is important to form building, because it prevents users from bouncing around randomly from form control to form control on the page. By default, if no tab index is set for form controls, the browser tabs top to bottom, meaning that a form control closest to the top will have a lower tab index by default. As the user presses the Tab key, the next form control, closest to the previous form control, is tabbed into. To override the default tab order, you can manually set the tab index here. A form control with a lower `tabindex` will be highlighted before a form control with a higher `tabindex` as the user tabs through the form.

❑   `readonly` — Associate a value with this property to prevent users from being able to type text into the text field. When left blank, the browser interprets this value as false, meaning "allow the user to type text into this text field." To overwrite this value, enter the text **true**. This guarantees that the text field will be read-only, preventing users from typing text into it.

❑   `disabled` — Like the `readonly` property, enter either a true or false value to disable or enable the text field. By default, the browser renders this property as true, meaning that the browser can read values from it and the user can physically type into it. If you'd like to disable the text field, enter the value **false** here.

Now that you have an understanding of the properties associated with text fields, let's add two more text fields to handle the collection of the user's phone number and e-mail address. Again, select the Input (Text) control from the Toolbox Task Pane and drag it into the second cell of the second column. Repeat this process to add a third text field within the third cell of the second column. This time, name the second and third text field **phone** and **email,** respectively. You should also set the size properties to **40** for both text fields.

Text Area

You can use the Text Area form control in scenarios where you want to allow your users to enter a large volume of text. Additionally, while the text field allows the user to enter text across a single line only, the Text Area, on the other hand, allows the user to enter text on multiple lines. The perfect scenario for the Text Area form control would be if you needed to add a questions/comments area within your Web page.

Try It Out   **Adding a Text Area**

To explore the use of the Text Area, let's add it to the `contactus.htm` page. To do this, follow these steps:

1.   In the fourth cell of the first column, add the text **Questions:**.

2.   Select the Text Area control from the Toolbox Task Pane and drag it into the fourth cell of the second column. The new Text Area will appear, similar to Figure 9-6.

3.   With the Text Area selected, switch over to the Tag Properties Task Pane and assign the name "questions" to the Text Area.

As you can see from Figure 9-6, the Text Area form control looks slightly different than the text field form control. While they both collect input from the user, the Text Area allows the user to enter large amounts of text and on multiple lines. It's for this reason that the scrollbars appear just to the right of the Text Area.

Similar to the text field and other input controls, the Text Area offers properties for assigning a unique name; associating a CSS class; and determining whether the Text Area should be read-only or not, disabled or not, and more. Following are the properties that are unique to the Text Area:

❑   `cols` — Associate a numeric value with this property to set the width in characters for the Text Area. For the purposes here, enter the value **32**. This will allow it to match up closely with the other text fields.

❑   `rows` — Associate a numeric value with this property to set the height in rows for the Text Area. As you can see, Expression Web defaults this value at 2. For the purposes here, enter the value **4**.

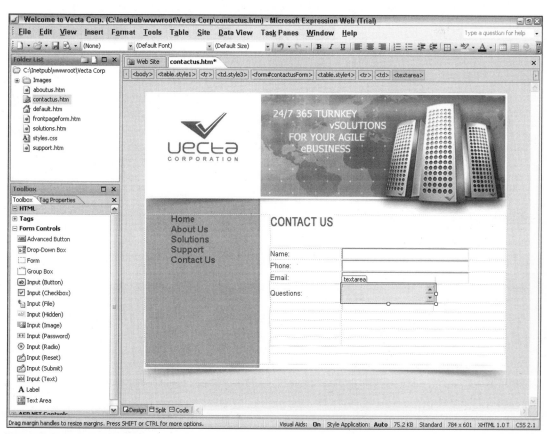

Figure 9-6: New Text Area

Input (Checkbox)

Checkboxes, similar to the ones that appear in numerous Expression Web dialog boxes, allow you to enable or disable selections within forms. More important, however, checkboxes enable you to select multiple options from a group of options. For example, in the contactus.htm page, you'll want to ask the users what their current server configurations are. Assuming that they're interested in one of Vecta Corp's solutions, it will be important for a sales representative at Vecta Corp to identify the user's server configuration before proceeding with a call back to the user. And, because a user's organization could potentially have a disparate server configuration such as Windows, Mac, Linux, or UNIX, you'll want to allow the user to select multiple items by enabling multiple checkboxes. If the user has only one item, fine. But, at the very least, you want to provide the user with the opportunity to select multiple items. Collecting as much information as possible from users will help the sales representative better serve their needs.

Try It Out   Adding Checkboxes

To demonstrate how checkboxes are added to a Web page, follow these steps:

1. Place your cursor in the fifth cell of the first column and enter the text **Servers:**.

2. Now find the Input (Checkbox) control from within the Toolbox Task Pane, select it, and drag it into the fifth cell of the second column.

3. Place your cursor to the right of the checkbox and enter the text **Windows**. Press Enter to create a line break.

4. Repeat Steps 2 and 3 three more times, adding a checkbox and entering the text **Mac**, **Linux**, and **Unix**. Once you've finished, the page should resemble Figure 9-7.

5. Now switch over to the Tag Properties Task Pane and provide the same name for each of the four checkboxes. Name them all **servers**.

Again, looking at the Tag Properties Task Pane for each checkbox reveals numerous properties that are shared by not only other form controls, but by other HTML elements as well. Following are the properties that are unique to the checkbox:

❑   *value* — The value you enter here is the value that will be sent to the server for processing. For the four checkbox controls, you'll want to enter values of **Windows**, **Mac**, **Linux**, and **UNIX**, respectively.

❑   *checked* — You can set the state of the checkbox control to either checked or unchecked when the form loads for the first time. By default, the browser renders this value as false. However, if you'd like a checkbox's state to appear checked when the page loads, enter the value **true** here.

Input (Radio)

Similar to the checkbox control, the radio button control allows users to select options within a form. The difference between radio buttons and checkboxes, however, is that with radio buttons, users can select only one option from a group of options. You can apply the concept of a radio button to this example by asking users if they're already a client of Vecta Corp. Because radio buttons allow you to select only one option from a group of options, the user is forced to answer either "Yes" or "No."

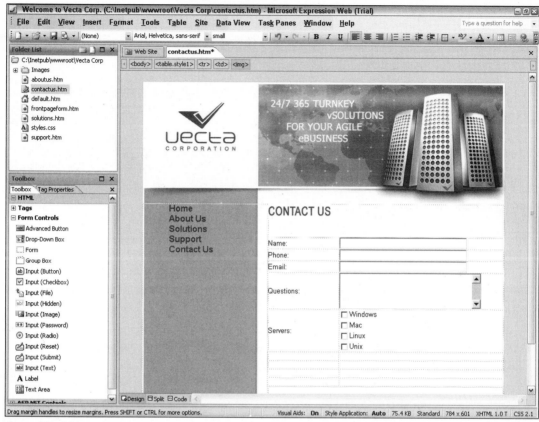

Figure 9-7: Adding checkboxes

Try It Out | Adding Radio Buttons

To see how radio buttons can be applied to a Web page, follow these steps:

1. Place your cursor in the sixth cell of the first column and enter the text **Current Customer?**.

2. Find the Input (Radio) control from within the Toolbox Task Pane, select it, and drag it into the sixth cell of the second column.

3. Place your cursor to the right of the radio button and enter the text **Yes**.

4. Repeat Steps 2 and 3 one more time, adding a radio button and entering the text **No**. Once you've finished, the page should resemble Figure 9-8.

5. Switch over to the Tag Properties Task Pane and provide the same name for both radio buttons. Name them **currentcustomer**.

6. The radio button, like the checkbox control, uses a value property to store the value that the server-side processing application will collect and ultimately use. For the purposes of this exercise, select the first radio button (the one with the "Yes" label next to it). Switch to the Tag Properties Task Pane and associate the text "Yes" within the value property. Repeat this process for the second radio button, associating the text "No" as the value in this case.

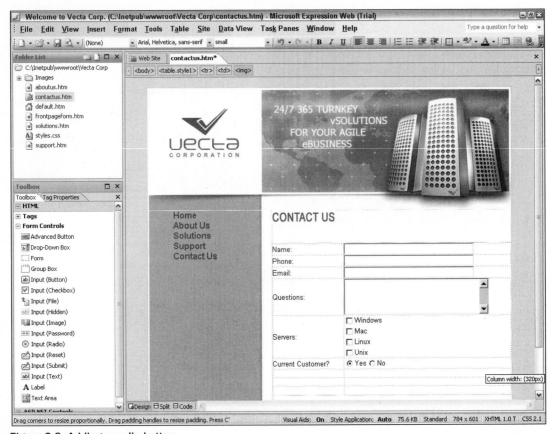

Figure 9-8: Adding a radio button

Drop-Down Box

In terms of selecting choices from a group of options, you're not restricted to simply using the checkbox and radio button form controls. Instead, you may decide to use the drop-down menus or list boxes to accomplish the same task. Available via the Drop-Down Box form control, you can use the drop-down menu as a way to store numerous values in one expandable and collapsible menu. Alternatively, modify the "multiple" property for the Drop-Down Box and the drop-down menu becomes a scrollable boxed pane that can store numerous values (otherwise known as a *list box*). Furthermore, depending on how you configure the list box, users navigating the list box can hold down the Ctrl key and click to select multiple options within the list. For the purposes here, configure the Drop-Down Box to allow users to choose which Vecta Corp solutions they're interested in.

Try It Out   Adding a Drop-Down Box

To see how Drop-Down Box form controls can be used as either a drop-down menu or a list box, follow these steps:

1. Place your cursor in the seventh cell of the first column and enter the text **Which solutions are you interested in?**.

2. Find the Drop-Down Box control from within the Toolbox Task Pane, select it, and drag it into the seventh cell of the second column.

3. Switch over to the Tag Properties Task Pane and provide the name for the Drop-Down Box as "solutions." So far the, Drop-Down Box will resemble Figure 9-9.

4. Now, switch over to the Tag Properties Task Pane and provide the name **solutions**.

5. For the most part, the Drop-Down Box form control outlines the same properties as other controls that you have used thus far. The only major difference here is that you are able to associate the `multiple` value with the `multiple` property within the Tag Properties Task Pane. Leaving this option blank, which is equivalent to a `false` value, causes the Drop-Down Box control to appear as a drop-down menu. Adding the `multiple` value here converts the Drop-Down Box to a list box control. For the purposes of this exercise, select the `multiple` value here. Instantly, the Drop-Down Box becomes a list box control.

6. The next step is to add items to the list box. You can do this by right-clicking the list box and choosing the Form Field Properties option from the context menu that appears. The Drop-Down Box Properties dialog box will appear, as shown in Figure 9-10.

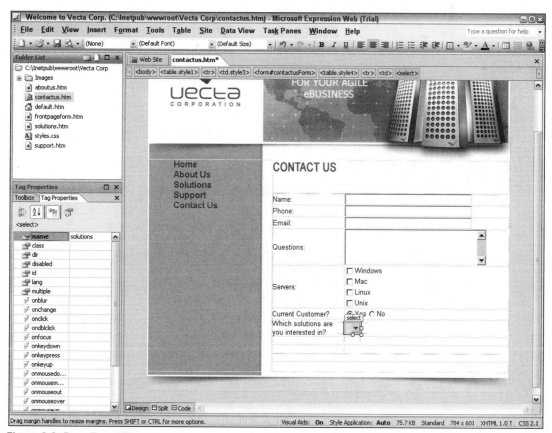

Figure 9-9: Drop-Down Box

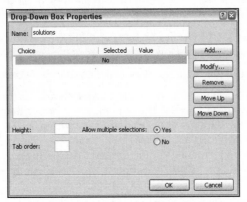

Figure 9-10: Drop-Down Box Properties dialog box

As you'll notice from the Drop-Down Box Properties dialog box, most of the properties that you can set here can easily be set from within the Tag Properties Task Pane. What can't be set from the Tag Properties Task Pane, however, are the items that should appear within the control. The Drop-Down Box Properties dialog box is where this task can be accomplished. To do this, follow these steps:

1.   From within the Drop-Down Box Properties dialog box, click the Add button. The Add Choice dialog box will appear.

2.   Within the Choice text box, add the text **vProspect 2.0.** You'll notice that the value is automatically populated for you. If you'd prefer to enter your own value, simply choose the Specify Value checkbox and replace the value within the text box with your desired value. Furthermore, if you'd like this choice to be initially selected, choose the Selected radio button.

> **The difference between Choice and Value boils down to how the server-side processing application handles values. Typically, you'd enter a value when the text contained within the text choice can't be used by the server-side processing application. Months of the year are a perfect example. Inherently, server-side code can't work with text labels for months of the year. It can, however, work with numbers. Most users, however, understand text labels for months better than they do numeric values. For this reason, you could enter the text label January within the Choice text box and then enter the numeric value 01 within the value text box. Users get to see the text, while the server-side processing application gets a crack at the numeric value.**

3.   Click OK to close the Add Choice dialog box. You'll see that the new choice appears within the Choices list.

4.   Repeat Steps 1–3, adding the choices **vConvert 2.0** and **vRetain 1.0**, respectively.

5.   Once the three items have been added to the choices list, select the first, blank item within the list and click the Remove button. The result of the finished Drop-Down Box Properties dialog box resembles Figure 9-11.

6.   Click OK to close the Drop-Down Box Properties dialog box. The three choices will now appear within the list box control on the page.

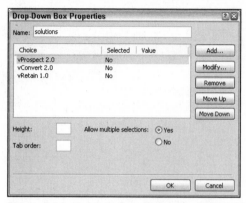

Figure 9-11: Finished Drop-Down Box Properties dialog box

Input (Button), Input (Submit), and Input (Reset)

Possibly the simplest form control to use and understand is the button. As you saw in Chapter 8, the generic Button control was used to interact with various behaviors within your Web page. Because the Button control has no default action associated with it, it's the perfect choice to use with a variety of client-side tasks.

The Submit button, on the other hand, does have a default action associated with it. The Submit button, when clicked, initiates the transfer of the form to the processing application outlined in the form's action. It's that simple! All you have to do is supply the form's action, insert a Submit button, and when the button is clicked, the browser instantly sends all of the form controls and their values to the server-side processing application. The Reset button can be used when you want to simply clear the values out of the controls within the form.

To demonstrate how the Submit and Reset button controls operate, let's add them to the Contact Us page now.

Try It Out   Adding Submit and Reset Buttons

To demonstrate how Submit and Reset buttons can be added to the page, follow these steps:

1. Find the Input (Submit) control from within the Toolbox Task Pane, select it, and drag it into the ninth cell of the second column.

2. Find the Input (Reset) control from within the Toolbox Task Pane, select it, and drag it into the ninth cell of the second column, next to the Submit button. The result of adding the buttons resembles Figure 9-12.

Again, like most of the controls in Expression Web, the Submit and Reset buttons use and share properties of other controls covered thus far. The one property that you'll want to be aware of is the value property. Changing this value effectively changes the text that appears on the button itself.

For example, by default, the "submit" and "reset" buttons appear lowercase. If you'd prefer to capitalize the first letter on both buttons, simply select the button, and change the value property to read "Submit" and "Reset," respectively.

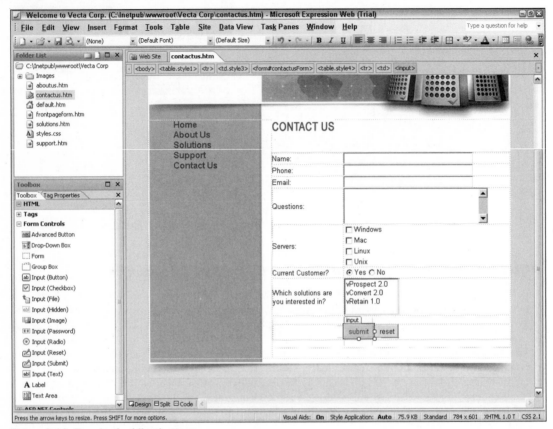

Figure 9-12: Result of adding buttons

Testing the Form

The form is taking shape nicely and is now ready for testing within the browser. To see how users will interact with your form, save your work and preview the page in the browser. When the page appears, fill out the form controls, entering text into the text fields, picking options from the checkboxes and radio buttons, and making selections from the list box. When you've finished, click the Submit button.

Instantly, the browser sends the form values to the server-side processing application (the Microsoft ASP page residing on the Vecta Corp server) outlined within the Action property for the form. The result is a simple confirmation page that thanks you for contacting Vecta Corp and outlines the values that you've entered/selected in the form. At first glance, it may seem confusing as to what exactly happened. The process of sending form information to the server for processing will be cleared up beginning in Chapter 10. For now, let's cover the process at a basic level.

As mentioned in the beginning of the chapter, forms exist as a way for organizations to collect information from their end users (clients). By clicking the Submit button, the user can send the form and the form control's values to an application (server), defined in the form's Action field, for processing. Figure 9-13 diagrams this process.

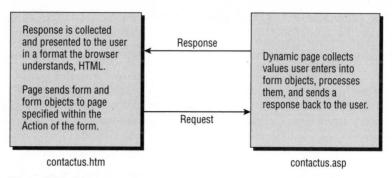

contactus.htm

contactus.asp

Figure 9-13: Form process

This approach is central to the way thousands of organizations (also known as *application service providers*) do business on the Web. In this scenario, the contactus.htm form page (which is what the client interacts with) is what you've just created. The application, contactus.asp, has already been created and resides on the server (www.vectacorp.com). The application's sole purpose is to collect the values in the form controls and simply redisplay them in the client's browser in a readable format. As you'll learn in Chapter 10 and moving forward, these applications can get much more complex than the simple example presented here. For now, this should give you an idea about the role of forms and form controls.

Other Controls to Consider

For the most part, the controls covered up to this point will be the ones you use most often within your forms. It's important to note, however, that other controls also exist for extending the functionality outlined by your forms. For example, rather than using the standard, generic browser-specific Submit button, maybe you decide to use your own custom image as the Submit button's style. If this is the case, then you'd use the Image Field control [Input (Image)]. Additionally, maybe you'd like to offer a field that allows users to browse for, select, and upload a file from their computers to the server. When this is the case, then you'd use the File Field control [Input (File)].

The remaining sections of this chapter shed some light into the following lesser-used form controls:

❑ The Advanced button

❑ The Image field

❑ The File field

❑ The Hidden field

❑ The Group Box

❑ Labels

Input (Image)

The drawback to using form buttons is that they all look alike. If you look at Figure 9-12, for example, the form buttons have a standard grey, beveled look that is only slightly different depending on the operating system you are using. Really, the only way to differentiate form buttons is by the text that appears on the button. And while you can create CSS styles to reformat the look of form controls including buttons, there is a quicker way to control the look of the Submit button in the image button control.

The image button control makes it easy to customize the look of your Submit buttons by allowing you to associate the submit action with a customized image that you are responsible for creating. What this means is that you can now create an image that fits into the overall look and feel of your Web site, and then use it to represent the submit action for your forms. In this example, the Submit and Reset buttons don't match the overall aesthetics of the site. To remedy that, remove the Reset button and replace the Submit button with your own custom image using the image button represented by the Input (Image) control within the Toolbox.

Try It Out   Adding an Image Field

To add an image field control to the page, follow these steps:

1. Because the Submit and Reset buttons don't flow with the overall design of the Vecta Corp Web site, start by selecting and removing them from the `contactus.htm` page.

2. Select the Input (Image) control from within the Toolbox and drag it into the ninth cell of the second column (where the Submit and Reset buttons used to be). The control will appear as a broken image icon. The reason for this is simple: You haven't associated the image to use with this control yet.

3. With the image field selected, switch to the Tag Properties Task Pane and locate the `src` property. Once you've identified the property, click the button icon that appears within the value field to launch the Select File dialog box. With the dialog box open, navigate to the Image folder of the site, locate the image `imagefield_submit.gif`, select it, and click Open. The Select File dialog box will close and the image button's look is instantly changed to appear similar to the look of the image shown in Figure 9-14.

Once again, the properties offered by the image control are the same as those covered up to this point. The only unique property here is the `src` property. As you saw in Step 3, the `src` property represents the path to the image file that should be associated with the control.

The Advanced Button

As you've undoubtedly noticed, the Submit and Reset buttons that you added and tested in the previous sections were limited in terms of customization. For the most part, you added the buttons, and the three-dimensional, generic, operating system–styled button appears within the browser. While the image field aims to solve this problem to a certain extent, the issue remains that you still have to have some knowledge of image-editing programs to be able to customize the button to your liking.

The Advanced Button, also available from the Form Controls section in the Toolbox Task Pane, allows you to add the standard operating system–styled button, yet allows flexibility in terms of customization through styles. The term "Advanced Button" is actually slightly deceiving. Perhaps a better name for the button should be "Stylized Button."

To give you an idea as to how the Advanced Button can be added and styled on a Web page, select the button from the Toolbox Task Pane and drag it into your page. If you switch to the Tag Properties Task Pane, you'll notice that there aren't any new properties offered by this control that you haven't seen revealed by other form controls in Expression Web to this point. What makes the Advanced Button control unique is that you can freely type text directly onto the button, including the ability to add line breaks and spaces from directly within the button. Furthermore, you can style the text on the button by changing the color, size, background color, weight, and much more. When you're ready to set the action of the button, simply select one of the three button types (button, reset, or submit) from the type menu within the Tag Properties Task Pane.

Input (File)

One of the most under-used form controls available in Expression Web is the file field control. (Its lack of use is outlined near the end of the section.) You can use this control as a way of enabling your users to browse their hard drives for a file in an effort to upload it to the server for processing or storage.

To demonstrate a perfect use of the file field control, you need only to turn to a favorite Web site of mine: stock.xchnge (www.sxc.hu). If you're not familiar with stock.xchnge, it's a completely royalty-free stock image Web site. Not unlike Web sites such as Corbis, Getty Images, or Photodisc that charge hundreds of dollars for users to download high-resolution images, stock.xchnge allows users to freely create an account and begin uploading personal, high-resolution images that they'd like to share with other stock.xchnge users. Other users browse the millions of images on the stock.xchnge server in hopes of freely downloading the perfect image to use within their Web and graphic design projects.

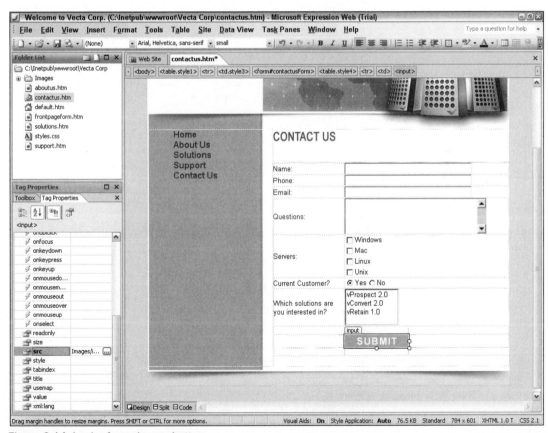

Figure 9-14: Look of new image button

Once you register as a user with stock.xchnge, you can immediately begin uploading images to share with the rest of the world. Figure 9-15 shows the five file fields that stock.xchnge offers from the My Account page, enabling users to upload five files at a time to stock.xchnge's servers.

You, too, can add the file field control to your Web page by simply selecting the Input (File) control in the Toolbox and dragging it out onto your Web page. From a client-side perspective, there isn't much that you need to do to get the control to show the Select File dialog box. To get the file from the client to the server, however, is a different story. The complexity and sheer volume of code involved in getting the control to work server-side are the primary reasons why the control is rarely used.

> Remember the `enctype` property of the form? By default, the browser transmits data using the `application/x-www-form-urlencoded` enctype. One instance where you'd use the `multipart/form-data` `enctype` is when working with file field controls.

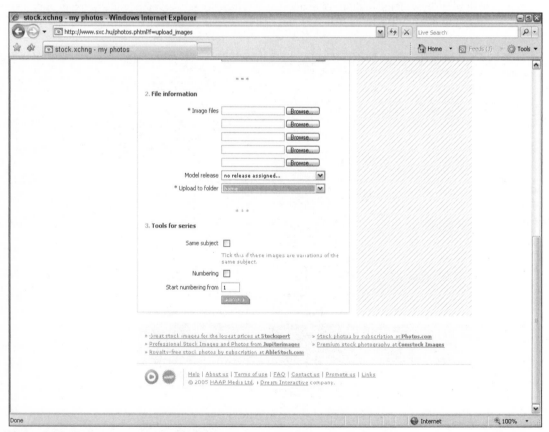

Figure 9-15: My Account page properties

Input (Hidden)

The Marketing department's friend, the hidden field control, is a common way to persist client-side data from page to page without the end user seeing or even realizing it. This form control is the Marketing department's friend because it was used to death in the late 1990s dot com Web-marketing crusade to sell unneeded and worthless software to unsuspecting Web newbies.

The scam was simple and involved nothing more than forms, form controls, and a couple of hidden fields. Typically, starting with an e-mail (spam) advertising the next best "free" software, unsuspecting users would click the accompanying link to visit the site offering the "free" software. Initially, the offer seemed legitimate, asking the users only for their e-mail address with a button promising that the next step was the download. The unsuspecting users would click the button to download and instantly be taken to a second page requiring more information such as name, address, and so on. Users, believing that the company already had their e-mail addresses and that they would get spammed if they didn't complete the process, cautiously entered more information and clicked yet another button that promised the next step was, in fact, the download. But to no avail; the users were now required to enter a credit card number and expiration date to purchase the $4.99 software, which they initially thought was free. Fearing retaliation from the company, the user was left feeling that $4.99 and worthless software were a fair trade for not sharing the personal information they just entered into all the form controls.

You've seen this before, right? Although not everyone is fooled into actually purchasing the software, some inexperienced Web users didn't know better and actually completed the purchase, much to their own disdain. If you were a culprit at one time, you could have easily closed the browser and been fine.

The personal information was not actually sent to the server when you clicked the Continue button to move from page to page, but was, in fact, stored in hidden field controls. On the first page, the user would enter an e-mail address and click Continue. The value (the e-mail address) was stored in a hidden field while the user entered more values. When the user clicked Continue on that second page, the new information was stored in a new series of hidden fields. The process would go on until the last page, at which time the user would finally pay for the software and then the personal information was taken from the hidden fields and stored by the company. Figure 9-16 diagrams the process.

Fortunately, this scam isn't widely used anymore. Now that we're in the twenty-first century, we've graduated to pop-up ads and spyware!

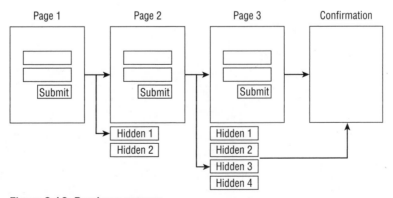

Figure 9-16: Purchase process

Group Box

The Group Box is rendered as the HTML `<fieldset>` tag in code; you can use it as a handy way to group similar form controls within a bordered container. The Group Box, in conjunction with its corresponding `<legend>` tag, helps users distinguish different form controls as they relate to specific functionality on the page.

Try It Out   **Adding a Group Box**

The Group Box is one of those simple HTML-based design elements that you'll find yourself using more often than not. To learn how the Group Box can be added to your Web pages, follow these steps:

1. With the `contactus.htm` page open, place your cursor anywhere in the form and select the `<form#contactusForm>` tag from within the Tag Selector. The entire form should be highlighted, similar to Figure 9-17.

2. Temporarily cut the form out of the page by choosing Edit ➪ Cut or by pressing Ctrl+X.

3. Select the Group Box control from the Toolbox and drag it into the area that the form used to be in. The Group Box appears on the page.

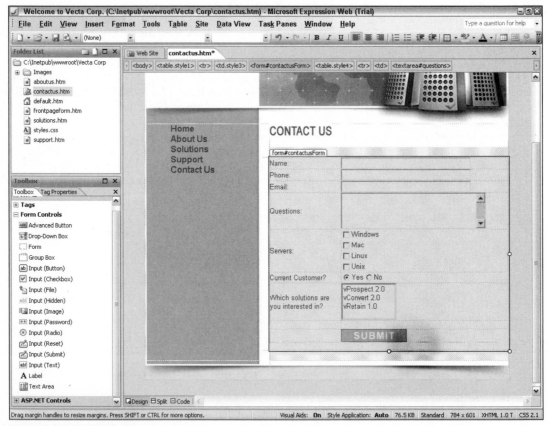

Figure 9-17: Highlighted form

4. Replace the default "Group box" text with your own custom text. Enter the text **Contact a Sales Representative**.

5. Place your cursor within the Group Box and choose Edit ➪ Paste or Ctrl+V to paste the form and its form controls back onto the page within the Group Box.

6. Save your work and preview the result in the browser by pressing F12.

As you can see from Figure 9-18, the form controls are outlined with a clean, bordered pane complete with the text label, "Contact a Sales Representative".

Label

The final element, conveniently stored within the Form Controls section of the Toolbox Task Pane, is the Label. If you've already tried dragging a label onto the page, you'll probably notice that nothing appeared. The reason for this is simple. Labels are meant to be used in code, not in the designer. Essentially, they're used as a way to define a unique association between text and a form element within the form that the text belongs to.

Figure 9-18: Bordered form controls

For example, the following HTML code outlines a checkbox form element as it would appear within the code view of Expression Web:

```
<form>
<input type="checkbox" name="moreinfo">
</form>
```

If you want to uniquely associate the text label "Name" with this control, you can wrap it within a `label` like this:

```
<form>
<label for="moreinfo">
More Info? <input type="checkbox" name="moreinfo">
</label>
</form>
```

While the label doesn't mean much to the browser, from a user standpoint, the control now becomes easier to work with. Now, rather than having to click the checkbox to enable it within the browser, you could also click on the text area "More Info?" within the browser. Clicking the text area would also enable the check box control just as if you were to click the control itself.

Summary

This chapter is the beginning of a higher level of Web development. Creating forms to interact with an end user really starts to show the strengths of the Web and offers endless possibilities. As you get deeper into this book, you'll start building forms that interact with server-side applications. As you'll see, forms, in conjunction with server-side applications, begin to push the envelope for more-engaging experiences for Web users.

In this chapter, you learned all about forms and form objects, including text fields, text areas, checkboxes, radio buttons, list boxes, drop-down menus, and more. You learned how to configure the action of forms so that their data is sent to a server-side script for processing.

Chapter 10 continues with much more depth on the topic of server-side scripting technologies by discussing the ever-growing topic of Web applications. As you'll see, forms and form controls play a crucial role in building these server-side Web applications.

Exercise

In this exercise, you use some of the concepts that you learned in this chapter to rebuild the Vecta Corp `contactus.htm` page. Specifically, you should do the following:

1.   Open the `contactus.htm` page and add a form to the page. Configure the form so that it sends the form to the `contactus.asp` script residing at `http://www.vectacorp.com/scripts/contactus.asp`.

2.   Add a table to the form to organize text and form controls within the form.

3. Add three text fields and name them **name**, **email**, and **phone**.

4. Add a text area field and name it **questions**.

5. Add four checkboxes and name them **servers**. Next to the checkboxes, add the text labels **Windows**, **Mac**, **Linux**, and **UNIX**.

6. Add two radio buttons and name them **currentcustomer**. Next to the radio buttons, add the text labels **Yes** and **No**.

7. Add a list box and name it **solutions**. Add the three choices **vProspect 2.0**, **vConvert 2.0**, and **vRetain 1.0** to the list box.

8. Test the results in the browser and ensure that the submission is sent and processed by the script.

Introduction to Web
Application Development

What is a Web application? That's the question this chapter will try to answer. Anyone who has spent any amount of time with Web applications might tell you that Web applications consist of many Web pages all working harmoniously together to facilitate interaction between a user and a Web server. You might have a Web site that consists of HTML, CSS, and JavaScript. Additionally, you might have a Web server with an installed server-side technology (such as ASP.NET) that responds to requests or interactions between the Web site and the Web server. Furthermore, you might employ some sort of data-storage mechanism that takes the form of a database, XML file, or other data source.

The simple fact is that Web applications encompass many different technologies, languages, platforms, and needs. For this reason, there's no simple definition for the term. Some say that Web applications are like Windows applications in that they allow you to store, query, and, in general, interact with data in and from a database. Although that may seem like the traditional and basic definition of a Web application, the truth is, Web applications extend well beyond that.

This chapter demystifies the term "Web application," clearing up terms introduced in previous chapters such as "client-side development" and "static Web pages." Additionally, some new concepts are introduced such as "server-side development," "databases," and much more. By the end of the chapter, you should have a firm grasp on what Web applications are, what purpose they serve and, more important, how they're implemented within the scope of Expression Web. Nearing the end of the chapter, the dynamic portions of the Vecta Corp Web site are introduced, including the dynamic pages that you'll end up building for it.

This chapter serves as an introduction to a whole new world as it relates to building Web pages. Specifically, you will do the following:

❑   Learn about Web applications and the terminology that surrounds Web architecture

❑   Understand the role of the Web server, including Expression Web's built-in development Web server

❑   Review the role of client-side technologies such as HTML, CSS, and JavaScript

❑ Learn about .NET and the .NET Framework

❑ Understand how Expression Web uses ASP.NET as the server-side technology of choice

❑ Explore the various database options, including the free SQL Server 2005 Express Edition that comes bundled with Expression Web

❑ Review how the Structured Query Language (SQL) is used to communicate between ASP.NET and the database

❑ Examine the dynamic pages that you'll build for the Vecta Corp Web application

Terminology

The introduction to this chapter teased you about what a Web application is, but stopped short of actually defining it. Simply put, a *Web application* is a Web site that contains static and dynamic pages working together to facilitate interaction between a user and a Web server. That clears it all up, right?

To sum up this rather lame attempt at defining Web applications, think of what you've done so far in the book. You've built simple Web pages (*static ones*), pressed F12 and, magically, the page appeared in the browser window as it was intended. Nothing special was required from you. You didn't have to install anything on the computer to get it to work (aside from Expression Web), and, best of all, you didn't have to manually write any code in the Code view of the Web page. If you were to diagram the process involved for a user browsing to your simple static Web page (assuming that it was hosted by a Web hosting provider rather than by your computer), the process might resemble what's shown in Figure 10-1.

As you can see from Figure 10-1, two major components make up static Web pages: the client and the Web server. The *client* makes a request by typing the URL of your Web site into the address bar of a browser and clicking Enter. At this point, a request is made to the *Web server*. The Web server, recognizing this request, sends HTML back to the client, whose browser parses the content out of the HTML tags and displays the text, images, and media (what the original developer of the page intended to be seen) to the user. As a developer, this process is often referred to as *client-side development* because you're using simple client-side technologies such as HTML, CSS, or JavaScript meant to be processed by the client browser, technologies that require very little (if anything) from the actual Web server.

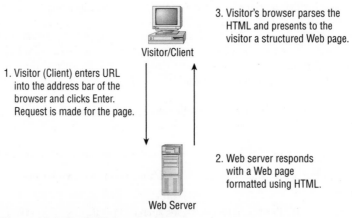

3. Visitor's browser parses the HTML and presents to the visitor a structured Web page.

Visitor/Client

1. Visitor (Client) enters URL into the address bar of the browser and clicks Enter. Request is made for the page.

2. Web server responds with a Web page formatted using HTML.

Web Server

Figure 10-1: Static Web page process

Dynamic pages, on the other hand, work differently and, to a certain extent, are a bit more complex in their implementation. Dynamic pages contain instructions in the form of a server-side scripting language or, in the case of ASP.NET (the server-side technology used by Expression Web), a full-blown object-oriented programming language that gets processed on the Web server. Sometimes the instructions or code is self-contained, sometimes it's mixed in with HTML code, but ultimately that code is processed and executed by a Web server. If you were to diagram the process involved for a user browsing to your dynamic Web page (assuming that it was hosted by a Web hosting provider rather than by your computer), it might resemble the process shown in Figure 10-2.

As you can see from Figure 10-2, dynamic Web sites, like static Web sites, rely on a client and a Web server, just as was the case in Figure 10-2. The fundamental difference, however, is that the server has much more to do for dynamic Web pages than it did for static Web pages. Although the user still makes a request for the initial page, dynamic Web pages rely on user interaction (typically through form elements discussed in Chapter 9) for further requests to be made to the server. With static Web sites, a single request is made to the page. Unless the user links to another page, the browser considers its work done and hands off the rest of its work to the client's browser. From there on out, it's the browser responsibility to render HTML tags, stylize pages using CSS, etc. Dynamic Web sites, on the other hand, wait for interaction from the user (a button press, a selection from a drop down menu, etc.) before being processed. Ultimately, there could be dozens, possibly hundreds, of requests made to the server by way of form controls, hyperlinks, and so on.

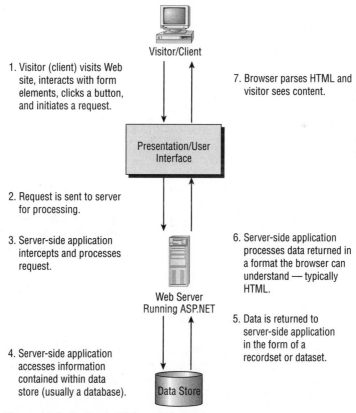

Figure 10-2: Dynamic Web page process

The process is actually quite simple. The user interacts with form controls (maybe types a username and password into a series of text boxes), clicks a Submit button, and the request is sent to the server for processing. The server recognizes that a request is being made and uses a server-side technology such as ASP.NET to process that request (maybe compare the values of the text boxes with a username and password stored in a database), and then sends a response back to the client. The response could be a page redirection to the main page once the user has logged in successfully, or it could be a message indicating that the username and password combination the user typed in are invalid.

That's the point with dynamic Web pages. You write the code in a page that figures out how to handle requests coming from the client. The pages are said to be dynamic because they're not just sitting on the client's browser waiting to be read or clicked. Rather, the information is dynamic; it facilitates user interaction and responds accordingly. Better yet, dynamic pages can use conditional logic and mathematical equations, send e-mails, write to the file system, and even interact with file storage mechanisms such as relational databases and XML files.

Introduction to Web Applications

The previous section outlined the differences between static client-side and dynamic server-side Web pages. You learned that dynamic server-side Web pages welcome interaction from the end user by offering a series of carefully crafted form controls. When the user submits the form (containing the form controls) to the Web server for processing, the dynamic portions of the page kick in and, in turn, process the incoming request. The result of the processing is ultimately piped back to the user in a friendly format that the browser understands (HTML).

Dynamic Web pages, however, are merely cogs within a grander system. They are individual pages that make up a part of the whole if you will. In the Web development world, dynamic Web pages are parts of a Web application. Ultimately, a Web application consists of many dynamic Web pages that perform numerous operations, depending on various factors built into the pages. Figure 10-3 illustrates this example with more detail.

As you can see from Figure 10-3, a Web application could consist of numerous dynamic Web pages, each performing its own unique task. In the Vecta Corp example, you may decide to make dynamic Web pages available for the knowledgebase, discussion forum, and patch download pages of the site. Doing so would allow Vecta Corp users to visit the Vecta Corp Web site in an effort to download software patches, find answers to their questions via the knowledgebase, and even participate in a discussion forum in an effort to communicate with other Vecta Corp users.

From an administrative standpoint, creating dynamic pages for the Vecta Corp site allows administrators to centrally manage all of the knowledgebase articles, patch downloads, and even forum discussion messages and user permissions. If you were an administrator, you'd need to be identified by the Web application. This prevents users who are not administrators from accessing content that they're not supposed to see.

To accommodate logins, you may decide to provide a login page, which is yet another dynamic page. If the user logs in correctly, you take her to the admin page (were administrators can centrally manage dynamic pages for the Vecta Corp site). If the login attempt fails, however, users are redirected back to the login page where they're shown an error message.

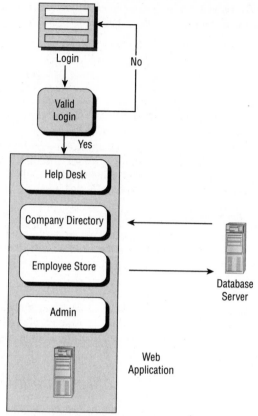

Figure 10-3: Many dynamic Web pages performing numerous operations

As you can see, all of these dynamic pages (knowledgebase, download patches, discussion forum, admin, and login) have the potential of working together in an effort to make life easier for not only the Vecta Corp user, but also the Vecta Corp administrator. All of the dynamic pages outlined here are discussed in more detail later in the chapter. They make up the Vecta Corp Web application.

As mentioned, Web applications are made up of various objects, otherwise known as *tiers*. These tiers make up the Web architecture of your site. Ever heard of the term three-tiered Web application? In this scenario, the term "tiered" refers to the number of these various related objects that make up the Web application as a whole. At the very least, you'll almost always have a two-tiered Web application: The first tier is that of your users (clients) who will visit your site. The second tier is the Web server on which the Web application is hosted. The third tier could be the data tier, or where your data storage mechanism (database) resides.

For the most part, the following tiers represent a traditional three-tiered Web application's architecture:

❑ *Presentation* — The presentation tier is everything that your users will see. Everything from the user interface (UI), images, media, JavaScript (client-side logic), and CSS make up the presentation tier.

❑ *Business Logic* — The business logic is the code running on the server that contains processing instructions utilizing technologies such as ASP.NET.

❑ *Data* — The data tier should (and will) be the lifeblood of your organization. Represented by a database (or, in some cases, a flat file such as an XML file), the data tier contains all the information that you'll want presented within your dynamic Web pages.

All in all, Web applications serve a valuable purpose in Web development. Many Web developers find it more convenient to use Web applications in place of static pages. Although the time-to-market is slower for Web applications than for static pages, maintenance and return on investment (ROI) far outweigh the time it takes to develop the application. After the Web application has been developed, updating content within a database that ultimately appears within the browser is a snap. Furthermore, the look and feel (design) of the site can easily be separated from the content, essentially disconnecting the designer and the developer, and ultimately making each portion of the Web application autonomous.

The previous nine chapters have discussed the many facets of Expression Web that facilitate client-side Web page development. As you've seen, working with Web pages within the development window in Expression Web is simple. Flanked by the numerous Task Panes, menu bars, and toolbars, it's hard to disagree that working with static Web pages in Expression Web is a breeze. Making the switch to dynamic Web development is not easy.

For this reason, an introduction to the different tiers of a Web application and an in-depth discussion of the various parts is necessary before you make the leap to dynamic Web development. The next few sections dissect each of these tiers, discussing and detailing the various objects that make up each tier. Specifically, the discussion outlines the following:

❑ Client-side technologies

❑ The Web server

❑ Server-side technologies (ASP.NET)

❑ Database options

❑ The Structured Query Language (SQL)

By the end of this chapter you should have a solid understanding of the technologies that go into building a Web application. More important, you'll have gained valuable insight into how Expression Web eases the development of Web applications through its simple-to-use Task Panes. The idea is that with the knowledge you acquire in this chapter, you'll be ready to build dynamic Web pages in Chapter 11 and moving forward.

Client-Side Technologies

The presentation tier (or, more specifically, what your users interact with) comprises many different client-side Web technologies, all serving a specific purpose depending on the developer's intentions.

As you've seen throughout the book thus far, client-side development can include the following technologies:

❑ *HTML* — Generally considered the foundation for all that is the Web, HTML (and, more recently, XHTML) serves as the structural markup for client-side Web pages. HTML is hard to ignore when working with Web sites because it's the only structural markup language that the browser can render. Even if you're solely working with server-side Web applications, HTML is what is ultimately sent back to the client from the server.

❑ *CSS* — As you've seen throughout the book, Cascading Style Sheets (CSS) provide the look/design and in some cases, the structural makeup of the client-side Web page. Using CSS, designers can control the look of text, links, form objects, the page, and more.

❑ *JavaScript* — Often referred to as *client-side logic,* JavaScript written within a `<script>` tag nested within the `<head>` tag of the HTML document offers unique properties for working with conditional logic, calculations, validation, and more in a Web page.

❑ *Media elements* — Embedded into the Web page using the `<embed>`/`<object>` HTML tags, media elements such as Flash, video, audio, and more enhance the user experience by incorporating a unique multimedia experience that can be engaging and stunning.

At the risk of rehashing technologies and languages covered for the past nine or so chapters, suffice it to say that client-side elements are still extremely important when working with server-side technologies. Server-side technologies are merely responsible for processing requests from the client. What the client sees in the response is ultimately going to be formatted using the "client-side" technologies already covered in the book.

The Web Server

Previous sections made reference to the fact that users interact with Web applications through a series of carefully crafted form controls presented to the user in the browser window. The user interacts with the form controls and then typically clicks a Submit button, in turn, expecting to see results. What hasn't been discussed, however, is how those results are returned to the user.

In general, servers rely on a piece of software that is crucial in the HTTP request/response process. This piece of software, the Web server, is primarily responsible for managing various Web sites, FTP sites, a mail client, and more on the server. Working in conjunction with the server-side technology (covered later), the Web server is also responsible for facilitating the handoff between the client's request, the server-side technology used to handle the request, the collection of the responses from the server-side technology, and the subsequent handoff of the response back to the client's browser.

Internet Information Services (IIS) is Microsoft's Web server solution. IIS comes bundled with most Microsoft server–based operating systems, including Windows NT 4 Server, Windows 2000 Pro, Windows 2000 Server and Advanced Server, Window 2003 Server, Windows XP Pro, and Windows Vista. In some cases, IIS installs when the OS is installed, but in other cases, you must manually walk through the process of setting it up on your own.

While the installation and configuration of IIS on your development computer certainly will be discussed, for now, it's important to determine whether or not your computer will even support the installation of IIS. The following table outlines the major Windows operating systems and shows whether the operating system supports IIS, and whether or not it comes preinstalled.

OS	Supports IIS?	Preinstalled?
Windows 95, 98, ME, XP Home	No	No, must use Expression Web's built-in Web server
Windows XP Pro	Yes	No, IIS 5.1
Windows NT 4 Server	Yes	Yes, IIS 4
Windows 2000 Pro	Yes	No, IIS 5
Windows 2000 Server & Adv. Server	Yes	Yes, IIS 5
Windows 2003	Yes	Yes*, IIS 6
Windows Vista	Yes	Yes, IIS 7

* Windows Server 2003 Web Server comes with IIS preinstalled. Other versions of Windows Server 2003 require the addition of the application server role to have IIS installed.

> A unique feature to visual editors, Web application development in Expression Web isn't dependent on whether you have IIS installed or not. While your Web server will ultimately need IIS to serve dynamic ASP.NET pages, development in Expression Web can still be done on your computer using Expression Web's built-in Web server. What this means is that if you have an operating system that doesn't support an installation of IIS for development purposes, Expression Web's built-in Web server will do the trick.

If you're not sure whether IIS is preinstalled on your computer, you can use one of these three methods to find out:

❑ Check for a folder called Inetpub located in the root of your system (typically C:\) drive. If you have that folder, as well as the wwwroot folder within it, chances are you're fine. Now, this isn't the best method for identifying whether or not IIS is installed on your computer. The reason for this is simple. If you ever uninstall IIS from your computer, these files are left behind. What that means is that relying on this method for identifying whether or not IIS is installed on your computer shouldn't be enough.

❑ Select Start ⇨ Settings ⇨ Control Panel ⇨ Administrative Tools. If you have a menu item for Internet Services Manager, IIS is indeed installed.

❑ Navigate to http://localhost in a browser. If you see the IIS Welcome screen, IIS is installed and running.

Again, if you have an operating system that supports IIS and you've tried one of the three previously mentioned methods for finding IIS on your machine and it's just not there, then your next step it to install it. The next section will walk you through the process of installing IIS. Remember that if you have Windows 95, 98, ME, XP, or Home Edition, you're not out of luck. You can still use Expression Web's built-in Web server for building Web applications. While the development process is transparent to the developer either way, the downside is that you won't able to simulate the environment of your Web server.

Installing IIS

As you saw in the previous section, IIS comes with most versions of server-based Windows operating systems, but it's not installed automatically in all versions, which is why it might not be present on your computer. If you've come to the conclusion that IIS isn't installed on your computer, and you have a compatible operating system similar to the ones listed in the table in the previous section, then you'll need to install it.

Try It Out   **Installing IIS**

While application development in Expression Web isn't dependent on IIS, it certainly helps to simulate the environment that your Web applications will be running on as much as possible. To install IIS on your computer, follow these steps:

1. Access the Control Panel by choosing Start ⇨ Settings ⇨ Control Panel.

2. In the Control Panel, select Add or Remove Programs.

3. Choose Add/Remove Windows Components. The list of components becomes visible within a few seconds.

4. In the list of components, enable the Internet Information Services (IIS) option.

5. Click Next (Windows may or may not prompt you to insert the Windows CD) to install IIS.

6. After IIS is installed, close the Add or Remove Programs dialog box.

You can check to see whether IIS installed correctly by running through one or all three of the bullet points highlighted in the previous section.

You are now ready to begin running Web applications from your local computer. Although this discussion won't cover how to configure IIS for external use, it will show you how to configure IIS to support local ASP.NET application development using Expression Web so that the applications that you build and test locally may later be uploaded to your external Web host provider.

Configuring IIS

Although little configuration needs to be done to begin working with IIS, this section introduces some basic features and functionality within IIS. Reading this section will help you better troubleshoot problems that may arise later in development. This section explains the following topics:

❑   Where to keep files on the Web server

❑   Using Localhost

Where to Keep Files on the Web Server

Now that you have IIS up and running, let's take a closer look at where the files for your Web applications are kept on the computer. Up to this point, you've been saving projects in the `My Document\My Web Sites\Vecta Corp` directory. This works fine for static Web pages because you're merely testing the functionality of the pages in the browser. IIS however, works a bit differently. By default, IIS reads and processes the code in the file from the `C:\Inetpub\wwwroot\` folder. If you open this folder and compare it to the folder tree in IIS, you'll notice some similarities. Although it is not a requirement to keep applications in this folder, it is generally considered a good repository for storing and managing your Web applications.

> **Technically, your files don't have to be in `C:\Inetpub\wwwroot\`. You can also create what's called a *virtual directory*. A virtual directory is essentially an alias within IIS that points to a folder somewhere else on your computer. To make things easier, however, you'll work with `C:\Inetpub\wwwroot\` for the rest of the book. Furthermore, if you're using Expression Web's built-in Web server, you may decide to keep your files within the `My Document\My Web Sites\Vecta Corp` directory. Again, the `C:\Inetpub\wwwroot\` directory more closely simulates a real Web server environment.**

Try It Out   Creating a Web Page Within the Web Root

So that you can test how the Web server works, let's create a new folder within `C:\Inetpub\wwwroot` and add a simple HTML page to the new folder. Follow these steps:

1. Open Windows Explorer and navigate to the root of `C:\Inetpub\wwwroot`.

2. Within `wwwroot`, create a new folder called `Vecta Corp`.

3. Open the `Vecta Corp` folder.

4. Right-click an empty area in the folder and choose the New ⇨ Text Document option from the context menu that appears.

5. After you select the New Text Document option, you can immediately rename the file. Change the name, including its extension, to `default.htm`. This action converts the text document to a HTML file.

6. Right-click the file and choose Open With ⇨ Notepad from the context menu. The file opens in Notepad.

7. In the document, add the following basic HTML:

```
<html>
<head>
<title>Sample HTML Page</title>
</head>
```

```
<body>
<h1>Hello World</h1>
</body>
</html>
```

8. Save the page and close Notepad.

That's it! You've just created your first basic page within the context of the Web server. The next section explains how to browse to the page using the default name of the Web server.

Using Localhost

Now that you have a new file in `C:\Inetpub\wwwroot\Vecta Corp`, your Web server has access to it. If you've been developing static HTML Web pages for a long time, habit may drive you to open files directly in your browser.

Dynamic pages can't be opened directly from the browser because your Web server needs to have a crack at the file before it is sent to your browser for display. If the Web server doesn't get the chance to interpret the request coded into a dynamic page, the code behind the dynamic page is never converted into the HTML that your browser can understand. Instead, you'll have to open the browser and navigate to the Web directory using the local Web address for your computer, also known as `http://localhost` (or by the IP address `http://127.0.0.1`). More specifically, because the `Vecta Corp` folder is located in `C:\Inetpub\wwwroot\Vecta Corp` on your computer, you can access it directly from the browser by typing in the URL `http://localhost/Vecta Corp`. Figure 10-4 shows the result of the page request in the browser.

In this case, the process was simple. Because the default page is essentially an HTML file, nothing is really required of the Web server. Most of the work in this case is handled by the browser. The browser parses the literal text out of the HTML tags and presents the text "Hello World" to the user. Because the page contained only HTML, you could have just as easily opened the page directly in the browser, displaying the same results. Remember, however, that the Web server (IIS) is the only piece of software that can access your server-side ASP.NET code directly. For this reason, it's a good idea that you get into the habit of accessing your dynamic pages directly from `http://localhost/Vecta Corp` (if you don't plan on using the built-in Web server).

Figure 10-4: Accessing the Vecta Corp folder directly from the browser

Expression Web's Built-In Web Server

While using IIS is certainly an option, it's important to understand that it's not the only option. Some Expression Web users, for example, won't have the luxury of owning an operating system that supports an enterprise-level Web server such as IIS. If this is the case, then perhaps Expression Web's built-in development Web server is for you.

Expression Web's built-in Web server, like IIS, allows you to run dynamic pages within the context of a Web server, without actually owning the real thing. Later, when you're confident that all of your dynamic pages work (having been tested using the built-in development Web server), you can freely transfer them to your Web hosting provider that does have a full-blown Web server installed.

In the previous sections, you learned how to install and configure IIS. For the most part, unless you define what's known as a "virtual directory," IIS relies on Web sites defined within the `C:\Inetpub\wwwroot\` directory. The beauty of Expression Web's built-in Web server is that your Web sites can reside anywhere on your computer. For example, up until this chapter, you've been placing the Vecta Corp Web site files within the `My Documents\My Web Sites\Vecta Corp` folder. With Expression Web's built-in Web server, this is fine. Once you configure Expression Web to use its built-in Web server (covered in the next section) to preview pages, Expression Web will automatically take the file you're previewing, and run it in the browser using the URL `http://localhost:<randomportnumber>/Vecta Corp`. As you'll see, for security purposes, Expression Web uses a randomized port number at the instant that you preview your files.

Configuring the Web Server in Expression Web

Configuring Expression Web to use its built-in Web server to preview your files is easy, and is simply a matter of enabling a checkbox within the Site Settings dialog box in Expression Web. Once you configure Expression Web to use its built-in Web server, every time you press F12 or choose File ➪ Preview in Browser ➪ <your browser option>, Expression Web launches an instance of the built-in Web server, minimizes that instance to the task bar tray, and launches your Web site to run within the context of the Web server. The process is that easy!

Try It Out   Configuring Expression Web to Use Its Built-in Web Server

Customizing Expression Web to use its built-in Web server is easy. To configure your Web site to use the built-in Web server, follow these steps:

1. If you don't have Expression Web open, go ahead and open it now. Open your Web site as you've done throughout the book by choosing File ➪ Open Site and select the Vecta Corp Web site, which should reside within your `My Documents\My Web Sites\Vecta Corp` folder.

2. Now, choose Site ➪ Site Settings. The Site Settings dialog box will appear. Immediately choose the Preview tab. As you can see from Figure 10-5, the Preview tab outlines options for enabling the built-in development Web server when pages are previewed.

3. Ensure that the "Preview using Web site URL" radio button is selected and then Click the "Use Microsoft ASP.NET Development Server" check box. The page type radio buttons will now become enabled.

Figure 10-5: Site Settings dialog box

4. Next, select the "For only ASP.NET Web pages" radio button. This guarantees that the built-in development server will only be used for ASP.NET pages. If you prefer to use the Web server for all Web pages, simply enable the "For all Web pages" radio button.

5. Click OK to close the Site Settings dialog box.

That's it! The Vecta Corp site is now configured to run the built-in development Web server for all ASP.NET pages.

While using Expression Web's built-in Web server is certainly convenient, it's not always the ideal option. In certain scenarios, using your IIS installation to preview pages makes much more sense than the built-in Web server. This allows you to test your pages in a simulated environment that will closely resemble that of the production Web server.

Try It Out   Configuring Expression Web to Use IIS

Configuring Expression Web to use IIS as opposed to its built-in Web server is similar to configuring it to use the built-in Web server. The major difference, however, is that your Web site files will have to reside within the `C:\Inetpub\wwwroot` folder. To configure Expression Web to use your installation of IIS instead of its built-in Web server, follow these steps:

1. Before you even open Expression Web, open your `My Documents\My Web Sites` folder. Select the `Vecta Corp` folder and copy or cut it. Then open the `C:\Inetpub\wwwroot` folder and paste the **copied/cut** `Vecta Corp` folder in. Your files will now reside at `C:\Inetpub\wwwroot\ Vecta Corp`.

2. Now, within Expression Web choose Site ➪ Site Settings. The Site Settings dialog box will appear. Immediately choose the Preview tab.

3. This time, click the "Preview using custom URL for this Web site" radio button and type the URL **http://locahost/Vecta Corp** path within the provided text box.

4. Click OK to close the Site Settings dialog box.

That's it! The Vecta Corp site is now configured to use your Web server (IIS) to run all Web pages.

In the next few sections, you learn about ASP.NET, the server-side technology that you'll use to build dynamic pages within Expression Web. As the sections progress, you'll also build a simple ASP.NET page and test it within the context of the Web server you've just configured.

Server-Side Technologies

As already mentioned, server-side technologies are software components that handle most (if not all) of the business logic in a Web application. When a user submits data from a form run on the client, that data is then sent to the Web server for processing. The Web server, using a server-side technology, processes the form (maybe inserts data into a database), and then sends a response back to the client. The process is fairly straightforward and, save for a few minor details, the process is the same regardless of which server-side technology is being used to process the request.

Over the past ten years, as the Web has matured, dozens of different server-side technologies have appeared. Most server-side technologies have a lot in common. For example, most of them interact with relational databases. They can process complex requests from Web browsers, and can write files to and read files from a file system. While there are roughly six major technologies to choose from, Expression Web currently supports one: Microsoft's ASP.NET.

In 2000, Microsoft created a buzz in not only the Web development world, but in the Windows development world when it introduced the .NET initiative (covered with more detail in the next section). The initiative's aim was simple: develop a line of products, platforms, and services that are interoperable for the developer, and easy to use and integrate for the ordinary user. Flanked by platforms such as the .NET Framework (which includes ASP.NET); products such as Visual Studio, Live, Office, and more; and Web services built directly into Live such as Passport, .NET has risen as an initiative worthy of its hype.

The next few sections review many of the foundation-level concepts that you'll need to understand before working with ASP.NET within Expression Web. Specifically, the discussion examines the following:

❑ .NET and the .NET Framework

❑ Installing the .NET Framework

❑ Creating a simple ASP.NET page

❑ Expression Web's ASP.NET integration

.NET and the .NET Framework

For the past several years, Microsoft has run a series of commercials that show executives interacting with software that is perceived to make the user feel as if the software is revolutionizing the way they do business. At the end of the commercial, the tag line says: "That's business with .NET." Great! What's .NET? To many, these commercials are vague and open themselves to too many questions: What is .NET? What is business with .NET?

When .NET was introduced to the public, there was such an overwhelming bombardment of marketing information that it was difficult to figure out what .NET was, and what kind of advantage it could provide for an organization. Fortunately, the dust has settled, and a clear definition of what .NET truly is has emerged.

.NET is Microsoft's new strategy for delivering software as a service. By reinventing the Application Service Provider (ASP) business model, Microsoft hopes to achieve independence from the long-standing "boxware" paradigm. Following are the key features that make up .NET:

❑ *.NET platform* — The .NET platform includes the .NET Framework and tools to build and operate the services, clients, and so on. ASP.NET, which is the focus of this section, is a component of the .NET Framework.

❑ *.NET products* — .NET products (which include Live, Office, and Visual Studio) provide developers a rich environment for creating Web services that use programming environments such as C++, Visual Basic .NET, ASP.NET, C#, and so on.

❑ *.NET services* — .NET Services are a set of user-centric XML Web services currently being provided by a whole host of partners, developers, and organizations hoping to build vertical market applications for devices, applications, and the Internet. The collection of My Services currently extends to Passport, Messenger, favorite Web sites, and much more.

As you can see, .NET is merely a strategy, and not a tool or service. It's no coincidence that Microsoft pulled the ending tag line from those commercials and replaced it with, "Solutions for the agile business."

The .NET Framework (which is a standalone, installable Windows application of sorts) is the environment for which .NET applications are built. The .NET Framework is specifically designed for Windows and Web applications, but supports development across a larger spectrum. Following are the three main parts of the .NET Framework:

❑ The Common Language Runtime (CLR)

❑ The Framework Class Library

❑ ASP.NET

Although the .NET Framework is just a small piece of the pie, it lays the foundation for .NET applications and Web services. Remember, the .NET Framework, although crucial in the .NET strategy, is only a small piece of the .NET platform, and the .NET platform is just one-third of the .NET initiative.

Installing the .NET Framework and ASP.NET

Unlike ASP (Microsoft's predecessor to ASP.NET), the .NET Framework (which includes ASP.NET) doesn't come preinstalled on most operating systems. In fact, Windows Server 2003 and Vista are the only operating systems that come with the .NET Framework preinstalled. However, this doesn't mean that installing the .NET Framework will be a pain. On the contrary, in most cases, installing the .NET Framework is as simple as visiting the Microsoft Windows Update Web site.

> To clarify, Windows Server 2003 comes preinstalled with an older version of the
> .NET Framework in 1.1. Vista, on the other hand, comes preinstalled with a much
> newer version of the .NET Framework in 2.0.

If you don't have Windows Server 2003 (which most of us probably don't), you'll need to install the .NET
Framework (which includes ASP.NET) manually. The best method of acquiring the .NET Framework is to
download and install it directly from the Web, or more specifically, the Microsoft Windows Update Web
site. The reason for this is simple. Windows Update will not only alert you of the fact that you don't have
the .NET Framework installed (assuming you don't); it will also allow you to download and install it. It's
like a detection and installation utility, all in one.

To use Windows Update to install the .NET Framework, follow these steps:

1. Open your browser and visit the Windows Update Web site located at
   `http://update.microsoft.com`.

2. When the site opens, you'll have the opportunity to choose from an Express installation or a
   Custom installation. Choose the Custom Install option. Windows scans your computer. This is
   the detection utility mentioned earlier.

3. When Windows Update has finished running through the detection utility, choose the Select
   Optional Software Updates link from the left navigation menu. If the .NET Framework Redistributable option appears in the list, you don't have the .NET Framework or ASP.NET installed
   on your computer. Select the checkbox next to the option now. If this option is not in the list, you do
   have .NET Framework and ASP.NET installed and you're ready to begin working with ASP.NET.

4. Assuming that you don't have it installed, click the "Go to Install Updates" link.

5. Click the Install button. The Installing Updates dialog appears and begins installing the .NET
   Framework. When finished, the .NET Framework Redistributable is installed along with
   ASP.NET. You may or may not have to reboot your computer.

That's it! You're now ready to begin working with ASP.NET.

> You can also download the .NET Framework Redistributable from `www.asp.net`.
> This is the official Web site for ASP.NET and is yet another good choice for down-
> loading the necessary and optional tools for building Web applications using
> ASP.NET. Furthermore, you can also download the .NET Framework Software
> Development Kit (SDK) from this site. The .NET Framework SDK contains debug-
> gers, compilers, sample code, and more. Be aware, however, that file is over 300MB
> in size, so be prepared to wait while it downloads.

Creating a Simple ASP.NET Page

Now that you've had a formal introduction to the .NET Framework and ASP.NET and you've had a chance to install ASP.NET, let's walk through the process of creating a simple ASP.NET page. Not only will this process help familiarize you with the technology, but you'll also get a basic understanding of how IIS or Expression Web's development Web server and the .NET Framework handle the processing of a dynamic ASP.NET page.

To create a simple ASP.NET page, follow these steps:

1. Open Expression Web if it's not open already and choose File ➪ New ➪ ASPX.

2. In the document, switch to Code view, and replace all of the existing code with the following code:

```
<html>
<head>
<title>Sample ASP.NET Page</title>
<script runat="server" type="text/vb">
Sub Page_Load()
     theTime.Text = Now()
End Sub
</script>
</head>

<body>
<h1>
The Date and Time is: <asp:label id="theTime" runat="server" />
</h1>
</body>
</html>
```

3. Save your work as `sample.aspx`.

To test your work, simply press F12. Regardless of which Web server you've configured within Expression Web, the page is launched within the browser. As you can see from Figure 10-6, the text "The Date and Time is:", along with today's actual date and time, appear on the page.

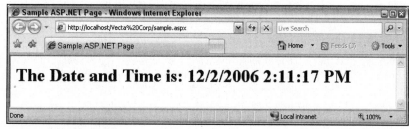

Figure 10-6: ASP.NET page

As you can see from the code snippet, there really wasn't much to creating an ASP.NET page. Look at the code again and see whether you can pick apart the dynamic portions of the page. In the example, you'll notice a Web control that's been added next to the literal text within the <h1> tag. Web controls, as you learn throughout the book, are Microsoft's reinvention of form controls (discussed in Chapter 9). In this case, the Label control is used as a way to display today's date and time as follows:

```
<asp:label id="theTime" runat="server" />
```

The label control, as is the case with every other ASP.NET control, has two distinct attributes: the id and the Runat server attributes. The id is a way to uniquely identify the control on the page; the runat="server" attribute and value tells the browser (and ultimately the Web server) that the Web server should process this portion of the page.

Near the top of the page, notice a code declaration block containing one event handler: Page_Load:

```
<script runat="server">
Sub Page_Load()
End Sub
</script>
```

It's called an event handler because it handles the page's load event and responds with code accordingly. In this case, you identify the label control by name and set its built-in Text property to today's date using the built-in Now() function:

```
theTime.Text = Now()
```

The result, as you've seen, is text that is parsed by the browser and today's date, which is fed to the browser by the .NET Framework. Under the hood, the page is fed through IIS. IIS, recognizing that a code block with runat="server" attributes exists, intercepts the request and calls for help from the .NET Framework (running as an operating system level process called aspnet_wp.exe in the background). To see this process, simply press Ctrl+Alt+Delete, click the Task Manager option, and choose the Processes tab from the Windows Task Manager dialog. As you'll see, the aspnet_wp.exe worker process runs silently in the background.

The .NET Framework processes the request and takes the code to mean, "Print out the date and time within the page." The .NET Framework converts the label control to a <span> tag (legitimate HTML) and responds back to IIS with plain old text and HTML tags. IIS then feeds that response back to the client browser, where you see the result in a clean and legible format.

If you don't believe that the .NET Framework always converts code to HTML, try viewing the source of the page in the browser by choosing View ⇨ Source (in IE). As you can see from Figure 10-7, the code declaration block (<script> tag) is removed from the page, the label control is converted to a <span> tag, and the date and time is rendered as literal text.

That's ASP.NET in a nutshell. In this example, you manually wrote the ASP.NET code. Again, the beauty in using Expression Web is that you don't have to do your own coding. Expression Web writes all the necessary code for you.

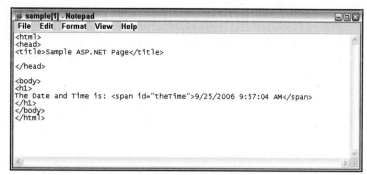

Figure 10-7: Source of the page

Expression Web's ASP.NET Integration

In the previous section, you got a taste of what ASP.NET can offer. Notice the word "taste," because the example outlined in the previous section was a simple example of ASP.NET. In reality, ASP.NET takes years to master. The complexity that the technology offers can't be outlined in one short chapter, or even one book. The upside to Expression Web, however, is that, regardless of the learning curve required to learn ASP.NET, Expression Web throws it all out the window by offering numerous Task Panes, menu items, and Toolbox options that, in general, make life easier in your ASP.NET Web application development endeavors. All in all, Expression Web outlines numerous features that facilitate the development of ASP.NET Web pages, including the following:

❑   *New dialog box* — As is the case with standard client-side development options such as HTML, CSS, JavaScript, and more, the New dialog box (shown in Figure 10-8 with the ASP.NET category selected) offers options for creating new ASP.NET (.ASPX) pages, ASP.NET Master Pages, Web User Controls (.ASCX), Web Configuration files (Web.Config), and Site Map files. While the New dialog box offers numerous options for creating ASP.NET-related files, in reality, the ASPX option is the one that you'll be using most often. To make life easier, you may also decide to create a new ASP.NET page by choosing File ➪ New ➪ ASPX.

❑   *Toolbox Task Pane* — As you learned in the previous chapters, the Toolbox Task Pane offers a series of visual icons that represent HTML tags, HTML form controls and, more important for this chapter and moving forward, ASP.NET controls. As you can see in Figure 10-9, the ASP.NET Controls node within the Toolbox Task Pane shows a series of sub-nodes that offers visual icons representing standard Web server controls, data controls, validation controls, navigation controls, login controls, and WebPart controls. While covering every subcategory is outside the scope of a book of this size, the discussion does cover some of the more widely used options such as the standard, data, validation, and login control sets.

❑   *Tag Properties Task Pane* — As is the case with every element in Expression Web, the Tag Properties Task Pane can be used to manipulate properties for elements that you add to the development area. Of course, this holds true for ASP.NET controls as well. As you'll see throughout the rest of the book, whenever you add an ASP.NET control, you'll immediately turn to this Task Pane to format unique properties that each control offers.

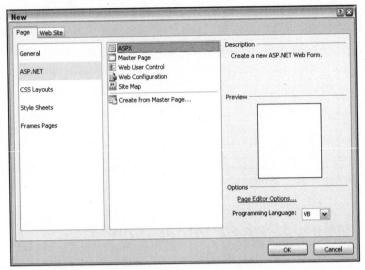

Figure 10-8: New dialog box

Figure 10-9: ASP.NET control node

❑ *Data Source Library Task Pane* — Before you begin working with database data dynamically within Expression Web, your first task is to define a connection to the database server (even if your database happens to reside on your development machine). The Data Source Library Task Pane facilitates connections to databases and XML files through a convenient and visual wizard-based interface.

❑ *Data Source Details Task Pane* — Once you've established a connection to a database or XML file, the Data Source Details Task Pane conveniently offers up all of the important information that the database or XML file outlines. For example, if you've established a connection to a SQL Server database, the Data Source Details Task Pane would outline all of the tables, fields, stored procedures, and more, outlined by the database. Even better, you could drag and drop fields from this Task Pane directly onto your ASP.NET page to create what are known as *bindings* (covered in more detail in Chapter 11).

As you can see, four major interface components are built into Expression Web for working with ASP.NET pages. But don't let this relatively small number fool you. These four interface components represent large development integration in Expression Web. The rest of the book is devoted to these four components and the subcategories/components that make them up.

The Database

Yet another tier of the overall Web architecture (discussed earlier in the chapter) is the data storage tier. As you begin to build Web applications (regardless of whether you're using Expression Web or not), it will become increasingly obvious that you'll need to store data in some sort of storage mechanism and allow its access through your Web application. Whether you are building a small Web application for displaying dynamic knowledgebase articles, product patches, and a discussion forum (such as what you'll be building for the Vecta Corp application), or a Web store that millions will visit, you will need some system for storing all the data that will be dynamically shown via those pages.

You might not want to stop there, however. You might want to include some way of tracking how many of a certain item you have left in your inventory (assuming you were building a Web store). You might even need to determine how many items you're selling during a particular week of the month. If that's the case, you will need some way of determining sales transactions. Like a filing cabinet that stores files and, subsequently, data within those files, you will need some mechanism of storing all your data for easy access and quick retrieval. That mechanism is the database.

In 1970, E. F. Codd, an employee with IBM, proposed his idea for what would become the first relational database design model. His model, which proposed new methods for storing and retrieving data in large applications, far surpassed any idea or system that was in place at that time. His idea of "relational" stemmed from the fact that data and relationships between them were organized in "relations," or what you know today as tables. Even though Codd's terminology for what are referred to as *tables, columns,* and *rows* was different, the premise behind the relational model has remained consistent. Although the model has undergone revisions and changes over the past 35 years, the idea of storing and retrieving information in large applications has not changed, solidifying the need for the relational database model.

Now that the history lesson is out of the way, what exactly is a database and how can you use it in conjunction with the Vecta Corp Web application? The best way to think of a database is in terms of a filing cabinet. The filing cabinet contains drawers, the drawers contain folders, and the folders contain documents that have information on them. A database is similar in concept. A database contains drawers, otherwise known as tables; those tables contain folders, or columns, which in turn contain rows of information pertaining to the particular column that they're in.

For a moment, let's take the Vecta Corp Web application and break it down to see exactly what kind of information you would need and just how you could break it up to make it manageable with a database:

❑ *Administrators* — You need some way to keep track of all your administrators. When a user attempts to log in to the admin page of the Vecta Corp application, this list is checked. If users exist as administrators, let them in to the admin page. If not, deny them access.

❑ *Patches* — Most software development companies maintain a Web site devoted to upgrades and patches for software they release. You may think about keeping a list of patches that includes older versions of software for Vecta Corp solutions.

❑ *Knowledgebase* — Possibly one of the most dynamic components of the Vecta Corp application is the knowledgebase. The knowledgebase maintains a list of frequently asked questions (FAQs), and directs users to answers for those questions.

Technically, the Webmaster of the Vecta Corp Web site could manually connect to and maintain the information within these pages. Every time a new patch was released or a new FAQ was introduced, the Webmaster could connect to the Web host, copy the static HTML file over to the local computer, make the change, and then upload the modified file back to the Web host for the public to see. While this process closely resembles what you've done thus far, it's far from flexible, especially when you have the potential of working with large amounts of data, as could be the case with some of the pages outlined in the previous bullet points.

Instead of working with static pages, you may decide to store all of the information for the knowledgebase, patches, and users centrally within a database. Doing so would allow you to centrally manage all of that data without having to connect to the Web host provider and copy the file down every time you needed to make a change. Furthermore, because the data is contained within a database, it's not limited to being shown via a Web page. Because you're pulling the data from a central data storage mechanism such as a database, you can now display the data via wireless devices, Windows applications, Flash-based presentations, and more.

Now that you're beginning to see the benefits of a database, let's outline some of the main components that make up the functionality of a database. When working with databases, the following are major concepts that you should understand:

❑ *Database management system* — The database management system (DBMS) represents the framework from which you design, store, and manage all the databases, tables, and columns that you design. To a certain extent, every database has some sort of interface for managing the potentially large volume of databases that your organization may employ. Typically, this is the DBMS. Some smaller databases (such as Access, for example) don't have a DBMS. As you'll learn, Access is a file-based database. For this reason, Access offers a unique file-based interface that you can use for managing the various components of the database.

❑ *Database* — In most cases, the database is the backbone of the organization. Especially, if your organization sells items online, the database is where everything relating to the company (its products, inventory, orders, customers, and more) is stored. While databases are managed via the DBMS, the database consists primarily of tables, columns, and more important, rows and rows of data within tables.

❑ *Tables* — After a database has been created, you might want to begin storing information relevant to a specific part of your organization within separate tables. As mentioned earlier, tables are very similar to file cabinet drawers. For example, in a Web store, it would be a mistake to store all the information about inventory, products, customers, and even transactions in one drawer; instead, you'll break these categories of information out and create different drawers (tables) to store all this information. For the Vecta Corp example, you'll break information relevant to users, patches, and knowledgebase articles out into their own separate database tables.

❑ *Columns* — After you outline all your tables, your next step is to decide what information to include within those tables. For example, you might want to include first name, last name, username, and password for all administrators who might access the Vecta Corp application within a users table. Additionally, you might want to include columns for a patch name and a patch download path within the patches table. Finally, the knowledgebase table could be made up of a unique knowledgebase number, the question, and an answer to that question. Theoretically, columns represent bits of information or more detailed descriptions of the table in which they are contained.

❑ *Rows* — Think back to the example mentioned earlier regarding the documents within the folders and the folders within the drawers contained within the filing cabinet. Rows represent the actual data in those documents. Similar to the columns within the tables, rows represent the actual data within the columns. Database tables have the potential for containing millions of rows. Technically, this is your data. The many rows of information contained in your database tables are what you'll ultimately display in your Web applications. Whether you're displaying knowledgebase articles or using database data to store credential information, the rows in your databases tables and the data contained within those rows are what you'll ultimately be interacting with inside the Web application.

Now that you've had a formal introduction to databases and you understand the structure of a database, you have some decisions to make. Technically, Expression Web supports connecting to many different types of databases. This book covers two: Access and SQL Server 2005 Express Edition. Let's discuss these options next.

Database Options

Numerous databases exist for you to work with. In fact, more databases exist than do server-side Web technologies. Like server-side technologies, the database you choose is ultimately up to you because most are interoperable with the various server-side Web technologies on the market today. Factors for choosing a database include reliability, support for the server-side technology you plan to use, scalability (how easy is it to scale up as your company grows), and extensibility (how easy is it to back up information, restore it in case of failure, merge data in and out, and automate processes).

As with server-side technologies, dozens of databases are available, but only the ones used in this book are examined here. Each database has its own strengths and drawbacks. Some are free and some cost thousands of dollars to license. For the sake of simplicity, the database options to be discussed include the following:

❑ Access

❑ SQL Server 2005 Express Edition

It's important to note that other database options exist. SQL Server 2000, Oracle, MySQL, IBM's DB2, PostGre Ingres, Sybase, dBase, and FileMaker Pro are all viable alternatives. Because of size constraints, this book limits development to the two Microsoft databases, Access and SQL Server 2005 Express Edition.

Access

Access is Microsoft's database solution for developers and small companies alike who want to build or house data within a small, yet reliable, store. Because Microsoft Access is cheap and easily attainable, it's usually the perfect choice for discussion and use in books such as this one. If you're a small company, looking for something cheap, reliable, and easy to use, then Access is for you. You can find more information on Access from Microsoft's Web site at `www.microsoft.com/office/access`. Here you can find the latest updates, news, and purchase information for Microsoft Access.

If you plan on purchasing Access, you might consider purchasing the Microsoft Office bundle (which includes Access, Word, Outlook, PowerPoint, and Excel) instead. For the price of about $550, you'll get more bang for your buck, as opposed to buying Access alone, which usually sells for about $400.

Because of its simplicity and attainability, Access is an excellent choice for the completion of projects within this book. If you look within the included files for this chapter, you'll notice the `VectaCorp.mdb` file. This is the Access file that you can use for the examples throughout the rest of the book should you decide on Access as your database of choice.

SQL Server 2005 Express Edition

SQL Server 2005 is Microsoft's database solution for medium to large companies and enterprises. It's quite a bit more expensive than Access, generally requires its own "database server," and, at times, requires the hiring of a certified database administrator (DBA) to maintain. With that said, SQL Server 2005 offers a robust and scalable solution for larger Web applications partly because of its unique core of features, including online transaction processing (OLTP), indexing, data transformation services, profiling, a query analyzer, and a robust and intuitive DBMS. If you'd like more information regarding SQL Server 2005, visit Microsoft's Web site at `www.microsoft.com/sql`.

This discussion assumes that, if you're reading this book, you probably don't want to invest in something as massive as SQL Server 2005 and that your needs are better suited to something free (but just as powerful). If this is the case, Microsoft's SQL Server 2005 Express Edition is perfect for you. Express Edition is Microsoft's free database alternative to SQL Server 2005. It functions and stores data exactly as SQL Server 2005 does, the only catch is that your database may not exceed 5GB (plenty of space for our application). Once it does, you'll need to upgrade to the full-blown Enterprise level solution. For more information about SQL Server 2005 Express Edition, visit Microsoft's Web site at `http://msdn.microsoft.com/vstudio/express/sql/download/`.

Try It Out   **Installing SQL Server 2005 Express Edition**

For the most part, if you have Office, you have Access installed, so let's not go into the details of installing that product. SQL Server 2005 Express Edition, however, is a bit of a different animal.

To install SQL Server 2005 Express Edition, follow these steps:

1.   Begin by visiting the SQL Server 2005 Express Edition download site at `http://msdn` `.microsoft.com/vstudio/express/sql/download/`. If you have the .NET Framework 2.0 already installed, click the Download button located under the Install Microsoft SQL Server 2005 Express Edition subheading in Step 3.

2.   When the File Download dialog box appears, save the file to your computer, preferably somewhere where you can easily access the file.

3.   Once the download completes, double-click the file to launch the Installer. Accept the license agreement and proceed through the wizard until the installation finishes. For the purposes of this discussion, accept all of the default options as you progress through the wizard. This will prevent errors from occurring as you progress through the examples in the chapters.

> **While installing SQL Server 2005 Express Edition is certainly easy, help is also available for less experienced users. For more information on installing SQL Server 2005 Express Edition, please visit the SQL Express forum at:** `http://` `forums.microsoft.com/MSDN/ShowForum.aspx?ForumID=385&SiteID=1`

Now, it's important to understand that SQL Server 2005 Express Edition isn't a software application that you launch as you do Access or Expression Web. Rather, it's a service that runs silently in the background of the operating system, much like the .NET Framework. To see this service in action, right-click your My Computer icon on your desktop and choose the Manage option from the context menu that appears. This will launch the Computer Management window. From the category nodes on the left, expand the "Services and Applications" node and choose the Services option from the list that appears. Scroll down the pane on the left until you find SQL Server (SQLEXPRESS), as shown in Figure 10-10.

As you see from Figure 10-10, SQL Server 2005 Express Edition is running silently as a service of the operating system.

The Vecta Corp Database

Now that you have a generic understanding as to what a database is and what purpose it serves within the context of a Web application, let's quickly review the pre-built database that you'll be using for the dynamic pages of the Vecta Corp Web site. The idea is that you become familiar with the various tables and the information within the tables that you'll eventually make available within the dynamic Vecta Corp Web pages so that you're prepared to work with the data using the various Task Panes in Expression Web. Specifically, the examination outlines the following tables:

❑   The Knowledgebase table

❑   The Patches table

❑   The Users table

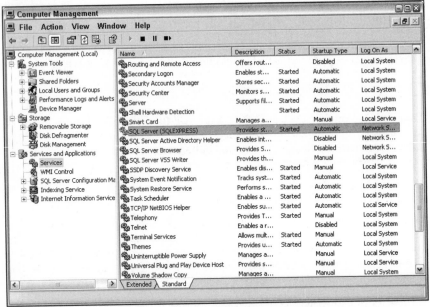

Figure 10-10: SQL Server in the Computer Management window

The Knowledgebase Table

You'll use the Knowledgebase table to store FAQs and general articles about Vecta Corp solutions for your users. The Knowledgebase table will consist of the columns shown in the following table.

Column Name	Data Type	Description
KBID	AutoNumber	A unique number that automatically increments when new knowledgebase articles are added. This number guarantees that each row in the table is unique.
CategoryID	Number	A numeric value that represents the category (software, hardware, network) for the knowledgebase article. This field will have a direct relationship to the Categories table.
Question	Text	The question that a Vecta Corp user could ask.
Solution	Text	The solution to the question.

The Patches Table

You'll use the Patches table to store patch and upgrade information for Vecta Corp solutions. The idea is that users will be able to come to the support page of the site and download patches and upgrades that they may need for solutions that they've purchased. The Patches table will consist of the columns shown in the following table.

Column Name	Data Type	Description
PatchID	AutoNumber	A unique number that automatically increments when new patch and upgrades are added. This number guarantees that each row in the table is unique.
SolutionID	Number	A numeric value that represents one of three Vecta Corp solutions (vProspect, vConvert, vRetain). This field will have a direct relationship with the Solutions table.
Version	Decimal	The version number for the patch or upgrade.
DownloadPath	Text	The file path to the download location of the file on the server. The idea is that this value is dynamically associated with a hyperlink on the Web page. That way, when the user clicks the link, the file on the server can be downloaded to the user's computer.

The Users Table

You'll use the Users table to store credential information for users who are able to access the admin page. Eventually, this table can grow to include users for the discussion board, should you decide to add one later. The Users table will consist of the columns shown in the following table.

Column Name	Data Type	Description
UserID	AutoNumber	A unique number that automatically increments when new users are added. This number guarantees that each user in the table is unique.
Name	Text	The user's name.
Username	Text	The user's username used to gain access to the admin page.
Password	Text	The user's password used to gain access to the admin page.

The Categories Table

The Categories table is considered a lookup table because it's used primarily by the Knowledgebase table. Also, you will use this table in later chapters to populate drop-down menus with knowledgebase categories. This way, when users need to view a particular knowledgebase article, they only need to select the appropriate category from the drop-down menu. The application, knowing that this item is selected, then retrieves data from the Knowledgebase table based on the category that's been selected from within the drop-down menu. The Categories table will consist of the columns shown in the following table.

Column Name	Data Type	Description
CategoryID	AutoNumber	A unique number that automatically increments when new categories are added. This number guarantees that each category in the table is unique.
Category	Text	The specific category with which knowledgebase articles will be associated. Unless more categories are added by the administrator, the only categories for which Vecta Corp will have knowledgebase articles associated with will be software, hardware, and network.

The Solutions Table

The Solutions table, like the Categories table, is also considered a lookup table because it's used primarily by the Patches table. More than likely, data contained within this table will seldom change. Also, you will use this table in later chapters to populate drop-down menus with Vecta Corp solutions. This way, when users need to view a particular patch, they only need to select the appropriate solution from the drop-down menu. The application, knowing that this item is selected, then retrieves data from the Patches table based on the solution that's been selected from within the drop-down menu. The Solutions table will consist of the columns shown in the following table.

Column Name	Data Type	Description
SolutionID	AutoNumber	A unique number that automatically increments when new Vecta Corp solutions are added. This number guarantees that each Vecta Corp solution in the table is unique.
Solution	Text	The specific solution for which patches and upgrades within the Patches table will be associated with. Unless Vecta Corp decides to sell more vSolutions, the only solutions that this table will contain will be vProspect, vConvert, and vRetain.

The Structured Query Language

Information contained within a database is useless unless you have the means of extracting it. The Structured Query Language (SQL) is the language that does just that. It allows for quick, but sophisticated, access to the database data through the use of queries. Queries pose questions and return the results to your Web application. But don't think of SQL as simply a way of extracting information. SQL can accomplish a variety of tasks, allowing you to not only extract information from a database, but to add, modify, and delete information as well.

SQL has its origins in a language developed by IBM in the 1970s called SEQUEL (for Structured English QUEry Language), and is still often referred to today as "sequel." It's a powerful way of interacting with current database technologies and the tables that make them up. SQL has roughly 30 keywords, and is the language of choice for simple and complex database operations alike. The statements you'll construct with these keywords range from the simple to complex strings of subqueries and table joins.

> Although all databases support basic SQL, others go well beyond the basics and incorporate their own proprietary syntax to support structured data, variables, error handling, flow control statements, loops, conditionals, transactions, and more. For example, Microsoft's implementation of SQL is known as Transact-SQL or T-SQL. Oracle's implementation of SQL is known as Procedural Language SQL or PL/SQL. The list goes on and on.

As this book progresses, you'll no doubt see how these statements are constructed. Queries, which are the backbone of dynamic Web applications, rely on basic SQL statements to operate. As the Vecta Corp Web application gets more complex, you'll see how to use insert, update, and delete statements to dynamically manipulate database data via a Web application running in a Web browser.

The Dynamic Vecta Corp Web Site

Up to this point, I have used various Web pages in the Vecta Corp Web site as examples of how to work with basic page formatting techniques, tables, CSS, forms and form controls, behaviors, layers, and more. The process has been simple. You create a new page, add some images and text to the page, format it with tables or layers, and then save it for viewing in the browser. While this process is fine for most of the pages in the Vecta Corp site, it's not, however, for most of the Support pages, where content has the potential of changing on a daily basis.

Think about it. Depending on how intricate the software is, your knowledgebase could become lengthy. Compound that with the fact that most software companies release patches, upgrades, and support documentation for their software, and you have the potential of working with dozens (if not hundreds) of files. And that's just within the Support section of the Vecta Corp Web site.

Dozens? Hundreds of files? You're probably thinking to yourself, job security right? When you're dealing with so many files on a Web site, maintenance tasks become enough to keep you busy all day, leaving little time for your talents and skills elsewhere on the Web site. Rather than taking a design or development role as it relates to the Web site, you might be stuck in maintenance mode, constantly adding, updating, and removing data from the support pages of the Web site.

This is where dynamic Web pages and Web applications come into play. Using a series of carefully crafted dynamic Web pages, you could easily streamline your workflow such that it begins to model the following workflow process:

❑   *Knowledgebase* — Rather than manually adding, removing, and deleting knowledgebase articles and FAQs, you simply tie a page (called `support_knowledgebase.aspx`) to the database. As you've seen, the Knowledgebase table within the database contains information such as knowledgebase ID, category, question, and solution. The rows contained within this table will be dynamically presented within the support_knowledgebase.aspx page.

❑ *Patch downloads* — Similar to the knowledgebase page, the patch download page (support_patches.aspx) will offer a list of patches and upgrades for Vecta Corp solutions. Tied to the Patches table, the support_patches.aspx page will offer functionality that will allow the user to view a patch ID, solution, version number, and download path.

❑ *Admin* — As the Web developer/administrator, you'll want a centralized interface for adding, modifying, and deleting knowledgebase articles and patches. This is where the admin.aspx page comes in. By creating a digital dashboard of sorts, you can easily fulfill these tasks without ever having to connect to your Web site manually within Expression Web.

After reviewing this process, you're probably starting to wonder about that job security. The downside to using dynamic Web pages and databases is that you're effectively taken out of some of the processes you've become accustomed to dealing with. The upside is that you can now focus on building more applications for your organization. Even better, you can now focus on designing and developing the fun stuff! And while the initial setup and development time is greater for the Web application than for the equivalent static pages, the benefits down the line far outweigh the time it would take to develop the application. Keep in mind that Expression Web cuts your development time in half. Because you're working with an intuitive visual editor and not coding by hand, creating the dynamic Vecta Corp pages in Expression Web will be fast.

Summary

This chapter was an important crossroad between client-side Web development and server-side Web application development. Throughout the chapter, you learned crucial concepts as they relate to Web architecture. You saw how modern-day Web applications function in a tiered architecture model. Specifically you learned about the various components that make up what we know as a tiered architecture model in that you have a client, the application/Web server, and a data store. As you progressed through the chapter, you learned about the role client-side technologies such as HTML, CSS, and JavaScript play in the architecture model. You also saw how server-side technologies such as ASP.NET and databases such as Access and SQL Server 2005 Express Edition fit into the model.

Aside from the theoretical material provided in this chapter, you also learned how to install and configure Microsoft's Web server IIS. You learned about Expression Web's built-in Web server. You also saw how to build a simple ASP.NET page that runs within the context of the Web server and uses the .NET Framework running on the server for processing. Additionally, you looked at database options such as Access and SQL Server 2005 Expression Edition, including getting Express Edition installed and running on your development machine.

While this chapter introduced what seems like a ton of concepts, terminology, and so on, it's merely a stepping stone for what's to come. In Chapter 11 and moving forward, you'll build on these concepts by putting together some of the dynamic Vecta Corp Web pages.

Accessing and Displaying Database Data

Throughout the book, you've learned about numerous important introductory-level concepts as they relate to dynamic server-side Web development. First, you learned about dynamic Web pages and what Web applications are. Next, you saw how databases such as Access and SQL Server 2005 Express Edition can serve as a backbone for data in your organization. You learned some introductory database concepts such as what databases are, and what role tables, columns, and rows serve. Finally, you reviewed the structured query language and, more specifically, how SQL provides the means for extracting, inserting, modifying, and deleting information from the database.

What you haven't learned to this point, however, is how to take all those foundation-level concepts and bring them together using Expression Web to create a truly dynamic, database-driven page. That's where this chapter comes in.

This chapter takes all the concepts you've learned up to this point and puts them into practice. You'll see how to connect Expression Web to your specific database using the Data Source Library Task Pane. Next, you'll learn about extracting data from the database using DataSource controls to create the Download Patches page for the Vecta Corp Web site. As this chapter progresses, you'll learn about the many features available for displaying data within a Web page, such as the GridView and DataList controls.

Starting to get excited? Good! This is where the previous chapters begin to come together to form Web applications.

This chapter serves as the beginning for a whole new world of Web development. By the end of this chapter, you should have a firm understanding of what it takes to connect to, extract from, and display database data within a Web page. To summarize, in this chapter you will do the following:

❑ Connect to a database using the Data Source Library Task Pane

❑ Use DataSource controls to extract data from a database

❑ Present database data within a Web page using both GridView and DataList controls

Connecting to a Data Source

With the database built, your first step to working with dynamic data is to actually connect Expression Web to the data source. On the surface, the process is as simple as opening the Data Source Library Task Pane and establishing a connection to either an Access or a SQL Server 2005 Express Edition database. Under the hood, however, the process is slightly more involved, and requires a bit more explanation before you dive in.

Chapter 10 outlined the major components of the .NET Framework. If you remember, the discussion in that chapter made reference to the fact that the .NET Framework offers three major components: ASP.NET, the CLR, and, most important, the .NET Framework Class Library. Note the importance of the .NET Framework Class Library here because everything in ASP.NET (from something as simple as a text box, to something more complex such as the classes used to connect to databases) is represented by a class. Those classes (and thousands more) are all contained within the .NET Framework Class Library. When you need to work with those classes, you simply import the necessary namespace (a hierarchal approach to organizing classes) into your Web page.

> If you recall, the Base Class Library was also outlined. The Base Class Library is Microsoft's way of acknowledging some classes you have to work with. For instance, Web controls, numbers, strings, the page, and more are all members of the Base Class Library, and are, therefore, out of sight and out of mind, and are not required to be imported.

Once the namespace has been imported into the page, you can either manually write code or use ASP.NET 2.0's newest layer of abstraction in `DataSource` controls to extract data and, more important, bind that data to either `List Bound` controls (drop-down menus, list boxes, checkbox lists, radio button lists, and more) or `Data` controls (`GridView`, `DataList`, `DetailsView`, `FormView`, and more). Visually, the process of connecting to, extracting from, and binding data to elements on your page will begin to mirror the diagram shown in Figure 11-1.

As you can see from the technical framework outlined in the diagram, the elements that you'll use to satisfy the various components in the hierarchy are as follows:

❑ *Database* — Of course, the database is already built. Whether you're using Access or SQL Server 2005 Express Edition for the examples in this book, the foundation for data access in Expression Web begins with the database.

> Remember, while databases are the most common mechanisms for storing data, they're not the only one. Technically, you can also store your organizations data within a XML file. As you'll see in Chapter 15, Expression Web has built-in functionality that allows you to connect to and extract data from XML files as well.

❑ *Data providers* — In ASP.NET 2.0, data providers are simply a fancy, technical term for the namespaces, classes, and members of a class used for connecting to a particular data source. Data providers offer the necessary functionality that Expression Web needs to successfully connect to the data source. In Expression Web, the process of connecting to a data source is handled using the Data Source Library Task Pane.

❑ *Data Source controls* — Once your connection has been established, your next step is to configure a DataSource control (either the AccessDataSource control when working with Access, or the SqlDataSource control when working with SQL Server 2005 Express Edition) to act as the intermediary between the data provider and List Bound / Data control. In previous versions of ASP.NET, this step was handled in code. Again, Expression Web makes this step of the development process easy, too. What used to take 20 or so lines of code is now conveniently handled using a simple control (AccessDataSource or SqlDataSource located within the ASP.NET controls subsection of the Toolbox Task Pane), and configured using a series of dialog boxes within a wizard.

❑ *List Bound and Data controls* — The presentational aspects of the page are handled using controls. If you want to present data from a database within a list box, drop-down menu, checkbox list, and so on, then you'd simply bind to what's known as a List Bound control. If you'd prefer to display your database data within a clean, grid-like view, then maybe the GridView control is more up your alley. As you'd expect from Expression Web, working with these controls is a snap, and is covered in more detail later in this chapter.

Classes, namespaces, DataSource controls, Data controls, List Bound controls, it's all a big blur, right? Again, the beauty in Expression Web is that you don't have to concern yourself with the technicalities of what's happening under the hood. This description merely provides an outline for how Expression Web handles the various tiers of the data binding hierarchy. As you can see, all of the technical terms that programmers would have to know and understand are handled in Expression Web using a familiar approach in controls, Task Panes, and wizards. More important, no code is required by you.

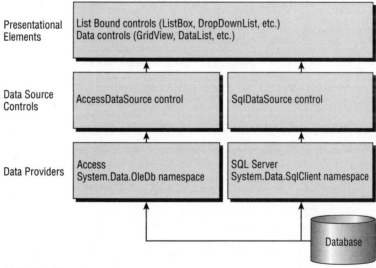

ASP.NET 2.0 Data Binding

Figure 11-1: Process of connecting to, extracting from, and binding data to elements on your page

Connecting to an Access Database

Chapter 10 introduced you to Access, Microsoft's personal and small-business database solution. If you recall, the database was created and conveniently stored within a `Database` folder in the Vecta Corp Web site. While the database resides within the `Database` folder, the Vecta Corp Web application has no idea it's there. In this section, you establish that reference between the Web application and the database by creating a connection to your data source.

Data source connections in Expression Web are handled using the Data Source Library Task Pane. Available by choosing Task Panes ⇨ Data Source Library, the Data Source Library Task Pane, shown in Figure 11-2, facilitates the process of creating new ASP.NET (database) and XML connections with a simple click of a link.

Once you click the provided link, the process of creating a database connection is as simple as proceeding through an intuitive series of dialog boxes.

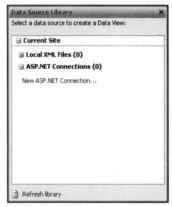

Figure 11-2: Data Source Library Task Pane

Try It Out   Connecting to an Access Database

To connect your Web application to an Access database, follow these steps:

1.   Open the files for this chapter by choosing File ⇨ Open Site. Browse to the Vecta Corp Web site and choose Open.

2.   Included in the project files is a file called `support_patches.aspx`. Open it by double-clicking the file within the Folder List Task Pane.

3.   Open the Data Source Library Task Pane by choosing Task Panes ⇨ Data Source Library.

4.   Select the New ASP.NET Connection link located within the Data Source Library Task Pane. The Choose Data Source Library dialog box appears, as shown in Figure 11-3.

5.   Choose the Microsoft Access Database File option from the "Data source" pane, clear the "Always use this selection" option, and click OK to proceed to the Connection Properties dialog box, shown in Figure 11-4.

6. Within the Connection Properties dialog box, click the Browse button to browse to and select `VectaCorp.mdb` (Access database file) located within the `C:\Inetpub\wwwroot\Vecta Corp\Database\` folder. For the sake of simplicity, you didn't specify a username and password for the database file, so leave those options as is. To test and ensure that Expression Web can successfully connect to your database without failure, click the Test Connection button. A small "Test connection succeeded" dialog box appears. Click OK to close it. Now, click OK to close the Connection Properties dialog box and proceed to the New Connection dialog box shown in Figure 11-5.

7. The New Connection dialog box is where you get to uniquely name the connection that Expression Web will make to your database file. This becomes advantageous when you start working on numerous ASP.NET files within your Web application. Rather than creating a new connection for every page in your application, you need to do this only once. Expression Web stores the connection (with the name that you provide here) within a `web.config` file (shown at the end of this section) for access from other Web pages in your application. While this discussion will definitely present the `web.config` file that is created for you in a minute, for now, enter a simple name within this text box like **vc_conn**. Click OK to close the New Connection dialog box.

That's it! You've successfully created a connection to your Access database within Expression Web. You'll immediately notice two changes within Expression Web: first, the `web.config` file is added to the Folder List Task Pane, and second, the `vc_conn` connection name is outlined within the Data Source Library Task Pane, similar to Figure 11-6.

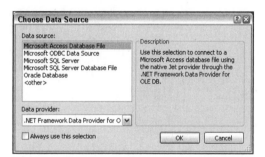

Figure 11-3: Choose Data Source Library dialog box

Figure 11-4: Connection Properties dialog box

As you can see in the lower left of Figure 11-6, the new connection vc_conn is created under the ASP.NET Connections subcategory within the Data Source Library Task Pane. If you'd like to remove the connection or even relaunch the dialog boxes to configure some of the many properties available for the connection, simply select the connection name within the Task Pane to access the submenu of options that allows you to do just that.

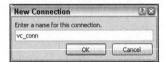

Figure 11-5: New Connection dialog box

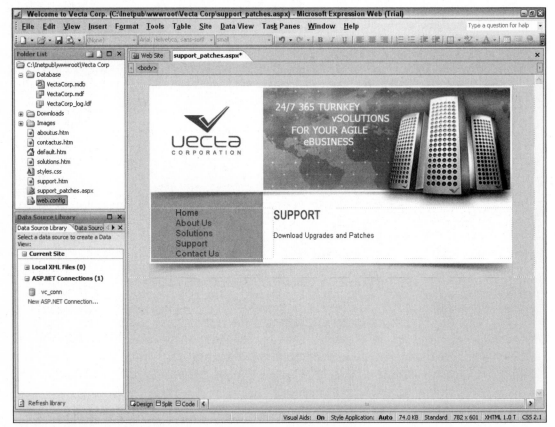

Figure 11-6: Successful connection to your Access database within Expression Web

The second change that you'll notice is the new `web.config` file that's created for you within the Folder List Task Pane. Aside from simply storing the connection string and provider type to the Web application, the `web.config` file is important because it stores application-level configuration settings for the Web application. Functionality such as security implementation, state management, custom error information, encoding, and more, are all outlined within this file.

To see what the file looks like, simply double-click it within the Folder List Task Pane to open the file within its own document window. Immediately, you'll notice that the file is an XML file that initially contains a node for connection strings. Within the connection strings node you'll see the new connection string `"vc_conn"` created in the earlier steps. Beyond that, you'll also see the connection string that Expression Web will use to connect to the database, as well as the provider type (outlined earlier in this chapter) that will be used when connecting to the database. Again, because you are using an Access database, the `System.Data.OleDb` namespace is used.

Now that a connection has been established to the database, you're ready to build the Download Patches page. Before doing that, however, let's review the process of connecting to a SQL Server 2005 Expression Edition database. As you'll see, some similarities exist in terms of creating a connection to both databases. The SQL Server 2005 Expression Edition database, however, requires just a few more properties to be configured.

Attaching your SQL Server 2005 Express Edition Database

Connecting to a SQL Server 2005 Express Edition database is similar to connecting to an Access database within Expression Web. The primary reason for this is the new simplistic nature of "attaching" and "detaching" database files built into the framework of SQL Server 2005. In previous versions of Microsoft development tools, the process of establishing a connection to a SQL Server database was much more complex. In SQL Server 2005, however, the process mirrors that of an Access database file. When you select the `.MDF` file (the SQL Server 2005 database file) to use, Expression Web is smart enough to "attach" the database file to the SQL Server database engine running as a service of the operating system for you. From a user standpoint, very little has to be done. Let's take a look.

Try It Out　　**Attaching Your SQL Server 2005 Express Edition Database**

To connect your Web application to a SQL Server 2005 Express Edition database, follow these steps:

1. Open the files for this chapter by choosing File ⇨ Open Site. Browse to the Vecta Corp Web site and choose Open.

2. Included in the project files is a file called `support_patches.aspx`. Open it by double-clicking the file within the Folder List Task Pane.

3. Open the Data Source Library Task Pane by choosing Task Panes ⇨ Data Source Library.

4. Select the New ASP.NET Connection link located within the Data Source Library Task Pane. The Choose Data Source Library dialog box appears, as shown previously in Figure 11-3.

5. Choose the Microsoft SQL Server Database File option from the "Data source" pane, uncheck the "Always use this selection" option, and click OK to proceed to the Connection Properties dialog box shown in Figure 11-7.

6. Within the Connection Properties dialog box, click the Browse button to browse to and select the VectaCorp.mdf (SQL Server 2005 Express Edition database file) located within the C:\Inetpub\ wwwroot\Vecta Corp\Database\ folder. In terms of security, SQL Server 2005 Express Edition offers two different options. The first, Windows Authentication, relies on your Windows credentials for access to the database file. For development purposes, this is the easiest method to use to connect to a SQL Server database file and the method you'll use for this example. The second, SQL Server Authentication, requires you to open SQL Server 2005 Express Edition's DBMS and manually configure a user and password that can be used here to access the database. Again, for the purposes of this discussion, leave the Use Windows Authentication option checked.

> It's important to note that, while you will use the file-based attachment method for "attaching" the SQL Server 2005 Express Edition database to the project, it may or may not be supported by your Web host provider. In certain cases, some Web host providers require you to use their SQL Server database installed on their servers. When this is the case, most Web host providers will supply a Web-based DBMS that you can use for working with the supplied database.

7. To test and ensure that Expression Web can successfully connect to your database without problems, click the Test Connection button. This time, you should experience a small lag before the "Test connection succeeded" dialog box appears. This is primarily because Expression Web attempts to attach the database file to the SQL Server engine running as a process of the operating system. After a few moments, however, Expression Web successfully attaches the file to the database engine and the "Test connection succeeded" dialog box will appear. Click OK to close it. Now, click OK to close the Connection Properties dialog box and proceed to the New Connection dialog box shown in Figure 11-5.

Figure 11-7: Connection Properties dialog box

8. As was the case in the previous section, the New Connection dialog box is where you get to uniquely name the connection that Expression Web will make to your database file. This becomes advantageous when you start working on numerous ASP.NET files within your Web application. Rather than creating a new connection for every page in your application, you need to do this only once. Expression Web stores the connection (with the name that you provide here) within a `web.config` file (shown at the end of the previous section) for access from other pages in your Web application. Enter a simple name within this text box like **vc_conn**. Click OK to close the New Connection dialog box.

That's it! You've successfully created a connection to your SQL Server 2005 Express Edition database within Expression Web. Again, as was the case in the previous section, Expression Web stores the connection information within an XML configuration file called `web.config` and places that file within the root of the Web application. Again, this file becomes visible within the Folder List Task Pane. Additionally, the new connection name `"vc_conn"` is conveniently listed within the Data Source Library Task Pane. If you'd like to remove the connection, or even edit properties that the connection outlines, simply select the connection name within the Task Pane to reveal a submenu containing Remove and Properties options.

With your SQL Server 2005 Express Edition database now connected and ready to use, you're ready to move forward and begin building the Download Patches page. The rest of the chapter is devoted to doing just that.

> **Again, it's important to understand that while Expression Web allows you to connect to and extract data from a variety of databases, this book only support two: Access and SQL Server 2005 Expression Edition. For the sake of simplicity, the rest of the book's examples assume that you're using SQL Server 2005 Express Edition. While most of the processes can be followed if you are using Access, some of the onscreen prompts and dialog boxes may or may not include different options, depending on the database that you're connecting to.**

Building the Download Patches Page

With new connections established to your database, you're now ready to begin building the Download Patches page (`support_patches.aspx`). As mentioned in Chapter 10, the idea behind this page is simple. It will enable Vecta Corp users to download upgrades and patches that they may need in support of solutions they may have purchased from the company.

To view the data contained within the `Patches` table in the database within the page, you'll need to perform the following few steps:

1. *Add a Data Source control* — Initially, you'll need to add a `DataSource` control to the page. The `DataSource` control allows you to define the SQL that you'll need to extract the necessary data from the database. It acts as the intermediary between the database and the presentational elements that you will include.

2.   *Add a presentational control* — Include a presentational element such as a Data or List Bound control to act as the component that will reveal the data contained within the database to the user. Initially, you will use a GridView control to display the upgrades and patches within a grid-like format. A bit later, you'll learn about other presentational controls such as the DataList control that can be used to display data within a Web page in a memo-list style format.

Of course, these two steps are outlined broadly. As each section unfolds, you'll begin to see the complexity and flexibility that DataSource controls and presentational controls such as Data or List Bound controls offer. What you can see here, however, are the final two tiers outlined within the technical diagram shown in Figure 11-1.

If you look at the diagram again, the development/addition of each component is coming together. The database was outlined in Chapter 10. The data provider (which acts as the bridge of communication between the database and the DataSource controls) was defined in the previous few sections. The DataSource controls (which outline the necessary SQL statements that you must extract the data from the database, as well as the presentational elements that are responsible for actually displaying the data) are outlined in the rest of this chapter.

Using DataSource Controls

Data extraction for most Web applications follows a simple pattern. The server-side technology fetches data from a data source, manipulates that data to fit into a nice-looking HTML layout, and then the result is piped back to a browser, which renders the output and presents to the user what the developer intended to be shown. With older versions of ASP.NET, developers had to write about 20 to 30 lines of code to connect to, issue a command to, and extract data from the data source.

For years, developers aiming to extract and present database data to users within a browser window would follow the same model. As developers, we got used to it. You'd maintain code snippets of the code that you'd reuse over and over, and paste it into your page when you needed to perform data extraction tasks. Sounds tedious, right?

With Expression Web (which relies on the newer, more modern ASP.NET 2.0), that 20–30 lines of code has been consolidated into zero lines of code. That's right! Code is no longer required when working with Web pages that connect to and extract data from data sources. How is this possible, you ask? The answer lies in the DataSource control.

DataSource controls, which take the form of the AccessDataSource (control for working with Access databases) and SqlDataSource (control for working with SQL Server databases) controls, were introduced as a method for essentially eliminating the same 20–30 lines of code that developers had to write to extract data from data sources. And they couldn't come at a better time. With Expression Web's introduction to the Web design/development marketplace, and with the promise of simplifying design and development tasks for the user, DataSource controls play right into the hands of not only Expression Web but, more important, the end user.

The idea is simple. You drag a DataSource control onto your Web page (which is visible only when working with your page in Expression Web and not within the browser), configure its properties to connect to your data source, specify a command to use for either retrieving data from, inserting data into, updating data within, and/or deleting data from the data source, and, finally, bind a presentational element such as a `GridView` control (mentioned later in this chapter) directly to the `DataSource` control for display within the browser. Before getting too far ahead, let's add a `DataSource` control to the page and configure its properties for data extraction now.

Try It Out   **Adding and Configuring a Data Source Control**

Now that the connection has been established to your data source, you can use a `DataSource` control to pull data from that data source and make it available for a presentational element such as a `GridView` control (covered later in the chapter) on the page. To add and configure a `DataSource` control, follow these steps:

1.   With the `support_patches.aspx` page open, switch to the Toolbox Task Pane, and expand the Data set of controls contained within the ASP.NET Controls subcategory. Find the `SqlDataSource` control and drag it out onto the page (assuming you're working with a SQL Server 2005 Express Edition database — if you're not, select and drag out the `AccessDataSource` control instead), as shown in Figure 11-8.

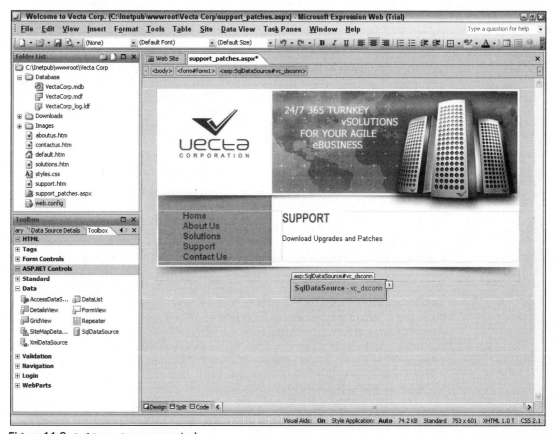

Figure 11-8: `SqlDataSource` **control**

2. The next step will be to uniquely name the DataSource control so that its name is slightly more meaningful than SqlDataSource1. To rename the control, open the Tag Properties Task Pane by choosing Task Panes ⇨ Tag Properties. Within the ID column, change the name of the DataSource control from SqlDataSource1 to something that you can relate to like **vc_dsconn** (short for Vecta Corp Data Source Connection).

3. Now that the DataSource control has been added and uniquely identified within the page, it's time to configure its properties so that it identifies itself with the vc_conn connection and so that it pulls data from the Patches table in the Vecta Corp database. To configure the DataSource control, begin by selecting the small expander arrow icon located just to the right of the control when it's selected. You'll receive a small submenu with the link that reads "Configure Data Source." Click that link to launch the Configure Data Source Wizard, shown in Figure 11-9.

4. As you can see from Figure 11-9, the first screen that's presented to you within the Configure Data Source Wizard is the Choose Your Data Connection screen. It's within this screen that you're able to configure the DataSource control to use either a preconfigured data connection or, if you prefer, to establish a new connection from scratch by clicking the New Connection button. Because you've already established a connection (vc_conn), select it from the drop-down menu. You may also expand the "Connection string" node to see a sample of the connection string that's created automatically for you. All of this is also visible in Figure 11-9. Click Next to proceed to the "Configure the Select Statement" screen.

5. Based on your connection, the Configure Data Source Wizard will then physically connect itself to the database and present you with a list of tables that the database contains within a drop-down menu in the "Configure the Select Statement" screen. From this drop-down menu, select the Solutions table and then click the checkbox with the asterisk (*) symbol next to it from within the Columns pane. Remember that the asterisk (*) symbol represents "all fields." As you can see from the read-only sample SELECT statement, the asterisk (*) symbol is combined with the table name and the SELECT and FROM keywords to form a SQL SELECT statement. This is the all-important command that is issued to the database in an effort to extract the data from the database. The result of the selections you'll want to make should resemble Figure 11-10.

The options that you have configured within this screen represent the most basic extraction from a database table. The following features are also offered within this dialog for working with more complex extractions:

❑ *Specify a custom SQL statement or stored procedure* — In the example outlined in Step 5, you selected "Specify columns from a table or view," picked a table from the database menu, and then chose from a list of fields in the Columns pane to automatically have Expression Web construct the necessary SQL statement for you. While this example works great for simple data extractions, it falls short when you need to work with complex queries that make use of joins. Furthermore, if you prefer to rely on a stored procedure for data extraction, then this option is more up your alley. Selecting this radio button and then clicking Next will direct you to a screen that allows you to either manually type your SELECT, INSERT, UPDATE, and DELETE statements, or simply pick a stored procedure to use from a drop-down menu instead. When you select this option, all other features in this screen are disabled.

❑ *Specify columns from a table or view* — As you saw in Step 5, this radio button facilitates the visual selection of tables and columns within those tables to include in your SQL statement.

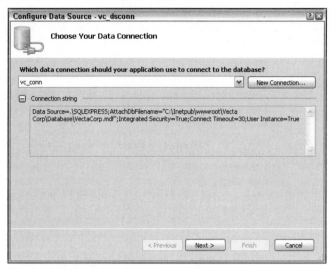

Figure 11-9: Configure Data Source Wizard

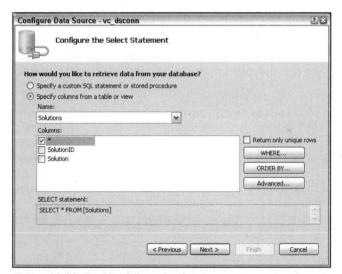

Figure 11-10: Result of the selections

- ❑   *Name* — As you saw in Step 5, selecting the "Specify columns from a table or view" radio button enables and then populates this menu with a list of tables/views within your database. Again, for this example, the Solutions table should be selected.

- ❑   *Columns* — As you saw in Step 5, selecting the "Specify columns from a table or view" radio button enables and then populates the name menu with a list of tables/views within your database. Once you select a table from the Name menu, this pane populates itself with the columns in the particular database table. You can then choose the check-boxes next to each column to either include all columns (the asterisk (*) symbol) or each individual column within your SQL statement.

❑ *Return only unique rows* — Click this checkbox to add the DISTINCT keyword to your SQL statement. Doing this would allow you to extract unique data from a table where the potential for duplicate values exists.

❑ *WHERE* — Click the WHERE button to launch the Add WHERE Clause dialog box. It's from within this dialog box that you're able to limit your data extractions based on a filter. This feature will be discussed in more detail later in this chapter.

❑ *ORDER BY* — Click the ORDER BY button to launch the Add ORDER BY Clause dialog box. It's from within this dialog box that you're able to create sorting criteria for the extracted data in either ascending or descending order.

❑ *Advanced* — Click the Advanced button to launch the Advanced SQL Generation Options dialog box. It's from within this dialog box that you're able to have Expression Web automatically generate INSERT, UPDATE, and DELETE statements (covered in more detail in Chapter 12). Furthermore, the dialog also allows you to set whether or not the DataSource control should use optimistic concurrency. As you'll see in Chapter 12, *optimistic concurrency* is especially useful in relational databases as a mechanism for detecting whether UPDATE or DELETE statements issued to the database conflict with already committed transactions or currently executing transactions. If they do, the UPDATE or DELETE is aborted, preventing redundant data from being added to the database.

❑ *SELECT statement* — As you configure options within the Configure the Select Statement dialog, this read-only label maintains a view of what your SQL statement looks like.

As the book unfolds, so, too, will other features offered here. Because this chapter is meant as an introduction to DataSource controls, for now, let's keep it simple. Click Next to proceed to the Test Query screen.

6. The Test Query screen is the final screen that you'll come to within the Configure Data Source Wizard. It's within this screen that you're able to test the result of the connection and, most important, the SQL statement that you configured in the previous screen. To test the query, click the Test Query button. As you can see in Figure 11-11, the data contained within the Solutions table is displayed within the preview pane. In the next few sections, you will use List Bound and Data controls to present a view similar to this within a Web page. Click Finish to close the Configure Data Source Wizard and return to your Web page.

With your DataSource control now configured to extract data from the database, you're ready to present that data within a Web page. This is where List Bound and Data controls come in.

Using List Bound Controls

With the DataSource control now set to extract the list of Vecta Corp solutions from the database, you now need some method for presenting that data within a Web page. Sure, you've set up a connection using the Data Source Library Task Pane and you've configured a DataSource control to tie itself to that connection and extract the solutions from the database. What you need now, however, is some mechanism for extracting data from the database for use on the Web page.

This is where List Bound and Data controls come in. While Data controls will be examined in more detail later in this chapter, List Bound controls, which are the subject here, are ideal for presenting data in Web pages within a checkbox list, radio button list, drop-down menu, list box, and bulleted list. With that said, the set of List Bound controls that you may decide to use within your Web pages includes the following:

- ❑ BulletList control

- ❑ CheckBoxList control

- ❑ DropDownList control

- ❑ ListBox control

- ❑ RadioButtonList control

Like all other Web controls, you can find this set of controls within the Standard section of the ASP.NET Controls set in the Toolbox Task Pane. For the purposes here, you will use the DropDownList control as a way of displaying all three Vecta Corp solutions to the user. The idea is that the user should be able to select for which solution they want upgrades or patches from a list of solutions (solutions stored within the Solutions table in the database). Later, this functionality is examined more closely, along with the available downloads to the user within a Data control. For now, let's explore how to add a List Bound control to the page and, more important, how to configure it to use the DataSource control outlined in the previous section.

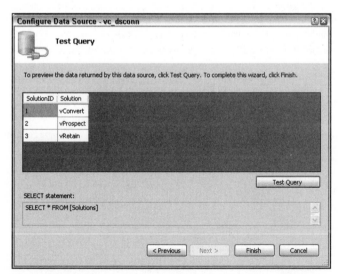

Figure 11-11: Data contained within the Solutions **table**

Try It Out   **Adding a List Bound Control**

While five different types of `List Bound` controls exist, the one that you'll want to use here is the `DropDownList` control. The idea is that you'll display all three Vecta Corp solutions to your users within a single pick-list menu. The user should then be able to select the solution that he or she is interested in to see all downloads available. To add a `DropDownList` control and configure it to bind to the `DataSource` control outlined in the previous section, follow these steps:

1. With the `support_patches.aspx` page open, switch to the Toolbox Task Pane, and expand the Standard controls contained within the ASP.NET Controls subcategory. Find the `DropDownList` control and drag it out onto the page. Immediately switch over to the Tag Properties Task Pane and name the `DropDownList` control **ddlSolutions**.

2. Notice that the `DropDownList` control on the page currently has the Unbound value associated with it. To bind it, you must access the Data Source Configuration Wizard. To do this, click the small expander arrow icon that appears just to the right of the control and click the Choose Data Source link from the menu that appears. The Data Source Configuration Wizard will appear, similar Figure 11-12.

3. As you can see from Figure 11-12, the wizard offers three different drop-down menus (ironically, the same type of menu that you're currently working with). The first allows you to select the `DataSource` control to bind the `DropDownList` control to. The second drop-down menu allows you to specify which field (from the extracted data) to use as the text value within the `DropDownList` control. Finally, the third drop-down menu allows you to specify the value field that should be associated with the `DropDownList` control. This value is extremely important because it will be the filtering criteria that you will use within a new `DataSource` control that you'll configure in the next section. For the purposes of this exercise, select the `vc_dsconn` data source from the "Select a data source" menu. Then, select the `Solution` and `SolutionID` options, respectively, from the next two drop-down menus. Your selections should resemble those shown in Figure 11-12. Click OK to close the Data Source Configuration Wizard.

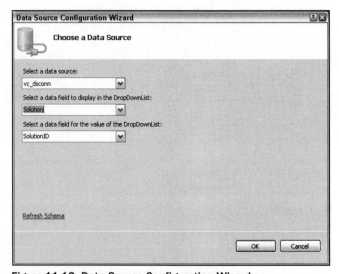

Figure 11-12: Data Source Configuration Wizard

4. Look at the `DropDownList` control. It should have the `Databound` value associated with it now. Save your work. To test your work in the browser, press F12. Immediately, Expression Web's built-in Web server kicks in, and your page becomes visible in the browser. More important, however, the `DropDownList` control appears on the page with the three Vecta Corp solutions listed, as shown in Figure 11-13.

See how easy that was? You were able to establish a connection to the database, extract data from a table within the database, and then present that data within a Web page by binding to a `List Bound` control. All of this functionality was accomplished just by using visual wizards and dialog boxes and, more important, writing zero lines of code! While this example represents the most basic and generic form of data extraction and binding, it's a big step forward.

The next few sections explore some slightly more advanced concepts. Specifically, you will create a new `DataSource` control that filters data extraction using the `WHERE` clause and bases the filter on the value being passed in from this `DropDownList` control. Then, the resulting data will be explored using more advanced presentational elements in `Data` controls.

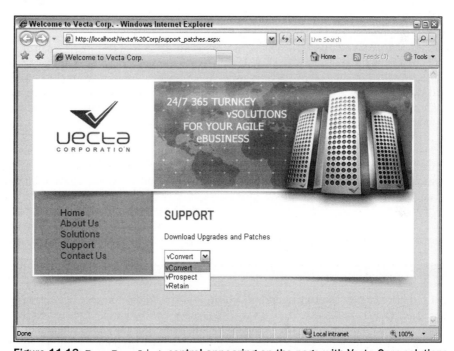

Figure 11-13: `DropDownList` **control appearing on the page with Vecta Corp solutions**

Using Data Controls

Now that you have a basic understanding as to how you can connect, extract, and present data using the Data Source Library Task Pane, `DataSource` controls, and `List Bound` controls, let's take a look at another set of controls aimed at facilitating not only data presentation, but data management as well. `Data` controls, like `List Bound` controls, are meant to display database data within a Web page. However, `Data` controls offer an advanced set of functionality that, unlike List Bound controls, provide features for editing, inserting, updating, deleting, sorting, paging, and more directly from within the control. Data controls available to you within Expression Web include the following:

❑ Repeater control

❑ GridView control

❑ DataList control

❑ FormView control

❑ DetailsView control

All five of these controls offer a unique visual interface. Furthermore, depending on which control you decide to use, features for various data management tasks will vary. The remainder of this chapter discusses some of the basic data presentation and management features offered via the GridView and DataList controls, including the two most popular Data controls available within Expression Web. Chapter 12 discusses the FormView control, the control used primarily when inserting data is necessary.

Working with the GridView Control

One of the most flexible and easy-to-use Data controls is the GridView control. The GridView control solves the problem that has plagued developers for years — centralizing data presentation and data management. In data management scenarios of years past, developers would create separate Web pages for viewing data, editing and updating data, and deleting data. Because a GridView displays data much like a spreadsheet does, information within a GridView is presented in a cleanly formatted tabular structure that is easy to read and aesthetically pleasing for the user.

Beyond the simplicities of data presentation, however, the GridView contains headers for field names that ultimately allow for sorting. Furthermore, the GridView also allows for paging (moving from one set or page of data to the next), the ability to customize the overall look with style templates, and even robust data management features (update and delete) directly from the GridView.

Gone are the days of having to create numerous pages for viewing, editing, and deleting data. The GridView control allows you to perform all of these tasks and more directly from within the control.

Try It Out   **Adding a GridView Control**

Now that you have an idea as to what kinds of features the GridView control can offer, let's add one to the support_patches.aspx page. This section will provide you with more practice in terms of inserting and configuring Data Source controls (because you will need one now to extract data from the Patches table), including using filtering criteria to limit the data extractions from the Patches table to patches and upgrades that are relevant to the selection the user makes from the drop-down menu. Additionally, this section will give you a clear understanding in terms of how easy it is to insert and work with the GridView control.

To add new DataSource and GridView controls, follow these steps:

1. As was the case with the DropDownList control, you must add a new DataSource control to the page before you can add the GridView control. You will add a new DataSource control to extract data from the Patches table. In this case, however, let's use the WHERE button to limit the data extraction based on the Vecta Corp solution that the user selects from the drop-down menu. To add a new `DataSource` control, begin by expanding the Data set of controls available from the ASP.NET Controls subcategory in the Toolbox. Find the `SqlDataSource` control and drag it out onto the page, next to the existing `vc_dsconn` control. Immediately switch to the Tag Properties Task Pane and uniquely name the new `DataSource` control (that is, change the `ID` property) **vc_dsconn_patches**.

2. Configure the `DataSource` control so that it extracts data from the `Patches` table. To do this, click the small expander arrow icon that appears just to the right of the control and choose the Configure Data Source link from the small submenu that appears. The Configure Data Source Wizard appears.

3. The first screen that you're presented within the Configure Data Source Wizard is the Choose Your Data Connection screen. From the menu that appears, choose the `vc_conn` option and click Next to proceed to the Configure the Select Statement screen.

4. Choose the "Specify columns from a table or view" radio button, select the `Patches` table from the Name menu, and click the asterisk (*) checkbox from within the Columns pane. Your SQL statement should read `SELECT * FROM Patches`. While this SQL statement may seem correct, it is, in fact, not. What you need to do is limit the data extraction to just grab data from the `Patches` table that's relevant to the user's selection in the Solutions drop-down menu. To do this, you must set up a filter using the `WHERE` clause. To set this up, click the WHERE button now. The Add WHERE Clause dialog box will appear, similar to Figure 11-14.

5. As you can see, the Add WHERE Clause dialog box offers features to allow you to customize the filtering criteria for the `DataSource` control. Specifically, Add WHERE Clause offers the following functionality:

   ❑ *Column* — The column from the database table on which you want to perform filtering. In this case, you want to filter the results based on the `SolutionID` column. Depending on which option the user selects from the drop-down menu, the value that's associated with the drop-down menu (1, 2, or 3) will serve as the filtering criteria here. Choose the `SolutionID` option from this menu now.

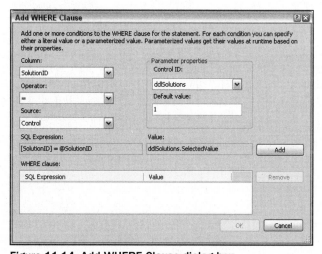

Figure 11-14: Add WHERE Clause dialog box

❏ *Operator* — The operator dictates how the conditional logic between the parameter being passed in and the column's value should be performed. Should the parameter being passed in be equal (=), greater than (>), less than (<), greater than or equal to (>=), less than or equal to (<=), or not equal to (<>) the column's value? This is where you get to specify that. For this example, choose the equal (=) sign.

❏ *Source* — This menu outlines all of the possible locations that the filtering parameter could come from. Options include None, Control, Cookie, Form, Profile, QueryString, and Session. Because you know that your parameter will be coming in based on the user's selection in the `DropDownList` control, choose Control now.

❏ *SQL Expression* — A read-only text label that outlines what the SQL expression looks like as you build it from the selections that you make in the dialog box.

❏ *Parameter properties* — Outlines the possible parameter names based on the option that you select from the Source menu. For example, in this case, you choose the Control option from the Source menu. Because only one control exists on the page (`ddlSolutions`), it's the only option that will appear within the Control ID drop-down menu. Choose it now. Just under the Control ID drop-down menu is the "Default value" text box. This is where you get to specify the default value of the parameter when the page loads for the first time. Because you want to display the patches and upgrades for the first solution in the list, enter the numeric value **1** here.

❏ *Value* — A read-only text label that outlines the code used for extracting the value for the parameter being passed into the `WHERE` clause. The modifications that you've made thus far will resemble those shown in Figure 11-14.

❏ *WHERE clause* — As you construct the `WHERE` clause, you can commit the modifications by clicking the Add button. Once you do, the `WHERE` clause is added to this list and the options outlined here reset themselves for you to be able to construct another. Click "Add" now to commit the changes you've made.

Now that the `WHERE` clause has been configured, click OK to close the Add WHERE Clause dialog box and return to the Configure the Select Statement screen. This time, notice the read-only `SELECT` statement pane. You'll notice that the statement now has the `WHERE` clause appended to it. Click Next to proceed to the Test Query screen.

6. In the previous section, you clicked the Test Query button and were presented with a complete list of items within the `Patches` table. In this case, because you set up a `WHERE` clause, the list that you'll get in return will be only a subset of all of the data within the `Patches` table. To demonstrate this, click the Test Query button. As you can see from Figure 11-15, the Parameter Values Editor dialog box appears. It's from within this dialog box that you're able to manually enter a value that represents the column that you've specified within the Add WHERE Clause dialog box. Because you specified the default value of 1, this number is automatically populated for you within the value column. Click OK to commit the test. You'll notice that the results that are produced within the list are limited to just vConvert downloads. Because vConvert is the option where the `SolutionID` is equal to 1, its data is the only data presented to you.

7. Click Finish to close and finish the configuration for the new `DataSource` control.

Figure 11-15: Parameter Values Editor dialog box

Now that the new DataSource control has been added and configured to present data from the Patches table, the next step is to add and configure the GridView control so that it uses this new DataSource control. Believe it or not, this process is much simpler than adding and configuring the DataSource control. To add the new GridView control, follow these steps:

1. Add some space after the DropDownList control by placing your cursor just to the right of the control and pressing Enter twice. Now, add the text **Available Downloads and Patches** and press Enter twice again.

2. Find the GridView control, available from the Data subset of controls within the ASP.NET Controls category in the Toolbox. Once you've selected it, drag it out so that it appears just under the text that you entered in the previous step. The result will appear, similar to Figure 11-16.

3. With the GridView control now on the page, the next step is to bind the GridView control to the DataSource control, added in the previous series of steps. To do this, choose the small expander arrow icon that appears just to the right of the GridView control. Once you click the expander arrow, a series of options (most of which are covered throughout this chapter and Chapter 12) appears within a submenu. For now, choose the vc_dsconn_patches option from the Choose Data Source menu. Immediately, the GridView will configure itself to match the data outlined within the Patches table in the database, similar to Figure 11-17. You'll also notice that the options available to you within the submenu have grown. Again, these options are discussed in great detail as this chapter and the one that follows unfold.

4. The last step to perform before you can test the page in the browser is to enable AutoPostBack for the DropDownList control. Without getting into too much technical detail, AutoPostBack forces the browser to post back the selected option within the DropDownList to the server for processing once a selection has been made by the user. The reason why you must do this is that the DataSource control is relying on the selected value of the DropDownList. To collect that selected value, the DropDownList control must post the selection back to the server. To enable AutoPostBack for the DropDownList control, simply click the expander arrow icon for the DropDownList control and click the Enable AutoPostBack checkbox.

5. Save your work and test the page in the browser by pressing F12.

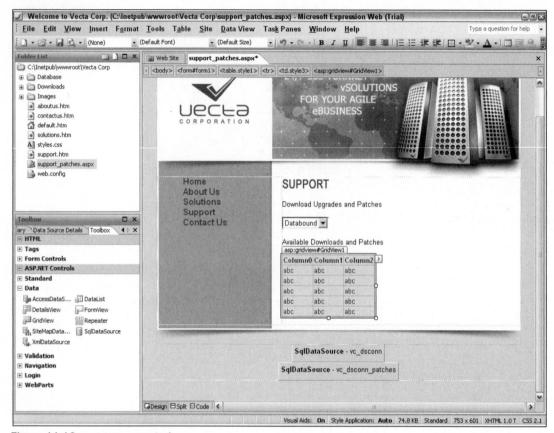

Figure 11-16: GridView **control**

As you can see from Figure 11-18, the GridView initially displays information for the first item selected in the DropDownList.

Again, this is possible because of the default value that you configured within the Add WHERE Clause dialog box. To see results for a different solution, simply choose a different option from the Solution drop-down menu. Depending on which option you select, the GridView configures itself to display the data associated with that option from the Patches table.

As you've seen, adding and displaying database data within a GridView control is easy. Not much is really required from you, aside from simply adding and configuring which DataSource control to bind the GridView to. The only downside to what you've done so far is that unneeded data is currently being presented to you within the GridView. For example, PatchID is probably a column that you don't need to display to the user. Furthermore, the SolutionID's 1, 2, and 3 don't mean much to the user, so you can probably eliminate that column. Also, the download path shouldn't be displayedto the user. Instead, you'll want to display a hyperlink here so that, when clicked, the ZIP file is down loaded

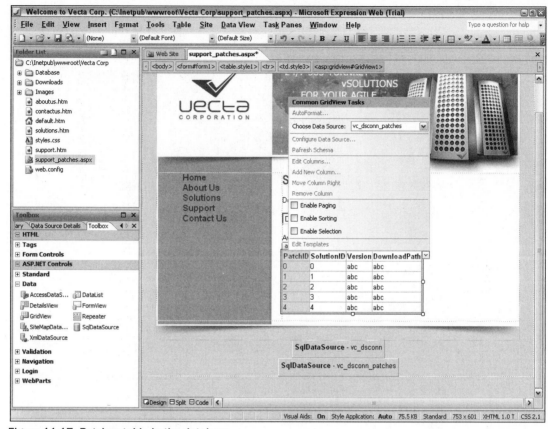

Figure 11-17: Patches table in the database

based on the path that's specified. Additionally, you might want to customize the header for the user so that, rather than seeing a header named "DownloadPath," the users see a header called "Download Now." All of this and more is possible simply by editing these columns. Let's do that next.

Editing Columns

As mentioned in the previous section, the GridView contains two columns that you are probably better off not displaying to the user. For example, users could care less what the ID is for the patch that they're downloading. Furthermore, the SolutionID is meant for the filtering mechanism only, and isn't something you need to show to the user. Additionally, the download path should be associated with a hyperlink rather than physically being shown to the user. All of these columns can be easily configured by either not showing them or configuring their contents to display something other than text (that is, a Hyperlink control rather than the download path). Configuring each column within the GridView will allow you to finely tune the control to appear more usable to your end users. Let's do that next.

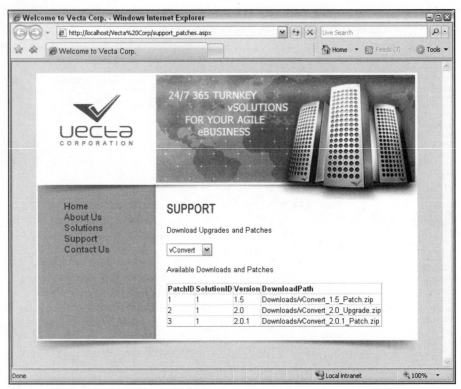

Figure 11-18: `GridView` **initial display**

Try It Out Editing the GridView Control's Columns

You can customize the columns within your `GridView` by following these steps:

1. Click the small expander arrow icon located just to the right of the `GridView` control and choose the Edit Columns option from the submenu that appears. The Fields dialog box will appear, as shown in Figure 11-19.

The Fields dialog box offers the following options:

❑ *Available fields* — This pane displays a list of fields that you can include within your `GridView`. For every field that you include within this list, a new column is created within the `GridView` to display the field's data. As you can see from the pane, you can either include all of the fields, an individual field from the collection of `BoundFields` (fields from the `DataSource` control), a `CheckBoxField`, a `HyperLinkField`, an `ImageField`, a `ButtonField`, a `CommandField`, and a `TemplateField`. While all of these possibilities certainly cannot be outlined in a book of this size, let's use at least one to give you an idea as to how adding these fields affects the usability of the `GridView` control. Because you'll need a hyperlink to allow the user to download the patch/upgrade, find the `HyperLinkField`, select it, and click the Add button. You'll notice that the field is added to the list of Selected fields.

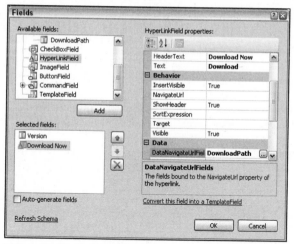

Figure 11-19: Fields dialog box

❑ *Selected fields* — Displays a list of fields currently bound within the GridView control. When you create a GridView control for the first time, by default, it simply creates bindings for all of the fields within the DataSource control. This is where you get to remove the ones that you don't need to show. Select the PatchID field and click the Remove Field icon represented by the button with the X on it. Repeat this process for SolutionID and DownloadPath. DownloadPath will be replaced by the HyperLinkField that you added in the previous bullet point.

❑ *BoundField properties* — All of the properties offered by bound fields can be manipulated here. While you'll leave the Version field alone, you definitely want to customize properties for the HyperLinkField that you added in the previous bullet points. Specifically, you'll need to customize the HeaderText (the text that should appear as the header), Text (the text that should be visible to the user), and DataNavigateUrlFields (the property associated with path of the hyperlink) properties. For HeaderText, enter the text **Download Now**, for Text, enter the text **Download**, and for DataNavigateUrlFields, enter the text **DownloadPath** (the field that contains the download path in the database).

❑ *Auto-generate fields* — If you prefer to simply bind all of the fields in the DataSource control to the GridView, simply click this checkbox. This option is enabled by default when you add and bind a GridView control to a DataSource control.

❑ *Refresh Schema* — The field structure contained within your DataSource control makes up the schema for the DataSource control. If that schema ever changes (maybe you configure the DataSource control to join other tables), click this link to refresh the look of your GridView. This option is also available from the submenu that appears when you click the small expander arrow icon from the GridView control.

❑ *Convert this field into a TemplateField* — In certain scenarios, the options offered within the field's dialog box just aren't enough to meet the needs of your potentially complex GridView structures. Clicking this link converts your fields into what's known as a TemplateField. TemplateFields are used by advanced ASP.NET developers who require more flexibility out of the fields within the GridView. You'll work with this option more in Chapter 12.

2. The completely formatted Fields dialog box should now resemble Figure 11-19. Click OK to close the Fields dialog box now. The structure of the GridView will change to accommodate the fields that you added, removed, and customized within the Fields dialog box.

3. Save your work and test the page in the browser by pressing F12. As you can see from Figure 11-20, the design of the GridView is much cleaner.

Also, try to click the Download link for a particular patch/upgrade. Immediately you should be presented with the File Download dialog box.

With the GridView functioning more as you need it to, you can now focus your attention on customizing how the GridView looks.

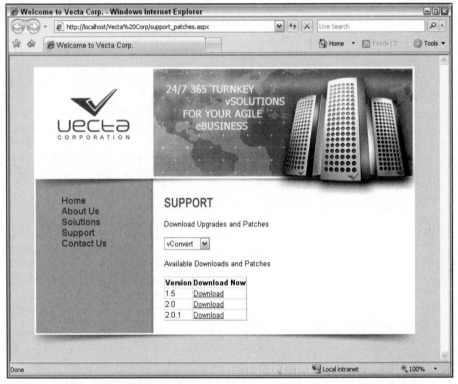

Figure 11-20: Design of the GridView

Formatting the GridView Control

In the previous sections, you added and configured fields within the GridView control mainly to improve the usability of the data outlined by the control. Although the example functioned well, it wasn't very aesthetically pleasing. Of course, you can fix this problem by customizing the many properties that are offered by the control.

You can customize the look of your `GridView` control in one of two ways. First, you can customize properties for the `GridView` offered in the Tag Properties Task Pane. This provides the most complete and advanced method for `GridView` customization. Second, you can format the look of the `GridView` quickly using the AutoFormat dialog box that becomes available when you choose the AutoFormat option from the submenu that appears when you select the expander arrow icon. For now, let's focus on the Tag Properties Task Pane.

Like controls in Expression Web, the `GridView` controls offers a set of customizable properties, each available and waiting to be modified via the Tag Properties Task Pane. The difference between the `GridView` and other controls, however, is that the `GridView` offers more than a hundred different properties and sub-properties that control everything, including the look of the `GridView`'s font, font size, color, background color, and so on, and properties that control each individual portion of the `GridView`, such as each row in the `GridView`, every other row, the footer, the header, and much more.

To give you an idea as to how vast the properties offered by `GridView` are, open the Tag Properties Task Pane now. You'll quickly notice that the `GridView` offers properties that are common across all controls such as `Font`, `Visible`, `Width`, `Enabled`, and even others that are specific to the `GridView` itself, such as `GridLines` (show or hide the grid-like lines surrounding the `GridView`), `CellPadding`, `CellSpacing`, `BackColor`, `BorderColor`, `BorderStyle`, `BorderWidth`, `ForeColor`, `Height`, `Width`, and much, much more.

While these properties enable you to customize the `GridView` control as a whole, they do little in terms of allowing you to customize the various components of the `GridView`. For this, you must access the particular component's style template. In all, eight different style templates exist for customizing the look of the eight different areas of the `GridView` control. Take a look at the Tag Properties Task Pane and you'll see the following expandable nodes, each representing the particular style template for the different areas within the `GridView`:

❑ `RowStyle` — The generic look of all rows within the `GridView`.

❑ `AlternatingRowStyle` — The look of every other row within the `GridView`.

❑ `EditRowStyle` — The look of the selected row in the `GridView` when the `GridView` is in edit mode. This is covered in more detail in Chapter 12.

❑ `EmptyDataRowStyle` — The look of the row within the `GridView` when the Data Source control that the `GridView` is bound to doesn't contain any rows.

❑ `FooterStyle` — The look of the footer row (bottom) within the `GridView`.

❑ `HeaderStyle` — The look of the header row (top) within the `GridView`.

❑ `PagerStyle` — The look of the paging row within the `GridView` when the `GridView` supports paging. This is covered with more detail in the next section.

❑ `SelectedRowStyle` — The look of the row when the particular row has been selected.

While you're certainly free to explore the customization of these properties, for our purposes, let's focus on a customization method that saves you time by allowing you to customize the look of the `GridView` using an easy-to-use visual approach in the AutoFormat dialog box.

To access the AutoFormat dialog box, click the small expander arrow icon located just to the right of the `GridView` control and choose the AutoFormat link from the submenu that appears. The AutoFormat dialog will appear, as shown in Figure 11-21.

As you can see from Figure 11-21, 17 different schemes exist for customizing the look of your `GridView`. For purposes of this discussion, choose the Professional option and click OK. You'll immediately notice that the appearance of the `GridView` control on the page is changed to coincide with the scheme that you picked. Save your work and test the page in the browser by pressing F12. As you can see from Figure 11-22, the appearance of the `GridView` control looks much better, and even matches the color scheme of the Vecta Corp site.

The best part about the AutoFormat feature is that the style templates previously outlined are automatically constructed for you based on the scheme that you choose within the AutoFormat dialog box. To give you an idea of what this means, select the `GridView` control, and immediately switch to the Code view for the Web page within the Expression Web. You'll notice the following style templates are included for you within the `GridView` control in code:

```
<FooterStyle BackColor="#5D7B9D" ForeColor="White" Font-Bold="True" />
<RowStyle BackColor="#F7F6F3" ForeColor="#333333" />
<EditRowStyle BackColor="#999999" />
<SelectedRowStyle BackColor="#E2DED6" ForeColor="#333333" Font-Bold="True" />
<PagerStyle BackColor="#284775" ForeColor="White" HorizontalAlign="Center" />
<HeaderStyle BackColor="#5D7B9D" ForeColor="White" Font-Bold="True" />
<AlternatingRowStyle BackColor="White" ForeColor="#284775" />
```

If it weren't for the AutoFormat dialog, all of these properties would have had to be customized manually within the Tag Properties Task Pane.

> While the previous statement is technically true, styles created within a CSS document may also be applied to a `GridView`. All controls, including the `GridView` control and the various components within the `GridView` control offer a `CssClass` property. Associate that `CssClass` property to a class selector within your style sheet to enhance the look of your `GridView` and its controls.

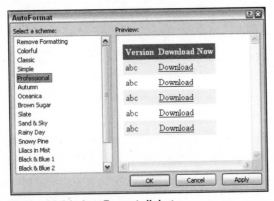

Figure 11-21: AutoFormat dialog

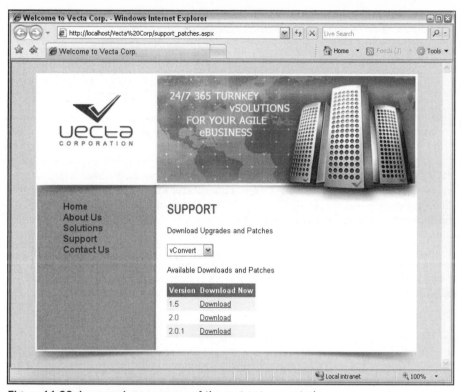

Figure 11-22: Improved appearance of the `GridView` control

Paging and Sorting the GridView

One of the last set of features that you may decide to add to your `GridView` control includes paging and sorting capabilities. From a usability standpoint, *sorting* provides your users with the ability to click on the column header in an effort to sort the data within the column in either ascending or descending order. From a presentation standpoint, *paging* allows you to limit the data shown within your `GridView` to a certain number of records. If the data within the `GridView` exceeds the number you specify, a padding widget appears as a footer of the `GridView` complete with either next or previous links, or numeric links that allow the user to page to the next set of records.

Try It Out   **Adding Paging and Sorting Capabilities to the GridView Control**

In previous versions of ASP.NET, adding paging and sorting capabilities to a `DataGrid` (the `GridView`'s predecessor) required about a dozen or so lines of code. In the most recent version of ASP.NET (2.0), there's no code to write. Instead, you set two properties. Like most features in Expression Web, accessing and setting these properties is simply a matter of enabling a checkbox. To enable paging and sorting for the `GridView` control, follow these steps:

1. Click the small expander arrow icon located just to the right of the `GridView` control and enable both Enable Paging and Enable Sorting checkboxes. Immediately, the only column that can be sorted (Version) is underlined and appears as a hyperlink. Additionally, you'll notice that the size of the GridView in design mode changes from five rows to ten rows. By default, when paging is enabled on the GridView control, the capacity of the rows within the GridView is governed by the PageSize property in the Tag Properties Task Pane.

2. You can change the capacity of the GridView by modifying the PageSize property. To do this, ensure that the Tag Properties Task Pane is open. Scroll down the Task Pane until you find the PageSize property and change the value of the PageSize property from 10 (the default) to 5. The GridView will collapse down to display five rows.

3. Save your work and test the page in the browser by pressing F12.

Click the Version link within the header for the column. You'll notice that as you click the link, the data within the GridView is sorted in ascending and then descending order based on the data within the column. What you won't see, however, is the paging control that you can clearly see within the design view. The reason for this is simple: you have only three rows of data. The paging control won't appear until the data within the GridView exceeds five rows.

In Chapter 12, you build an admin page that will allow you to manually add rows of data to the database from a Web page. Using that functionality, you can add more data to the Patches table so you can see the functionality offered by the paging control. Of course, you could also switch back to Expression Web and change the PageSize property from 5 to 2. Because you have three rows, the paging control will appear.

So far, you've seen how modifying the PageSize property can affect how many rows of data are displayed within the GridView control before the paging control appears. While the PageSize is certainly one property examined here, it's not the only one. The following list of properties represents the most common for manipulating the look and functionality offered by the GridView control for paging and sorting:

❑ AllowPaging — Enables or disables the paging feature within the GridView. Setting this option to true is equivalent to clicking the checkbox within the submenu that appears when you click the expander arrow icon within the GridView.

❑ AllowSorting — Enables or disables the sorting feature within the GridView. Setting this option to true is equivalent to clicking the checkbox within the submenu that appears when you click the expander arrow icon within the GridView.

❑ PagerStyle — As mentioned in the previous section, the GridView offers a set of eight customizable style templates that represent the eight different areas within the GridView. Because the Pager is one of those eight areas, expand this node to customize everything from the font, wrapping, border, alignment, and more for the GridView's pager component. Because you used the AutoFormat text box in the previous section, these settings are pre-populated for you.

❑ PageSize — Represents the GridView's row capacity before the paging control appears. Also dictates how many records are shown within the GridView per page.

❑ PageIndex — Represents the numeric index of the page that the GridView should display initially when the page is loaded (0 represents the first page, 1 represents the second, 2 the third, and so forth).

❑ PagerSettings — Expand this node to reveal further properties for customizing the look of the paging control. For example, the Mode property offers options for setting the pager to display next and previous links, numeric links (default), next and previous with first and last links, and numeric with first and last links. Additionally, you may also decide to customize the vertical and horizontal positioning of the pager; whether to show it on the top, bottom, or both of the `GridView`; and more.

Working with the DataList Control

The `DataList` control, like the `GridView` control, facilitates data presentation within a Web page. By simply binding the `DataList` to a configured `DataSource` control, you can easily present data from a table in your database within a Web page. The biggest difference between the `DataList` and the `GridView`, however, is that the `GridView` is meant to display data in a tabular, grid-like format (much like a spreadsheet) whereas the `DataList` control is meant to display data in a list view.

To imagine how the `DataList` presents data, think of your Contact list within Outlook. If you look at the list, contacts are shown in columns rather than rows, as is the case with the `GridView` control. Because of the column-based approach, each contact can contain different information independent of other contacts. Some contacts may have the address visible, others just a phone number, while other contacts may display the address and multiple phone numbers. Alternatively, other contacts may show just the e-mail address. These views are all possible with the `DataList` control.

Admittedly, usage of the `DataList` control will be far less within your Web pages than is the case with the `GridView` control. The `DataList` control certainly has its place and warrants discussion within the scope of this project.

To demonstrate the use of the `DataList` control, a file called `support_patches_datalist.aspx` has been created for you. What you'll do within this file is create a new `DataSource` control, configuring its properties to extract data from both the `Patches` and `Solutions` tables. Then you'll add the `DataList` control, binding it to the newly created `DataSource` control. Beyond this section, the discussion will explore how to configure the `DataList` control within Expression Web. You'll see how using Templates and the Property Builder within Expression Web can really bring the `DataList` to life.

Throughout this chapter, you've created `DataSource` controls as the mechanism for extracting data from your database tables. The controls discussed thus far bind to the `DataSource` controls and present the data that the `DataSource` control is responsible for extracting. In the previous sections, you saw how to add and configure a basic `DataSource` control by simply extracting data from the `Patches` table. Then the process got a just a bit more advanced by using `WHERE` clauses to limit the data returned based on a parameter passed in from the `DropDownList` control.

This section provides yet a more advanced look at extracting data from database tables using joins within the `DataSource` control. So, even if you have no interest in the `DataList` control, read on. At the very least, you'll learn how to create complex joins using the Query Builder within the Configure Data Source Wizard.

Try It Out   Creating Complex Joins Using the Query Builder

As was the case with the `DropDownList` and `GridView` controls, a `DataSource` control must be added and configured before you can work with the `DataList` control. To add and configure a `DataSource` control to be used with the `DataList`, follow these steps:

1. With the `support_patches_datalist.aspx` page open, switch to the Toolbox Task Pane, expand the Data set of controls contained within the ASP.NET Controls subcategory. Find the `SqlDataSource` control and drag it out onto the page.

2. Rename the DataSource control to something more meaningful than SqlDataSource1. To rename the control, open the Tag Properties Task Pane by choosing Task Panes ⇨ Tag Properties. Within the ID column, change the name of the DataSource control from SqlDataSource1 to something that you can relate to, such as **vc_dsconn** (short for Vecta Corp Data Source Connection).

3. Now that the DataSource control has been added and uniquely identified within the page, it's time to configure its properties so that it identifies itself with the vc_conn connection and so that it pulls data from both the Patches and Solutions tables in the VectaCorp database. To configure the DataSource control, begin by selecting the small expander arrow icon located just to the right of the control when it's selected. You'll receive a small submenu with the link that reads "Configure Data Source." Click that link to launch the Configure Data Source Wizard.

4. The first screen that's presented to you within the Configure Data Source Wizard is the Choose Your Data Connection screen. Because you've already established a connection (vc_conn), select it from the drop-down menu and then click Next to proceed to the Configure the Select Statement screen.

5. Configure the SELECT statement to extract data from both the Patches and Solutions tables. In the previous sections, you simply selected the "Specify columns from a table or view" radio button, chose which table in the database you wanted to extract data from within the Name menu, and then chose which fields you wanted to include in the statement within the Columns pane. While this process is fine for individual tables, it doesn't work when you need to extract data from multiple tables. For this, you must configure a SELECT statement manually. To do this, select the "Specify a custom SQL statement or stored procedure" radio button and click Next to proceed to the Define Custom Statements or Stored Procedures screen.

6. Within the Define Custom Statements or Stored Procedures screen, you have the option of manually writing the SQL statement to use for extracting data from your database tables. This is the route that you should take. Enter the following SQL into the SELECT statement text box:

```
SELECT Solutions.Solution, Patches.Version, Patches.DownloadPath
FROM Solutions INNER JOIN Patches
ON Solutions.SolutionID = Patches.SolutionID;
```

The result will resemble Figure 11-23.

7. Click Next to accept the SQL statement and proceed to the Test Query screen. Within the Test Query screen, click the Test Query button. This time, not only does the data for Version and DownloadPath appear, but the data for Solution appears as well. Again, this is possible because of the join created above. Click Finish to close the Configure Data Source Wizard and return to your Web page.

With the DataSource control configured, let's now focus on adding the DataList control.

Try It Out   Adding a DataList Control

You can add a DataList control and subsequently bind it to the DataSource control created earlier by following these steps:

1. Switch to the Toolbox Task Pane and expand the Data set of controls contained within the ASP.NET Controls subcategory. Find the DataList control and drag it out onto the page just under the text that reads "Download Upgrades and Patches."

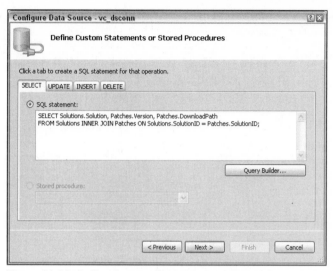

Figure 11-23: Define Custom Statements or Stored Procedures dialog

2. As soon as you add the `DataList` control to the page, you'll immediately notice that, by default, the `DataList` appears as a simple grey box. Before you can begin to see what the `DataList` will look like, you'll need to bind it to the `DataSource` control. To do this, select the small expander arrow icon located just to the right of the `DataList` control and choose the `vs_dsconn` option from the Choose Data Source menu located within the submenu that appears. Instantly, the `DataList` control configures itself to display the `Solution`, `Version`, and `DownloadPath` within a list format, similar to Figure 11-24.

3. Save your work and test the page in the browser by pressing F12. As you can see from Figure 11-25, all of the data is presented within a clean, list-like format.

Like the `GridView` control, the `DataList` can be further configured to show hyperlinks, formatted to be more aesthetically pleasing, and more. This can be accomplished via the Property Builder, as well as by manipulating templates offered by the `DataList` control. Both of these topics are covered in the next few sections.

Using the Property Builder

When working with the `GridView` in previous sections, you were able to format the control to make it look more appealing. You did this by manipulating some of the many properties offered by the control directly within the Tag Properties Task Pane. Additionally, you were able to choose the AutoFormat option in an effort to quickly and easily add a pre-built scheme to the control, making it more aesthetically pleasing to the end user. While the `AutoFormat` option is also available for the `DataList` control, there's another feature that's unique to the `DataList` in the Property Builder. The Property Builder, like the properties listed within the Tag Properties Task Pane, allows you to customize the look and functionality of the `DataList`. The main difference with the Property Builder, however, is that properties are organized into categories, and selecting and applying properties to the `DataList` is centered around a visual approach that, again, is unique to the `DataList` control.

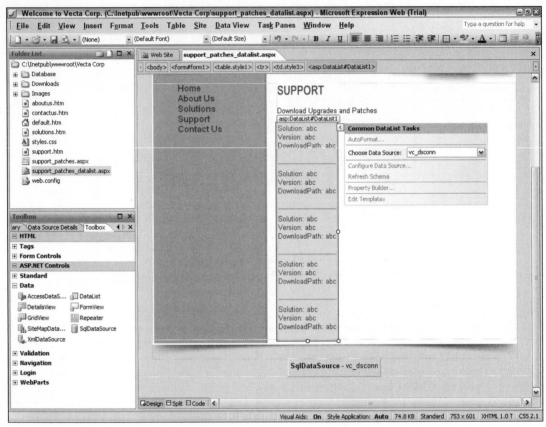

Figure 11-24: `Solution`, `Version`, **and** `DownloadPath`

Try It Out   **Formatting the DataList Using the Property Builder**

To demonstrate how easy the Property Builder makes configuring properties for the `DataList` control, let's use it now to format the background color of every other item within the `DataList`. To do this, follow these steps:

1. Launch the Property Builder for the `DataList` control by clicking the small expander arrow icon located to the right of the `DataList` and choose the Property Builder link from the submenu that appears. The Property Builder dialog will appear.

2. Click the Format category from the pane on the left side.

3. With the Format category selected, expand the Items node within the Objects pane and choose the Alternating Items option.

4. Choose the Silver option from the "Back color" menu. The result of the formatted dialog box will appear, similar to Figure 11-26.

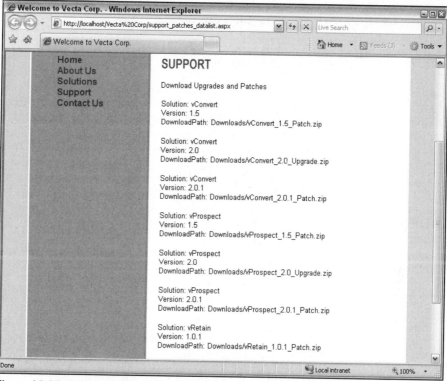

Figure 11-25: Data presented within a clean, list-like format

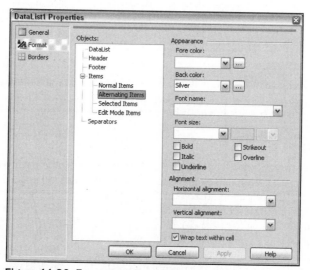

Figure 11-26: Formatted dialog box

5.   Click OK to close the Property Builder. Immediately, the `DataList` is formatted to reflect the silver color that you've associated with every other item in the list.

6.   Save your work and test the page in the browser by pressing F12. You'll notice that every other item in the list has its background color set to gray.

As you can see, the Property Builder makes editing properties for the `DataList` control easy by offering a simple, visual interface for customizing properties. In this example, you simply configured the background color of every other item within your `DataList`. As you moved through the Property Builder, however, you probably noticed that other properties existed for extending the look and functionality offered by the `DataList`. In summation, these properties (organized by category) are listed as follows:

❑   *General* — Offers simple properties for customizing how the `DataList` should show data. For example, you may decide to show or hide the header and footer of the `DataList`. If this is the case, simply enable or disable the "Show header" and/or the "Show footer" checkboxes. Also, remember that the `DataList` has the capability of displaying data much like your contacts in Outlook. The General category also offers a Columns text box that allows you to specify how many columns to use for displaying the list data. Additionally, you can customize the direction of the data presentation. By default, this value is set to Vertical. However, if your Columns text box is set to 2 or more, then this property should be set to Horizontal instead.

❑   *Format* — Offers options for customizing the look of the eight different areas within the `DataList`:

❑   *Objects* — Select one of the eight different areas within this list to customize its appearance within the Appearance pane. Options include the `DataList` as a whole, the header, footer, normal items, alternating items, selected items, items when they're in edit mode, and the separator.

❑   *Appearance* — Once you've selected one of the eight different areas from the Objects pane, you can customize the look from the options offered here. For the most part, these options are generic and represent changes that you can make for customizing the forecolor, background color, font name, font size, font weight, font style, and horizontal alignment.

❑   *Borders* — You can add borders (including border color and width), cell padding, and cell spacing to the `DataList` by customizing properties offered here.

Again, it's important to understand that every property offered for every control cannot be covered within a book of this size. The goal here (as it is with all the chapters in this book) is to provide you with a basic understanding of the topic. The idea is that, with the introduction, you'll branch out on your own and apply the basics learned in this book with more advanced concepts in your own projects.

DataList Templates

One of the topics yet to be discussed is templates. Templates are used in `Data` control (such as the `GridView`, `DataList`, and others) to extend the functionality offered by the control. In previous sections, you added a `GridView`/`DataList` control by simply dragging the control onto the page and then binding it to a preconfigured `DataSource` control. Save for a few properties that you modified using the Edit Columns dialog (`GridView`), the Property Builder (`DataList`), or the Tag Properties Task Pane, there really wasn't much expected of you. You added the control to the page, bound it to a `DataSource` control, and previewed the page in the browser, and the control displayed data in either a grid-like or list view. For most basic data extraction tasks, the processes reviewed up until this point will work just fine. It's when you want to extend the functionality of these controls that you'll need to rely on templates.

Templates (which vary depending on the Data control that you use) extend the functionality of the control by allowing you to specify what (additional) content should appear within the template of the control. The content displays only when either the browser or the user accesses a piece of functionality within the control that causes the template to become enabled.

Consider the areas in between each item within the DataList. Currently, the way the DataList displays, it shows the Solution, then the Version, then the DownloadPath, and finally a space in between the item and the beginning of the next item. What if you wanted to include some sort of image, or even something as simple as a horizontal line that clearly marks the division between items in the DataList? The way that the DataList is set up, without the use of templates, there is no way to accomplish this task.

While templates vary depending on Data control, the seven that are consistent across the board are as follows:

❑ ItemTemplate — The content that should appear within each cell of the DataList.

❑ AlternatingItemTemplate — The content that should appear within every other cell of the DataList.

❑ SelectedItemTemplate — The content that should appear within each cell of the DataList when a cell in the DataList is selected.

❑ EditItemTemplate — The content that should appear within each cell of the DataList when the DataList is in edit mode.

❑ HeaderTemplate — The content that should appear within each header cell of the DataList.

❑ FooterTemplate — The content that should appear within each footer cell of the DataList.

❑ SeparatorTemplate — The content that should appear in between cells of the DataList.

The DataList is unique in a sense that it relies entirely on templates. Even when you simply bind the DataList to the DataSource control, Expression Web automatically generates an ItemTemplate within the DataList in code, and creates the bindings to the fields within the DataSource control.

To prove this point, switch to Code view. As you can see from the highlighted code in Figure 11-27, the DataList control contains an ItemTemplate.

While the ItemTemplate is included within the DataList automatically, others you include at your leisure. One such template is the SeparatorTemplate. The SeparatorTemplate tells the browser to render content contained within that area in the browser. The SeparatorTemplate is the area in between each item in the DataList. Using some basic template editing techniques, you could simply add a horizontal line within that template and expect that element to also appear within the browser. Let's try it!

Try It Out   Adding a Separator to the DataList Using Templates

To learn how to add a horizontal line as a separator between items in the DataList, follow these steps:

1. Click the small expander arrow icon located to the right of the DataList and choose the Edit Templates link from the submenu that appears. The appearance of the DataList will immediately change to support template editing.

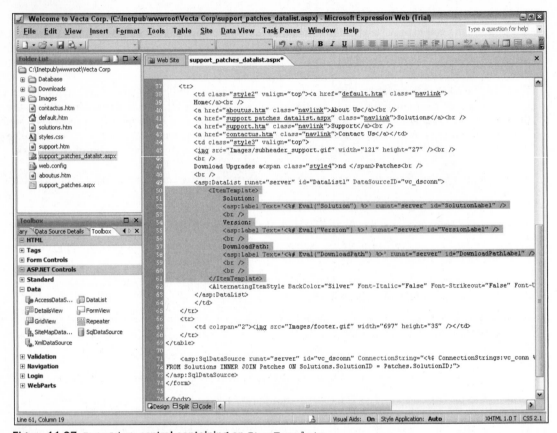

Figure 11-27: `DataList` **control containing an** `ItemTemplate`

2. Initially, the `DataList` displays in edit mode, allowing you to modify the `ItemTemplate`. In this case, leave the `ItemTemplate` alone and instead switch over to the `SeparatorTemplate`. To do this, select the Separator Template option from the Display drop-down menu. The appearance of the `DataList` switches to support editing within the `SeparatorTemplate`.

3. Place your cursor within the `DataList` and choose Insert ➪ HTML ➪ Horizontal Line. The horizontal line appears within the `DataList`.

4. You can exit template editing mode by choosing the End Template Editing link that appears within the submenu below the Display drop-down menu. The `DataList` reverts back to its original state.

5. Save your work and test the page in the browser by pressing F12. As you can see from Figure 11-28, a horizontal line appears between each item in the `DataList`.

As you can see, templates provide an extended level of flexibility for customizing the look and functionality for the `Data` controls that you decide to use on your pages. This section has merely scratched the surface, discussing the `SeparatorTemplate` at an introductory level. Chapter 12, however, expands on concepts learned here by introducing the `ItemTemplate` and `EditItemTemplate` in more detail.

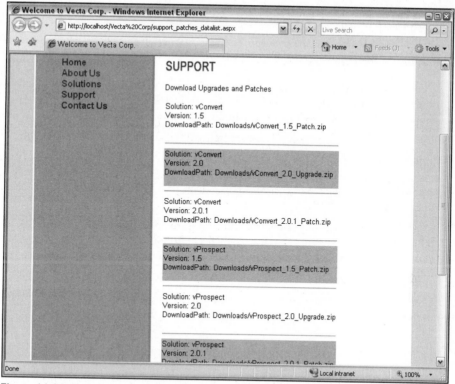

Figure 11-28: Horizontal line appearing between each item

Summary

This chapter served as a crucial starting point for working with dynamic Web pages in Expression Web. The concepts covered in this chapter will prove invaluable as you build Web applications both in future chapters, as well as in your own projects.

In this chapter, you learned how to connect to an Access/SQL Server 2005 Express Edition data source using the Data Source Library Task Pane. Then, you learned how to connect to and extract data from that data source using DataSource controls. Finally, and more important, you learned how to present that extracted data within both List Bound (DropDownList) and Data controls (GridView and DataList). For every control that you worked with, you learned how to format the DataSource control to progressively extract data from one table, filter data from a table, and then join data from two tables.

While this chapter served as a starting point for working with dynamic database data, Chapter 12 will build on the introductory concepts learned here by introducing data management. Specifically, you'll learn how to extend the DataSource controls to allow for inserting, updating, and deleting. Additionally, you'll learn how to configure the GridView for data management (that is, allowing the user to edit, update, and delete records in the database directly from the GridView control). Finally, Chapter 12 introduces a new Data control in the FormView control, used specifically for creating an interface to allow your users to insert data into the database directly from the Web page.

Exercise

In this exercise, you use some of the concepts that you learned in this chapter to build the support_ knowledgebase.aspx page. Specifically, you should do the following:

1. Open the provided support_knowledgebase.aspx page and immediately establish a connection to the data source using the Data Source Library Task Pane. You will have to perform this step only if you weren't following along with the examples in the chapter.

2. Add a new DataSource control and configure it to extract data from the Categories table.

3. Add a DropDownList control to the page and bind it to the new DataSource control so that the categories are presented as text within the DropDownList control and the category ID is set as the DropDownList control's value. Don't forget to enable AutoPostBack for the DropDownList control.

4. Create a second DataSource control and configure it to extract data from the Knowledgebase table based on the category that the user selects from the DropDownList control. Remember that you'll have to configure the DataSource control to use a WHERE clause.

5. Add a DataList control and bind it to the second DataSource control.

6. Configure the DataList control using the Property Builder so that it fits in with the color scheme of the Vecta Corp Web site.

Inserting, Editing, and Deleting Database Data

Chapter 11 introduced you to a critical component in building Web applications: data extraction and presentation. You learned how to establish a connection to the database and configure a DataSource control to act as the bridge of communication between the database and your presentational elements, and you learned how to drag out and bind presentational elements (such as the drop-down list control, GridView control, and DataList control) to your DataSource controls for the sole purpose of displaying database data within your Web pages.

While Chapter 11 introduced crucial concepts and generally laid a foundation for working with database data, the reality is that simple data extractions will get you only so far. To take your Web applications to the next level, you want to offer functionality that allows your users to insert new, modify existing, or delete data from the database directly from within a Web page.

By the end of this chapter, you'll have acquired the skills necessary to build a full-functioning dynamic Web application — one where all of the company's data is centrally housed within a database and presented to users dynamically within Web pages using ASP.NET controls. Furthermore, you'll have acquired the skills to be able to insert new, modify existing, and delete data within the database centrally from a Web page, without the need to use traditional FTP methods. In this chapter, you will do the following:

- ❑ Create the Vecta Corp administration page
- ❑ Build on the DataSource configuration skills that you've acquired thus far by manipulating the DataSource control to allow database inserts, updates, and deletes
- ❑ Use the FormView control to insert data into the database
- ❑ Insert and configure a GridView control to support editing, updating, and deleting

Building an Administration Page

In Chapter 11, you were able to establish a connection to the database, manipulate a DataSource control to extract data from the database, and then add and bind a presentational element (such as a List Bound or Data control) to the configured DataSource control. While the examples covered in Chapter 11 worked well for simple data extractions and presentations, they do not allow you to insert, modify, and delete data from a database. Although the presentation of data within the Web pages is dynamic, modification of that data is still reliant on a user physically entering a database to make the necessary changes.

This chapter remedies this problem by offering an administrative page that users (administrators) may access to insert new, modify existing, and/or delete data from the database centrally from a Web page. The process will mirror the one diagrammed in Figure 12-1.

As you can see from Figure 12-1, methods for extracting data and presenting it within the Knowledgebase (support_knowledgebase.aspx) and Patches (support_patches.aspx) pages won't change. The data is still being extracted from the database (via DataSource controls) and presented to the user within each page using List Bound and Data controls.

What will change, however, is the way that the data is added, modified, and deleted within the database. By building an administration page (admin.aspx), you could easily allow your users to manipulate the data contained within the database centrally. From a user's standpoint, the process is transparent. Users are simply viewing the information that they came to the site to find. From a development perspective, however, the process is much more dynamic. All of the company's crucial data is conveniently stored within the database and dynamically presented through List Bound and Data controls within the appropriate pages. The content becomes much more dynamic because an administrator gets to manipulate that data centrally via an administrative console. To achieve this, you will perform the following steps:

1. Open the provided ASP.NET page titled admin.aspx.

2. Add and configure a new DataSource control so that it supports inserts, updates, and deletes.

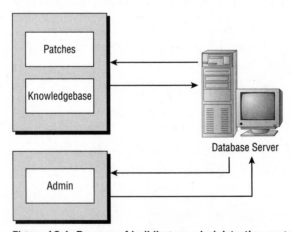

Figure 12-1: Process of building an administration page

3. Add and configure a `FormView` control. The `FormView` control is the ideal control to use when inserts are required.

4. Add and configure a `GridView` control to use for data management purposes. In Chapter 11, you saw how the `GridView` control presents data within a tabular grid-like format. Additionally, the `GridView` supports modifications and deletions of data directly from within the control.

As you'll see, creating an administrative page in Expression Web will be a quick and relatively painless process of working with and configuring controls. Let's get started!

Configuring a Data Source Control to Allow Inserts, Updates, and Deletes

As you saw in Chapter 11, the first step to working with dynamic data (aside from establishing a connection to the database using the Data Source Library Task Pane) is to add and configure a `DataSource` control to extract data from the necessary database table. In Chapter 11, you added the `DataSource` control and then configured it to simply extract data from a table (`Patches` and `Knowledgebase`).

In this chapter, you will still perform the same process, but with one additional step to allow you to configure the `DataSource` control to support inserts, updates, and deletes.

Try It Out　　**Adding and Configuring a Data Source Control to Support Inserts, Updates, and Deletes**

Before you can begin adding and using the `FormView` and `GridView` control, you must add and configure a new `DataSource` control to support inserts, updates, and deletes. To do this, follow these steps:

1. If you haven't done so already, open the `admin.aspx` page included with the download files for this chapter. With the `admin.aspx` page open, switch to the Toolbox Task Pane, and expand the Data set of controls contained within the ASP.NET Controls subcategory. Find the `SqlDataSource` control and drag it out onto the page. (This assumes you're working with a SQL Server 2005 Express Edition database. If you're not, select and drag out the `AccessDataSource` control instead.)

2. Give the `DataSource` control a name that is slightly more meaningful than `SqlDataSource1`. To rename the control, open the Tag Properties Task Pane by choosing Task Panes ⇨ Tag Properties. Within the ID column, change the name of the `DataSource` control from `SqlDataSource1` to something that you can relate to, such as **vc_dsconn** (short for Vecta Corp Data Source Connection).

3. Now that the `DataSource` control has been added and uniquely identified within the page, it's time to configure its properties so that it identifies itself with the `vc_conn` connection and so that it pulls data from the `Patches` table in the `VectaCorp` database. To configure the `DataSource` control, begin by selecting the small expander arrow icon located just to the right of the control when it's selected. You'll receive a small submenu containing a link that reads "Configure Data Source." Click that link to launch the Configure Data Source Wizard.

4. The first screen that's presented to you within the Configure Data Source Wizard is the Choose Your Data Connection screen. Because you have already established a connection (`vc_conn`) to your database in Chapter 11 using the Data Source Library Task Pane, the connection should be

conveniently available for you within the drop-down menu. Select the vc_conn option from the drop-down menu now. Click Next to proceed to the Configure the Select Statement screen.

5. Based on your connection, the Configure Data Source Wizard will then physically connect itself to the database and present, within a drop-down menu, a list of tables that the database contains. From this drop-down menu, select the Patches table and then click the checkbox with the * symbol next to it from within the Columns pane. Remember that the * symbol represents "all fields." As you can see from the read-only sample SELECT statement, the * symbol is combined with the table name and the SELECT and FROM keywords to form a SQL SELECT statement. This is the all-important command that is issued to the database in an effort to extract the data from the database.

6. As you've no doubt noticed, the process outlined in the previous steps hasn't changed since Chapter 11. But now the process begins to change. Because you need the DataSource control to not only help you with data extractions, but also to facilitate inserts, updates, and deletes, you must specify a setting that allows the DataSource control to automatically generate these statements for you. To do this, start by clicking the Advanced button. The Advanced SQL Generation Options dialog box appears, as shown in Figure 12-2. It's from this dialog box that you're able to specify whether the DataSource control should support inserts, updates, or deletes.

7. Because you want the DataSource control to support insert, updates, and deletes, click the "Generate INSERT, UPDATE, and DELETE statements" checkbox, and then click OK to close the dialog box and return to the Configure Data Source Wizard.

8. Click Next to proceed to the Test Query screen. As you may recall, the Test Query screen is the final screen that you'll come to within the Configure Data Source Wizard. It's here that you're able to test the result of the connection and, most important, the SQL statement (minus the INSERT, UPDATE, and DELETE statements) that you configured in the previous screen. To test the query, click the Test Query button. The data contained within the Patches table is displayed within the preview pane. Click Finish to close the Configure Data Source Wizard and return to your Web page.

Now that you have a configured DataSource control on the page, you're ready to add the necessary Data control to facilitate inserts, updates, and deletes. The first control you learn about here is the FormView control. You'll use the FormView control when you want to quickly and easily build a form that facilitates the insertion of data into the database table outlined within the DataSource control.

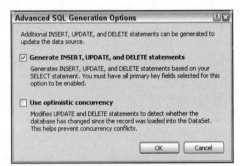

Figure 12-2: Advanced SQL Generation Options dialog box

Working with the FormView Control

In the previous chapters, you looked at data presentation using the DataList and GridView controls. These controls were ideal in scenarios that required quick binding and presentation of database data in either a list or grid-like format. While these controls worked well for data presentation, they fall short in one area: providing an interface for quickly inserting content into the database. This is where the FormView control comes in.

Whereas the DataList and GridView controls are meant to display multiple records from a database in either a list or grid-like view, the FormView control is meant to display a single record at a time. More important, for the purposes of this discussion, the FormView control is ideally suited when inserting new records into your database is a requirement. Rather than adding multiple text labels and then adding the numerous form controls needed to collect the data from the user, a developer only needs to drag a FormView control onto the page and bind it to a DataSource control, and the FormView control instantly creates the text labels (based on the database table's column names) and corresponding form controls for you. The FormView control is yet another time-saving control built into Expression Web that minimizes the amount of time required to create the same type of functionality using traditional methods and, more important, it does not require that you write any code to use it.

Customizing the user interface of the FormView control is much like customizing the interface for a DataList control in that the FormView control relies on templates. As you did with the DataList control in the previous chapter, you can use the Edit Templates mode by clicking the expander arrow icon offered by the FormView to manipulate the following:

- ❏ ItemTemplate (the default content that's offered by the FormView)
- ❏ EditItemTemplate (the content that should appear when the FormView is in edit mode)
- ❏ FooterTemplate (the content that appears in the FormView's footer)
- ❏ HeaderTemplate (the content that appears in the FormView's header)
- ❏ PagerTemplate (the content that appears in the FormView's paging row)
- ❏ InsertItemTemplate (the content that appears in the FormView when the control is in insert mode)

Later in this section, you see how to switch to Edit Templates mode so that you can extend and customize the functionality offered by the FormView control.

Finally, like all Data controls, you can also customize the aesthetic look of the FormView control by using style properties such as EditRowStyle, EmptyDataRowStyle, FooterStyle, HeaderStyle, InsertRowStyle, PagerStyle, and RowStyle. If you recall, these properties are available as expandable nodes within the Tag Properties Task Pane. When you expand the nodes, properties for customizing font, font size, back color, fore color, width, height, alignments, and more are revealed. Additionally, you may also take the quick route and use the AutoFormat dialog, as you saw in the previous chapter, to quickly customize the look of the FormView control by applying pre-built schemes to the various style properties automatically.

Now that you have a general idea of how the FormView control works and how it can be used within the scope of the admin page, let's use it to create the insert functionality for the Patches table in the database. The idea is that administrators should be able to use the FormView control offered within this `admin.aspx` page to insert new patches, complete with a version number and download path into the `Patches` table within the database. Later, you'll use a `GridView` control to allow administrators to edit and delete the data contained within the `Patches` table.

Try It Out   **Adding a FormView Control**

Follow these steps to add and configure a `FormView` control:

1. Open the Toolbox Task Pane, expand the ASP.NET Controls category, expand the Data subset of controls, locate the `FormView` control, and select it. Drag it out onto the page just under the text "Insert and Modify Patches."

2. You'll need to uniquely identify the control so that it makes more sense than the default `FormView1`. To uniquely identify the control, switch to the Tag Properties Task Pane and rename it by changing the text in the right column next to the word ID with the new ID **fvPatches**.

3. The next step is to bind the `FormView` control to the `DataSource` control that you configured in the previous section. To do this, click the small expander arrow icon located to the top right of the `FormView` control. The Common FormView Tasks submenu will appear. Choose the `vc_dsconn` option from the Choose Data Source menu. Instantly, the `FormView` control's appearance changes to reflect the fields offered by the `DataSource` control.

4. As you may have noticed, the default view of the `FormView` control is set up to display a single record of data. The key word here is "display." By default, the `FormView` control is set up to initially load and display `ItemTemplate`. Of course, you don't want to use this control to view data; you want to use it to insert data. For this reason, you'll need to adjust the `FormView` control so that `InsertItemTemplate` is the default template that is shown to the user. You can switch to `InsertItemTemplate` by locating the `DefaultMode` property within the Tag Properties Task Pane and selecting the Insert option from the submenu that appears. The `FormView` control's appearance changes to support data inserts using text boxes, as shown in Figure 12-3.

5. You'll notice two quick issues with the `FormView` control. First, the `SolutionID` displays with a text box next to it. Obviously, this isn't going to work because you can't expect your users to guess a numeric value to insert within that text box. Instead, you'll need to add a drop-down menu in that area and populate that drop-down menu with the list of solutions from the `Solutions` table. Second, you'll notice a Cancel link located next to the Insert link. For the purposes of this exercise, there's nothing to cancel, so this link can be eliminated. Let's do the latter first. To eliminate the Cancel link, click the small expander arrow and choose the Edit Templates link. The `FormView` control will switch to edit templates mode. Next, choose the `InsertItemTemplate` option from the Display menu. The `FormView` control's appearance changes to show the content within the `InsertItemTemplate`. Select the Cancel link and click Delete to remove it.

6. The next step is to change the functionality for the `SolutionID`, replacing the text box with a drop-down menu. To do this, start by adding a new `DataSource` control to the page. Switch to the Toolbox Task Pane, find the `SqlDataSource` control available from the Data set of controls within the ASP.NET Controls category, and drag it out onto the page. Immediately switch to the Tag Properties Task Pane and uniquely identify the new `DataSource` control as **vc_dsconn_ solutions**. Next, click the small expander arrow icon and choose the Configure Data Source link from the submenu that appears; the Configure Data Source Wizard will appear. Choose the `vc_conn` option from the connection drop-down menu and click Next to proceed to the Configure the Select Statement screen. Now, choose the Solutions option from the Name menu,

click the checkbox next to the * symbol within the Columns pane, and click Next to proceed to the Test Query screen. Click Finish to close the Configure Data Source Wizard.

7. Select the SolutionID text box within the InsertItemTemplate in the FormView control and click the Delete key to remove the text box. You can now replace that text box with a DropDownList control. To do this, expand the Standard subset of controls contained within the ASP.NET Controls category in the Toolbox, locate the DropDownList control, and drag it out and into the area where you just removed the text box from. The result should resemble Figure 12-4.

8. With the DropDownList control selected, switch to the Tag Properties Task Pane and change the id property from the default DropDownList1 to something a bit more meaningful like SolutionID.

9. The last step is to bind the DropDownList control to the DataSource control that you added and configured in Step 6. You can do this by choosing the small expander arrow icon located to the right of the DropDownList control and choosing the Choose Data Source link from the submenu that appears. The Data Source Configuration Wizard will appear. Select the vc_ dsconn_solutions option from the data source menu. Choose the Solution option from the "Select a data field to display in the DropDownList" menu. Finally, leave the SolutionID option selected in the "Select a data field for the value of the DropDownList" menu. The configured Data Source Configuration Wizard dialog box will resemble Figure 12-5. Click OK to close the Data Source Configuration Wizard.

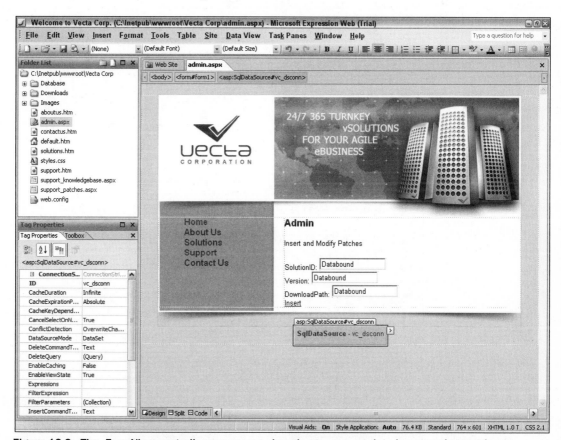

Figure 12-3: The FormView control's appearance changing to support data inserts using text boxes

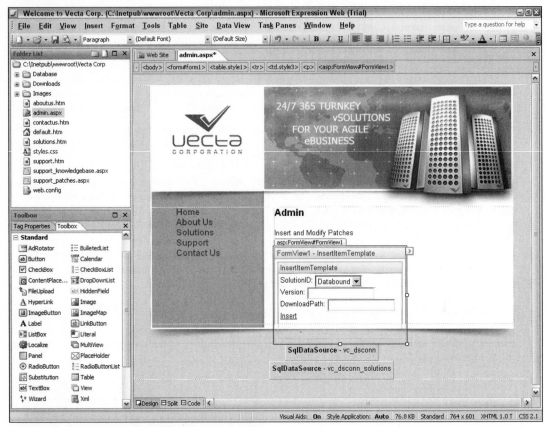

Figure 12-4: Dragging the DropDownList control

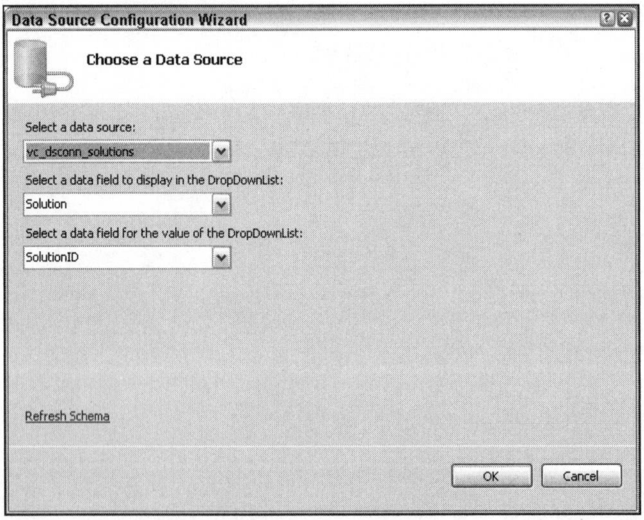

Figure 12-5: Configured Data Source Configuration Wizard dialog box

10. You must dynamically set the SelectedValue property for the DropDownList control. To do this, choose the Edit DataBindings link. The DataBindings dialog box will appear. Locate the SelectedValue option from the Bindable properties pane, choose the SolutionID option from the "Bound to" menu, and then click the "Two-way databinding" checkbox. The result of the formatted dialog box will resemble Figure 12-6. Click OK to close the DataBindings dialog box.

11. To exit Edit Template mode, select the small expander arrow icon from the FormView control and choose the End Template Editing link from the submenu that appears. Save your work and test the page in the browser by pressing F12. The admin.aspx page will appear in the browser, supporting inserts to the Patches table, similar to Figure 12-7.

To test the functionality, select a solution from the SolutionID drop-down menu, add a fictitious download version, and include a download path similar to the one shown in Figure 12-7. Click the Insert link. The page should simply refresh itself. It won't be immediately noticeable that a new record was inserted, but rest assured, it has been. In the next section, you'll add a GridView control that will not only allow you to view the data you've inserted, but modify it as well.

Modifying and Deleting Database Data Using the GridView Control

In Chapter 11, you used the GridView control in an effort to quickly and easily present database data within a Web page. You created a DataSource control, added a GridView to the page, and then bound the GridView to the DataSource control using the Choose Data Source drop-down menu available by clicking the expander arrow icon for the GridView control. The process was simple and required little effort. For the most part, the work came in configuring the DataSource control, and even that wasn't all that difficult.

While presenting database data within a Web page using the GridView control was certainly easy, it also remains one of the most basic tasks you can perform within the GridView control. You can extend the functionality offered by the GridView control to allow users (in this case, administrators) to not only see database data in a grid-like format, but also to interact with that data by offering features that allow for modifications and deletions of data directly from within the control.

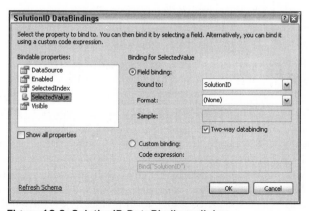

Figure 12-6: SolutionID DataBindings dialog

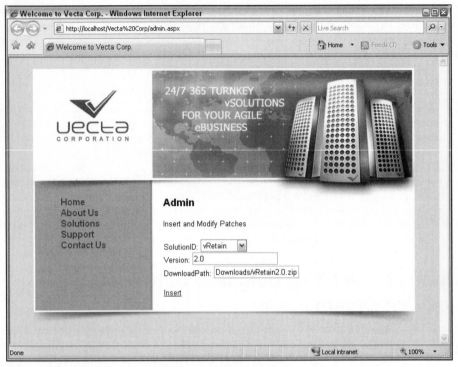

Figure 12-7: admin.aspx page appearing in the browser

Try It Out   Extending the GridView to Support Modifying and Deleting

You can extend the `GridView` control to support modifications and deletions of database data directly from within the control. To do this, follow these steps:

1. Place your cursor just after the `FormView` control and add a couple of line breaks by pressing the Enter key. This will give you some space between the `FormView` control and the new `GridView` control that you'll add in the following steps.

2. Expand the Data set of controls available from the ASP.NET Controls set in the Toolbox Task Pane. Select the `GridView` control and drag it into the page under the `FormView` control.

3. Switch to the Tag Properties Task Pane and uniquely identify the `GridView` control as **gvPatches** by replacing the ID property.

4. With the `GridView` control selected, click the expander arrow icon. Choose the `vc_dsconn` data source from the Choose Data Source menu. Immediately you'll notice that the submenu of items this time is much more extensive than it was in Chapter 11. The reason for this is simple. Because you had the `DataSource` control generate INSERT, UPDATE, and DELETE statements automatically, the `GridView` recognizes this, and provides options that allow you to set whether or not to allow updates and deletions directly from within the `GridView`. Click both the Enable Editing and Enable Deleting checkboxes. Immediately, the `GridView` appears with Edit and Delete hyperlinks as the first two columns within the `GridView`, similar to Figure 12-8.

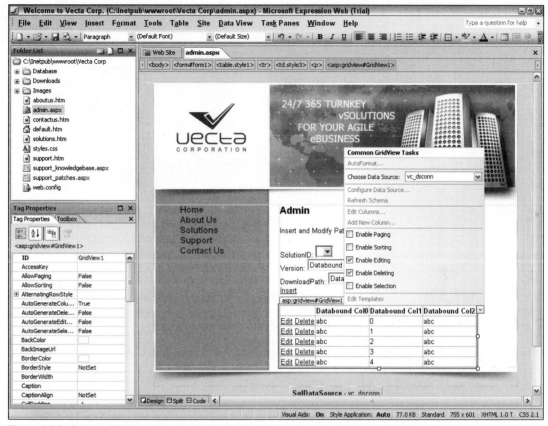

Figure 12-8: Edit and Delete hyperlinks as the first two columns within the GridView

5. For the most part, these two selections are all you need to get the functionality working. Before you test it in the browser, however, you'll edit the columns so that PatchID doesn't appear as a viewable column within the GridView. To do this, click the small expander arrow icon and choose the Edit Columns link from the submenu that appears. The Fields dialog box will appear.

6. Within the Fields dialog box, choose the PatchID option from within the "Selected fields" pane and then click the "Remove field" icon (the small icon with a red X on it). The field is immediately removed. Select OK to close the Fields dialog box and return to the Web page.

7. Save your work and test the page in the browser by pressing F12.

When the page appears in the browser, select a Solution from the menu, add a fictitious version number in the text box, and include a fictitious download path (also in the provided text box). Click the Insert hyperlink. Immediately, the item appears at the bottom of the list in the GridView. Now, to interact with that data, click the Edit hyperlink for the item that you just added. Immediately, the GridView's row becomes editable by revealing text boxes for each cell within the row, as shown in Figure 12-9.

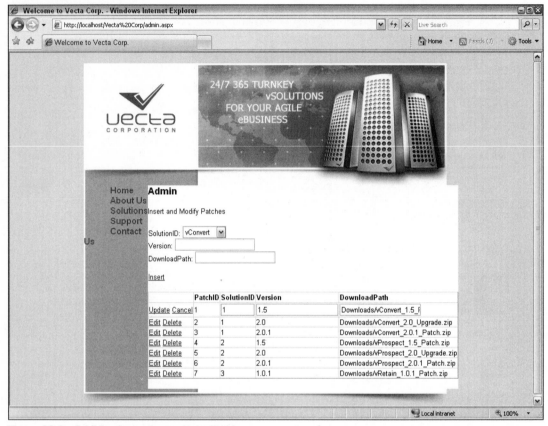

Figure 12-9: GridView's row becoming editable

You'll also notice that the Edit and Delete hyperlinks are temporarily replaced with Update and Cancel hyperlinks. Obviously, Cancel cancels the editing of the row and, when clicked, returns the GridView back to its normal state. To see how Update works, try changing the version number and click Update. Immediately, the change that you make is written to the database, the GridView exits edit mode, and you're returned to the normal mode of the GridView with the change in place.

While the additions were quick to implement, and the functionality is relatively smooth, there are still some minor issues that you must address. First, the width of the GridView is too large when you're in edit mode. Second, the solution IDs appear within text boxes. The correct functionality would have the solutions appear within a drop-down menu, as was the case in the FormView control. These are two minor issues that should be addressed now.

First and foremost, let's address the issue of the solution IDs appearing within a text box. As you did in the FormView example, you added a DataSource control that extracts data from the Solutions table. Then, you switched to the InsertItemTemplate and replaced the text box with a DropDownList control. Finally, you bound the DropDownList control to the DataSource control. With the GridView, the process is shortened because the DataSource control already exists — you can simply use the one you created for the FormView control. All you really have to do is convert the SolutionID column into a

TemplateField (because GridView controls don't use templates by default as the DataList and FormView controls do), switch to the EditItemTemplate, replace the TextBox control with a Drop-DownList control, and then bind it to the existing DataSource control.

To do this, follow these steps:

1. Select the small expander arrow icon that appears when the GridView control is selected and choose the Edit Columns link from the submenu that appears. The Fields dialog box will appear.

2. Select the SolutionID field from the "Selected fields" pane and choose the "Convert this field into a TemplateField" link. Click OK to close the Fields dialog box.

3. Once you close the Fields dialog box, the GridView's options submenu should still remain visible. Immediately click the Edit Templates link. From the Common GridView Tasks sub-menu, choose the EditItemTemplate option from the Display menu. The GridView's appearance will change to display the EditItemTemplate.

4. Select the text box that resides within EditItemTemplate and remove it by selecting the Delete key. Now find the DropDownList control available from the Data subset in the ASP.NET Control category within the Toolbox and drag it into the EditItemTemplate.

5. Once you've dragged the control in, the Common DropDownList Tasks submenu appears. Select the Choose Data Source link. The Data Source Configuration Wizard appears. Pick the vc_dsconn_solutions option from the "Select a data source" menu, pick the Solution option from the "Select a data field to display in the DropDownList" menu and, finally, ensure that the SolutionID option is selected from the "Select a data field for the value of the DropDownList" menu. Choose OK to close the Data Source Configuration Wizard.

6. The next step is to set the selected value for the DropDownList control. Doing this guarantees that the selected value of the drop-down menu is equivalent to the SolutionID contained within that field. To do this, you must edit the DataBindings, similarly to the way you did it in the FormView example. Click the Edit DataBindings link from the submenu that appears from DropDownList. The DataBindings dialog box appears.

7. Choose the SelectedValue option from the Bindable properties pane, choose the "Field binding" radio button, and select the SolutionID option from the "Bound to" menu. Click OK to close the DataBindings dialog box.

8. Click the End Template Editing link to exit template editing. Save your work and test the page in the browser by pressing F12.

When the page appears in the browser, again click the Edit link for a row in the GridView. This time, a DropDownList control displays within the editable Field in the SolutionID column. Notice that because you set the SelectedValue in the DataBindings dialog box, the correct item is preselected for you in the drop-down menu.

With the SolutionID issue taken care of, let's next focus on changing the physical widths of the Version and DownloadPath text boxes. This will allow you to ultimately restrict the width of the GridView control as a whole. To do this, follow these steps:

1. Select the small expander arrow icon that appears when the GridView control is selected and choose the Edit Columns link from the submenu that appears. The Fields dialog box will appear.

2. Now select the Version field from the "Selected fields" pane and choose the "Convert this field into a TemplateField" link. Click OK to close the Fields dialog box.

3. Once you close the Fields dialog box, the GridView's options submenu should still remain visible. Immediately click the Edit Templates link. From the Common GridView Tasks submenu, choose the EditItemTemplate option from the Display menu for the Version column. The GridView's appearance will change to display the EditItemTemplate for the Version column.

4. Select the text box, open the Tag Properties Task Pane, and enter a value of **40** for the Width property.

5. Click the End Template Editing link to exit template editing. Save your work and test the page in the browser by pressing F12.

This time when you click the Edit link, the width of the GridView control doesn't auto-adjust to compensate for the oversized Version text box.

Summary

As you have seen, Expression Web makes data insertions, modifications, and deletions from a Web page a simple matter of configuring DataSource controls, and then enabling functionality offered by various Data controls (including the FormView and GridView control). In this chapter, you did just that. You configured DataSource controls to automatically generate INSERT, UPDATE, and DELETE statements. As you saw, just by enabling a checkbox, Data controls that you added to the page then revealed options for setting whether or not to allow the user to be able to insert (FormView control) or modify and delete data (GridView control) directly from within the Web page.

The downside of the current approach taken here is that anyone can access the admin.aspx page. Obviously, this could pose a serious threat because normal Vecta Corp users would be able to freely add and remove patch and upgrade information for Vecta Corp solutions. Instead, you'll want to password-protect that page. In Chapter 13, you'll do just that.

Exercise

In this exercise, you use some of the concepts that you learned in this chapter to build the interface that allows you to insert and manage knowledgebase data. Specifically, you should do the following:

1. Add a new FormView and GridView control to the admin.aspx page, under the existing controls, used for the Patches functionality.

2. Add a new DataSource control that extracts data from the Knowledgebase table. Enable the "Generate INSERTS, UPDATES, and DELETES" checkbox.

3. Bind both the FormView and GridView controls to the DataSource control. Enable Editing and Deleting of data for the GridView control.

4. Bind both the FormView and GridView controls to the DataSource control. Enable Editing and Deleting of data for the GridView control.

5. Add a new `DataSource` control that extracts data from the `Categories` table.

6. Modify the `InsertItemTemplate` for the `FormView` control so that the Category field displays a `DropDownList` control, bound to the `DataSource` control added in Step 5, instead of a text box.

7. Convert the `CategoryID` field into a `TemplateField` for the `GridView` control. Modify the `EditItemTemplate` so that a `DropDownList` control, bound to the `DataSource` control created in Step 5, appears instead of a text box.

Validating User Input

In Chapter 12, you created an administrative page within the Vecta Corp site in an effort to offer functionality to administrators that allowed them to insert, modify, and delete database data directly from a Web page. The process was simple, and generally involved little more than adding the `FormView` control (for inserting data) and the `GridView` control (for modifying and deleting data) to the page, and binding the controls to a preconfigured `DataSource` control. If you've worked with Web applications in the past, then you know administrative pages like the one you created in Chapter 12 are common. The one and only downside to the application that you created, however, was the fact that you didn't add measures to the administrative page that validated the user's input before sending it to the database.

Validation (or ensuring user-entered information is correct) is common, and is a measure that most Web developers implement within their Web applications. Why would you want to do this? Imagine a user entering the text "one.five" within the Version text box as opposed to the numeric value "1.5". Furthermore, imagine the user leaving the text boxes blank before clicking the Submit button and sending inconsistent data (or worse, no data at all) to the database. Of course, you wouldn't want your database filled with data that you can't use. Instead, you can circumvent these issues by performing validation on the form elements to ensure that the user always enters at least a value into every text box and that every text box accepts only a specific type of value — perhaps a value that is consistent with the data type of the field in the database.

The only knock on validation techniques is that, traditionally, working with validation scripts has been problematic for Web developers and programmers alike. For years, Web developers have borrowed, stolen, and reused scripts that would have otherwise taken hours (perhaps days) to create from scratch. Because of ASP.NET and Expression Web's integration of ASP.NET, this is no longer the case.

ASP.NET provides a set of controls in Validation controls that ease the problems that have beset Web developers in the past. This chapter will teach you everything there is to know about Expression Web's handling of validation. Specifically you will do the following:

❏ Learn the difference between client and server-side validation.

❏ Use ASP.NET Validation controls including the `RequiredFieldValidator`, the `CompareValidator`, the `RegularExpressionValidator`, the `ValidationSummary`, and more within the Vecta Corp Web site.

Client-Side Versus Server-Side Validation

Traditional form validation (that is, form validation as it was handled in traditional ASP, ASP.NET's predecessor) can be accomplished in one of two ways. You can write JavaScript code (client-side) that becomes lengthy and unmanageable, or you can use VBScript (server-side) and validate the user input when the form is processed on the server. Either way, scripts look archaic and hacked.

Client-side validation has its benefits in that it provides instant feedback to your users. If the user fails to enter a name in a text box, the user can be provided with an error message without a roundtrip to the server. It's quick and efficient, and good for the overall user experience. The problem with client-side validation is twofold.

First, the user must have JavaScript enabled in his or her browser. Second, the developer almost always has to write code that supports multiple browser versions. What works in Netscape doesn't necessarily work in Internet Explorer. The headaches increase when developing for small form factor devices such as PDAs and phones.

For these reasons, creating JavaScript validation scripts always seemed like a chore and wasn't always the obvious choice. To gauge the complexity that is JavaScript, take a look at the following code example, which demonstrates what a typical client-side validation script could resemble:

```
<html>
<head>
<title>Client-Side Validation Sample</title>
<script type="text/javascript">
function validate() {
    if (document.form1.username.value == "" ||
        document.form1.password.value == "")
    {
        alert("Username and Password are required!");
        return false;
    } else {
        return true;
    }
}
</script>
</head>
<body>
<form name="form1">
Username:<br />
<input name="username" type="text" id="username"><br /><br />
Password:<br />
<input name="password" type="text" id="password"><br /><br />
<input type="button" name="Submit" value="Submit" onClick="validate()">
</form>
</body>
</html>
```

In this instance, the user clicks the Submit button, the `Click` event is raised, the `validate()` function is called, and the form fields' values are checked. Although client-side validation would be a great and viable solution for performing validation tasks, its complexity and learning curve pose drawbacks to the beginning and even intermediate Web developer looking to create quick scripts with minimal effort. The client-side route becomes even less desirable when users browsing to your site have JavaScript disabled in their browsers.

For this reason, a second method exists in server-side validation. Because server-side validation functions equally in all browsers (regardless of whether or not the user disables JavaScript), it is considered a safer alternative. The downside with server-side validation is that the application must make a roundtrip to the server before the user is alerted of any errors. The following example closely resembles a typical server-side validation script using traditional ASP:

```asp
<%
If (Request.Form("Submit") = "Submit") Then
    If (Request.Form("username") = "") Then
        blnUsername = True
    End If
    If (Request.Form("password") = "") Then
        blnPassword = True
    End If
End If
%>
<html>
<head>
<title>Server-Side Validation Sample</title>
</head>

<body>
<form method="post" action="index.asp">
Username:<br />
<input name="username" type="text" id="username"><br />
<% If blnUsername Then %>
You must enter a username!
<% End If %><br />
Password:<br />
<input name="password" type="text" id="password"><br />
<% If blnPassword Then %>
You must enter a password!
<% End If %><br />
<input type="submit" name="Submit" value="Submit">
</form>
</body>
</html>
```

As you can see, it's unlikely that you'll be able to steer clear of complex and unmanageable code. Fortunately for you, ASP.NET Validation controls virtually eliminate the need to know JavaScript and eliminate the dependency on server-side coding that was common in traditional VBScript (ASP).

ASP.NET's set of Validation controls, supported in Expression Web, allows you to simply add an object to the page and configure some simple properties. The previous "login" pages could be rewritten (in code) using Validation controls as follows:

```
<html>
<head>
<title>Validation Controls Sample</title>
</head>
<body>
<form runat="server">
Username:<br />
<asp:textbox id="username" runat="server" /><br />
<asp:requiredfieldvalidator id="rfvUsername" ControlToValidate="username"
ErrorMessage="Username is required!" runat="server" /><br />
Password:<br />
<asp:textbox id="password" runat="server" /><br />
<asp:requiredfieldvalidator id="rfvPassword" ControlToValidate="password"
ErrorMessage="Password is required!" runat="server" /><br />
<asp:button id="btnSubmit" Text="Submit" runat="server" />
</form>
</body>
</html>
```

If you use Validation controls, the code is cleaner, easier to read, and much more manageable because your code is written with familiar markup as opposed to a client-side scripting language in JavaScript or a server-side scripting language such as VBScript (ASP).

Figure 13-1 shows the functionality within the browser. When you click the Submit button, you instantly receive error messages alerting you that you forgot to type a username and password.

While the following example outlines what Validation controls might look like in code, the nice part about Expression Web is that all you have to do is drag the control onto the page from the Toolbox and then configure two basic properties (in most cases) to get the control to work.

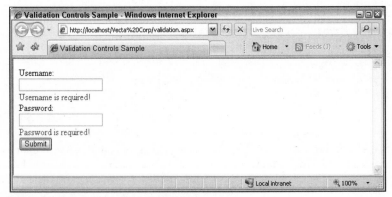

Figure 13-1: Functionality within the browser

Using Validation Controls

Now that you have an understanding of what Validation controls can do, let's have a look at the different controls included with ASP.NET. In general, the following six controls make up the Validation controls set, also offered within the ASP.NET subcategory of controls within the Toolbox Task Pane:

- ❑ The `RequiredFieldValidator` control
- ❑ The `CompareValidator` control
- ❑ The `RangeValidator` control
- ❑ The `ValidationSummary` control
- ❑ The `RegularExpressionValidator` control
- ❑ The `CustomValidator` control

As you saw in the previous section, even in code, Validation controls are easy to work with. Because they are similar to Web controls in that they are inserted as tags, Validation controls are a snap to use, regardless of whether you work with them in code or via the designer. Once a Validation control is inserted, it validates an existing control on the page and presents an error message to the user if the user completes an action that fails validation. Are you beginning to see the benefit? All you'll ever have to do is insert a control — no JavaScript or clumsy server-side code ever has to be written by hand!

The `RequiredFieldValidator` control, for example, will resemble the following markup:

```
<asp:requiredfieldvalidator
    id="rfv1" runat="server"
    ControlToValidate="txtEmail"
    ErrorMessage="Email address is required!">
</asp:requiredfieldvalidator>
```

You'll notice two important properties associated with the `RequiredFieldValidator` control. First of all, the `ControlToValidate` property specifies which Web control this Validation control will validate (in this case, a fictitious control with an ID of `txtEmail`). The second property is `ErrorMessage`. This property displays a customized error message in red if the user does not enter a value into the Web control that the `RequiredFieldValidator` is bound to.

In general, the `ControlToValidate` and `ErrorMessage` properties are the two most important properties that you'll need to configure to get Validation controls to work on your page. While these are the two that you'll work with most often, every Validation control varies — that's what makes this set of controls so flexible.

The rest of this chapter examines the set of Validation controls integrated into Expression Web. For now, let's look at the most important (the one that you'll use most often) — the `RequiredFieldValidator` control.

The RequiredFieldValidator Control

Possibly the most used control included within the Validation control set is the `RequiredFieldValidator`. The `RequiredFieldValidator` control does exactly what it says. It ensures that a user enters a value into a specific Web control (typically a text box). Although it does nothing more, it does play a vital role in form validation because it guarantees that a user enters a value into a Web control before submitting the data.

Try It Out   Adding a RequiredFieldValidator Control

The `RequiredFieldValidator` control is one of the most important controls included within the Validation controls set. To see how the `RequiredFieldValidator` can be added and configured to work with your Web pages, follow these steps:

1. Create a new ASP.NET page by choosing File ➪ New ➪ ASPX. Immediately save the page as `validation.aspx`. Within the form, type the text **Email:**.

2. Add a `TextBox` control to validate just below the Email text that you added in the previous step. You can do this by switching to the Standard set of controls contained within the ASP.NET Controls category in the Toolbox Task Pane, finding the `TextBox` control, and dragging it out onto the page (preferably within the form that's provided for you and under the Email text). Switch to the Tag Properties Task Pane and change the ID of the TextBox control to `txtEmail`. Also, add a couple of spaces below the `TextBox` so that you have some room to add a `Button` control.

3. Add a button that you'll use to initiate the validation of the `RequiredFieldValidator`. To do this, find the `Button` control, again located within the Standard set of controls contained within the ASP.NET Controls category in the Toolbox Task Pane. Select it, and drag it out into the area below the `TextBox`. Switch to the Tag Properties Task Pane and change the Text property for the button to **Submit**.

4. Add the Validation control. To do this, switch to the Validation set of controls contained within the ASP.NET Controls category in the Toolbox Task Pane, find the `RequiredFieldValidator` control, select it, and drag it out onto the page, preferably just next to the `TextBox` control. You'll notice that the `RequiredFieldValidator` control's color is red by default. Obviously, red usually means error, and because these controls are meant to display as errors, the color choice makes sense.

5. The final step is to configure a couple of basic properties for the `RequiredFieldValidator` control, specifically the `ControlToValidate` and `ErrorMessage` properties. To do this, select the control and immediately switch to the Tag Properties Task Pane. Find the `ErrorMessage` property and replace the default value (the name of the control is the default value) with the error message **Your email is required!**. Also, find the `ControlToValidate` property and choose the `txtEmail` option from the submenu that appears in the second column, next to the `ControlToValidate` property. The result will resemble Figure 13-2.

6. That's it! Save your work and test the page in the browser by pressing **F12**.

With the page now appearing in the browser, try clicking the Submit button without including a value within the text box first. Immediately, the error message appears. See how easy that was? Even better, the error message will clear itself out automatically as soon as you type something into the text box. To demonstrate this, type a value into the text box and tab out (by pressing the Tab key) when you've finished. Immediately, the error message disappears automatically.

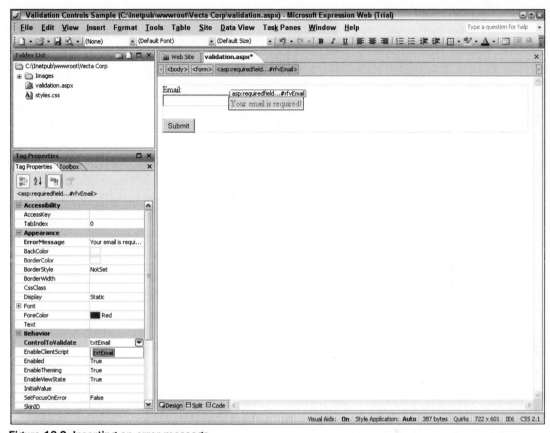

Figure 13-2: Inserting an error message

For the most part, the `ID` and `Runat` properties are required properties for all ASP.NET controls. The `RequiredFieldValidator` is no different. The `RequiredFieldValidator` builds on these required properties and forces you to configure the `ErrorMessage` and `ControlToValidate` properties as well. While these are required, others are optional. The following is a list of properties that you might think about configuring when working with the `RequiredFieldValidator`:

❑ `ControlToValidate` — Specifies the ID of the Web control that you want to validate.

❑ `Display` — Shows how the error message within the Validation control will be displayed. Possible values are `Static`, `Dynamic`, and `None`. The default is `Static`. At its default `Static` state, the control consumes space within your design. For example, if you have the control wedged in between a text box and a table's cell containing in the text box, the table's cell may be adjusted to fit the Validation control. To override this, you can use the `Dynamic` option. This option is ideal when you don't want the Validation control to consume space within your design. The control will consume space only when the error message appears.

❑ `EnableClientScript` — Enables or disables client-side validation. By default, the value is set to `True` (enabled). If you prefer to disable client-side validation, and prefer to have the form validated on the server, choose the `False` option. ASP.NET will automatically run and process the Validation controls on the server as opposed to the client. This is ideal when you want to make your Web application backward-compatible with older browsers.

❑   `Enabled` — Enables or disables the Validation control.

❑   `ErrorMessage` — Specifies the error message that will be displayed to the user in its default red color.

❑   `ID` — Uniquely identifies the Validation control. Expression Web will automatically provide an ID for you. Because this ID is rarely used outside of the control, the default value provided for you doesn't need to be changed.

❑   `SetFocusOnError` — Set this property to `True` when you want the user's cursor to automatically be placed within the Web control that caused the error.

❑   `Text` — Allows you to set an initial text value for the Validation control. This text value is then replaced with the error message if an error is caused.

❑   `ValidationGroup` — Allows you to specify a text value that indicates the validation group that this control should be a part of.

For the most part, these properties are accessible with all Validation controls. Some Validation controls, however, build on these controls by offering their own that relate to the type of functionality offered by the control. These properties are discussed as they become relevant to the discussion.

The CompareValidator Control

One of the most useful Validation controls is the `CompareValidator` control. At its heart, the `CompareValidator` control performs a comparison between a value entered into a primary `TextBox` with the value entered into a secondary `TextBox`. Of course, this control is ideal when you want to offer a Password and Confirm Password set of `TextBox` controls. Using this control would allow you to check whether passwords match in both text boxes. Beyond the simplicity of comparing values, however, the `CompareValidator` control also allows you to perform data type checks. For example, assume that you have a text box for Age. The `CompareValidator` control can also be used to guarantee that the user enters numeric values (for example) within that `TextBox`.

Try It Out   Adding a CompareValidator Control

The `CompareValidator` control is by far one of the most dynamic controls included within the Validation controls set. To see how the control can be used, follow these steps:

1.   With the `validation.aspx` page open, add a couple of line breaks after the `RequiredField-Validator` control and add the text **Password**. Then, switch to the Standard set of controls contained within the ASP.NET Controls category in the Toolbox Task Pane. Find the `TextBox` control, and drag it out just underneath the Password text. Switch to the Tag Properties Task Pane and change the ID of the `TextBox` control to `txtPassword`.

2.   Repeat Step 1, adding a couple of spaces after the `TextBox` control, and adding the text **Confirm Password**. Switch to the Standard set of controls contained within the ASP.NET Controls category in the Toolbox Task Pane, find the `TextBox` control, and drag it out just underneath the Confirm Password text. Switch to the Tag Properties Task Pane and change the ID of this `TextBox` control to `txtConfirmPassword`.

3. Let's perform Step 1 one more time. This time, add a couple of spaces after the Confirm Password `TextBox` control, and add the text **Age.** Switch to the Standard set of controls contained within the ASP.NET Controls category in the Toolbox Task Pane. Find the `TextBox` control, and drag it out just underneath the Age text. Switch to the Tag Properties Task Pane and change the ID of this `TextBox` control to `txtAge`.

4. You'll add two `CompareValidator` controls. To do this, switch to the Validation set of controls contained within the ASP.NET Controls category in the Toolbox Task Pane. Find the `CompareValidator` control, select it, and drag it out onto the page, preferably just next to the `txtConfirmPassword` `TextBox` control. Repeat this step one more time, adding a `CompareValidator` control next to the Age `TextBox` control.

5. Configure the properties for the `CompareValidator` controls, specifically the `ControlTo-Validate`, `ControlToCompare`, and `ErrorMessage` properties. To do this, select the `Compare-Validator` control associated with the `txtConfirmPassword` `TextBox` and immediately switch to the Tag Properties Task Pane. Find the `ErrorMessage` property and replace the default value (the name of the control is the default value) with the error message **Your passwords don't match!**. Also, find the `ControlToValidate` property and choose the `txtConfirmPassword` option from the submenu that appears in the second column. Additionally, locate the `ControlToCompare` property and choose the `txtPassword` option from the submenu that appears in the second column. This configuration should effectively compare the two `TextBox` values and produce an error message if the two don't match.

6. Configure the data type check for the second Age `CompareValidator` control. To do this, select the `CompareValidator` control and immediately switch to the Tag Properties Task Pane. Find the `ErrorMessage` property and replace the default value (the name of the control is the default value) with the error message **Age must be numeric!**. Also, find the `ControlToValidate` property and choose the `txtAge` option from the submenu that appears in the second column. In this case, you are not comparing anything, so leave the `ControlToCompare` property alone. What you do want to configure is the `Operator` property. Locate the `Operator` property and choose the `DataTypeCheck` option from the submenu that appears. This sets what type of validation the control will perform. Next, you must set the type of data that the control will validate. Locate the `Type` property and choose the `Integer` option from the menu that appears. Your controls should now be fully configured and should resemble Figure 13-3.

7. Save your work and test the page in the browser by pressing F12.

To test the functionality, try entering two different values within the Password and Confirm Password text boxes. Immediately, the error message should appear. Now, try entering text values within the Age text box. Again, the error message will appear because the value is not numeric.

For the most part, the `CompareValidator` uses the same properties that other Validation controls use. Following are the ones that are somewhat unique to the `CompareValidator`:

❑ `ControlToCompare` — The control to compare against. The value of this control is compared to the value of the control set by the `ControlToValidate` property.

❑ `Operator` — Sets the type of validation that will be performed by the control. Options include `Equal` (default), `NotEqual`, `GreaterThan`, `GreaterThanEqual`, `LessThan`, `LessThanEqual`, and `DataTypeCheck`.

❑   `Type` — Sets the type of data that the control should expect when performing validation. Options include `String` (text), `Integer` (numeric), `Double` (decimals), `Date`, and `Currency`.

❑   `ValueToCompare` — If you have a preset value that you'd like the control to compare against, you may enter that value here.

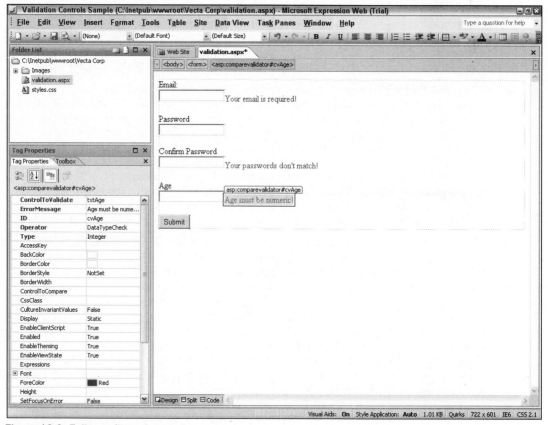

Figure 13-3: Fully configured controls

The RangeValidator Control

You could use the `RangeValidator` control when you want to check whether the value of a form field falls between a minimum and maximum range value. For example, assume that you're building a survey system in which a user taking the survey must fall between a certain age range, and perhaps even a certain salary range. You could use the `RangeValidator` control as a way of comparing a value within a control to ensure that it falls between a certain age, and even a particular salary range.

Try It Out   **Adding a RangeValidator Control**

In the previous example, you added an Age text box and then used the `CompareValidator` control as a way of guaranteeing that what a user types into that text box is numeric. Now, you'll use the

RangeValidator control to ensure that what a user types into that text box falls between the numeric values 18 and 24. To do this, follow these steps:

1. With the validation.aspx page open, add a RangeValidator control by switching to the Validation subset of controls within the ASP.NET Control category in the Toolbox Task Pane. Find the RangeValidator control, select it, and then drag it onto the page, preferably next to the existing CompareValidator control associated with the Age text box.

2. Switch to the Tag Properties Task Pane and associate the txtAge option for the Control-ToValidate property.

3. Associate the numeric value **24** within the MaximumValue property. Additionally, associate the value **18** within the MinimumValue property.

4. Enter the text **Your age doesn't fall between our age range!** within the ErrorMessage property. Also, select the Integer option from the Type property's submenu. The result of adding the RangeValidator controls should resemble Figure 13-4.

5. Save your work and test the page in the browser by pressing F12.

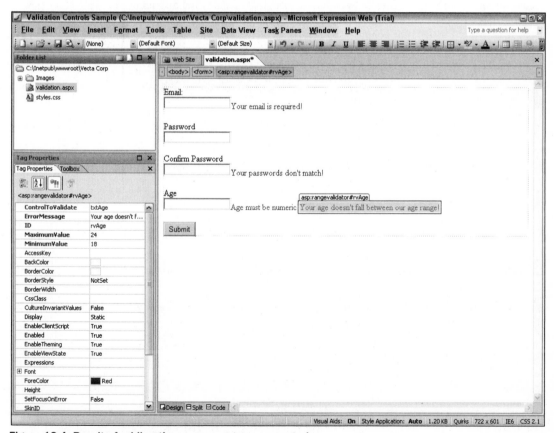

Figure 13-4: Result of adding the RangeValidator controls

When the page appears in the browser, enter a value that clearly doesn't fall within the age range that you want. As soon as you click the Submit button, the error will appear.

You'll also notice that error message appears with some noticeable space between the text box and error message. This is because the `CompareValidator` control (which is currently not visible) is taking up space. Remember that you can eliminate this consumption of space by modifying the `Display` property for the `CompareValidator` control that exists in between the text box and the `RangeValidator` control.

To do this, close the browser and switch back to Expression Web. Select the `CompareValidator` on the page, open the Tag Properties Task Pane, and select the `Dynamic` option from the `Display` property's submenu. Again, save your work and test the page in the browser by pressing F12. This time, when the error message appears, it appears just to the right of the text box, without the space that appeared previously.

The ValidationSummary Control

You use the `ValidationSummary` control when you want to present all of the errors within the page to a user at the same time. Imagine that you have a form that contains 100 different form fields; if the page contains errors, it can be difficult for a user to figure out which control caused that particular error because the page is so big. The `ValidationSummary` control alleviates this problem by presenting the user with a list of form fields that caused errors at the bottom of the page. You can even set the `ValidationSummary` control to present the user with a message box error that contains a list of form fields that caused errors within it.

Try It Out	Adding a ValidationSummary Control

The `ValidationSummary` control is an important usability control that greatly enhances the user experience. To add the `ValidationSummary` control to your page, follow these steps:

1. With the `validation.aspx` page open, place your cursor next to the Submit button and enter a couple of spaces by pressing the Enter key twice.

2. Add a `ValidationSummary` control by switching to the Validation subset of controls within the ASP.NET Control category in the Toolbox Task Pane. Find the `ValidationSummary` control, select it, and then drag it onto the page, preferably into the area that you just cleared space for. The result of the addition will resemble Figure 13-5.

3. Switch to the Tag Properties Task Pane and choose the `True` option from the `ShowMessageBox` property's submenu.

4. That's it! As you can see, this is an easy control to work with. Save your work and test the page in the browser by pressing F12.

Once the page appears, enter information within the form that you know will cause errors. Once you click the Submit button, the errors that are produced within the page are displayed within a red bulleted list of errors below the Submit button. Additionally, a pop-up message containing errors also appears.

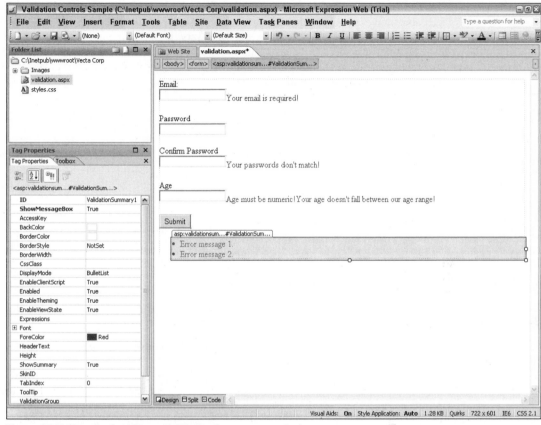

Figure 13-5: Result of adding a ValidationSummary control

The RegularExpressionValidator Control

Suppose, for a moment, that you wanted to be able to validate an e-mail address entered into a text box. The problem with validating an e-mail address is that there are so many different possibilities for a user to enter.

What about a phone number? Technically, users should be able to enter phone number formats of 555-555-5555, (555) 555-5555, or even 5555555555. Furthermore, what if you wanted to validate a user's Social Security Number? You know that Social Security Numbers will always contain nine digits, but the user could potentially enter those digits within a text box using the format 555555555 or even 555-55-5555. The question you face is how to perform validation tasks on text boxes when data input can vary.

Enter the RegularExpressionValidator control. Using the RegularExpressionValidator control, you can specify a combination of possible values by setting a regular expression to handle the validation. Essentially, a *regular expression* is a special string set by the user to check for and replace patterns in another string. While writing regular expressions is no easy task, like everything else, Expression Web makes the process of working with regular expressions simple for you by providing a set of pre-built regular expressions for validating the following types of inputs:

❏ Internet e-mail address

❏ Internet URL

❏ Phone number

❏ Social Security Number

❏ ZIP code

For the most part, the RegularExpressionValidator control is simple and easy to work with. All of the properties that you'll need to configure are similar to the ones discussed up to this point. The only property that is unique to the RegularExpressionValidator control is the ValidationExpression property. This is the property that accepts the custom regular expression string to use on the control that the RegularExpressionValidator control will validate.

Try It Out   Adding a RegularExpressionValidator Control

To add and configure the RegularExpressionValidator control on your page, follow these steps:

1. With the validation.aspx page open, add a RegularExpressionValidator control by switching to the Validation subset of controls within the ASP.NET Control category in the Toolbox Task Pane. Find the RegularExpressionValidator control, select it, and then drag it onto the page, preferably next to the existing RequiredFieldValidator control that resides just to the right of the Email TextBox control.

2. Switch to the Tag Properties Task Pane and set the ErrorMessage property with the text **Invalid email address!**.

3. Select the txtEmail option from within the ControlToValidate property's submenu.

4. It's time to pick the regular expression that you'll use. Because you'll be validating an e-mail address, you'll pick a regular expression suited for that task. To do this, click the button (with the three dots on it) in the second column for the ValidationExpression property. Immediately, the Regular Expression Editor dialog box will appear, as shown in Figure 13-6.

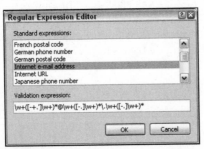

Figure 13-6: Regular Expression Editor
dialog box

5. As you can see, the Regular Expression Editor dialog box offers numerous pre-built regular expressions. Because you want to validate an e-mail address, choose the "Internet e-mail address" option from the Standard expressions list and click OK.

6. That's it! The `ValidationExpression` property will now be set with the regular expression used for validating e-mail addresses. Save your work and test the page in the browser by pressing F12.

When the page appears in the browser, try entering an e-mail address that you know is invalid — for example, **z@z**. Once you've entered the poorly formatted e-mail address, click the Submit button. Immediately, the error message will appear, as shown in Figure 13-7.

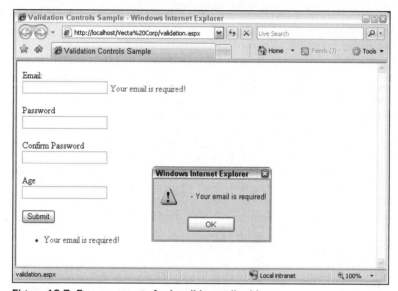

Figure 13-7: Error message for invalid e-mail address

The CustomValidator Control

The Validation controls included with ASP.NET allow you to handle nearly all kinds of validation. Certain types of validation, however, cannot be done with the controls provided. This is where the `CustomValidator` comes in handy.

The `CustomValidator` control offers all of the properties that you're accustomed to seeing from the other controls such as `ErrorMessage`, `ControlToValidate`, and more. However, the `CustomValidator` control exists specifically for your custom validation needs. With the `CustomValidator`, you're not tied to requiring a value, comparing a value, checking ranges, and so on, but rather, you're responsible for creating your own validation. Using some client-side scripting techniques and then pointing the `ClientValidationFunction` property offered by the `CustomValidator` to that client-side script, you can easily create validation functions that respond to validation tasks that you want performed.

For example, as you've seen thus far, a Validation control doesn't exist to check whether the user selected an item from a drop-down menu. Assuming you have a drop-down menu complete with cities in a state, and an extra item that simply displays a "SELECT ONE" choice, how can you validate that control to ensure that a user selects any choice other than the "SELECT ONE"?

The answer lies in the `CustomValidator` control. To see how a `CustomValidator` can be used with a drop-down menu, take a look at the following code sample:

```
<asp:DropDownList ID="ddlCity" runat="server">
    <asp:ListItem Value="0">SELECT ONE</asp:ListItem>
    <asp:ListItem>Los Angeles</asp:ListItem>
    <asp:ListItem>Sacramento</asp:ListItem>
    <asp:ListItem>San Diego</asp:ListItem>
</asp:DropDownList>
<asp:CustomValidator
    ID="cvCity" Runat="server"
    ClientValidationFunction="validateCity"
    ControlToValidate="ddlCity"
    ErrorMessage="Please select a city!" />
```

As you can see, the `DropDownList` code is fairly generic. For that matter, so is the `CustomValidator` control that's associated with the `DropDownList` control. The one property that you haven't seen from other controls thus far is the `ClientValidationFunction`. As you can see, the value associated with this property outlines a function called `validateCity`. The `validateCity` function is a client-side scripting function that you would be responsible for creating within a client-side code declaration block near the top of the page. That code could resemble the following:

```
<script type="text/javascript">
function validateCity(oSrc, args) {
    args.IsValid = (args.Value != 0);
}
</script>
```

As you can see, the `validateCity` function accepts two parameters: `oSrc` and `args`. These two parameters automatically get passed in by the `CustomValidator` control. While you are not using the `oSrc` parameter, the `args` parameter outlines the control that the `CustomValidator` is validating. Essentially, the following code does all the work:

```
args.IsValid = (args.Value != 0);
```

This line of code is responsible for making a determination as to whether the parameter `args`, or the control to be validated, has a selected value of 0 (the first item in the drop-down list). If it doesn't, the error message should appear. However, if it does, the "SELECT ONE" value is still selected in the `DropDownList` control, and the error message should appear.

Summary

As you have seen, ASP.NET Validation controls in Expression Web are powerful and, more important, easy to use. This chapter taught you how to validate required form fields with the `RequiredFieldValidator` control, compare form fields with the `CompareValidator` control, check for a numeric range within form fields with the `RangeValidator` control, provide a user with a summary of errors with the `ValidationSummary` control, check for e-mail addresses with the `RegularExpressionValidator` control, and perform your own custom validation with the `CustomValidator` control.

Chapter 14 introduces yet another important concept as it relates to dynamic Web development: security. Throughout Chapter 14, you learn how to secure pages within your site (such as `admin.aspx`) in an effort to prevent users who are not authorized to access particular pages from viewing those pages.

Exercise

In this exercise, you use some of the concepts that you learned in this chapter to validate user input on the `admin.aspx` page. Specifically, you should do the following:

1. Open `admin.aspx`, select the `Patches FormView` control, and choose the `InsertItemTemplate`.

2. Add a new `RequiredFieldValidator` control such that it validates the Version text box. Also, add a `RequiredFieldValidator` to validate the `DownloadPath`.

3. Add a `CompareValidator` and perform a `Double DataTypeCheck` on the Version text box.

4. Repeat the process for the `Knowledgebase FormView` control.

Securing Your Web Applications

In previous chapters, you added interactivity to the Vecta Corp site by developing portions of the site as dynamic. Essentially, you created `Knowledgebase` and `Patches` tables within a database and dynamically extracted that data to be presented within `support_knowledgebase.aspx` and `support_patches.aspx` pages, respectively. As an administrator, you were able to simply browse to a page called `admin.aspx` in an effort to centrally manage the data that was to be presented to the users.

Conceptually, the process was simple, and ended up being transparent to both the Vecta Corp user and the Vecta Corp administrator. One problem remains. Technically, there's nothing stopping a Vecta Corp user from browsing to the `admin.aspx` page and making changes that are meant only for Vecta Corp administrators. This is where security comes into play. By implementing certain security measures, you could easily password-protect the `admin.aspx` page, essentially preventing unwanted visitors from gaining access to the company's data.

Of course, the topic of security is nothing new. On the contrary, it's been at the forefront of Web development for quite some time and still remains one of the hottest topics, so much so, in fact, that hundreds of Web sites, articles, ads, and books exist related to the subject. Many companies, consultants, and organizations are dedicated to helping protect you and/or your company's vital asset — its data. It's not a downside by any stretch of the imagination. In fact, major online news sites, portals, and even government agencies have been invaded in one form or another, all the while employing some measure of security.

Although this chapter cannot begin to cover all there is to know regarding the subject, it can help you better understand the basic framework involved in securing your Web applications using some simple techniques offered by Expression Web. Specifically, you will do the following:

❑   Learn about ASP.NET 2.0's methods for handling Web application security

❑   Configure Application Services to install the necessary database tables within your local instance of SQL Server 2005 Express Edition to begin working with authentication

❑   Configure forms authentication

❑   Create a login page

❑   Work with `Login` controls (including `Login`, `CreateUserWizard`, `LoginName` and `LoginStatus`, `PasswordRecovery`, and `ChangePassword` controls)

Using ASP.NET 2.0, in combination with some simple wizard-based configuration processes, you will see just how easy it is to secure your Web applications in Expression Web. There's much to do in this chapter so let's get started.

> For the most part, all of the chapters up until this point relied on Expression Web's built-in Web server to operate. Validation and authentication, on the other hand, function a bit differently in that they rely on application domains to operate. Since this is the case, you'll need to run the examples in this chapter within the scope of IIS. IIS is required for this chapter.

Securing the Vecta Corp Site

As mentioned, the current development setup leaves much to be desired in terms of security. At the very least, you'll want to password-protect the `admin.aspx` page so that Vecta Corp users don't accidentally stumble onto the page and begin making changes to data contained within the company's database. Figure 14-1 diagrams this process.

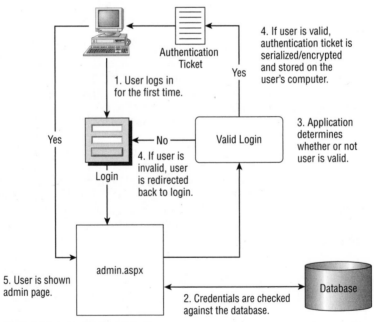

Figure 14-1: Protecting the site

As you can see from the diagram, a much safer alternative for the `admin.aspx` page would be to move it out of the Vecta Corp Web site root and relocate it within a separate folder (still within the root) called `Admin`. When a user visits `www.vectacorp.com/Admin/admin.aspx`, the general idea would be for the user to be presented with some sort of interface that facilitates the collection of his or her username and password. The user would then be responsible for entering these credentials — in which case, the credentials are validated against a storage mechanism of some sort. If the user's credentials exist within the storage device, the user is allowed to proceed to the admin.aspx page. If the user enters the wrong credentials, however, the user is automatically redirected to the main Vecta Corp site.

Conceptually this sounds simple right? For the most part, configuring authentication, creating a login page, and working with ASP.NET 2.0 Login controls within Expression Web is easy. Before moving too far forward, however, let's take a step back and discuss the types of authentication methods that you may decide to employ for Vecta Corp's security needs.

If you've studied the diagram in Figure 14-1, it's easy to tell that you need some sort of method for authenticating the user. In other development environments (and even previous versions of ASP), these methods consisted of archaic and non-secure credential-storage mechanisms accessed by sloppy code that seemed inconsistent and hacked up, depending on the developer. In ASP.NET, this problem was remedied by offering three easy-to-work-with authentication methods:

❑ *Windows Authentication* — Windows authentication uses IIS in conjunction with operating system-level permissions to allow or deny users access to your Web application.

❑ *Forms Authentication* — Offering the most flexibility, forms authentication allows for the most control and customization for the developer. Using forms authentication, the developer is completely responsible for building the login page and may choose from a variety of credential-storage methods for authorization. These include an XML file, a database, coded directly into the page, the Web.Config file, cookies, and even ASP.NET 2.0's newest method for credential storage and authorization, the Membership and Role Providers.

❑ *Passport Authentication* — By far the newest addition to user validation methods, passport authentication, is the centralized authentication service provided through the .NET initiative by Microsoft. Because a user relies on MSN or Hotmail e-mails as a passport, developers need never worry about storing credential information on their own servers. When users log in to a site that has passport authentication enabled, they are redirected to the passport Web site where they enter their passport and password information. After the users' information is validated, they are automatically redirected back to the original site.

Although these are three great authentication methods, this discussion will focus on one: forms authentication. Forms authentication is by far the most popular authentication method because of its flexibility for the user. Whereas Windows authentication relies on operating system–level permissions to be set up by an administrator on the Web server, and passport authentication relies on Microsoft-built components for authentication and authorization, forms authentication relies on the traditional "you build it" concept where the developer is responsible for building a login page and then "hooking" that login page into the credential-storage mechanism of choice.

In general, configuring and working with forms authentication within your Web applications is simple and involves this simple four-step process:

1. *Configure application services.* As mentioned earlier, ASP.NET allows you to use numerous credential-storage mechanisms, including an XML file, a database, the Web.Config file, and more. In ASP.NET 2.0, Microsoft added a new mechanism to an already extensive list of options. This new method, the Membership Provider, is a framework built by Microsoft meant to streamline the way developers store and manage users' credentials for their Web applications. By simply running a configuration utility included for you with the .NET Framework download, a database and an extensive framework of database tables are added for you within your

local instance of SQL Server 2005 Express Edition. Then, as long as forms authentication is configured and `Login` controls are used, usernames, passwords, security questions, security question answers, and more are automatically managed for you within the database by ASP.NET. As you'll notice, the great part about ASP.NET 2.0's application services is that you don't have to be a database developer or an ASP.NET programmer to work with Web application security!

2. *Configure forms authentication.* Out of the box, ASP.NET allows access to everyone who visits your ASP.NET Web applications. Similar to the previous step, you must run some configuration steps to first enable forms authentication, and second, to deny access to all anonymous users to the Web application. As you'll see, this can be easily accomplished by running a configuration utility within IIS.

3. *Create a login page.* Probably the simplest part of the four-step process is to create the login page. As you'll see, once you configure your application to use forms authentication, by default, ASP.NET will rely on a page called `login.aspx` to redirect unauthenticated users to. To accommodate ASP.NET's redirection, you will build this page and add some `Login` controls, mentioned in the next step.

4. *Implement* `Login` *controls.* By far the most feature-rich set of components included with ASP.NET 2.0 are `Login` controls. `Login` controls work hand-in-hand with application services (including the Membership Provider) by offering a set of easy-to-use controls for logging in users, creating new users, displaying the login status and name of the user, allowing the user to recover a password, and allowing a user to change a password. All of these controls will be covered extensively later in the chapter.

Once application services are enabled, forms authentication is configured, and the login page is created, password-protecting your site is a simple matter of working with a set of visual controls known as `Login` controls. Before jumping too far ahead, however, let's begin with the crucial step of configuring application services.

Configuring Application Services

As you saw in the previous section, the first step to working with security in ASP.NET and Expression Web is to enable and configure application services. But what exactly are "application services"?

Application services (often referred to as *building block services*) are a set of useful core frameworks included with the .NET Framework, and are useful when working with common Web application scenarios (such as security and membership management, role management, personalization, profiling, and more). In the end, these building block application services save the developer an extensive amount of development time by including features and functionality that a developer would have had to account for otherwise.

For example, in this chapter, you'll employ some techniques for password-protecting the `admin.aspx` page within the Vecta Corp Web application. Traditional methods of accomplishing this task would have you manually designing a credential-storage table within the database that includes a user's name, e-mail address, username, password, a hashed version of the password, the salted hashed version of the password, a security question, a security answer, a "login tries" counter, and more. Additionally, you'd need to add significant amounts of code just to log in a user. Furthermore, you would also want to build a mechanism for allowing users to recover and change their passwords, which in itself would require considerable amounts of code.

Because of application services, all of the work is already done for you. All you really need to do is run through a simple-to-follow configuration wizard (available by running a provided executable), in which case the .NET Framework configures your database instance with the necessary tables it needs for your Web applications to be able to store and access credential information, role information, profile information, personalization information, and more.

Configuring Application Services

Configuring application services to work with your Web applications is as simple as running an executable and proceeding through a simple-to-follow wizard. To configure application services for your Web application, follow these steps:

1. Open Windows Explorer and browse to `C:\WINDOWS\Microsoft.NET\Framework\ v2.0.50727`. Within the folder, double-click the file `aspnet_regsql.exe`. Doing so will launch the ASP.NET SQL Server Setup Wizard, as shown in Figure 14-2.

2. The first screen that's presented to you within the wizard is a simple message describing what the wizard will accomplish. Click Next. The second screen within the wizard allows you to specify whether to configure application services or remove application services. Select the first radio button, "Configure SQL Server for application services," and click Next.

3. The third screen in the wizard allows you to specify the location of your SQL Server database instance, whether to use Windows or SQL authentication to log in to the database, and the database to install the necessary tables into. In this case, because you are using SQL Server 2005 Express Edition, append the text **\SQLEXPRESS** to the value that appears within the Server text box. Additionally, leave the Windows authentication option selected, and leave the <default> option selected from within the Database menu. By leaving the <default> option selected, the wizard will automatically create a database with the name `ASPNETDB` within your SQL Server 2005 Express Edition instance. Your settings should resemble those shown in Figure 14-3. Click Next.

4. The final screen that's presented to you within the wizard is the Summary. Click Next to proceed with the configuration of application services on your computer. Once this step is finished, the wizard will advance you to the Confirmation screen. Click Finish to close the wizard.

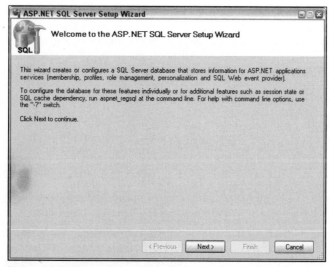

Figure 14-2: Server Setup Wizard

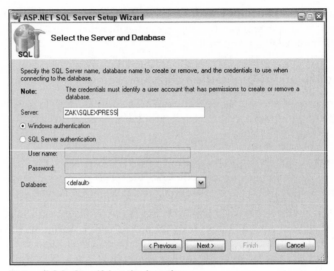

Figure 14-3: Specifying the location

That's all there is to it! You won't notice much right away, but rest assured, you now have a new database called ASPNETDB within your local instance of SQL Server. Furthermore, all of the tables required for working with membership, roles, personalization, profiles, and more are set to go within that database.

The next step is to configure forms authentication for your Web application. As you'll see, this process, like the process of configuring application services, is wizard-based and mostly intuitive.

Configuring Forms Authentication

With application services now configured, you can now turn your attention to configuring forms authentication for the Web application. Traditionally, this could be done by modifying the Web application's Web.Config file, which resides in the root of your Web application. The Web.Config file, which is automatically placed into the root directory of your application when you define a connection to a database, has the potential for storing global application-level settings, including custom error messages, the connection string to the database you're using, the default language for the page, settings for handling session and state management and, more important for you, settings that define what authentication and authorization schemes to support.

Unfortunately, diving right into an XML-based file and expecting to know which nodes to manipulate right off the bat isn't all that realistic. Fortunately for you, the .NET Framework 2.0 installs an easy-to-use and intuitive tool available directly from within IIS, where you can visually manipulate the various nodes that could potentially exist within a Web application.

Before you dive in and start to work with this tool, there is some prep work that you must first perform. Specifically, you must move the admin.aspx page out of the root of the Vecta Corp Web site and into its own folder called Admin. Remember that you want all users to be able to view all of the pages within the Vecta Corp root, but you must isolate the pages that should require authentication. Because you have only one, `admin.aspx`, you can make this easy on yourself by simply moving that file into a new folder. Let's do that now:

1. Open Windows Explorer and browse to `C:\Inetpub\wwwroot\Vecta Corp`.

2. Create a new folder within the root by choosing File ➪ New ➪ Folder. Call the new folder `Admin`.

3. Select the `admin.aspx` page and drag it into the `Admin` folder.

4. Since the `Admin` folder will have its own separate permissions from the root of the Web application, it will need its own `Web.Config` file. To make this easy, simply copy the `Web.Config` file located at the Vecta Corp root, and paste it into the `Admin` folder. The two folders side by side should resemble those shown in Figure 14-4.

Now that you have the `admin.aspx` page isolated from the main Vecta Corp site, you can now focus your attention to setting permissions on the site as a whole. This can be done by opening the tool mentioned previously and manipulating the authentication and authorization dialog boxes within the tool. Let's do that now.

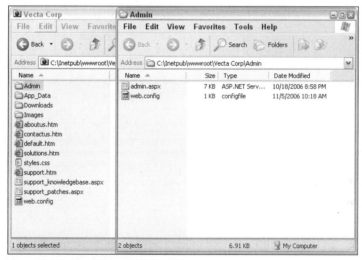

Figure 14-4: Two folders side by side

Try It Out   Configuring Forms Authentication

With the `admin.aspx` page now isolated from the rest of the Vecta Corp files, you can now focus your attention on manipulating authentication and authorization sections for the `Web.Config` files that reside in the root and within the `Admin` folders. To do this, follow these steps:

1. Start by opening IIS. You can do this by selecting Start ➪ Settings ➪ Control Panel ➪ Administrative Tools ➪ Internet Information Service. IIS will launch.

2. Expand your computer node, expand the Web Sites nodes, and expand the Default Web Site node. The Vecta Corp Web application will be listed. Right-click the application and choose Properties from the context menu that appears. The Vecta Corp Properties dialog box will appear.

3. Click on the ASP.NET tab and then immediately click the Edit Configuration button that appears within the dialog box when the tab is selected. The ASP.NET Configuration Settings dialog box will appear. This is the tool mentioned earlier for visually manipulating the `Web.Config` file. As you'll notice, the dialog box is divided into seven major configurable sections. The sections you care about most, however, are Authorization and Authentication.

4. Of course, you must configure options within both tabs. However, for the Vecta Corp application's settings (what you're configuring now), all you really care about is setting the authentication mode. Because this folder is the top of the hierarchy, all settings that you make here trickle down to child folders (such as `Admin` and ultimately `admin.aspx`). With that said, choose the Authentication tab. A series of authentication options will appear.

5. As you'll notice, the Authentication tab offers options for setting the authentication mode (the default is Windows authentication), specifying the cookie name that should be created and used when forms authentication is enabled (the default is .ASPXAUTH), assigning the login page that forms authentication will redirect to when forms authentication is enabled (the default is `login.aspx`), setting the type of encryption (if any) to use for the cookie, setting the expiration time of the cookie (the default is 30 minutes), and setting which provider to use for Membership and Role management. For the purposes of this exercise, simply select the Forms option from the Authentication mode menu, shown in Figure 14-5.

6. Also, take note of the filename contained within the Login URL text box. As you can see, `login.aspx` is the page that users will automatically be redirected to if they try to access a page that they're not authorized to view. Of course, you can change this value if you want, but `login.aspx` is a common name and intuitive for both the developer and user. Click OK to close the ASP.NET Configuration Settings dialog box. Again, click OK to close the Vecta Corp Properties dialog box.

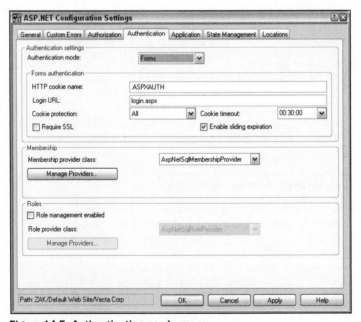

Figure 14-5: Authentication mode menu

That's it! Forms authentication is now configured for the Vecta Corp Web site. What you haven't done yet, however, is set authorization or, more specifically, which folder/pages within the site people can access. Let's do that now.

Configuring Forms Authorization

With forms authentication now enabled for the site, you can now focus on configuring which portions of the site users are allowed to access. By default, all users are allowed to visit all pages within your site. For the root directory, this approach is fine. For the Admin folder, however, it's not. Remember that Web.Config file that you copied into the Admin folder? You'll now modify that Web.Config file (using the tool that you used to set Forms authentication) to modify authorization for the Admin folder. To do this, follow these steps:

1. Open IIS if it's not already open. You can do this by selecting Start ▭ Settings ▭ Control Panel ▭ Administrative Tools ▭ Internet Information Service. IIS will launch.

2. Expand your computer node, expand the Web Sites node, and expand the Default Web Site node. The Vecta Corp Web application will be listed. Now, expand the Vecta Corp node. This time, right-click on the Admin folder and choose Properties from the context menu that appears. The Admin Properties dialog box will appear.

3. Click the ASP.NET tab and then immediately click the Edit Configuration button that appears within the dialog box when the tab is selected. The ASP.NET Configuration Settings dialog box will appear.

4. This time, click the Authorization tab. You'll notice that the Authorization dialog box is split into two lists: "Inherited authorization rules" (those directly inherited from the Vecta Corp parent folder) and "Local authorization rules" (those that you are responsible for creating). Unfortunately, you're not able to remove inherited rules, but you can add your own. Those that you add, by default, override inherited permissions. And that's a good thing, considering the inherited permissions call for allowing all users access to the site. Well, you don't want to allow all users access to the Admin folder, so you'll set a new rule here, manually. To do this, click the Add button. The Edit Rule dialog box will appear, as shown in Figure 14-6.

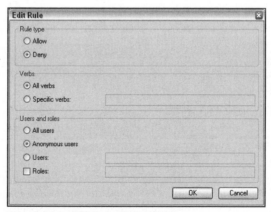

Figure 14-6: Edit Rule dialog box

5.   In this case, you want to deny unauthenticated (anonymous) users from accessing the Admin folder. Because this is the case, choose the Deny option from the "Rule type" set of options. Additionally, select the "Anonymous users" option from the "Users and roles" set of options. The result of the selection will appear similar to Figure 14-6. Click OK to close the Edit Rule dialog box.

6.   Once you close the Edit Rule dialog box, the new rule will appear within the "Local authorization rules" list, similar to Figure 14-7. You'll notice that the Users column appears with a question mark (?). This is the symbol that represents "anonymous users." Click OK to close the ASP.NET Configuration Settings dialog box. Also, Click OK to close the Admin Properties dialog box.

7.   Close IIS.

Forms authentication and authorization are now fully configured for the Vecta Corp site. You can now move forward with creating the page that forms authentication that you will use for collecting user credentials: login.aspx.

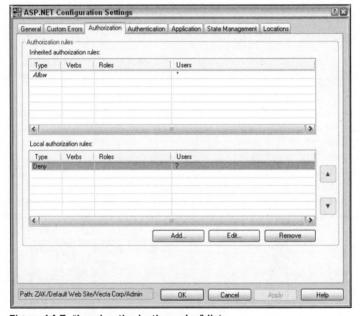

Figure 14-7: "Local authorization rules" list

Creating the Login Page

The beauty in ASP.NET forms authentication lies in how easy it is to actually get password-protection functionality working on your site. Like most concepts in ASP.NET, you haven't done any coding. Everything up to this point has involved the manipulation and configuration of wizards and dialog boxes.

In this chapter, for example, you simply ran an executable that configured application services within your computer. Behind the scenes, a complex framework of code and an extensive network of database tables were installed so that other components (specifically Login controls) could interface directly with. In the previous section, you used the built-in ASP.NET Application Configuration dialog box to quickly configure forms authentication and authorization for the site and folders within the site.

While you are well on your way to fully creating an authentication mechanism for the site, the functionality that you've implemented thus far can, at the very least, be tested. Doing so will provide a preview for the basic functionality involved in forms authentication. To test what you have thus far, follow these steps:

1. Start by opening a Web browser. Now, browse to the Vecta Corp site located at http://localhost/Vecta Corp/. You'll immediately notice that the page comes up without asking you to log in. Again, this is by design. The root Web site is for public use and shouldn't require a login.

2. Now try browsing to the page http://localhost/Vecta Corp/Admin/admin.aspx. This time, the result is much different. Rather than displaying the admin.aspx page that you built in Chapter 12, a page with a generic "The resource cannot be found" error appears, as shown in Figure 14-8.

Before you panic, thinking you did something wrong, note that everything is indeed functioning properly. Remember that you configured forms authorization for the Admin folder. What this means is that all pages that reside within the Admin folder will require authentication first. The application, recognizing that this page requires authentication, is trying to redirect you to login.aspx (the Login URL that you were asked to make note of within the Authentication tab). Because you haven't created login.aspx yet, a generic "resource (the login page) cannot be found" error appears in its place.

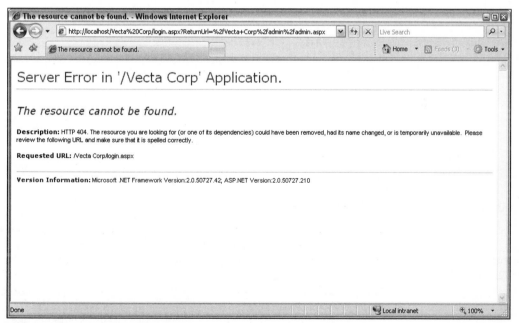

Figure 14-8: Generic error on page

To fix this problem, you only need to create a new page (login.aspx) within the root of the Web application. Let's do that next:

1. Close the browser and reopen Expression Web if it's not already open.

2. Select File ➪ New ➪ ASPX. Save the new page as login.aspx, placing it within the root of the Vecta Corp site (not the Admin folder).

3. Type some generic text within the page. Enter the text **To visit the Admin page, you must login first**.

4. Save your work. Again, reopen the browser and try browsing to the http://localhost/ Vecta Corp/Admin/admin.aspx page once more. Again, you're denied access to the Admin folder by being redirected to the login.aspx page. This time, because the file (login.aspx) exists, it's presented to you within the browser (along with the error message), as shown in Figure 14-9.

While that was certainly easy, you are far from being finished. You'll next need to add functionality that allows the user to log in, administrators to create accounts, and so on. All of this functionality can be accomplished using a series of controls known as Login controls.

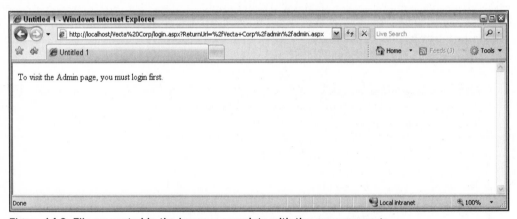

Figure 14-9: File presented in the browser complete with the error message

Working with Login Controls

Now that you've performed most of the configuration steps, you can now focus on adding functionality that allows users to log in, create accounts, view their login status, view their login name, recover their passwords if they've forgotten them, and change their passwords if they so desire. Again, like most features in ASP.NET 2.0, all of this functionality is provided for you, thanks to application services and Login controls.

Login controls are a set of pre-built controls that offer rich functionality meant for logging in a user; creating user accounts using strong passwords, security questions, and security answers; allowing users to recover and change passwords; and even allowing users to view their login status (whether they're logged in or not) and login name. The Login controls discussed here include the following:

- ❏ The Login control
- ❏ The CreateUserWizard control
- ❏ The LoginStatus control
- ❏ The LoginName control
- ❏ The PasswordRecovery control
- ❏ The ChangePassword control

When it comes to forms authentication, these controls are crucial because they offer functionality that would have otherwise taken the developer weeks (if not months) to build by hand. As you'll see, like most components in ASP.NET, Login controls are easy to use and, most important, require no code to implement.

The Login Control

Possibly the most important Login control is the Login control itself. The Login control performs exactly as its name implies. It offers text boxes to allow users to enter their usernames and passwords. By simply clicking a button, the Web application then compares the values of the username and password text boxes with values specified within the ASPNETDB database (created for you automatically when you configured application services). If the values match up, users are allowed to proceed to their intended page. If they don't match up, however, users are presented with an error message and are asked to log in again.

Additionally, the Login control offers a Remember Me checkbox. Users are optionally encouraged to enable this checkbox when they want the application to remember them the next time they visit the application. This prevents users from having to log in every time they visit the page.

The Login control is easy to work with and, at its heart, requires nothing more than dragging the control from the Toolbox Task Pane into the page.

Try It Out   Adding a Login Control

Adding a Login control is easy and requires just a few steps. To add a Login control to your page, follow these steps:

1. Open the login.aspx page within Expression Web if it's not already open.

2. Switch to the Toolbox Task Pane, expand the ASP.NET Control category, and expand the Login subset of controls. Locate the Login control, select it, and drag it into the page. As you'll notice, the Login control offers username and password text boxes, a Remember Me checkbox, a Log In button, and two Validation controls for requiring username and password inputs.

3. You may also decide to format the look of the Login control by selecting the control, clicking the expander arrow icon, and choosing the AutoFormat option. This will launch the AutoFormat dialog box, enabling you to select a pre-built scheme for your Login control. To match the color scheme of the Vecta Corp Web site, choose the Professional scheme and click OK to apply it.

4. Save your work.

That's it! You now have the presentational component required to enable users to log in to and view the admin.aspx page contained within the Admin folder.

Before you test the functionality, however, let's outline some of the more important properties that the Login control offers. Setting these properties will further enhance the usability and functionality of the Login control. These properties include the following:

❑   CreateUserText — The text to be shown for the "create user" link. The CreateUserWizard control (discussed in the next section) allows you to create a page (createuser.aspx) where users can register for the Vecta Corp site.

❑   CreateUserUrl — The URL of the "create user" page. This is the URL that is associated with the CreateUserText property.

❑   DestinationPageUrl — The page to redirect to after a successful login. By default, this value is defined as default.aspx. If you do not plan on using the name default.aspx for your home page, then you'll need to set this value with the name you decide to use instead.

❑   DisplayRememberMe — Enables or disables the Remember Me checkbox. Setting this option to false is crucial in sites where security is of the utmost importance. The reason for this is simple. When this value is set to true, the cookie that forms authentication relies on sits on the user's computer, making it vulnerable to attackers. When this value is set to false, the cookie is removed from the user's computer as soon as the browser window is closed.

❑   FailureAction — The action that should be performed when a login attempt is unsuccessful. By default, the page is simply refreshed and the failure text is shown. However, you may choose the RedirectToLoginPage option, in which case, the user is redirected to the site's default login page (assuming more than one login exists).

❑   FailureText — The error message that should appear on an unsuccessful login attempt. The default text is "Your login attempt was not successful. Please try again."

❑   PasswordRecoveryText — The text to be shown for the password recovery link. The PasswordRecovery control (discussed later) enables users to recover their passwords. This is the text that appears within the Login control and is associated with the PasswordRecovery property.

❑   PasswordRecoveryUrl — The URL of the password recovery page. This is the URL that is associated with the PasswordRecoveryText property.

Again, this is not a complete set of properties. These are merely the properties that can be considered most important when working with the Login control.

Now that you're aware of some of the important properties that the Login control offers, let's test the control's functionality. To test the functionality, open the Web browser and browse to the page http://localhost/Vecta Corp/Admin/admin.aspx. Immediately, you are redirected to the login.aspx page, as shown in Figure 14-10.

But wait, there's a problem! How can you log in to view the admin.aspx page if you're not technically considered a user of the admin.aspx page yet? The answer is that you can't. Try it for yourself. Add a username and password into the provided text boxes and click the Log In button. After a few quick seconds, the error message "Your login attempt was not successful. Please try again" appears in red.

Obviously, the login attempt was unsuccessful because no users exist in the database to validate against. Of course, you can fix this problem by adding users.

To add users, you must use the `CreateUserWizard` control (discussed next). Once a user has been added, you can return to the `login.aspx` page and attempt to log in with the credentials that you create within the "create user" page.

> **Technically, you don't have to use the** `CreateUserWizard` **control to add users to the database. Instead, you might decide to use the configuration tool (mentioned earlier when discussing authentication and authorization) to manually add users. Assuming you want a Web-based approach (and since it's a perfect lead in to the** `CreateUserWizard` **control), adding users using the configuration tool isn't covered.**

Figure 14-10: Redirection to the login.aspx page

The CreateUserWizard Control

One of the most dynamic controls included within the `Login` controls set is the `CreateUserWizard` control. You can use this control as a front for adding users to the `ASPNETDB` database (the database used with application services and, in this case, authentication). Of course, the control goes well beyond allowing you to simply add users. It also allows you to add and confirm a user's password, add an e-mail address, a security question, and the security question's answer. Like the `Login` control, the `CreateUserWizard` control also performs validation on the text boxes that it offers. Most important, however, the `CreateUserWizard` control facilitates the collection of a "strong" password (that is, a password that contains a combination of letters, numbers, and special characters, all aimed at preventing hackers from stealing passwords that you add).

In most cases, the `CreateUserWizard` control is ideal when you want users to register themselves on your site. In this scenario, you'd create a new page (`createuser.apsx`) within the root of the Vecta Corp site. This way, all Vecta Corp users would be able to access this page and register themselves as new users. In this case, however, you don't want that. Because only one administrator (maybe two at the most) will be accessing the admin.aspx page, there's really no reason for you to add it to the root of the site. However, you also can't add it within the Admin folder. Because you have no registered users, you wouldn't be able to access that folder to get to this page anyway.

> One way around this dilemma is to temporarily shut off forms authentication. You could then access the Admin folder and the createuser.aspx page, quickly add a user, and then re-enable forms authentication. With the new user in the database, you would then be able to log in and gain access to both admin.aspx and createuser.aspx pages within the Admin folder.

What you will do instead is simply create the page at the Web applications root, knowing full well that in a "real world" scenario, this page would have to either be removed from the site, or moved into the Admin folder once an administrator has been created.

Try It Out   Adding the CreateUserWizard Control

To add a CreateUserWizard control to a new page, follow these steps:

1. Start by creating a new page in Expression Web by choosing File ➪ New ➪ ASPX. Save the page as createuser.aspx within the Vecta Corp root.

2. Switch to the Toolbox Task Pane, expand the ASP.NET Control category, and expand the Login subset of controls. Locate the CreateUserWizard control, select it, and drag it into the page. As you'll notice, the CreateUserWizard control offers text boxes for the username, password, password confirmation, e-mail, security question, and security question answer.

3. You may also decide to format the look of the CreateUserWizard control by selecting the control, clicking the expander arrow icon, and choosing the AutoFormat option. This will launch the AutoFormat dialog box, enabling you to select a pre-built scheme for your CreateUserWizard control. To match the color scheme of the Vecta Corp Web site, choose the Professional scheme and click OK to apply it.

4. Save your work.

That's it! You now have the presentational component required to allow users/administrators to add new users to the Vecta Corp site. Before you test the functionality, however, let's outline some of the more important properties that the CreateUserWizard control offers. Setting these properties will further enhance the usability and functionality of the CreateUserWizard control. These properties include the following:

❑ AutoGeneratePassword — Set this property to true when you want the application to automatically generate a random password for the user. Once the user finishes the wizard, a confirmation page and a random password are sent to the user using properties specified within the MailDefinition set of properties. Once the user comes back to the site, he or she would be able to change his or her password via a change password page that takes advantage of the ChangePassword control. Additionally, when this value is set to true, the password and password confirmation text boxes are removed. The default value for this property is false.

❑ CompleteSuccessText — The text that appears to users when their account has been successfully created. Default is "Your account has been successfully created."

❑ ContinueDestinationPageUrl — The URL to redirect users to when the Continue button is clicked. The text that you specify within the CompleteSuccessText property is shown to the users here. They would then click the Continue button to be redirected to the URL you specify here. For the purposes of this discussion, specify login.aspx here.

❑ LoginCreatedUser — Choose true when you want a created user to be automatically logged in. If you were an administrator creating accounts for users, you'd want to set this property to false. Otherwise, the application would log you out and immediately log you in as the newly created user.

❑ MailDefinition — A collection of properties to use when sending confirmation e-mails to users. Properties offered here include BodyFileName (an external, preformatted file that represents the body of the e-mail), CC, From, IsBodyHTML (whether the body should be HTML-based or text-based), Priority, and Subject. You'll notice that a To property isn't outlined. By default, the To value of the e-mail is preconfigured to use the user's e-mail specified within the control.

❑ RequireEmail — Specifies whether or not to require the user's e-mail address. Default is true. If the AutoGeneratePassword property is set to true, this property should also be left at its default of true as the AutoGeneratePassword property will rely on the e-mail when sending out the newly generated password.

Again, this is not a complete set of properties. These are merely the properties that can be considered most important when working with the CreateUserWizard control. There are literally dozens of properties that you may decide to configure with the CreateUserWizard control. You should review these properties and tinker with them at your leisure.

Now that you're aware of some of the important properties that the CreateUserWizard control offers, let's test the control's functionality. To test the functionality, open the Web browser and browse to the page http://localhost/Vecta Corp/createuser.aspx. A page (similar in design to the page you built in Expression Web) appears. Enter a username, a password and password confirmation, an e-mail address, a security question, and security question answer, as shown in Figure 14-11.

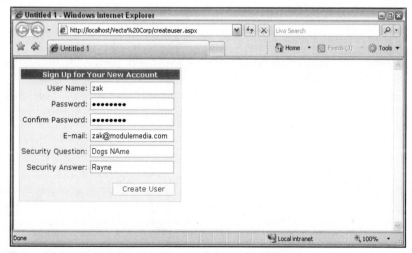

Figure 14-11: Testing functionality of the CreateUserWizard control

Now, click the Create User button. Immediately, the new user is created and the control changes to display the text that you outlined within the `CompleteSuccessText` property. Click the Continue button to be redirected back to the login page (the page you specified within the `ContinueDestinationPageUrl` property).

Back on the `login.aspx` page, try to log in again. Because the user that you're trying to log in with exists within the database now, you're granted access to the `admin.aspx` page!

The LoginStatus and LoginName Controls

Possibly the simplest controls that you can take advantage of within Expression Web are the `LoginStatus` and `LoginName` controls. By adding these two controls to the page, you can display the user's login status. For example, if a user is logged in, the `LoginStatus` control renders a Logout link. Clicking the Logout link logs users out of the application and redirects them back to the `login.aspx` page if you desire. If the user is not logged in, a Log In link is rendered instead. Clicking this link would redirect the user to the `login.aspx` page in an effort to log in to the application. The `LoginName` control simply displays the name of the user within a text label. This is ideal when you want to display a friendly message such as "Welcome <user>" to the logged in user.

Try It Out   **Adding the LoginStatus and LoginName Controls**

For the purposes here, adding the `LoginStatus` and `LoginName` controls to any page other than the `admin.aspx` page doesn't make much sense. Because users aren't required to log in to view the general Web site, displaying their login name would be pointless. Furthermore, adding the `LoginStatus` control would render a Login link to the user that, when clicked, would redirect the user to the `login.aspx` page. You would be safer if the user didn't even know that the `login.aspx` page existed.

With that said, let's add the `LoginStatus` and `LoginName` controls to the `admin.aspx` page. Follow these steps:

1. Open the `admin.aspx` page within Expression Web.

2. Switch to the Toolbox Task Pane, expand the ASP.NET Control category, and expand the Login subset of controls. Locate the `LoginStatus` control, select it, and drag it into the page, preferably just underneath the Contact Us link in the left navigation bar. You may also decide to attach the `.navlink` class to the `LoginStatus` control. To do this, open the Apply Styles Task Pane and with the `LoginStatus` control selected, choose the `.navlink` class from within the Task Pane. The link will conform itself to look just like the other navigation items.

3. Replace the Admin subheader with the text **Welcome:**. Locate the `LoginName` control, select it, and drag it into the page, preferably next to this text. The result will appear, as shown in Figure 14-12.

4. Save your work.

That's it! Now try browsing to the `admin.aspx` page again by opening a browser and entering the path **http://localhost/Vecta Corp/Admin/admin.aspx**. If you're asked to log in again, do so now. When you reach the `admin.aspx` page, your login name appears next to the Welcome text. Additionally, because you're logged in, a Logout link appears in the left navigation area, similar to Figure 14-13.

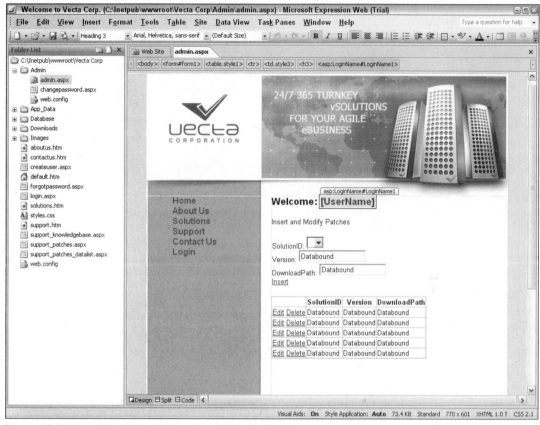

Figure 14-12: Dragging the LoginName control onto the page

The PasswordRecovery Control

You can use the `PasswordRecovery` control when you want to offer functionality that allows users to recover or reset forgotten passwords. Like the `CreateUserWizard` control, the `PasswordRecovery` control offers a set of `MailDefinition` properties that, when set, automatically e-mails users either a randomly generated password or their original password (depending on how the password is being stored in the database). By default, application services are configured such that passwords, password salts, and secret question answers are stored as unreadable hashed values. Because this is the case, there's no way for you or even application services to recover that password. When the user runs through the features offered within the `PasswordRecovery` control, application services instead will generate a randomized password, replace the existing value in the database with this new randomized value, and then send that value out to the user within an e-mail. (The e-mail address of the user is retrieved from the same database table.)

For the purposes of this discussion, you will create a new page called `forgotpassword.aspx`. Then, you will configure the `Login` control within the `login.aspx` page to offer a hyperlink that allows users to link directly to this page should they need to recover their passwords. Let's take a look.

Figure 14-13: Your username appears as well as a Logout link

Try It Out   **Adding the PasswordRecovery Control**

To create a new "forgot password" page and add the `PasswordRecovery` control to that page, follow these steps:

1. Create a new ASP.NET page. You can do this by choosing File ⇨ New ⇨ ASPX within Expression Web. Once the new page appears, save it as `forgotpassword.aspx` within the root of the Vecta Corp Web site.

2. Switch to the Toolbox Task Pane, expand the ASP.NET Control category, and expand the Login subset of controls. Locate the `PasswordRecovery` control, select it, and drag it into the page.

3. You may also decide to format the look of the `PasswordRecovery` control by selecting the control, clicking the expander arrow icon, and choosing the AutoFormat option. This will launch the AutoFormat dialog box, enabling you to select a pre-built scheme for your `PasswordRecovery` control. To match the color scheme of the Vecta Corp Web site, choose the Professional scheme and click OK to apply it.

4. Configure the From and Subject fields within the `MailDefinition` set of properties within the Tag Properties Task Pane. Choose the Tag Properties Task Pane, expand the MailDefinition node, and enter a fictitious e-mail address within the From field. Enter the bogus e-mail address **noreply@travelsite.com**. Now, enter the text **Your password has been reset** within the Subject field. With these two properties set, ASP.NET will now be able to generate an e-mail address and be able to successfully populate From and Subject fields for the newly created message.

5. The next step involves setting some generic mail properties within the `Web.Config` file. Because the `Web.Config` file stores application-level settings, the Web application will turn here first for help on how to send the e-mail. With that said, you'll set the following properties within the `Web.Config`, preferably within the `<system.web>` node:

```
<system.net>
    <mailSettings>
        <smtp>
            <network host="localhost" password="" userName="" />
        </smtp>
    </mailSettings>
</system.net>
```

6. As you can see from the markup in the Web.Config file (also shown in Figure 14-14), properties exist for telling the application how and what program to use for sending the e-mail. In this case, because we'll be using the local computers built-in SMTP service, the host name `Localhost` is supplied within a `<network>` tag.

7. Save your work and close the `Web.Config` file.

In terms of working with the `PasswordRecovery` control in Expression Web, that's it! Before you can call the functionality complete, however, there are still two tasks that you must first tackle.

First, you need to reopen the `login.aspx` page and provide a link from that page to the `forgotpassword.aspx` page. This can be done easily by simply configuring a property available from the `Login` control. Second, and most important, you must configure IIS to allow e-mail relaying from the local computer.

> **In ASP and ASP.NET 1.0, you could send e-mail without configuring e-mail relaying in IIS. In ASP.NET 1.1 forward, Microsoft enhanced IIS security by preventing automatic relaying of e-mails from your local IIS instance. Of course, this can be manually overridden by adding your computer's IP address, or 127.0.0.1, to the relay permitted list.**

Let's start by creating the link from the `login.aspx` page. Follow these steps:

1. Open the `login.aspx` page.

2. Select the `Login` control and then immediately switch to the Tag Properties Task Pane. Find the `PasswordRecoveryText` and `PasswordRecoveryUrl` properties and enter the values **Forgot Password?** and **forgotpassword.aspx**, respectively.

3. Save your work and close the `login.aspx` page.

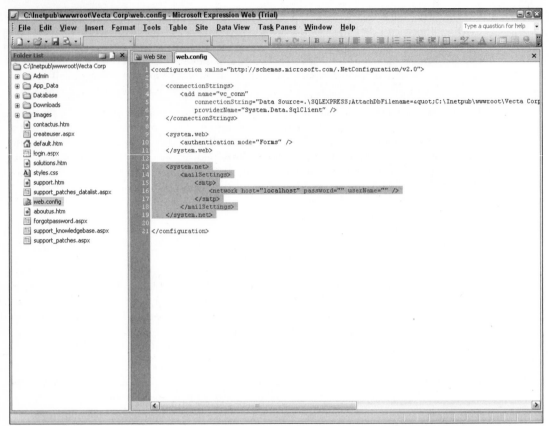

Figure 14-14: Markup added to the Web.Config file that specifies how the e-mail should be sent and more importantly, what computer to use for sending that e-mail

Now, when you visit the login page, you will have a convenient link to the "forgot password" page, available to you from under the Log In button. The final step is to configure IIS to allow relaying of e-mail through its built-in Simple Mail Transfer Protocol (SMTP) server. To do this, follow these steps:

1. Open IIS if it's not already open. You can do this by selecting Start ⇨ Settings ⇨ Control Panel ⇨ Administrative Tools ⇨ Internet Information Service. IIS will launch.

2. Expand your computer node and then right-click on the Default SMTP Virtual Server node; choose Properties from the context menu that appears. The SMTP Virtual Server Properties dialog box will appear.

3. Click on the Access tab.

4. Choose the Relay button.

5. Click the Add button.

6. Add the Localhost IP address: **127.0.0.1** and click OK. The Relay Restrictions dialog will resemble Figure 14-15.

7. Select OK and proceed to close IIS.

That's it! You can now test the functionality and, more important, expect an e-mail once you've completed the password-recovery process. To test the functionality, open your Web browser, and browse to `http://localhost/Vecta Corp/login.aspx`. You'll notice the small Forgot Password link that appears. Click it now to be redirected to the `forgotpassword.aspx` page.

When the page appears, enter your User Name in the text box provided and click Submit. The application will then query the database for users with that unique username and present a second dialog with the resulting security question. Enter the security answer that you provided now and click Submit. Assuming that you entered the correct security answer, the confirmation page appears and, most important, an e-mail with your new, randomly generated password will be sent out.

To see this in action, open your e-mail client and check your e-mail. As you'll see, an e-mail is successfully generated and sent to your account. You'll also notice that the e-mail contains a randomly generated password. Hang on to this randomly generated password. You'll use this value next to change your password to a new, easier-to-remember password.

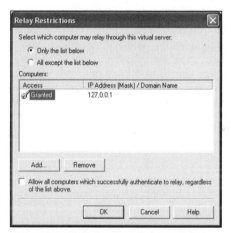

Figure 14-15: Relay Restrictions dialog

The ChangePassword Control

The final control that you will work with is the `ChangePassword` control. You can use this control (as the name implies) as a way of changing an existing password contained within the database. This control is ideally suited when you've used the `PasswordRecovery` control to wipe out and resend you a randomly generated password.

As you've seen, the randomly generated password is long and difficult to remember. You'll no doubt want to change it to something that's easier to remember. The `ChangePassword` control facilitates this process. It offers a Current Password text box along with New Password and New Password Confirmation text boxes, which make changing your password a snap.

Try It Out   **Adding the ChangePassword Control**

Because users must be logged in to change their passwords, you'll build out a new page called `changepassword.aspx` and place it within the `Admin` folder. Once a user logs in using the randomly generated password that's been returned, he or she may access this page in an effort to change the password to a friendlier, easier-to-remember format. To use the `ChangePassword` control, follow these steps:

1. Create a new ASP.NET page by choosing File ➪ New ➪ ASPX. Immediately save the page as `changepassword.aspx`, placing it within the `Admin` folder.

2. Switch to the Toolbox Task Pane, expand the ASP.NET Controls category, and expand the Login subset of controls. Locate the `ChangePassword` control, select it, and drag it into the page.

3. You may also decide to format the look of the `ChangePassword` control by selecting the control, clicking the expander arrow icon, and choosing the AutoFormat option. This will launch the AutoFormat dialog box, enabling you to select a pre-built scheme for your `ChangePassword` control. To match the color scheme of the Vecta Corp Web site, choose the Professional scheme and click OK to apply it.

4. Save your work.

That's it! Now, try browsing to the `changepassword.aspx` page again by opening a browser and entering the path **http://localhost/Vecta Corp/Admin/changepassword.aspx**. If you're asked to log in again, do so now. Remember that you'll have to use the randomly generated password that was provided for you in the auto-generated e-mail. Once you've logged in and you've successfully reached the `changepassword.aspx` page, paste the password that you copied from the e-mail into the Password text box. Now, enter a new password and confirm it. As soon as you click the Change Password button, the application confirms the change and provides you with a "success" message.

Summary

Incorporating password protection for your applications in Expression Web isn't all that difficult. For the most part, Microsoft has streamlined the process by requiring minimal work from the developer.

As you saw, the beginning of this process involved the configuration of application services, which, for the most part, were easily accessible by running an executable. Second, you configured forms authentication and authorization by running the ASP.NET Configuration Settings dialog for the application you needed to configure. From that dialog, you were able to set forms authentication for the site and, more important, configure forms authorization (or what folders/files in the application can and cannot be accessed). The third step involved creating the login page, the page that users are redirected to when they try to access a page that requires authentication. Finally, you looked at the myriad of `Login` controls included with Expression Web. Specifically, you looked at logging in users by using the `Login` control, creating new users using the `CreateUserWizard` control, allowing users to view their login name and login status with the `LoginName` and `LoginStatus` controls, and allowing users to recover and change passwords by utilizing both the `RecoverPassword` and `ChangePassword` controls, respectively.

Chapter 15 completely changes gears and focuses on a topic that is always trendy as it relates to Web development: XML data. Specifically, you'll look at the features built into Expression Web that facilitate the interaction between a Web application and XML data.

Working with XML Data

HTML, as you know, is the abbreviation for HyperText Markup Language. The "Markup" refers to the library of tags that describes how data should be laid out within a page. The browser then parses the information out of those tags and presents it to the user in a friendly and legible fashion. What HTML doesn't do, however, is give any information about what the data means, called *metadata* (data that describes other data). Without metadata, search engines and other data-filtering techniques have to rely on keyword searches or even content searches to retrieve information for the user.

The Extensible Markup Language (XML) is about metadata and the fact that different people have different needs for how they categorize and organize that data. Like HTML, XML is a set of tags and declarations. Rather than being concerned with how the data is structured and subsequently parsed by the browser, XML provides information on what the data means and how it relates to other data.

This chapter examines XML in much more detail, explaining the differences between XML and the XML style sheet language (XSL). Additionally, this chapter discusses Expression Web's XML integration. With even very little knowledge of XML, you can easily and effortlessly create data bindings between your XML files and your Web pages. Specifically, this chapter covers the following topics:

- ❑ An introduction to XML and XSL
- ❑ Exploring the XML options outlined within Expression Web
- ❑ Building your own XML file
- ❑ Binding XML data to a Web page
- ❑ Consuming and presenting data directly from an RSS feed

Introduction to XML and XSL

As mentioned, XML is about defining data. Whereas HTML's purpose is to structuring data, the goal of XML is to define what data means. In the short term, it provides an immediate opportunity for database-driven site development. As could be the case with the fictitious Vecta Corp company, departments (including even yours) may use the same database in different ways. Accounting needs payable and receivable information, Sales wants to monitor information by salesperson to figure out commission structures, and Marketing wants data organized by product and industry segment to figure out future release strategies. Using XML, you would be able to customize the presentation of the queried data in a fashion most useful to the person making the query.

Like HTML, XML's purpose is to describe the content of a document. Unlike HTML, XML does not describe how that content should be displayed. Instead, it describes what that content is. Using XML, the Web developer can mark up the contents of a document, describing that content in terms of its relevance as data. Take a look at the following HTML element:

```
<p>Cammy the Content Manager</p>
```

This example describes the contents within the tags as a paragraph. This is fine if all you are concerned with is displaying the words "Cammy the Content Manager" within a Web page. But what if you want to access those words as data? Using XML, you can mark up the words "Cammy the Content Manager" in a way that better reflects their significance as data:

```
<employee>Cammy the Content Manager</employee>
```

Notice the `<employee>` tag. Surely an `<employee>` tag doesn't exist within any markup language, does it? The beauty of XML is that it does not limit you to a set library of tags as HTML does. When marking up documents in XML, you can choose the tag name that best describes the contents of the element.

For example, in the preceding example, you may need to differentiate between the employee's name/title and his or her employee ID. This can be achieved by using an attribute to describe the employee ID. Because XML allows you to place attributes on tags, you could identify "Cammy the Content Manager" with the employee ID of `1001`, as shown here:

```
<employee id="1001">Cammy the Content Manager</employee>
```

As a second example, take a look at the following document, which describes employees working at Vecta Corp:

```
<h1>Vecta Corp Employees</h1>
<table>
    <tr>
        <td>Ada the Admin Assistant</td>
        <td>Cammy the Content Manager</td>
        <td>Damon the Developer</td>
    </tr>
</table>
```

This document provides information, but that information isn't too clear. Do these employees have unique employee IDs? Do they belong to a department? As it relates to describing data, the following code may be better suited for the preceding example:

```
<employees>
    <company>Vecta Corp</company>
    <employee>
        <name id="1001" department="Administration">Ada</name>
```

```
        <name id="1002" department="Marketing">Cammy</name>
        <name id="1003" department="Engineering">Damon</name>
    </employee>
</employees>
```

Because XML is concerned with how data should be defined, it does not make a good presentational language. If you created an XML document from the preceding example and tried to view it in the browser, you would get little more than a simple collapsible tree, as shown in Figure 15-1.

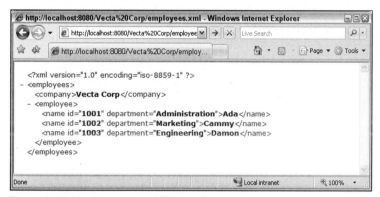

Figure 15-1: Viewing sample XML in a browser

As you can see, XML is not a presentational language. Instead, it is used to define how data is to be structured. Presenting XML data so that it can be viewed in the browser can be accomplished by using the eXtensible Stylesheet Language (XSL). XSL allows you to apply HTML-like features to an XML document so that it may be presented in a friendly format to the user within a browser window. In an effort to clarify XSL, let's take a look at another example. Consider the following data, which represents information about an employee (Cammy) within the fictitious Vecta Corp company:

```
<?xml version="1.0" ?>
<?xml-stylesheet type="text/xsl" href="employeesTransform.xsl"?>
<employees>
    <employee id="1001">
        <name>Cammy</name>
        <title>Content Manager</title>
        <department>Marketing</department>
        <email>cammy@vectacorp.com</email>
    </employee>
</employees>
```

While this is an example of a simple XML file, you could potentially have hundreds, perhaps thousands, of employees within your Vecta Corp XML file. With that said, you may need a way of presenting that data in a browser-friendly format. You could apply the following style sheet in this situation:

```
<xsl:stylesheet version="1.0" xmlns:xsl="http://www.w3.org/1999/XSL/Transform">
<xsl:template match="/">
<html>
<body>
```

```
<h2>Vecta Corp Employees</h2>
<table border="1">
    <tr bgcolor="Silver">
        <th align="left">Name</th>
        <th align="left">Title</th>
        <th align="left">Department</th>
        <th align="left">Email</th>
    </tr>
    <xsl:for-each select="employees/employee">
    <tr>
        <td><xsl:value-of select="name" /></td>
        <td><xsl:value-of select="title" /></td>
        <td><xsl:value-of select="department" /></td>
        <td><xsl:value-of select="email" /></td>
    </tr>
    </xsl:for-each>
</table>
</body>
</html>
</xsl:template>
</xsl:stylesheet>
```

As Figure 15-2 shows, the employee's data is now presented within a cleanly formatted HTML table.

As you can see, XML is about defining what data means. Unlike HTML (which deals with structuring data), XML deals with defining data. Unfortunately, without XSL, the XML data is of little use within a browser. And, as you've probably noticed, if you're not a seasoned XML/XSL developer, it may feel as though XML/XSL requires a steep learning curve. This is where Expression Web comes in.

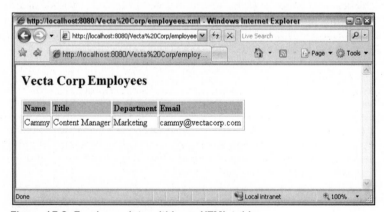

Figure 15-2: Employee data within an HTML table

Expression Web's Visual XML Authoring Environment

As you saw in the previous section, writing XML and XSL code by hand can become a chore. With the release of Expression Web, however, Microsoft brought about new and revamped features for building, interacting with, and binding XML and XSL files so that you don't have to it manually. Specifically, these features include the following:

❑ *Create XML files directly from the New Page dialog* — Built into the New Page dialog box is a template file for creating XML pages quickly and easily. Creating a new XML document from this template lays the framework for building XML files and subsequently generating XSL transformations effortlessly.

❑ *View XML files as data sources* — Expression Web will automatically read and display XML files in your defined site within the Data Source Library Task Pane. If you recall, previous chapters used the Data Source Library Task Pane to connect to and view relational data sources such as databases. XML files, however, also appear within this Task Pane, as long as they're located within the folder that you're currently working with.

❑ *Create bindings visually using the Data Source Details Task Pane* — Viewing the content within an XML file is easy. You simply choose the XML file directly from within the Data Source Library Task Pane and select the Show Data option from a submenu that appears. Immediately, the nodes outlined within the XML file become visually accessible directly from within the Data Source Details Task Pane as selectable elements. You can then click, hold, and drag out each individual element (or all of them at once) onto the Web page to instantly create data bindings.

❑ *Create XSL transformations intuitively* — Rather than manually creating XSL files to stylize XML content within a Web page, Expression Web does the heavy lifting for you. At the point at which you drag nodes from the Data Source Details Task Pane, Expression Web creates an XSL file for you automatically. Furthermore, you're given the option to save the XSL file at Expression Web's default location or within your project's folder.

❑ *Integrate RSS feeds directly into your Web site with little to no setup time* — By far, one of the coolest features integrated into Expression Web is the ability to tie directly into RSS feeds (covered with more detail later in this chapter). By simply pointing the Data Source Library Task Pane to a remote path of the RSS feed, Expression Web automatically generates a schema tree of nodes, elements, and more within the Data Source Details Task Pane. Once the schema tree has been created from the remote RSS feed, it's merely a matter of dragging and dropping the elements from the Bindings panel into your Web page, formatting the content, and then previewing the result in the browser.

As this chapter unfolds, the discussion will dive into all of these topics. Before doing that, however, let's begin by creating our first XML file.

Creating an XML Document

Before you can begin integrating XML data into your Web pages, you must first build the XML file that will contain the data to be offered within the Web pages. Once the XML file has been created, you can focus on working with the many other features built into Expression Web that facilitate and allow you to work with XML. Let's get started.

Keeping in line with the Vecta Corp application, let's build an XML file that defines data for Vecta Corp employees. What purpose this data will serve and which application it will be designed for are irrelevant at this point. What you do care about is creating the XML file that defines the name, title, department, and e-mail address for all of the Vecta Corp employees.

To create the XML file, start by choosing File ⇨ New. The New Page dialog box will appear. Choose the XML option from the General category and click OK. The XML file appears in Code view with the following line at the top of the page:

```
<?xml version="1.0" encoding="iso-8859-1"?>
```

As you can see, the first line of code defined in the XML file is the *XML declaration*. This declaration should be included at the beginning of each XML document. Not only does it specify the XML version to the browser, but it also outlines the character set to be used in the document. Now that the XML document has been created, add the following data, beginning at line 2:

```xml
<employees>
    <employee id="1001">
        <name>Ada</name>
        <title>Admin Assistant</title>
        <department>Administration</department>
        <email>ada@vectacorp.com</email>
    </employee>
    <employee id="1002">
        <name>Agnes</name>
        <title>Accountant</title>
        <department>Accounting</department>
        <email>agnes@vectacorp.com</email>
    </employee>
    <employee id="1003">
        <name>Cammy</name>
        <title>Content Manager</title>
        <department>Marketing</department>
        <email>cammy@vectacorp.com</email>
    </employee>
    <employee id="1004">
        <name>Dave</name>
        <title>Developer</title>
        <department>Engineering</department>
        <email>dave@vectacorp.com</email>
    </employee>
    <employee id="1005">
        <name>Ferris</name>
        <title>Founder</title>
        <department>Executive</department>
        <email>ferris@vectacorp.com</email>
```

```
        </employee>
        <employee id="1006">
            <name>Herb</name>
            <title>Representative</title>
            <department>Human Resources</department>
            <email>herb@vectacorp.com</email>
        </employee>
        <employee id="1007">
            <name>Mike</name>
            <title>Director</title>
            <department>Marketing</department>
            <email>mike@vectacorp.com</email>
        </employee>
        <employee id="1008">
            <name>Pat</name>
            <title>Programmer</title>
            <department>Engineering</department>
            <email>pat@vectacorp.com</email>
        </employee>
        <employee id="1009">
            <name>Tina</name>
            <title>Tech Writer</title>
            <department>Administration</department>
            <email>tina@vectacorp.com</email>
        </employee>
        <employee id="1010">
            <name>Wally</name>
            <title>Webmaster</title>
            <department>Marketing</department>
            <email>wally@vectacorp.com</email>
        </employee>
    </employees>
```

Looking at the data, you'll probably notice some interesting aspects. First and foremost, the tags say a lot about the data contained within them, right? This is XML at its finest. It's describing the data contained within the tags. You have a list of employees, hence the <employees> tag. Then you have groups of individual employees; therefore, you have various <employee> tags uniquely identified by the id attribute. Within each <employee> tag, you have tags that define the employees name (<name>), title (<title>), department (<department>), and e-mail address (<email>).

Second (and possibly the most obvious even if you're not an HTML developer), none of these tags are recognizable. Remember that with XML, you're responsible for defining the tags. XML is used to define data, not structure it. Ultimately, the browser doesn't care what tags you're using because it won't attempt to parse anything out of the file. This is where data binding comes in.

Save your file as employees.xml. As soon as you save your document, two things will happen. The first and most obvious is that the employees.xml file appears within the Folder List Task Pane. Obviously, because it's contained within your site's folder, it (and every other file within your site) is listed here. Second (and more important), the employees.xml file appears as a data source option within the Data Source Library Task Pane (Task Panes ⇨ Data Source Library), as shown in Figure 15-3.

Now that your XML file is listed within the Data Source Library Task Pane, you can freely work with the data that is available through that XML file. As you'll see in the next section, nodes within the XML file will become available to you within the Data Source Details Task Pane. From the Data Source Details Task Pane, XML nodes can then be freely dragged and dropped directly onto your Web page to create data bindings. Let's do that next.

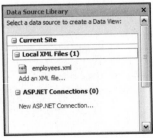

Figure 15-3: The employees.xml file appearing as a data source option within the Data Source Library Task Pane

Binding XML Data

Now that you've successfully created the XML file (which contains the data that you'd like offered within a Web page, defined using a series of nodes), you'll notice that the file's name appears within the Data Source Library Task Pane directly underneath the Local XML Files section. To reveal the nodes that the XML file contains within the Data Source Details Task Pane, you only need to select the file and choose the Show Data option from the submenu that appears. Immediately, the nodes that are offered by the XML file (id, name, title, department, and email) are shown within the Data Source Details Task Pane, as shown in Figure 15-4.

As you'll notice from Figure 15-4, the Data Source Details Task Pane, as it did for database data, outlines all of the nodes contained within the XML file. Additionally, it displays record-by-record a sample of the data contained within the XML file, starting with the first item or, in this case, the employee whose id is 1001 (Ada, the Admin Assistant).

Of course, you can scroll through the XML file to view the data contained within it by selecting the left/right arrow icons that appear just to the right of the employee node. As you'll notice, brackets appear, encasing a count of the records within the XML file and the numeric value of the record that you're on as you scroll through the XML file.

While being able to see a visual list of the nodes contained within the XML file in the Data Source Details Task Pane is certainly nice, it does very little in terms of allowing you to view that content within the Web page. What you must do next is create a binding.

The process of binding XML nodes to your Web page is similar in concept to that of creating bindings from relational data sources (such as a database), the only difference is that relational databases require some sort of intermediary server-side technology that can handle the data query and subsequent data presentation. XML files, on the other hand, need only an XSL file to handle the transformation from XML to structural presentation in HTML. Fortunately for you, the XSL files that the browser needs to present your XML data are automatically created for you by Expression Web. Let's take a look.

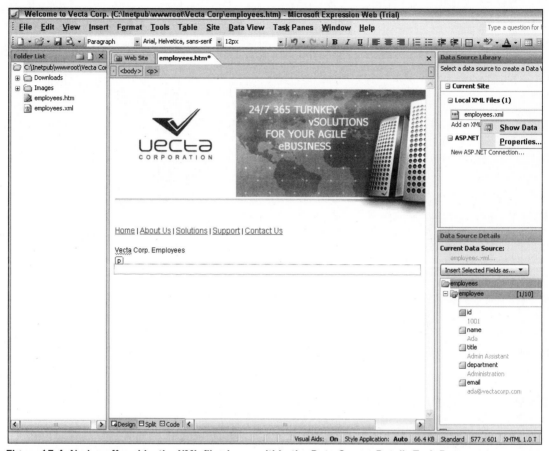

Figure 15-4: Nodes offered by the XML file shown within the Data Source Details Task Pane

Try It Out   Binding XML Data to a Web Page

With the XML nodes now visible within the Data Source Details Task Pane, you can freely drag and drop those nodes onto the Web page in an effort to create a data binding. To create a binding, follow these steps:

1.   Creating bindings for your XML data can be handled in one of a couple ways. First, you could select the node from the Data Source Details Task Pane and drag it out onto your Web page. (Go ahead and select the employee node now, and drag it out onto the page.) Doing this creates what's known as a *Multiple Item View*. The second option for creating a Multiple Item View is to simply highlight the specific node (employee) that you want to create the binding for, click the "Insert Selected Field as" menu, and choose the Multiple Item View option from the submenu that appears. Either method you choose produces the same result. A table is created within the Web page (for structuring purposes), the node name is added as the table's header, and your data is included as a separate row within the table, as shown in Figure 15-5.

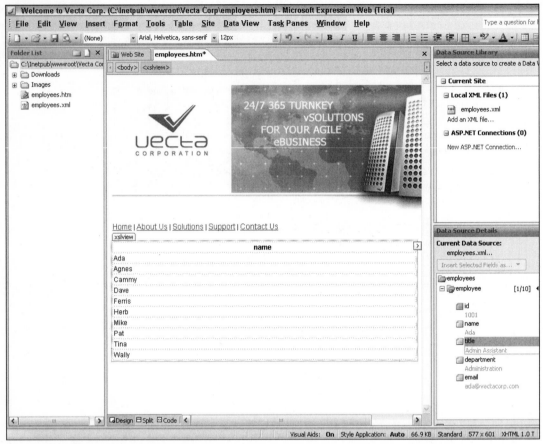

Figure 15-5: Result of creating bindings

2. Another method for creating a binding is to use the *Single Item View*. In this approach, the data appears within an HTML table as it did in the previous step, the only difference being that each text element has the node name next to it as opposed to being outlined within the table's header. To use the Single Item View, simply highlight the specific node that you want to create the binding for, click the "Insert Selected Field as" menu, and choose the Single Item View option from the submenu that appears. You'll notice that the data is added similarly to the first step, the only difference being that the node name appears next to each element.

3. For the purposes of this exercise, use the method outlined in Step 1. Your employees.htm page should resemble the one shown in Figure 15-5. The next step is to add sub-data to each name within the table. For example, you will want users to know which department an employee belongs to, what the employee's title is, and, more important, what the employee's e-mail address is. You can add these nodes directly within the table's cell by using sub-views, which create data

associations with already created nodes within the view on the page. To do this, place your cursor within the first cell, next to Ada's name. Now, select the title node from within the Data Source Details Task Pane, click the "Insert Selected Field as" button, and choose the Subview option from the menu that appears. Immediately, the employee's title will appear as a bulleted item directly below the employee's name.

4. Repeat Step 3, placing your cursor next to Ada's name, choosing the next node in the list (department, then e-mail address), choosing the "Insert Selected Field as" button, and then selecting the Subview option from the menu that appears. When you've finished, the employee's name will appear as the top-level item followed by e-mail, department, and title listed within bullets directly under the particular employee's name, as shown in Figure 15-6.

5. The last step before you test the page is to change the header of the table from "name" to "Vecta Corp Employees" so that it matches what's outlined in Figure 15-6. Once that's done, you're ready to test your work within a browser.

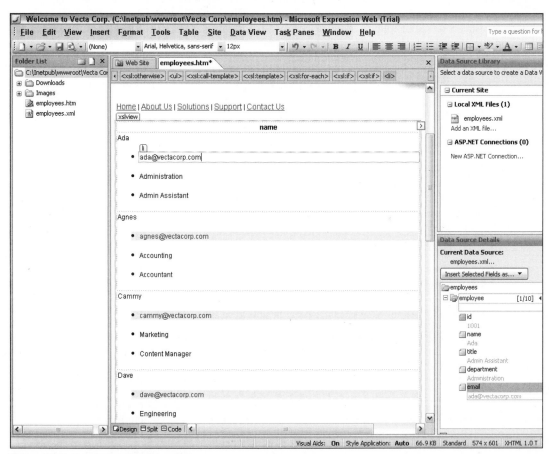

Figure 15-6: Employee data inserted

6. To preview your work in the browser, you must first save your document. Choose File ⇨ Save now. Almost immediately the Save Embedded Files dialog box appears with two files (`xslview.js` and `employees11.xsl`) listed within the "Embedded files to save" list. These are the JavaScript and XSL files that Expression Web creates automatically for you so that viewing your XML data within a Web page becomes possible. By default, Expression Web will save these files within the root of your project so click OK now. The Save Embedded Files dialog box will close and the two new files will appear within your Folder List Task Pane.

7. Preview your page in the browser by pressing F12. The page launches and the XML data will be presented within the page similarly to the way it was outlined within the page in Expression Web.

The simple seven-step process outlined thus far represents the most basic form of extracting and binding XML data to your Web pages. As you saw, that process was fairly simple, and involved nothing more than creating the XML file and then dragging and dropping individual nodes from the Data Source Details Task Pane into your Web page. In certain instances, however, you might want to take advantage of other, more advanced features offered by the XML view's submenu of options. To access these options, select the small expander arrow icon that appears in the upper-right corner of the XML view to reveal the following set of options:

❑ *Filter* — Click this button to launch the Filter Criteria dialog box. It's within this dialog box that you're able to specify filtering criteria for the XML data that is returned in the browser. For example, you may decide to create search functionality so that when a user enters a value into a text box and clicks the Submit button, that value is passed into a parameter that you're responsible for creating within this dialog box. The browser would then query and, in a sense, issue a WHERE clause to the XML document to retrieve data that matched the search criteria.

❑ *Sort* — Click this link to launch the Sort dialog box. It's within this dialog that you are able to specify how to sort the data that is returned by the XML file. Options include sorting by one or more of the nodes contained within your XML file and whether to sort them in either ascending or descending order.

❑ *Edit Columns* — Click this link to launch the Edit Columns dialog box. It's within this dialog box that you're able to show or hide specific nodes from appearing within the data view.

❑ *Change Layout* — Click this link to launch the Data View Properties dialog box with the Layout tab selected (also mentioned in the final bullet point). It's from this tab that you're able to configure your data to be presented in either an HTML or Datasheet view. When the HTML option is selected, various view styles appear for you to select from.

❑ *Data View Preview* — Select an option from this drop-down menu to either limit or not limit the results that are shown within the Web page by the XML file. Options include the ability to hide all filters (the default shows all the data in the XML file), one item, five items, ten items, or no items (in which case, the "No Matching Items" text is displayed instead).

❑ *Conditional Formatting* — Launches the Conditional Formatting Task Pane. It's within this task pane that you're able to outline conditions that should be met before data is presented within the Web page.

❑ *Refresh Data View* — Click this link to refresh the XML view. This should be done each time you make node changes to the XML file. When you refresh the data view, the data view's appearance will change to reflect the changes made in the XML file.

❏   *Data View Properties* — Click this link to launch the Data View Properties dialog box. From this dialog box, you are able to customize the layout of the data view, the path to the source of the XSL file, what kind of XSL processing Expression Web should force, and various general options that allow you to specify whether to show a header, footer, or a summary, and if text should be displayed when a user performs a search and no matching records are returned.

Working with RSS Feeds

One of the hottest trends in Web development today is that of RSS. Originally developed by Netscape, Really Simple Syndication (RSS) is an XML format for syndicating Web content. A Web site that wants to allow other sites to publish some of its content creates an RSS document and registers the document with an RSS publisher. A user who can read RSS-distributed content can then use the content on a different site.

Syndicated content includes such data as news feeds, events listings, news stories, headlines, project updates, and excerpts from discussion forums, or even corporate information. While numerous Web sites exist devoted to the topic of helping you publish and distribute RSS feeds, you need look no further than Expression Web. With Expression Web's built-in XSL transformation integration, consuming RSS feeds within your Web site is a snap.

Try It Out   **Consuming an RSS Feed**

As you'll see, working with RSS feeds in Expression Web is not only easy, it's extremely intuitive. To consume an RSS feed within your Web page, follow these steps:

1.   Locate the RSS feed that you want to consume within your Web page. A Web site that I know offers an RSS feed is the *Chicago Sun-Times* sports feed located at `http://www.suntimes.com/rss/sports/index.xml`. To see an example, browse to that Web site now. You're immediately presented with the RSS feed similar to Figure 15-7.

> **Depending on your browser, the formatting of the RSS feed will differ. Internet Explorer displays the basic structure of the RSS feed and asks you to subscribe to it. Firefox works similarly. Previous versions of Internet Explorer, however, will simply display the XML directly within the browser, as shown in Figure 15-1. In this case, the display shouldn't matter. What you care about is saving that feed as an XML file to your computer.**

2.   Your next step will be to save that RSS feed to the Vecta Corp directory as an XML file. Once this is done, you can import and work with the nodes outlined within the XML file within your Web page in Expression Web. To do this, choose File ➪ Save As. The Save As dialog box will appear. Browse to your working directory and save the file (with the XML extension) to that folder. The name you specify is irrelevant.

3.   Shift your attention back to Expression Web. Create a new Web page by choosing File ➪ New ➪ HTML. Immediately save the page as `rssfeed.htm`.

4.   Ensure that the Data Source Library Task Pane is open. By default, the new XML file (`Chicago Sun-Times Sports.xml`) should automatically appear. If it doesn't, click the "Add an XML File" link within the Task Pane now. When the Data Source Properties dialog box appears, browse to the `Chicago Sun-Times Sports.xml` file and click OK to manually add the file to the Data Source Library Task Pane.

5. As you did earlier in the chapter, select the XML feed from within the Data Source Library Task Pane and choose the Show Data option from the submenu that appears. Immediately, the elements outlined within the XML file become visible within the Data Source Details Task Pane as an expandable/collapsible tree.

6. Expand the node list until you find the item element. Select it and choose the Single Item View option from the Insert Selected Fields as sub menu. Expression Web creates a series of tables and dedicates a table for each item within the XML file. You'll also notice that a cell within each table is dedicated to the `title`, `link`, `description`, `author`, and `pubDate` element contained within the XML file similar to Figure 15-8.

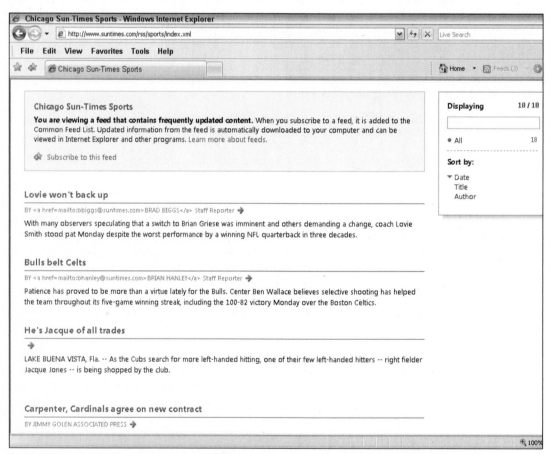

Figure 15-7: The Chicago Sun-Times XML sports feed

7. Save your work. The Save Embedded Files dialog box will appear. As you did earlier in the chapter, accept the default save paths and click OK.

8. To preview your page in the browser, press F12. The page, complete with today's news appears within the browser similar to Figure 15-9.

As you can see from Figure 15-9, the content of the RSS feed is displayed within the browser. You'll also notice that there's much formatting to be done. Most of the links appear with their raw HTML visible. Additionally, some of the element headings, like pubDate, aren't intuitive to the viewer. All of this and more can be configured directly within Expression Web with little additional work.

While this section provided a gentle introduction into the world of consuming RSS feeds, in reality, the door is open for you to explore. Expression Web introduced rich functionality for not only working with generic XML files, but third-party RSS feeds as well. With a bit more exploration, you'll no doubt be creative and consuming RSS feeds within your Web pages quickly and easily.

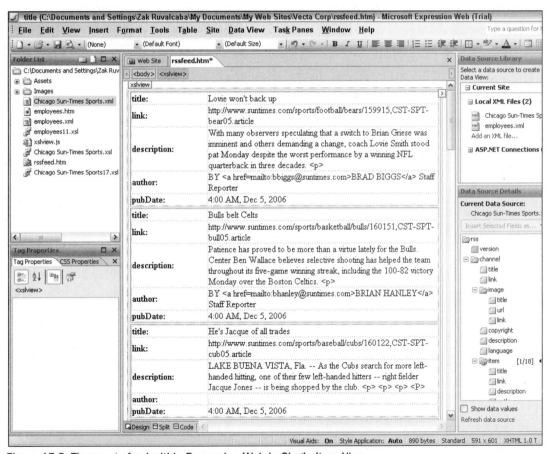

Figure 15-8: The sports feed within Expression Web in Single Item View

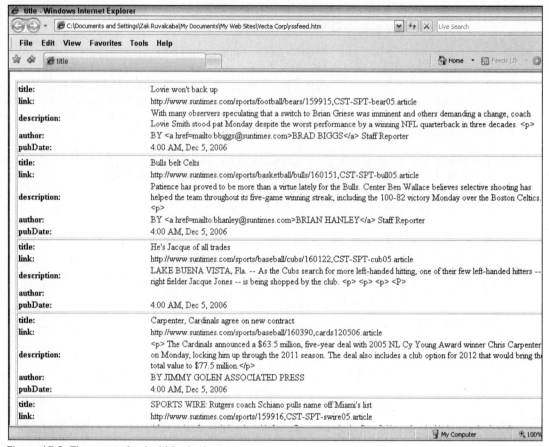

Figure 15-9: The sports feed within the browser

Summary

As you have seen, Expression Web's support for XML is abundant. In this chapter, you learned about XML, you explored the support for creating XML and XSL transformations within Expression Web, and you saw how to integrate third-party news feeds directly within your Web site. With Web development trends moving more and more in the direction of XML, it's hard to ignore its momentum. Fortunately, Microsoft has risen to the occasion and has included features and functionality for working with XML technologies directly from Expression Web's already feature-rich environment.

Building Accessible and Standards-Compliant Web Sites

There is an implicit promise in the name of the World Wide Web — the promise of an information network that can be used by everyone around the world. The Web succeeds at what it does because of its universality. A Web document is written in one or more Web languages designed to be cross-platform and interoperable with a wide variety of technologies.

Clearly, the Web is designed to be open to a broad range of users, and that's where things start to get tricky! The average Web user of moderate means in North America or Europe has a decently fast computer, a full-color monitor, a keyboard, a mouse, speakers, and a high-speed modem or a faster connection. But that's just the average user. People tend to be scattered all over the range of possibility, rarely conforming to the same capabilities. Welcome to designing on the Web!

This chapter explains what Web accessibility standards are, how they benefit both you and your users who have disabilities, and how you can use Expression Web to ensure that everyone can use your site. Specifically, the discussion outlines the following topics:

❑   Accessibility standards, including Web content accessibility guidelines (WCAG) and Section 508

❑   How to conform to standards

❑   Applying standards to your Web designs using various features built into Expression Web

❑   Accessibility reference that outlines various tests that you can perform on images, tables, colors, image maps, multimedia, and more

Accessibility Standards

The way you design a Web site determines, to a very large extent, who is able to access that site. If you're concerned only about those with the latest version of your favorite browser and the fastest hardware and connection, there's no guarantee that you'll make a Web site that can be used by anyone who falls outside of those parameters.

There's a very large group of users who tend to fall outside of nearly everyone's target audience when developers design for the Web: users who have disabilities.

Web users who have visual disabilities are often stymied by Web pages that rely on images, color, or visual layout to convey the meaning of the site's content. Those with limited vision will have difficulties with low-contrast colors or small fonts. Deaf or hard-of-hearing users won't hear the sound tracks of multimedia. Users with limited physical dexterity might not be able to drag and drop, or to do other activities requiring a mouse. Pages with complex text that lack illustrations and summaries will be very difficult for users with cognitive disabilities.

The Web isn't always easy to use if you have special needs. Some users, such as those who are blind, can rely on special assistive technologies such as screen readers, Braille displays, or screen magnifiers for Web access. However, these tools will work with your site only if you've carefully built your sites to allow access.

> To learn more about how people with disabilities access the Web, visit the site of the International
> Center for Disability Resources on the Internet, at www.icdri.org.

The process of creating a site that can be used by anyone regardless of disability is called *accessibility*. To properly create a Web site that is accessible, you'll need to know all about assistive technology, how people with disabilities use the Web, and how HTML and other Web languages function in browsers. You'll also need to be an expert on accessibility's close cousin, *usability*, which is the study of how people use computers effectively.

Sound like a lot of work? Well, it is, believe me, but fortunately, you won't have to do all that work yourself. The knowledge you'll need to construct accessible Web sites has been compiled into accessibility standards that function as a checklist of sorts so that all you really have to do is follow these simple rules to produce a site with no barriers to access.

Expression Web makes it even easier for you to follow those standards because they're built right into the software itself. By using Expression Web's accessibility features to create and check your work, you can greatly simplify the process of creating accessible Web sites.

Standards Resources

When it comes to the World Wide Web, there is one primary source for nearly all of the standards you'll use: the World Wide Web Consortium (W3C).

The W3C is an international association of some of the major players in the Web, from browser makers to research organizations. The official specifications for HTML/XHTML, XML, CSS, and other key Web technologies were created by the W3C's working groups and released as recommendations for adoption on the Web.

> *The W3C's Web site is located at* www.w3.org *and is the definitive source for Web specifications. However, most Web specifications are incredibly dry reading, and unless you're some sort of masochist, you won't want to dive right into them. A better idea is to start at the Web site of the Web Standards Project (*www.webstandards.org*), a group of expert Web developers who promote standards compliance.*

One branch of the W3C concerns itself exclusively with access by people with disabilities: the Web Accessibility Initiative (WAI). Just as the W3C has produced standards for the HTML language, so has the WAI produced standards for accessibility.

Web Content Accessibility Guidelines

For Web developers, the most important WAI standards are contained in the Web Content Accessibility Guidelines (WCAG), which are a set of guidelines, checkpoints, and associated techniques that describe how to ensure the accessibility of your Web site.

> *You can read the full WCAG recommendation and download a checklist for easy reference from the W3C's Web site at* www.w3.org/tr/wcag.

The WCAG recommendation lists 14 basic principles (or guidelines) that promote accessibility:

1. Provide equivalent alternatives to auditory and visual content.
2. Don't rely on color alone.
3. Use markup and style sheets, and do so properly.
4. Clarify natural language usage.
5. Create tables that transform gracefully.
6. Ensure that pages featuring new technologies transform gracefully.
7. Ensure user control of time-sensitive content changes.
8. Ensure direct accessibility of embedded user interfaces.
9. Design for device independence.
10. Use interim solutions.
11. Use W3C technologies and guidelines.
12. Provide context and orientation information.
13. Provide clear navigation mechanisms.
14. Ensure that documents are clear and simple.

Each of these guidelines is supported by one or more checkpoints. For example, the checkpoints for the second guideline, "Don't rely on color alone," are as follows:

❑ 2.1 Ensure that all information conveyed with color is also available without color (for example from context or markup).

❑ 2.2 Ensure that foreground and background color combinations provide sufficient contrast when viewed by someone having color deficits, or when viewed on a black-and-white screen.

Each checkpoint is given a priority value. A *priority 1* means that the failure to follow that checkpoint will exclude members of your audience with specific disabilities. *Priority 2* checkpoints are designed to reduce the difficulty of access by people with disabilities, and *priority three* checkpoints actively improve the quality of access for individuals with special needs.

In WAI terminology, if your site fulfills all the priority 1 checkpoints, it is said to be Single-A compliant with WCAG. Meeting all priority 1 and 2 checkpoints grants your site Double-A status, and successfully meeting all the checkpoints qualifies a site as Triple-A level.

WCAG compliance levels have been accepted by many public and private organizations as the minimum requirement for sites they control. For example, California community college Web sites must meet at least WCAG Double-A standards.

Section 508

In addition to being directly adopted, the WCAG standard has been used to create specialized Web accessibility policies. The most influential of these is the standard employed by the United States for most government Web sites.

The requirements for federal sites are described in Section 508, subsection 1194 of the 1998 amendments to the Rehabilitation Act. That's a mouthful to say at once, so everyone refers to the set of requirements simply as Section 508.

The aim of Section 508 is to ensure that government information technology is accessible to people with disabilities — both those working within federal agencies and those citizens who are using public Web resources.

The Section 508 requirements for Web sites are modeled after the priority 1 checkpoints in WCAG, with a few modifications. Specifically, Section 508 adds some new requirements and eliminates a few priority checkpoints, while generally rewriting from the technical recommendation language of the W3C to the form of bureaucratic regulation favored in government work.

The official Web site for Section 508 is www.section508.gov.

Which Standard to Follow?

It's been said that the great thing about standards is that there are so many to choose from. Despite the humor of this statement, there's still some truth to it. There's not one universal standard for accessibility but several, including Single-A WCAG, Double-A WCAG, Triple-A WCAG, and Section 508.

The overlap between *Single-A WCAG checkpoints* and *Section 508 requirements* remains significant, however, so the techniques used to make a site accessible by one standard will generally ensure that the other standard is met.

The *Double-A* and *Triple-A WCAG standards* are more difficult to meet because they go beyond basic accessibility and require that Web pages not be difficult to use.

In some cases, you may be able to choose which standard to follow. Most commercial and personal Web sites are unregulated and, thus, you can select your level of compliance. Many commercial sites will aim for Single-A compliance, but Double-A compliance improves site access for disabled users or employees. Private organizations or corporations that provide services to people with disabilities will want to achieve Triple-A compliance.

As mentioned previously, public sector Web sites may have legal requirements for accessibility, depending on the location and type of public entity. For example, U.S. federal agencies such as the Department of Forestry are required to meet the Section 508 requirements, and most universities for example, must meet WCAG Double-A. Your organization's legal or disability officer can advise you on specific regulatory obligations that apply to your Web site.

Conform with Standards

Conforming to accessibility standards provides many benefits. Besides reducing your potential legal complications (especially if you are subject to specific requirements), it can also improve the overall usability of your site because the considerations needed for producing an accessible Web site also lead to a site that is improved for everyone. For example, a transcript of an audio speech can benefit anyone accessing the Web from a quiet public library.

Accessible standards also encourage designs that can be used on a diversity of Web access devices, including set-top boxes, Internet appliances, and PDAs. The same techniques that guarantee access for non-visual browsers also improve access for users of text-only cell phones.

Creating an accessible Web site consists of ensuring that you've coded your site so that a broad audience can use it. Your audience will include not only traditional browsers and Web devices, but also specialized programs or hardware, collectively called *assistive technology*. Examples of assistive technology include screen readers, pointing devices, voice recognition software, screen magnifiers, Braille terminals, and onscreen keyboards.

Assistive technologies are usually very innovative and clever approaches to overcoming obstacles. However, like any computer feature, they can work only with what they're given, in terms of information.

If a Braille terminal encounters an image that isn't labeled properly (with an `alt` attribute), it cannot tell automatically if the image is a spacer GIF, a simple decoration, an important piece of content necessary for understanding the page, or a banner ad. As the author of a Web page, you can provide this necessary information so that assistive technologies can function properly.

For example, the following modified version of the Vecta Corp About Us Web page, although a straightforward design, nonetheless poses serious accessibility problems for users with disabilities:

```
<!DOCTYPE html PUBLIC "-//W3C//DTD XHTML 1.0 Transitional//EN"
"http://www.w3.org/TR/xhtml1/DTD/xhtml1-transitional.dtd">
<html xmlns="http://www.w3.org/1999/xhtml">
<head>
<title>Welcome to Vecta Corp</title>
<style type="text/css">
body {
      font-family: Arial, Helvetica, sans-serif;
      font-size: 12px;
}
a {
      color: #CC1C0D;
      font-size: 14px;
}
</style>
</head>

<body>
<p><img src="Images/header.gif" width="697" height="227" /></p>
<p>
      <a href="default.htm" class="navlink">Home</a> |
      <a href="aboutus.htm" class="navlink">About Us</a> |
      <a href="solutions.htm" class="navlink">Solutions</a> |
      <a href="support.htm" class="navlink">Support</a> |
      <a href="contactus.htm" class="navlink">Contact Us</a>
</p>
<p>
      <img src="Images/subheader_aboutus.gif" width="121" height="27" />
      <br /><br />
      <strong>Company Overview</strong>
      <br /><br />
      With innovative approaches and advanced methodologies, Vecta Corp
      provides scalable business solutions to help <br />
      companies achieve success through revenue increase, cost management
      and user satisfaction.<br />
</p>
</body>
</html>
```

So, what does the page look like in a browser? As you can see from Figure 16-1, it displays perfectly fine in a full-featured browser such as Internet Explorer.

Note, however, that the red color used on the navigation links doesn't reproduce well in a black-and-white screenshot. What would this site be like for blind users? To test, you can use a text browser named Lynx to view the page. Lynx displays all Web pages without images or colors, just as plain text. This is a useful approximation of what visually impaired users experience when accessing a Web page. Most users who can't see will use a screen reader program that reads aloud the text from a browser, or a Braille display with raised dots. Both of these methods are roughly equal to the text display of Lynx.

To install and view this page using Lynx, follow these steps:

1. Visit www.vectacorp.com/downloads and download the Lynx application by clicking on the provided link.

2. Once you've downloaded the ZIP file, extract the Lynx folder from the ZIP.

3. Double-click lynx.exe to start the Lynx browser.

4. When the Commands message appears, press the G key on your keyboard.

5. Type the location to your aboutus.htm page, or **http://localhost/Vecta%20Corp/aboutus.htm**. (The %20 renders as a space.)

As you can see from Figure 16-2, some minor problems are clearly visible. Initially, the banner at the top isn't identified beyond [header] and the subheading image for About Us displays the text [subheader_aboutus].

Figure 16-1: Page displayed in Internet Explorer

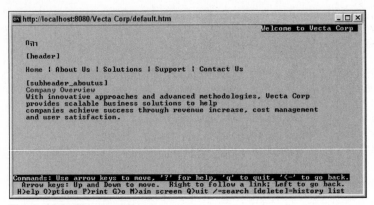

Figure 16-2: Minor problems

To correct these issues, you can revise the page to make it more accessible, as shown here. The changes to the source code are shown in bold.

```
<!DOCTYPE html PUBLIC "-//W3C//DTD XHTML 1.0 Transitional//EN"
"http://www.w3.org/TR/xhtml1/DTD/xhtml1-transitional.dtd">
<html xmlns="http://www.w3.org/1999/xhtml">
<head>
<title>Welcome to Vecta Corp</title>
<style type="text/css">
body {
      font-family: Arial, Helvetica, sans-serif;
      font-size: 12px;
}
a {
      color: #CC1C0D;
      font-size: 14px;
}
</style>
</head>

<body>
<p>
<img src="Images/header.gif" width="697" height="227"
      alt="Vecta Corporation" />
</p>
<p>
      <a href="default.htm" class="navlink">Home</a> |
      <a href="aboutus.htm" class="navlink">About Us</a> |
      <a href="solutions.htm" class="navlink">Solutions</a> |
      <a href="support.htm" class="navlink">Support</a> |
      <a href="contactus.htm" class="navlink">Contact Us</a>
</p>
<p>
      <img src="Images/subheader_aboutus.gif" width="121" height="27"
      alt="About Us" />
      <br /><br />
```

```
        <strong>Company Overview</strong>
        <br /><br />
         With innovative approaches and advanced methodologies, Vecta Corp
         provides scalable business solutions to help <br />
        companies achieve success through revenue increase, cost management
        and user satisfaction.<br />
    </p>
    </body>
    </html>
```

The major addition that you'll notice is that the `alt` attribute has been added.

The revised page is shown in Figure 16-3 in Lynx. Although the changes aren't dramatic, they are enough to allow a broader group of users to access the page.

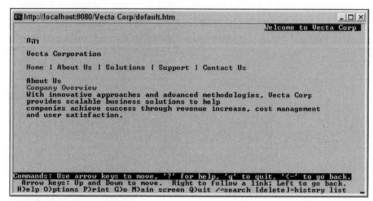

Figure 16-3: Revised page

Checking Accessibility

In general, it's more efficient to consider and implement accessibility measures as you build a site. However, in some cases, you may be dealing with older sites that need to be updated or even sites that you didn't design and have inherited responsibility for. Additionally, while this isn't generally recommended, you may even decide that you'd like to design your site first, and then allow Expression Web to point out your accessibility vulnerabilities, and then implement those practices manually later.

When the latter is the case, Expression Web assists you in bringing your Web pages up to compliance with accessibility standards through accessibility reports that analyze your page and look for specific problems. You can even run reports on all pages in one folder, on your hard drive, or on the Web site as a whole.

The Accessibility Task Pane, available to you from within Expression Web, allows you to scan your Web pages in hopes of tracking down accessibility flaws within your site, view accessibility reports that Expression Web produces, and then react by fixing these inconsistencies as they're presented to you within a list. As you'll see, Expression Web allows you to scan all pages, open pages, selected pages within the Folder List Task Pane, or the current page that's open. During the scan, you can have

Expression Web check for WCAG Priority 1, WCAG Priority 2, and Section 508 compliance. Additionally, you can have Expression Web present errors, warnings, and/or a manual checklist of compliancy issues.

Try It Out   Performing an Accessibility Check

So that you understand how accessibility checks are performed in Expression Web, let's perform one now on the original `aboutus.htm` page. If you recall, at the very least, you should receive missing `alt` attribute errors. Let's find out. To perform an accessibility check, follow these steps:

1. With the original `aboutus.htm` (the page represented by the code outlined earlier in this chapter, which was missing the `alt` attributes) page open, choose Tools ➪ Accessibility Reports. Immediately, the Accessibility Checker dialog box appears. As you can see from the dialog box, the Accessibility Checker offers options that allow you to scan all pages, open pages, selected pages within the Folder List Task Pane, or the current page that's open. Additionally, options exist for specifying the type of checks to perform on your pages including WCAG Priority 1, WCAG Priority 2, and Section 508 compliance. You also have options to present errors, warnings, and/or a manual checklist of compliancy issues. For the purposes of this exercise, check the appropriate boxes so that your dialog matches up with the one shown in Figure 16-4.

2. Click the Check button to perform the accessibility scan. Immediately, the Accessibility Task Pane appears with accessibility flaws listed, as shown in Figure 16-5.

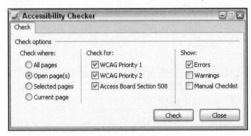

Figure 16-4: Completed dialog

As you can see from Figure 16-5, the Accessibility Task Pane is divided into three categories, each relevant to a particular action to take toward accessibility compliance on a page. For example, the left column of the Accessibility Task Pane is divided into the following features:

❑ *Run Accessibility Checker* — Click this small icon to re-launch the Accessibility Checker dialog box in an effort to refine or broaden your accessibility checking criteria. Once you click the Check button, however, the previous results are lost.

❑ *Next Result* — Click this icon to force your cursor to the exact line in code within the page that produced the error. The first time you click this, your cursor is automatically taken to the first accessibility issue within the list.

❑ *Previous Result* — Click this icon to force your cursor to the previous line of code that produced the accessibility error.

- ❑ *Refresh Changed Results* — Once you fix an accessibility error in code, the accessibility list isn't automatically updated for you. To update the list, click this icon.

- ❑ *Show Problem Details* — Select an accessibility issue from the list and then click this button to show a more detailed description of the error in question within a dialog box.

- ❑ *Generate HTML Report* — Click on this icon to have Expression Web generate an HTML-based report, similar to Figure 16-6.

Additionally, you'll notice five columns outlined within the Accessibility Task Pane that help describe the error (Problem Summary), what page it appears on (Page), the line number it appears on (Line), the type of issue (Error versus Warning) that is being presented (Issue Type), and the particular checkpoint it violates (Checkpoint).

To automatically have your cursor jump to the line number within the page that produced the error, simply double-click the error within the Task Pane. The page will immediately open (if it's not already open). Switch to code view, and then highlight the particular line number in question. Additionally, if you'd like more information as to the WCAG/Section 508 error that was produced, simply click on the hyperlink for the WCAG/Section 508 error within the Checkpoint column to automatically browse to the particular section within the W3C Web site.

> **Most of the options outlined here are also accessible by simply right-clicking onto the error within the list. The context menu provides similarly named options for the features outlined previously.**

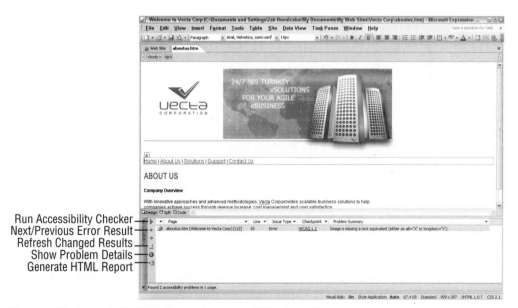

Run Accessibility Checker
Next/Previous Error Result
Refresh Changed Results
Show Problem Details
Generate HTML Report

Figure 16-5: Accessibility Task Pane with accessibility flaws listed

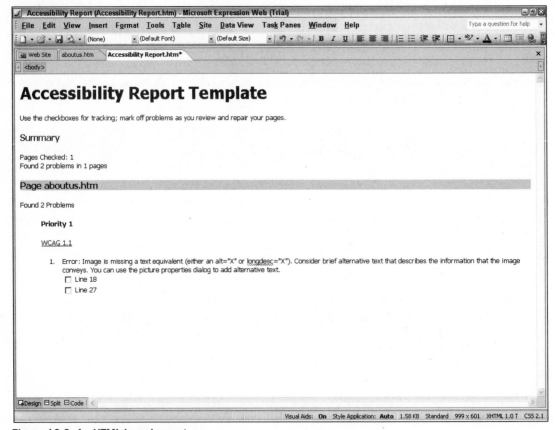

Figure 16-6: An HTML-based report

Now that you have an understanding of how the Accessibility Task Pane can be used, let's take advantage of the helpful list and fix those errors now. To fix the reported accessibility issues, simply perform the following steps:

1. Double-click the error within the list. The aboutus.htm page automatically switches to code view and highlights the particular code block in question.

2. As you'll see from the Problem Summary column, this particular tag is missing an alt attribute. Because alt attributes are ideal alternatives for the visually impaired, let's add it now. To do this, simply place your cursor within the tag and add the attribute and value:

   ```
   alt="Vecta Corporation".
   ```

3. While you know that this tag is now fixed, Expression Web isn't smart enough to figure out on its own that you've actually performed the fix, so it keeps the error within the list. To update the list, simply choose Refresh Changed Results icon from the left column of options. Immediately, the error disappears.

Accessibility Reference

The rest of this chapter is a reference to the checks performed by the accessibility checker in Expression Web. Each test is identified by a short title, but it's not always clear what each title means; the discussions that follow will clarify the meaning of the test titles.

Image Tests

Because images are inherently visual, they can present serious obstacles to users who can't see. There is also some danger that a strobing image could trigger seizures in photo-epileptic users. To avoid image-based accessibility issues, Expression Web can perform image-based tests, outlined in more detail in the following table.

WCAG	Section 508	Accessibility Test
1.1	1194.22(a)	Spacer IMG with valid ALT.
1.1	1194.22(a)	No LONGDESC for spacer IMG.
1.1	1194.22(a)	Non spacer IMG with valid ALT.
1.1	1194.22(a)	Non spacer IMG with equivalent ALT.
1.1	1194.22(a)	Non spacer IMG with valid LONGDESC.
1.1	1194.22(a)	Non spacer IMG needs LONGDESC.
1.1	1194.22(a)	Image OBJECT with valid CONTENT.
1.1	1194.22(a)	Image OBJECT with equivalent CONTENT.
7.1	1194.22(j)	GIFs do not cause the screen to flicker.

A *spacer image* is one that serves only to lay out the page and doesn't contain any useful information itself. Most of these are blank or transparent images. Any purely decorative image such as a spacer image should have an alt attribute value of alt="".

In the preceding table, some of these tests seem to be repeated with just a subtle change (for example, Non spacer IMG with valid ALT and Non spacer IMG with equivalent ALT). A valid alt attribute is simply one that exists. For example, if you include the alt attribute but purposely leave the attribute's value empty, this is considered **valid usage** of the alt attribute, despite the fact that it contains no value.

However, a *valid* alt **attribute** is not necessarily an *equivalent* alt attribute. Consider the top header image, which contained the text "Vecta Corporation." If the alt value was simply alt="Vecta", this would still be considered a valid alt attribute, but it would not be an equivalent value. An equivalent value in this case would be the much more descriptive alt="Vecta Corporation".

An *automatic program* (such as the accessibility checker in Expression Web) can check to see whether an `alt` attribute is valid, but only human judgment can determine if the value is equivalent. For this reason, there is a manual check that goes with some automatic checks. The `longdesc` attribute is another example. Only a human can determine if additional information is needed to convey the image content.

> **You may begin to think that images are the enemy of accessibility and should be avoided. Nothing could be further from the truth! Images, when given appropriate `alt` and `longdesc` attributes, are not an accessibility problem. In fact, lack of images may introduce accessibility hurdles for some people, including those with problems reading because of cognitive disabilities. A good descriptive illustration really is worth a thousand words, so don't be afraid to use them!**

Imagemap Tests

Imagemaps share all the possible pitfalls that can accompany images, and introduce several potential problems of their own. The special checks done on imagemaps in Expression Web are shown in the following table.

WCAG	Section 508	Accessibility Test
1.1	1194.22(a)	AREA with valid ALT.
1.1	1194.22(a)	AREA with equivalent ALT.
1.1	1194.22(a)	Links are needed for server-side imagemap.
9.1	1194.22(e)	No server-side imagemaps should be used.

There are two types of imagemaps in HTML:

❑   *Client-side imagemaps* that use `<area>` tags to define shapes

❑   *Server-side imagemaps* that require scripting to determine the outcome of a map click

Of the two, client-side maps are much more accessible because assistive technology programs can read the `<area>` tags and create a menu instead of an image with hotspots. However, each `<area>` must be marked with an appropriate `alt` attribute.

Server-side imagemaps present serious accessibility problems for users who can't see images and, thus, should be avoided whenever possible. If you do use a server-side imagemap, you should be sure to provide equivalent text links for every hotspot on the imagemap.

Color and Style Tests

As shown in the Vecta Corp About Us Web page example, the use of color can create accessibility problems when done carelessly. Contrast is important as well; blue links on light blue backgrounds are hard to see. Style sheets are almost always visual, and may have many of the same problems as color when used to convey specific information. The checks for color and style sheets in Expression Web are highlighted in the following table.

WCAG	Section 508	Accessibility Test
2.1	1194.22(c)	Color is not essential.
2.2	1194.22(c)	Colors are visible.
6.1	1194.22(d)	Style sheets should not be necessary.

Keep in mind that these checks are not saying "don't use color" or "don't use CSS." In fact, you most assuredly should use both of them, and use them regularly. Color provides many usability and comprehension benefits, and style sheets are a boon to accessibility. These tests merely ask you to ensure that the vital information of the page isn't conveyed only by a style or color choice, and is shown on the page in some other manner.

Form and Scripting Tests

Forms and scripts can present problems to assistive technology programs such as screen readers. The checks performed in Expression Web that deal specifically with forms and scripts are shown in the following table.

WCAG	Section 508	Accessibility Test
1.1	1194.22(a)	INPUT with valid ALT.
1.1	1194.22(a)	INPUT with equivalent ALT.
1.1	1194.22(a)	SCRIPT with valid NOSCRIPT.
1.1	1194.22(a)	SCRIPT with equivalent NOSCRIPT.
	1194.22(l)	Scripts are accessible.
6.5		No JavaScript links are used.
7.4	1194.22(p)	No auto refresh is used.

The requirement for `<input>` tags to have `alt` attributes applies only to image Submit buttons — those `<input>` tags with `type="image"`.

Scripts that have an effect (such as presenting new content) should have an equivalent `<noscript>` tag that either provides access to the content, or links to a page or server-side program that has the same effect. Scripts that validate input or produce cosmetic effects (such as mouseovers) aren't required to have `<noscript>` tags.

Links that are purely JavaScript actions (or pull-down menus that change the current location without a Submit button being pressed) can be very difficult for assistive technologies and should be avoided. Also, pages that automatically refresh based on `<meta>` tags can disrupt screen readers. Instead, use HTTP redirects in the server configuration or within an `.htaccess` file.

Table and Frame Tests

Tables and frames are visual ways of presenting content in specific locations. When used injudiciously, they can introduce serious accessibility errors for people with visual disabilities who may not be able to see the page at all, or who may be using a screen magnifier and can't see the entire layout at once. The tests for tables and frames performed in Expression Web are shown in the following table.

WCAG	Section 508	Accessibility Test
5.1	1194.22(g)	Data table should have headers.
5.1	1194.22(g)	Cell of data table should refer to headers.
5.1	1194.22(g)	Data tables should be defined by TABLE tag.
5.1	1194.22(g)	Multiple headers should be marked in data tables.
12.1	1194.22(i)	FRAME with valid TITLE.
12.1	1194.22(i)	IFRAME with valid TITLE.

The tests listed for tables apply to *data tables* or tables that have been inserted to display tabular columns of information (such as a bus schedule). Web accessibility standards distinguish between data tables and *layout tables*, which are tables used to lay out Web pages in two dimensions on the screen. Only data tables require special coding for headers, and then only when the table is complex.

> **Should you even use tables and frames for layout?** Tables used to be a more serious accessibility problem when screen readers would read across line by line, cutting cells in strange places. Current screen readers have improved this, and all you have to do is ensure that your table cells make sense when read in the order they appear in the source code.
>
> **Frames, however, are more problematic. Apart from potential accessibility hurdles, frames can introduce problems with bookmarking and usability. However, if labeled correctly, and if an appropriate `<noframes>` tag is provided, frames can be made accessible as well.**
>
> **This doesn't mean that they're the best solution. Often, a non-framed design with CSS for layout can accomplish as much as tables or frames and has even greater accessibility. Use tables and frames with care, if you decide to use them.**

As mentioned earlier, a `title` attribute is meant to be a human-understandable name, such as `title="Navigation Frame"` or `title="Banner Ad Frame"`. Avoid naming your tables by their location; `alt="Left Frame"` is useless because it doesn't describe the function, just the location.

Multimedia and Applet Tests

The term "multimedia," as used here, refers both to video and audio; embedded objects can include Java applets, Flash animations, and more. The tests for these types of content in Expression Web are shown in the following table.

WCAG	Section 508	Accessibility Test
1.1	1194.22(a)	Audio/video OBJECT with valid CONTENT.
1.1	1194.22(a)	Audio/video OBJECT with equivalent CONTENT.
1.1	1194.22(a)	OBJECT with valid CONTENT.
1.1	1194.22(a)	OBJECT with equivalent CONTENT.
1.4	1194.22(b)	Multimedia with synchronized alternative.
1.3	1194.22(b)	Multimedia with equivalent audio description.
1.1	1194.22(a)	Linked AUDIO with equivalent CONTENT.
	1194.22(m)	Link to plug-in is present.
1.1	1194.22(a)	APPLET with valid ALT.
1.1	1194.22(a)	APPLET with valid CONTENT.
1.1	1194.22(a)	APPLET with equivalent ALT.

In general, the easiest way to deal with multimedia is to provide a text transcript of the information. In addition to the dialog, action and events must be described. A synchronized alternative is a text or audio version that plays at the same time as the video, such as a caption or an audio description. The synchronization is usually accomplished by using the Synchronized Multimedia Integration Language (SMIL).

To learn more about SMIL, visit the W3C's multimedia page at www.w3.org/AudioVideo.

Other Accessibility Tests

Several other accessibility checks that are performed don't fall into separate categories, but nevertheless are very important for ensuring the accessibility of your site. These are shown in the following table.

WCAG	Section 508	Accessibility Test
13.6	1194.22(o)	Skip repetitive links.
7.1	1194.22(j)	Avoid causing the screen to flicker.
14.1		Use clear language for site's content.
4.1		Clarify natural language usage.
		Proprietary tags are used.
6.2	1194.22(k)	Text-only equivalent page may be needed.

Repetitive links are the pet peeves of many screen reader users. When a visual browser loads a Web page, a sighted user can instantly scan it in a glance, jumping to the content (usually in the middle of the page), and ignoring the navigation bars altogether. Screen reader users don't have this luxury; they have to listen to all the links on every page, again and again, before reaching the content. For this reason, the Web accessibility standards suggest a Skip Navigation link at the top of the page that will take the user directly to the main content, bypassing the navigation bars.

> For a great tutorial on creating skip navigation functionality, visit Jim Thatcher's Skip Navigation tutorial at www.jimthatcher.com/skipnav.htm.

In accessibility standards terminology, a *natural language* is any language that a human being speaks or writes. When part of a page is written in a different language, this could confuse screen readers or automatic translation software. Therefore, changes in natural language should be shown in the HTML tags. Use the lang attribute (and xml:lang in XHTML) to indicate changes in language, such as this:

```
<p>I counted to three:
<span lang="es">Uno, dos, tres.</span>
</p>
```

If you've tried everything and you can't make a Web page accessible, you can make an equivalent page that is simpler and presents the same information in straightforward markup and language. This is often called a *text-only page*, but in general, a text page isn't necessary! Nearly any page can be made accessible by adding a few extra tags and attributes.

Summary

By employing the techniques of accessible Web design, you can ensure that users with disabilities won't be shut out from accessing your Web site. These techniques are described in the Web accessibility standards.

The World Wide Web Consortium's Web Content Accessibility Guidelines define the technical considerations for creating accessible Web sites. The WCAG checkpoints provide you with a blueprint for your accessible Web site, and have been adopted (in modified form) by the United States government in the form of the Section 508 requirements.

Creating an accessible Web site shouldn't be an extra chore. It should be part and parcel of your good Web design practices. The special accessibility functions of Expression Web help make these important practices quick and easy to apply!

Index

I

V

W